"Something Has Gone Crack": New Perspectives on J.R.R.Tolkien in the Great War

"Something Has Gone Crack": New Perspectives on J.R.R. Tolkien in the Great War

edited by
Janet Brennan Croft
& Annika Röttinger

Walking Tree Publishers

2019

Cormarë Series No. 41

Series Editors:
Peter Buchs • Thomas Honegger • Andrew Moglestue • Johanna Schön • Doreen Triebel

Series Editor responsible for this volume: Peter Buchs

Library of Congress Cataloguing-in-Publication Data

Janet Brennan Croft & Annika Röttinger (eds.):
"Something Has Gone Crack": New Perspectives on J.R.R.Tolkien in the Great War
ISBN 978-3-905703-41-2

Subject headings:
Tolkien, J.R.R. (John Ronald Reuel), 1892-1973
World War, 1914-1918 – Great Britain – Literature and the war
War in literature
War and literature
The Lord of the Rings
The Hobbit
The Silmarillion

Cormarë Series No. 41

First published 2019

Set in Adobe Garamond Pro and Shannon by Walking Tree Publishers

Cover illustration by Matthias Fechner

Acknowledgments

When Walking Tree Publishers, in the years leading up to 2017, were discussing how they could commemorate their twentieth anniversary, the idea came up of organizing an international conference on Tolkien and the Great War, ideally in the North of France. However, given that 2017 would be just one year late for the real commemoration of an event that happened in 1916 (imagine the outcry "the Swiss are again one year late for the battle!") and the necessity of affiliating with one of the big Tolkien societies to help organizing the event, and France not being blessed with a large national-level Tolkien organization for us to work with, we decided to drop the alluring, promising, but probably fatal idea, and joined forces with the German Tolkien Society (DTG) for their Augsburg Conference.

Imagine our exaltation when, shortly later, we were contacted by Janet Brennan Croft and Annika Röttinger with the proposal of doing a volume with us on this very subject. Here it is! And the contributions offer a heady mix on a broad range of subjects, authored both by old hands of Tolkien studies and new talents.

Our thanks go to all those who worked with us to make this volume possible. First of all, of course, thanks to the two editors who did a splendid job on this and were a pleasure to work with. Secondly to our contributors without whom there would be no new ideas to share with our readers. Thirdly also to Rachel Naughton from the Melbourne Diocesan Historical Commission who gave us permission to use and supplied us with a fair scan of the Tolkien portrait by Frederick A. Farrell, and to Derek Clayton and Phil Mathison who provided us with maps on the battlefield of the Somme and the Tolkien Triangle in East Yorkshire.

A great 'thank you' also to Jessica Paesch and Larissa Zoller who were in charge of the layouting and proofreading of the text, respectively. The cover art is the work of Matthias Fechter, a new artist with Walking Tree Publishers. Also, I want to thank my colleagues at Walking Tree Publishers, Thomas Honegger, Andrew Moglestue, Johanna Schön, and Doreen Triebel for their valuable input on various matters and their help with the layout and the proofing.

Zolllikofen, August 2019
Peter Buchs, Series Editor

Table of Contents

Introduction

Introduction

In J.R.R Tolkien's body of work, the Great War serves as a source of imagery, motifs, and examples of military operations and strategy; of central themes about conflict, comradeship, duty, and the destruction of the environment; and of personal trauma which he worked out in meaningful symbolic form throughout his life. Like most educated young men going into the war as officers, Tolkien had a solid grounding in the classics of Greek and Roman antiquity, but he added to this a deep knowledge of the medieval literature and history of Northern Europe. From these sources and others he developed a long historical perspective on military strategy, the conduct and ethics of war, and varieties of heroism. The Officers Training Corps was also a part of his shared background with other young men of his class and education, training him in the materiel and daily life of the modern military.

The chronology which follows this introduction provides far more detail, but here in essence was Tolkien's war experience: After the war broke out in August 1914, Tolkien delayed his deployment through a program that allowed him to finish his BA while participating in officer training at Oxford. In March 1916 he married Edith Bratt. Tolkien embarked for France in June 1916, served as a signaler at the Battle of the Somme, and was invalided out with trench fever in October 1916 and sent back to England, where he spent the remainder of the war in hospitals and training camps. One close friend, Rob Gilson, died on the first day of the Somme in July 1916; another, Geoffrey Bache Smith, in December 1916.

Two films released in the wake of the one hundredth anniversary of the ending of the Great War in 1918 illuminate the importance of the war as an event in J.R.R. Tolkien's life. The use of the Battle of the Somme and the young officer's part in it as an opening framing device in *Tolkien* (2019), the biographical feature film directed by Dome Karukoski, suspends the audience in anxious anticipation of the moment when the war will impact the three main concerns of the young Tolkien's life: his Oxford studies, his relationship with Edith, and his deep friendships with his school mates in the "Tea Club and Barrovian Society" (TCBS). *Tolkien* is a fictionalization, not a documentary, and takes immense liberties with the timelines of Tolkien's entry into the war, his marriage to Edith, and the deaths of his friends. But the impact of the war on the sensitive and artistic young man, already traumatized by losing both of his parents, is sympathetically depicted, and his motivation as a writer in carrying on the high ideals of his lost friends is clear.

They Shall Not Grow Old (2018) is connected to Tolkien only because of its director, Peter Jackson, who also helmed the *Lord of the Rings* (2001-2003) and *Hobbit* (2012-2014) film trilogies. The film combines restored and colorized archival footage from the war with oral history voice-overs and audio and visual special effects in an intensely visceral experience for the viewer. The focus is on the experience of the average British enlisted man, with little to no attention paid to the causes and strategies of the war or to participants outside of this group. Those depicted in the film are primarily young or underaged working-class men from a rural or urban background who signed up early in the war out of a sense of duty or desire for adventure and, if not injured, saw the war through to the end. One might find parallels with Sam in particular in the attitudes of most of these soldiers: a determination to do the job they felt called upon to do, or a feeling that war service would "make him a man"; a sense of camaraderie with his fellows, and a lack of any sort of personal antipathy towards the individual German soldier on the other side; and an ability to come home more or less mentally intact, though perhaps still only able to really talk about his experiences with other veterans.

In this volume we collect a variety of perspectives on the war's impact on Tolkien's writing, organized into four sections. The first includes four papers that serve as an orientation to Tolkien's war experiences. Tom Shippey and John Bourne lay out the broad strokes of the landscape we will be exploring in their discussion of the British Army's recruitment and training practices and conduct of the war in general, as well as the specifics of Tolkien's own participation. Glenn E. Peterson examines in more depth the strategic blunders Shippey and Bourne allude to, and how they are reflected and critiqued in the First Age battles that were among Tolkien's earliest writings in the legendarium. Annika Röttinger catalogs and discusses Tolkien's references to the Great War, both direct and subtle, in *The Lord of the Rings*, keeping in mind Tolkien's own distinction between allegory and applicability. Tal Tovy explores the modern phenomenon of total war and how the context of the wars in which Tolkien and his sons served underlies a pervasive medieval/modern tension in his depiction of war in *The Hobbit* and *The Lord of the Rings*.

In the next section we are concerned with biography and how the personal becomes art. John Rosegrant insightfully assesses Tolkien's personal experience of the Great War in the context of the overall traumatic arc of his life: loss of parents, loss of friends, the frustration of his romance, frequent ill-health, and so on. Michael Flowers explores the landscape of Tolkien's period of recovery after being sent back from the front, and investigates traces of this time and place in his fiction. Wilhelm Kuehs compares Tolkien's experiences of war with those of German poet and essayist Ernst Jünger, and examines their highly contrasting artistic, philosophical, and political responses to the war, particularly in their constructions of heroism.

The following section traces major themes in Tolkien's legendarium that had their roots in, or were heavily influenced by, his war experiences. John Garth compares motifs of angelic beings, revenants, and supernatural intervention in Tolkien's works with popular folklore and superstition surrounding the war, a rich vein to mine indeed. The recurring motif of the watchful, ominous, or uncanny silence is explored by Łukasz Neubauer. Victoria Holtz Wodzak takes us underground to discover Tolkien's recurring theme of subterranean dangers and encounters. Molly Volanth Hall studies the way in which Tolkien explicitly links bodily trauma with the devastated landscape of war. Anna Smol continues the discussion of trauma but with a focus on death and the social construction of heroism in Tolkien's "The Homecoming of Beorhtnoth Beorhthelm's Son".

It is essential to any study of the Great War not to assume that only the most frequently heard voices are important. The often-overlooked experiences and viewpoints of participants outside the mainstream are also necessary to give us a full picture of the impact of war, and were not neglected by Tolkien. In our final section we explore issues of race, class, gender, and sexuality. Lynn Schlesinger examines the women who served in the Great War, and in particular those women who served in healing capacities and who provided models for some of the women in Tolkien's legendarium. Felicity Gilbert's discussion of masculinity and homoeroticism is continued by Alicia Fox-Lenz, who adds issues of class and the master/servant relationship to the mix. Finally, Giovanni Costabile writes at the intersection of gender, class, and ethnicity in an examination of Éowyn and a possible source for her heroic action on the Pelennor Fields.

At this point in the study of J.R.R. Tolkien's life and works, the centrally important topic of his Great War experience is by no means exhausted. There is still detective work to be done in discovering facts about his service and convalescence; there are themes and motifs still to be examined, particularly in the more recent posthumous volumes which have not yet been fully explored; other works of art or scholarship in other fields may illuminate aspects of Tolkien's work that have not yet been considered. Our hope is that this collection is by no means the last word on the topic, but instead sparks new ideas and future scholarship.

Janet Brennan Croft

Chronology

Chronology

Tabular overview: Tolkien in the Great War

1914	
October	Tolkien reports for military service, Oxford University Officers' Training Corps
1915	
June	Completes academic degree
28 June	Application for temporary commission for the duration of the war
29 June	Medical examination without findings
30 June	Application request is granted
8 July	Allocation as Second Lieutenant of the 13th Battalion of the Lancashire Fusiliers
from 19 July	Training in Bedford, Bedfordshire
August	Lichfield, Staffordshire
September	Whittington Heath Camp, near Lichfield, Staffordshire
October	Brocton Camp on Cannock Chase, Staffordshire
November	Rugely Camp on Cannock Chase, Staffordshire
December	Brocton Camp on Cannock Chase, Staffordshire
1916	
January	Specialization in signalling and coding
22 March	Marriage to Edith Bratt
13 May	Examination for Signalling Officer

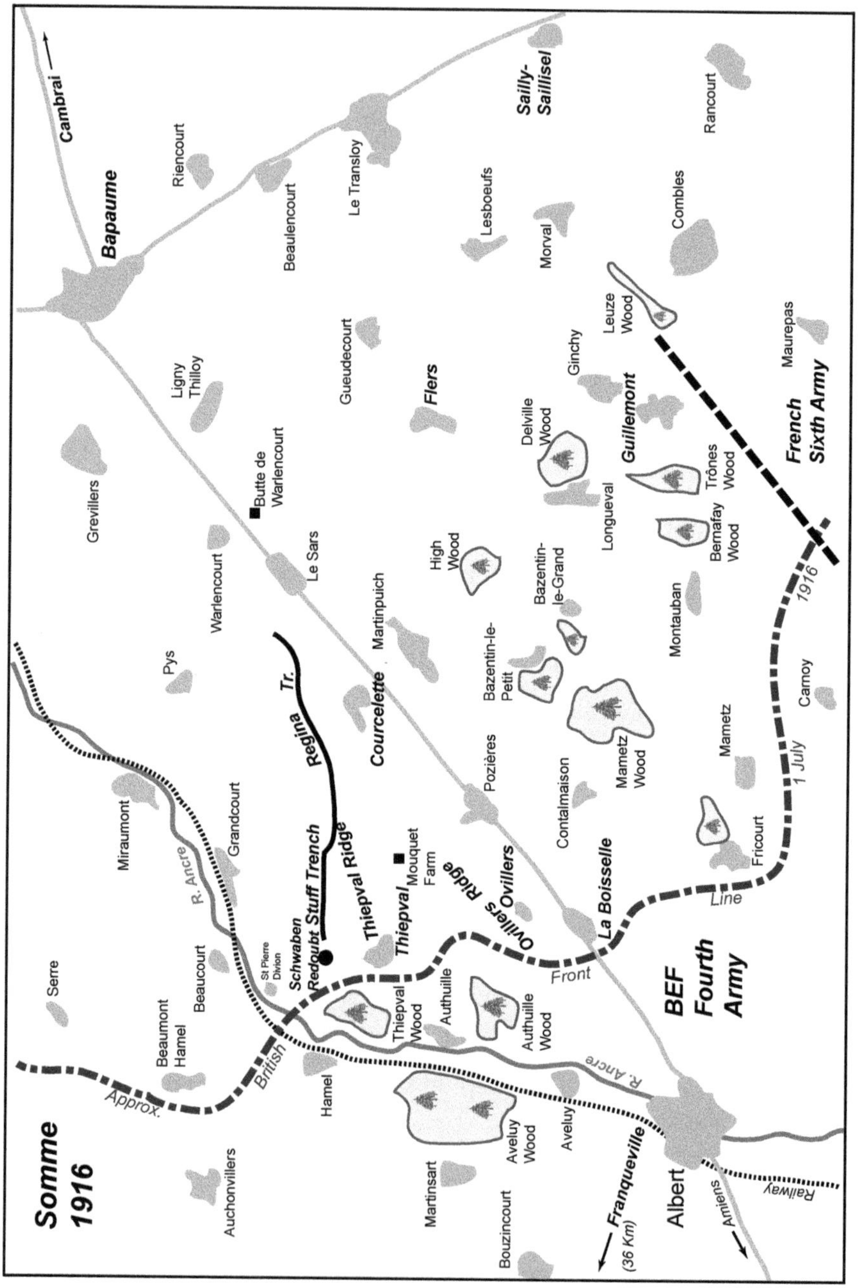

Derek Clayton: Map of the Battle of the Somme

2 June	Receives marching orders for France
4 June	London
5 June	Folkestone
6 June	Crossing to Calais; there allocation to camp no. 32 at Étaples
7 June	Allocation to camp no. 25 at Étaples, last instructions and toughening training; allotment to 11th Lancashire Fusiliers, 74th Infantry Brigade, 25th Division British Expeditionary Force
27 June	Amiens
28 June	Drilling and training in Rubempré
30 June	Warloy-Baillon
1 July	Standby position in Warloy
3 July	Bouzincourt, first time under fire
10 July	Senlis-le-Sec
12 July	Albert; back to Senlis-le-Sec
14 July	Usna Hill
15 July	Frontline at La Boisselle, possibly first encounter with corpses
16 July	Night assault on La Boisselle; during the day, assault on Ovillers
17 July	Trenches at Bouzincourt; on to Forceville
18 July	Beauval, cleaning operations and training
20 July	Tolkien becomes Battalion Signalling Officer (and probably acting Lieutenant)
22-23 July	Training in Bus-lès-Artois
24 July	Trenches at Maylly-Mayllet and Beaumont-Hamel
25-29 July	Trenches at Beaumont-Hamel and Auchonvillers
5-6 August	Camp between Acheux and Bertrancourt
7-9 August	Trenches at Beaumont-Hamel, Bertrancourt, Colinchamps

10-13 August	Cleaning operations and training in Bus-lès-Artois, signalling training
15 August	Drilling and training in Acheux-en-Amiénois
16-23 August	Signalling Officer's Training of the 25th Division
22 August	Bouzincourt
24 August	Hédauville, trenches at Thiepval
16 August	Bouzincourt
End of August	Trenches at Ovillers, Ovillers-la-Boisselle, repair works
6 September	Bouzincourt
7-11 September	March to Franqueville, via Léalvillers (7th September), Puchevillers (8th September), Beauval (10th September), Candas (11th September)
12-24 September	Larger training and drilling units in Franqueville
25-27 September	March back to the front line, via Forceville (25 September), Hédauville (26 September), Bouzincourt (27 September)
28 September	Trenches at Thiepval
End of September	Battle for 'Thiepval Ridge,' taking parts of the 'Stuff Redoubt' and 'Schwaben Redoubt,' encounter with German prisoner
1-5 October	Bouzincourt
6 October	Trenches at Ferme de Mouquet, 'Zollern Redoubt' and 'Hessian Trench'
9 October	Final capture of 'Stuff Redoubt'
14 October	Final capture of 'Schwaben Redoubt'
21 October	Assault on and capture of 'Regina Trench'
22 October	Setting up running trenches between 'Hessian Trench' and 'Regina Trench'
23 October	Inspection by Brigadier-General Bethell, Commander of the 74th Brigade; drive to Vadencourt, there inspection by Major-General Bainbridge, Commander of the 25th Division

24 October	Beauval
25-26 October	Inspection by Fifth Army General Gough and Field-Marshal Haig, Commander-in-Chief
27 October	Tolkien reports in sick with trench fever.
28 October	Officer's Hospital in Gézainvourt
29 October	Duchess of Westmorland Hospital in Le Touquet
8 November	Crossing to England; First Southern Hospital in Birmingham
Mid of December	Discharged from hospital; with Edith in Great Haywood, Staffordshire

1917

January	In a convalescence home in Harrogate, Yorkshire
February	Great Haywood, Staffordshire
End of February	Medical examination at Lichfield Military Hospital, found to be unfit for service
19 April	Tolkien is declared fit for service, allotment to 3rd Lancashire Fusiliers, is posted in Yorkshire
April	Stationed in Humber Garrison, Roos; further signalling training
1 May	Further medical examination: declared fit for home service, posted in Thirtle Bridge, Yorkshire
1 June	Declared fit for general service, stationed in Thirtle Bridge
July	Tolkien fails the signalling exam; has a high fever
Mid of August	Admission to Brooklands Officers' Hospital, Hull
16 November	Birth of first son, John Francis Reuel Tolkien
November	Ready for home service; with 3rd Lancashire Fusiliers stationed at Thirtle Bridge, Yorkshire

1918

April	Tolkien is considered ready for general duty; Rugeley Camp, Staffordshire
June	Brocton Camp, Staffordshire: taken ill with gastritis and admitted to Brooklands Officers' Hospital in Hull, Yorkshire
28 July	Marching orders for service in France
31 July	Withdrawal of the marching orders
September	In a recovery home in Blackpool; declared completely unfit for military service
October	War Office approves an employment outside the military
November	Position at *New English Dictionary*
11 November	Armistice; Tolkien is to remain stationed at Oxford

1919

16 July	Tolkien is officially demobilized

Section I:

The Conduct of War: Reading the Great War in Middle-earth's Wars

Tom Shippey and John Bourne

A Steep Learning Curve: Tolkien and the British Army on the Somme

The Lancashire Fusiliers?

If Tolkien, living as a boy in the village of Sarehole, had ever had occasion to walk, with his mother, to the village of King's Heath rather more than a mile away, he would probably have walked down from their address at 5 Gracewell into Wake Green Road, past Sarehole Mill where the Museum now is, and then turned west along what is now the B6146 road, along Swanshurst Lane, Coldbath Road, Brook Lane and eventually Addison Road. Parallel to Addison Road, for its last few hundred yards, and one block south of it, is Mossfield Road. Both roads meet the main Alcester Road which runs north-south through the centre of King's Heath.

About a hundred yards before the junction with Alcester Road, on the south side of Mossfield Road, there now stands an apartment building. A plaque on the wall, however, reminds one that this was once the drill hall of the *Comitatus Wigorniensis*. The old drill hall was less than 200 yards south of St Dunstan's Church, which Mabel Tolkien used to attend, and less than half a mile from 80 Westfield Road, to which the Tolkiens moved from 5 Gracewell sometime in late 1900 or early 1901. It seems likely that Tolkien at least knew of its existence.

The *Comitatus Wigorniensis*, one may well feel, was the regiment Tolkien should have joined some fifteen years later. *Wigorniensis* means, "of Worcestershire", the county Tolkien always regarded as home. As David Bratman has pointed out, while Sarehole is regularly identified as a Warwickshire village, at the time Tolkien lived there, before the boundary shift of 1911, it was a Worcestershire village (Bratman 7). Meanwhile *Comitatus* would become, for Tolkien, a familiar term of scholarship. It means "a body of companions", the *comites* who followed a leader, nearly always in scholarly use a barbarian Germanic leader. The term was picked up by scholarship from its use in the *Germania*, Tacitus's first-century description of the Germanic tribes which, as Joep Leerssen has pointed out, was probably the most influential Classical work of all those rediscovered during the Renaissance (41). Scholars (especially German scholars) were particularly impressed by Tacitus's admiring description of the way that members of a *comitatus* considered it a disgrace to survive the death of their leader in battle, if they could not avenge him.

As the works of Germanic antiquity began to be rediscovered and printed, they were even more impressed by the way that poems and sagas written many centuries later continued to show the behaviour described by Tacitus. The Old English poem *The Battle of Maldon*, written at some date not long after 991, and of course provided with a kind of sequel in Tolkien's playlet, "The Homecoming of Beorhtnoth Beorhthelm's Son", describes how Beorhtnoth's companions urge each other to fight till they die once their leader is dead. The Old Norse *Saga of Hrolf Kraki*, written much later but describing an event of the sixth century, describes how all King Hrolf's men fight till they are killed – except for one, who pretends to surrender, but only till he is given a sword on which to swear allegiance, and uses it to run through his master's bane, King Hjörvarth. The saga is the most important analogue of *Beowulf*, and the chief among Hrolf's champions is Böthvar Bjarki, or "Little Bear", very clearly the model for Tolkien's were-bear hero Beorn. The "*comitatus* spirit" became a very familiar term among scholars of the nineteenth and twentieth centuries.

In Mossfield Road, however, the regiment whose name was translated as *Comitatus Wigorniensis* was the Worcestershire Yeomanry (the Queen's Own Worcestershire Hussars). Yeomanry regiments were originally cavalry units raised from the upper ranks of the rural working class – men who could ride – and officered by the county gentry. One of their useful qualities (for some) was that the conservative rural working class could always be relied on to put down riots among the urban mob: they were what modern Americans might call "rednecks". In twentieth-century warfare they had a somewhat mixed reputation. One professional soldier recalls a colonel of Yeomanry being asked, very gently, by his commanding general, whether everything was in order. Ammunition? Gas-masks? The colonel replied, "Dash it, I don't know about any of that, George … but we've got forty dozen of champagne, well crated, and the pack of foxhounds is in fine fettle" (Masters 3.36).[1]

Local patriotism, however, obliges one of the current authors (TAS) to recall that it was a mounted sabre charge by the Dorset Yeomanry at the Battle of Agagia in North Africa on 26th February 1916, which overran enemy machine-guns and put an abrupt stop to the Senussi Rebellion.[2] Converted to tanks, Yeomanry regiments continued to perform well, the Nottinghamshire Yeomanry gaining a good reputation in the Battle of Normandy – as one of its members commented, largely because of "the unprofessional tactics of Yeomen who came from a long inheritance of shooting gentry and poaching peasants" (Tout 5.116). They knew how to stalk, even in a tank.

At Oxford in 1911 Tolkien enrolled in King Edward's Horse, a cavalry regiment recruited from those (like Tolkien) born overseas.[3] This might well have made him an acceptable recruit later on for the Yeomanry, though whether, as one who did not "ride to hounds", he would have been accepted as an officer is more doubtful. Also doubtful is whether joining the Yeomanry would have been advantageous to Tolkien. If Tolkien had joined it, he would have avoided the Western Front entirely, but might well have taken part in the disaster that befell the regiment at Qatia, near the Suez Canal, on St George's Day, 1916, when all the regiment's officers, except the CO, were captured and spent the rest of the war in an Ottoman prisoner of war camp.[4]

In any case, as we know, some time in June 1915 (or possibly a little earlier) Tolkien decided to follow his friend G.B. Smith into the Lancashire Fusiliers, hoping to join Smith's 19th Battalion, but eventually (9th July 1915) being posted to the 13th. (Smith had joined the army as a private soldier in October 1914 in the 8th (Service) Battalion Oxfordshire and Buckinghamshire Light Infantry, a unit raised in Oxford. He was recommended for a temporary

1 Note that with works many times reprinted, page numbers in references are often of little use. Where appropriate, we give chapter numbers as well.
2 There is a fine picture of "The Dorset Yeomen at Agagia", painted by Elizabeth S.T. Butler, in County Hall at Dorchester. The faces of the officers, whom Lady Butler knew personally, are all portraits. Her most famous painting, "Scotland Forever!", shows the charge of the Scots Greys at Waterloo.
3 The similarity of names is coincidental. The school was founded by King Edward VI, King Edward's Horse was renamed for King Edward VII.
4 See Bridgwater, ed., the memoir of Lieutenant Arthur Holyoake, Worcestershire Yeomanry, a solicitor from Bromsgrove, Worcestershire.

commission in December 1914 and was commissioned in the 19th Battalion Lancashire Fusiliers.)

Neither Tolkien nor Smith had, as far as we know, any connection at this time with Lancashire, and the decision to choose that regiment remains unexplained. Very probably, though, just as Tolkien was following Smith, so Smith – whose full name was Geoffrey Bache Smith – was following a close family friend of his family's, Herbert George Bache. H.G. Bache was one of six brothers who attended King Edward's School. He joined the 10th Lancashire Fusiliers as early as October 1914, and was killed by a sniper on 15th February 1916. He was a distinguished sportsman, and his father gave the Bache Cup in his honour to King Edward's: it is awarded every year to be held by the boy considered to be the outstanding sportsman of his year. Why Bache chose the Lancashires is not known: his five brothers all served in different regiments or units, one of them, his elder brother A.R. Bache, indeed in the Worcestershire Yeomanry.[5]

The many battalions of the Lancashires provide one hint of a reason for joining them. In 1914 the British Army suffered from a major disadvantage not shared by any of the other combatants. Britain had never had conscription, and its army, effectively a colonial gendarmerie, was tiny by comparison with all the others. Kaiser Wilhelm is often said to have described the British Expeditionary Force of 1914 as "a contemptible little army," an insult taken up by those insulted, to call themselves "the Old Contemptibles". It's unlikely that the Kaiser ever did say the phrase, but if he did, and said it in German as *eine verächtlich kleine Armee*, then the correct translation would be "a contemptibLY small army," which would have been perfectly true: the BEF consisted of six infantry divisions, rising to eight by the end of 1914, while the French and German armies on the Western Front were already fielding seventy-seven and eighty-two respectively.

The result was, of course, massive and rapid expansion. Regiments which normally consisted of two battalions (one home, one abroad) expanded till they had, like the Lancashires, nineteen or more. The county basis of the regiments also meant

5 I have been told (TAS) that the Baches, though established in West Bromwich, Staffordshire, in Tolkien's time, had Lancashire connections some generations back, but have not been able to confirm this. Bache is a village on the Cheshire/Lancashire border.

that rural counties, like Worcestershire, with their relatively small populations, raised fewer new battalions than counties with large and new urban centres, like Lancashire, with its many manufacturing towns. But if there were few trained men, there were even fewer trained officers and (possibly worse) even fewer trained NCOs. There was almost no-one, especially after the losses of the Regular Army in 1914, even to train the trainers.[6] In these circumstances, even men with the rudimentary military training offered by the King Edward's School cadet force and then King Edward's Horse, or the Oxford Officer Training Corps, were entirely acceptable as junior officers.

The New Army, Officers and Men

And senior officers? C.S. Forester's 1936 novel *The General* has been described as "a scathing criticism of the way the British fought the war," but it is also a rather sympathetic explanation of British failures.[7] Forester's hero is a characteristic example of the kind of general who later became the caricature so much loved by the BBC: a cavalry officer and Regular soldier, stiff, unimaginative, indifferent to casualties, with no initial experience of barbed wire, machine guns or heavy artillery, commanding from far behind the front line. Forester's point, however, is that just by the accident of surviving the battles of 1914, his hero Curzon, hitherto no more than second-in-command of a 600-man battalion, found himself promoted first to command of his battalion, then to command of an infantry brigade, a division, and within two years an army corps of 100,000 men. The incoming tide floated all the boats, and the tide from 1914 was massive expansion, from below. It is no surprise that the results were not always favourable.

As for the wave of completely untrained new recruits, opinions varied. One of the most popular books of the post-war period (now brushed out of memory by

---

6 There were fewer than 11,000 infantry officers on the active list of the Regular army in 1914, and close to 20 % of these became casualties in that year. "K3" units like Tolkien's battalion (we explain the term below) were low down the priority list for officers. His fellow-officers included public schoolboys, civil service and mercantile clerks, others with managerial backgrounds, and two promoted and decorated working-class rankers. At 24, Tolkien was average in age. Almost none of them had significant pre-war military experience or training.

7 Forester's novel was published in 1936. The comment quoted is on p. v of the "Preface" written by Colonel Merrill L. Bartlett of the US Marine Corps for a 1982 reprint.

the prevailing negative images of World War 1) was Ian Hay's *The First Hundred Thousand* (1915). This describes rather affectionately the raising and training of one of the first "New Army" divisions, amateur soldiers responding patriotically to Lord Kitchener's famous appeal for volunteers, "Your Country Needs YOU!" Opinions of the worth of New Army divisions (of which Tolkien's was one) varied considerably. Forester's Curzon meets scepticism from his superior officers when he brings his division to France – though Forester also notes that the raw material in the ranks was considerably better than that of the old Regular army, where joining the army was often a last resort for the unemployable. In his 1928 *Memoirs of a Fox-Hunting Man* – it would be followed by his 1930 *Memoirs of an Infantry Officer* – Siegfried Sassoon, later to be one of the most famous (and bitter) war-poets, describes his first sight of New Army troops on the march, and it too is markedly unfavourable:

> [W]e passed an infantry brigade of Kitchener's Army. It was raining; the flat dreary landscape was half-hidden by mist, and the road was liquid mud. We had fallen out for a halt when they passed us. Four after four they came, some of them wearing the steel basin-helmets which were new to the English armies then. The helmets gave them a Chinese look. To tell the truth, their faces looked sullen, wretched, and brutal as they sweated with their packs under glistening waterproof capes. Worried civilian officers on horses, young-looking subalterns in new rainproof trench-coats; and behind the trudging column the heavy transport horses plodding through the sludge [...]. It was the War all right, and they were going in the direction of it. (Sassoon, *Fox-Hunting Man*, "At the Front")[8]

"Sullen, wretched, and brutal," herded on by "civilian officers": readers of Tolkien may well recall Tolkien's description of orcs on the march in Mordor, passing Sam and Frodo sitting by the side of the road in their orc-gear and hoping to escape attention.

> The leading orcs came loping along, panting, holding their heads down. They were a gang of the smaller breeds being driven unwilling to their Dark Lord's wars; all they cared for was to get the march over and escape the whip. Beside them, running up and down the line, went two of the large fierce *uruks*, cracking lashes and shouting. File after file passed, and the tell-tale torchlight was already some way ahead. Sam held his breath. Now more than half the line had gone by. Then suddenly one of the slave-drivers spied the two figures by

8 Quoted here from *The Complete Memoirs of George Sherston* (1940), Part X/II, 249. George Sherston was the name Sassoon adopted for the publication of his slightly fictionalised autobiographical trilogy.

> the road-side. He flicked a whip at them and yelled: "Hi, you! Get up! [...] Don't you know we're at war?" (*LotR* VI.2.930-931)

The last phrase became almost a catch-phrase in reality, as Tolkien no doubt intended readers to grasp. Both Sassoon's and Tolkien's are images of a conscript army, but at least New Army officers were "worried" rather than "slave-drivers," and both men and officers (at this stage) were volunteers.

Tolkien's own introduction to and experiences of the war have by now been exceptionally well documented, by Wayne Hammond and Christina Scull, and further by John Garth:[9] his posting to the 13th (Reserve) Battalion of the Fusiliers in July 1915, after graduation from Oxford, his decision to become a Signals Officer, his arrival at the 11th Fusiliers on 28th June 1916 (three days before his friend Rob Gilson was killed in the disastrous first attack on the Somme), actions at Bouzincourt and La Boisselle, his becoming 11th Battalion Signals Officer on 20th July, and eventually the 18th Division attack on the Schwaben Redoubt in September, the 11th Fusiliers attack with 25th Division on Regina Trench on 21st October, and Tolkien's succumbing to "trench fever" (i.e a variety of typhoid) on 27th October. A question one might nevertheless ask is: what kind of battalion did Tolkien join?

An average one is perhaps the answer. Tolkien's battalion was a "New Army" unit, raised in response to Lord Kitchener's appeal for recruits in August 1914, and was in the third tranche of units raised, so-called "K3". "Average" is not meant critically. In World War One the Lancashire Fusiliers in fact won more Victoria Crosses (the highest British award for bravery) than any other regiment, more than the Guards, more than the Black Watch or other "crack" regiments – though it must be said that having so many battalions gave them many more opportunities. But when Tolkien wrote (in his 1936 lecture on *Beowulf*) that there were "men not ignorant of tragic legend and history," who "have heard of heroes and indeed even seen them," the "men" he meant were himself and C.S. Lewis, but the "heroes" were surely his comrades in the Fusiliers (*BMC* 16).

---

9 See Scull and Hammond 81-94, Garth 169-201.

Nevertheless, Robert Graves, in his 1929 memoir *Good-bye to All That*, gives an interesting account of his move from the Royal Welch Fusiliers, very much a crack regiment, to the Welsh Regiment, an "average" one. The former were both more professional and more ambitious. He notes that:

> The Second Royal Welch, unlike the Second Welsh, believed themselves better trench fighters than the Germans. With the Second Welsh it was not cowardice but modesty. With the Second Royal Welch it was not vainglory but courage: as soon as they arrived in a new sector they insisted on getting fire ascendancy. [...] They began with machine-guns firing at night. As soon as one started traversing down a trench the whole platoon farthest removed from its fire would open five rounds rapid at it. [...] The Welsh seldom answered a machine-gun. If they did, it was not with local organized fire, beginning and ending in unison, but in ragged confused protest all along the line. (Graves 14.113)

Graves's account makes the point – an important one – that individual experiences of the trenches varied a good deal depending on the unit, and on its commander. Tolkien's battalion commander was (Temporary) Lieutenant-Colonel Lennox G. Bird, a civilian when war broke out, an architect by profession, and aged only 38: the other three battalions in Tolkien's brigade were all commanded by Regular officers, one of them only 25. His brigade commander was, initially, Brigadier-General G.A. Armytage (an Old Etonian), replaced just before Tolkien's 21st October attack by H. Keppel Bethell, who would become (at 35) the youngest British divisional commander of the 20th century, and who was described by one of his staff officers as "the most insubordinate person I have ever come across," someone who "never took the slightest notice of any regulations" (Bond and Robbins 178, 218). Neither Bird nor Bethell, then, fitted the BBC stereotype of age and rigidity – though Bird, one should note, was eventually replaced in February 1917 and sent back to Britain to command a training battalion after a series of adverse reports.[10] Tolkien's divisional commander was Major-General E.G.T. Bainbridge, a pre-war Regular aged 48, shown by the divisional war diary to be a careful and reflective professional.

It's important, accordingly, to correct another misconception, now very deeply engrained in popular awareness, that the many disasters of the war were the result of thoughtlessness or indifference on the part of the generals and their staff. The classic case is 1st July 1916, when Rob Gilson was killed, which has

---

10 He later ran a successful property development company in Hong Kong.

left an image of straight lines marching forward into uncut barbed wire, to be scythed down by German machine-guns.[11] This certainly happened on occasion. But when it did this was to a large extent the result of the near-total lack of training for the new armies. Marching forward was about all the amateur British soldiery could be trusted to do, without total loss of control. Many of them could probably barely load their rifles (and one of the current authors, TAS, points out that even loading a Short Magazine Lee-Enfield is not immediately easy. If you do not load the cartridge-clip the right way, two rounds up, three rounds back, the rifle jams after the first shot.)

All generals, furthermore, British, French, German and in the end American, made the same mistake of over-rating the importance of spirit, morale, élan. In the case of General Pershing, one can see why. When he looked at his American divisions, up to strength in numbers as British divisions in 1917 were not, and moreover filled with six-footers, cowboys and lumberjacks, and compared them with the half-size British divisions filled out by undernourished conscripts from the slums – the British even formed two "Bantam divisions" from men who could not make the previous height requirement, which was itself only 5 foot 3 – he imagined that he could sweep the Germans aside by sheer impetuosity. But a machine-gun does not care whether its target is six-foot tall or five-foot, as the Americans found to their cost.

The Steep Learning-Curve

Experience is, however, a great if costly teacher, and by October 1916, when Tolkien and the 11th Lancashires made their attack on Regina Trench, the British army had gone a long way up the "steep learning-curve" of this article's title. It was no longer assumed that artillery would crush the opposition for the infantry to march forward unopposed and take possession. At the lowest level of sections and platoons, the infantry had been re-equipped. They were no

11 Modern scholarship has demolished the idea that the British infantry attacked in a uniform way on 1st July 1916 – slowly in orderly lines (see for example Prior and Wilson 171-84). In fact, a variety of infantry tactics was used. The key to success, however, was not what kind of infantry tactics was employed, but how effectively the artillery performed its task of cutting the Germans' barbed wire, destroying their trenches and strong points and silencing their guns. Across most of the front, the failure of the artillery doomed the infantry. This was certainly the case with the attack in which Gilson was killed.

longer undifferentiated masses of rifle-and-bayonet men. Every platoon carried Lewis guns, i.e. light machine-guns to give covering fire. They also had Stokes mortars to fire bombs into shell-holes and machine-gun nests, as well as rifle-grenades, these latter fired from special attachments which gave much greater range than hand-grenades. Even more important, in the future, would be close co-operation between artillery, infantry, tanks and ground-attack aircraft. But even in October 1916, Tolkien's tactics would have been very different from poor Rob Gilson's. They made it possible for even average battalions to out-perform the crack ones of the past.

One area, however, where improvements were not so readily made, and one which bears directly on Tolkien's own experience, was the area of signals, part of what would now be called "C3" – Command, Control, Communications. In some ways this was the perennial problem of trench warfare, and one which exacerbated all the others.[12] It is a problem now difficult to imagine. One has to remember, first, that there were no readily-portable radios, and few radios of any kind. Communication by telegraph was possible, using Morse code, as well as communication by telephone. (This was one reason why generals remained away from the front lines: the only way a general had any idea of what was happening was if he was on the end of a phone-line.) Phone and telegraph messages were however insecure, and readily intercepted. They were also dependent on phone-lines, and those on the surface were regularly cut by shellfire, or by vehicle traffic, while digging them in was slow, laborious, dangerous. In any case, when it came to making an attack, troops advancing under fire could hardly do so while trailing giant drums of cable. Once they had left their own trenches, communication by phone was over.

What was left? Much of Tolkien's training at the School of Signals (from August 1915), to be put into practice once he became Battalion Signals Officer on 20th July 1916, would have concerned the less effective, but less easily-disrupted methods: flares, Morse code signals by flashing light (not very useful in daylight), signal flags (though standing up and waving flags to semaphore was very likely suicidal on a battle-front), human runners (another highly dangerous activity – Hitler won his Iron Cross as a *Meldegänger* or runner), and, of course, last resort,

12 For which see in particular Hall 54-87.

carrier pigeons. As long as no-one dropped the basket! The 11th Battalion War Diary praises the work of the signallers as "excellent," and notes that "When a man carrying a basket of pigeons was hit in the open, another man recovered it and brought the birds safely to Regina Trench, whence a message was sent to Divisional Headquarters announcing the success of the attack."[13]

Nevertheless the 25th Division War Diary lays out the difficulties clearly. The system of runners "can be considered a failure." On the left of the Division front (which is where Tolkien was) visual signalling failed because "the whole terrain was under observation from the OVILLERS Ridge and forward signal stations drew such heavy fire that they had to be abandoned." Pigeons "were not sufficiently used" because commanders kept them back for emergencies, though sometimes their value "was fully demonstrated." Wireless was only used for test messages since it was certain to be tapped. The divisional diary also noted firmly that "Battalion Signal Officers must not be taken to replace Company casualties."[14] C3 was a major preoccupation for senior officers, and Signals Officers were not readily replaced: the qualities required, as far as one can now tell, were clarity of thought, a good memory, and a relatively high level of education and literacy. Tolkien's Oxford degree may well have led to him being chosen to train as a signaller, but when he deployed to France (after passing his course at the Signalling School in Otley), he was posted to A Company as a normal infantry officer. Since he was, however, "signals ready", when the Battalion Signals Officer was promoted to Brigade S.O., Tolkien filled his place.

Was being a Signals Officer a safer job than being a platoon commander? Possibly so, but not very much. At least two 11th Battalion signallers were awarded medals for bravery during 1916, Sergeant William Payne receiving the Military Medal for his actions on 7th July – though wounded, he "kept up communications [...] which necessitated not only working the instruments, but going out in the open, which was constantly shelled, and repairing the wires," so enabling reinforcements to be sent up. As noted already by Scull and Hammond, on

---

13 TNA: PRO WO95/2246, 11th Battalion War Diary. Ch. 4, "The Somme, 1916", 37. Garth also notes the incident (198), and see further Mackay and Warburton 37.

14 TNA: PRO WO95/2222, 25th Division War Diary. "Somme Battle, Appendix 1 on Communications", 3-4.

28th September, by which time Tolkien was Battalion Signals Officer, Lance-Corporal Albert Fletcher won the Distinguished Conduct Medal (generally regarded as a "near-miss" for a V.C.), for keeping up communication from a patrol, using a captured German flashlight (91).[15] The British communication system, including signals HQs and dugouts, was moreover a major target for German artillery and snipers.

Meanwhile, as mentioned already, the trench-experience was by no means the same for everyone. Even on the disastrous day of 1st July 1916, results were very different at various points along the long battle-front. In the north the attack was an abject failure, but at the southern end of the attack the 18th and 30th Divisions of XIII Corps took all their objectives, mainly because of a much more effective artillery bombardment than elsewhere, supplemented by the French Army on XIII Corps' right. The differences were noted, and became a major part of the British Army's "steep learning-curve".

The preceding paragraphs may then give us a rather different image from the standard one of Tolkien's October 1916 "over the top" experience, as presented notably, if conventionally, in Humphrey Carpenter's Tolkien biography: the "slow tramp forward" of 1st July, the "featureless desert of mud", "the same pattern: a rest period, back to the trenches, more attacks (usually fruitless), another rest period"(90-92). We would like to stress that Carpenter's adjective "fruitless" is – all too characteristically of British comment on WW1 – pure convention on his part. He had no idea whether attacks were fruitless or not, and probably no idea of what their purpose was, as we shall point out below.[16] It was a German staff officer who described the Somme as "the muddy grave of the German field army."[17]

What Carpenter's conventional image furthermore misses out, and even denies, is that the Fusiliers' attack of 21st October was strikingly successful: though it

15 Garth also notes that "One of Tolkien's runners [...] was later decorated for bravery" after the October attack (198).

16 One might also well recall Elrond's comment: "Fruitless did I call the victory of the Last Alliance? Not wholly so, yet it did not achieve its end. Sauron was diminished, but not destroyed. [...]" (*LotR* II.2.244).

17 The phrase was apparently used by a Captain von Hentig of the German General Staff, and quoted in the British Official History of the war, but there is some doubt as to where it first appeared. There is considerable online comment on the phrase.

should perhaps be considered a counter-attack, or even a counter-counter-attack. In putting it in context, it is important to realise two things. One is that – although eventual success depended on all-arms co-operation, including the re-armed infantry, the newly-invented tanks, and equally-novel ground-attack aircraft – the dominant arm of World War I was and remained the artillery – and successful use of artillery depended on observation positions.

The second thing is that, as a result of the way the front-line stabilised in 1914, the British Army on the Somme was effectively *fighting uphill*. On the rolling downlands of Picardy, of course, "hill" is a relative term. But even a slight eminence, a ridge, a fold in the ground,[18] was enough to hide one side from the artillery spotters of the other. Much attention has been given to the air war, and most of it has concentrated on the "aces" and their scores of shot-down opponents. The fighter-duels, however, took place for the most part to attack or protect the slow planes spotting and photographing for the artillery, or the tethered balloons used especially by the Germans for the same purpose: it says a lot that shooting down one of the heavily-guarded balloons counted double on a fighter-pilot's score-sheet.

What these two basic facts meant was that a lot of the "fruitless attacks" dismissed by Carpenter were aimed not at breakthrough but at securing observation points. On Tolkien's front,[19] the vital feature was the Thiepval ridge, which ran from the village of Thiepval to a point north-east of the village of Courcelette. It was guarded, for the Germans, by the Schwaben Redoubt behind the ridge. This was the pivot of the German line, and from it the Stuff and Regina Trenches ran some 3000 yards east towards Courcelette. If the British could gain and hold the ridge, they could then overlook a considerable depression from the north of Sailly-Saillisel towards Bapaume on the east and the Ancre valley to the west: as Garth notes, they would have a "panoramic view" of German-held territory (195). Both sides fought very determinedly for these vantage points. Thiepval village had in fact been taken by the Ulster Division as far back as

18 Or even an ancient burial mound. On Tolkien's front, the Butte de Warlencourt, an old tumulus about 60 feet high, became an important objective for both sides, changing hands more than once.

19 We are most grateful to Derek Clayton for drawing repeated maps of Tolkien's section of the battlefield, for which see p. x. Only a very detailed and large-scale trench-map could, however, give a complete image of the gains and losses, the almost insignificant features which became so vitally important and which were fought over so doggedly.

1st July 1916 – the "black day" of the British Army, when Rob Gilson was killed – but reinforcements failed to arrive and the Germans retook it (thus making the points made earlier about very different experiences even on 1st July, and about the result of failures in C3).

For the next four months the British attacked and the Germans defended, and by the end of September the British held the whole of the Schwaben Redoubt except for the north-east corner, but not the Stuff and Regina Trenches. In the first three weeks of October the Germans made eleven counter-attacks to regain lost ground, and a German Regimental order, dated 20th October, explained why:

> Men are to be informed by their immediate superiors that this attack is not merely a matter of retaking a trench because it was formerly in German possession, but that the recapture of an extremely important point is involved. If the enemy remains on the ridge, he can blow our artillery in the Ancre valley to pieces, and the protection of the infantry will then be destroyed. (Buchan 140, in ch. 2, sub-section 3, "The Fight for Thiepval Ridge")

During a short spell of fine weather, accordingly – frost, strong east wind, dry ground, good visibility – the Germans counter-attacked with a Bavarian division (26th Reserve) and Marines from the Naval Division. The counter-attack was held, apparently without great difficulty, and the British promptly (for their preparations had already been made, see again Scull and Hammond, 2006, 92-93) counter-counter-attacked along the whole length of Regina Trench, just after noon on 21st October, with New Army divisions, including Tolkien's, on the left and centre, and Canadians on the right. The attack was a complete success, taking the whole of Stuff and Regina Trenches (except for the extreme end of the latter, west of the Bapaume road), pushing out advanced posts north and north-east of Schwaben Redoubt, and establishing a position the whole length of the ridge eastwards from the Ancre river. The result was (as the German Regimental Order had foreseen) artillery domination of the whole upper valley of the Ancre, and the ground behind the German front line north and east from Beaumont Hamel.

By no means one of Carpenter's "fruitless" attacks, then, as the participants must have realised immediately.[20] Indeed, and very unusually, what happened once Tolkien's Fusiliers were relieved from their captured trenches was that they were paraded and congratulated first by their Brigade commander, Brigadier-General Bethell, and then their Division commander, Major-General Bainbridge, both on the 23rd. Then, on the 25th, by the Fifth Army commander, General Sir Hubert Gough, and finally, on the 26th, by the commander of all British forces in France, General Sir Douglas Haig himself. (One might suspect that all the commanders were not only delighted but also hugely relieved.)

And then, on the 27th Tolkien's active service career ended when he reported sick with trench fever, never to be passed fit for active service again.[21] It would be too much to say that Tolkien went out in a blaze of communal glory. But it would be fair to say, and important to say, that his retrospective view of his service was not the hopelessly bitter one (the "class-war" narrative beloved by the BBC) so often projected on to the trenches, and casually rubber-stamped by Carpenter.

Fact and Fiction

The next question, of course, is what effect Tolkien's relatively fortunate war-service had on his fiction. This one can only guess at, but should not ignore. One should at least avoid projecting on to his fiction the "ironic" attitude which came to dominate the post-war literary scene – or at least that part of the post-war literary scene which literary critics have ever since chosen to privilege.

Tolkien himself was rather sceptical about attempts to "map" his war-experiences on to his fiction. In many post-war memoirs and fictions the abiding horror of the trenches was the presence of the unburied dead, "hanging on the old

---

20 On Tolkien's front the British took 1100 prisoners and suffered 1200 casualties, the latter including wounded and walking-wounded, German casualties unknown. In the four months from July to October the British, on the attack, took 73,000 German prisoners and some 1500 guns, mortars and machine-guns, a set-off against the 20,000 dead they had lost on 1st July: for, from a war-fighting point of view, an enemy prisoner is as permanently out of action as a dead one, and more easily counted.

21 Tolkien was not the only 11th Battalion officer to succumb to trench fever round about this time.

barbed wire," as the popular song put it, or left over from old battles, even built into the parapets and revetments of the trenches themselves. It is not surprising, then, that the image of the Dead Marshes traversed by Frodo, Sam and Gollum has been thought to be a memory, even "a shorthand symbol for the trenches" (Garth 311): "They lie in all the pools, pale faces, deep deep under the dark water. I saw them: grim faces and evil, and noble faces and sad. Many faces proud and fair, and weeds in their silver hair. But all foul, all rotting, all dead" (*LotR* IV.2.628). Tolkien was less sure, though not to the point of absolute denial:

> Personally I do not think that either war [...] had any influence upon either the plot or the manner of its unfolding. Perhaps in landscape. The Dead Marshes and the approaches to the Morannon owe something to Northern France after the Battle of the Somme. They owe more to William Morris and his Huns and Romans, as in *The House of the Wolfings* or *The Roots of the Mountains*. (*Letters* 303)

This has regularly been taken to mean that the Dead Marshes owe something to William Morris, but John Garth has argued convincingly (in a private communication, which he allows me to cite here, to be published as "William Morris and the Western Front") that the section "Perhaps [...] the Somme" should be taken as a parenthesis by Tolkien: so that "They owe more"' is referring back to "the plot" and its "unfolding" rather than to the landscape. The Dead Marshes do, then, indeed "owe something" to the Somme, but not much else does (consciously) in *The Lord of the Rings*.

Another connection often made is with Tolkien's account of "The Fall of Gondolin", begun in 1917. This contains a description of the war-machines of Melko:

> Some were all of iron so cunningly linked that they might flow like slow rivers of metal or coil themselves around and above all obstacles before them, [...] and they blasted all that stood before them [...]; yet others were creatures of pure flame that writhed like ropes of molten metal [...]. (*LT II*, "The Fall of Gondolin", 170)

These do indeed sound like, first tanks (with their "cunningly linked" caterpillar tracks) and then flamethrowers (the "writhing" of flaming fuel has often been noted). Tanks were moreover first used by the British, not at Cambrai in November 1917 (which is the assault everyone remembers) but at the Battle of Flers-Courcelette, fought about five miles east of Thiepval between 15th and 22nd September 1916, while Tolkien was in reserve at Franqueville about twenty miles away: like the Battle of Guillemont, mentioned below, it was part of the slow British advance from the 1st July base-line. Flamethrowers meanwhile were first used by the Germans in 1915. Their use was so restricted by their short range that it is unlikely Tolkien ever saw one, though he must have heard about them.

One further comparison which might be made – and which has not been previously noted – comes from a famous German account of the Somme, written by Ernst Jünger, and translated into English as *Storm of Steel*. This describes the eerie effect of British warplanes, circling over the battlefield, and probably spotting for the artillery, but doing so while fitted with a siren:

> No sooner had day broken than a low-flying RAF plane whirled towards us, and, vulture-like, began drawing its circles overhead, while we fled into our holes and huddled together. The sharp eye of the observer must have noticed something anyway, because before long the plane began to emit a series of low, long-drawn-out siren tones, coming at short intervals. They put one in mind of the cries of a fabulous creature, hanging pitilessly over the desert. (Jünger 98)[22]

We have come across no other mention of this feature, but Jünger is quite explicit about it. Readers of Tolkien can hardly avoid comparing the effect of the siren on Jünger with that of the Nazgûl, mounted on its fabulous steed, on the hobbit Pippin:

> Suddenly as they talked they were stricken dumb, frozen as it were to listening stones. […] Pippin knew the shuddering cry that he had heard: it was the same that he had heard long ago in the Marish of the Shire, but now it was grown in power and hatred, piercing the heart with a poisonous despair. […] But now wheeling swiftly across [the Great River], like shadows of untimely night, he saw in the middle airs below him five birdlike forms, horrible as carrion-fowl yet greater than eagles, cruel as death. Now they swooped near, venturing almost within bowshot of the walls, now they circled away. (*LotR* V.4.808-809)

If there is any connection, did it come from life or from literature? Jünger's report comes from the Battle of Guillemont, fought 3rd-6th September 1916, no more than a few miles south-east of Thiepval, when Tolkien was at Ovillers-La

22 The original work, *In Stahlgewittern*, was first privately published in 1917. We comment below on its later history.

Boisselle about six miles away. He could have heard and remembered the same sirens as Jünger. On the other hand, Jünger's book, first privately published in 1917, was attracting more and more attention, being made public in 1920, with a major revised edition in 1924, and an English translation in 1929. Tolkien might well have been interested in an account of his own battlefield from the other side, and would not have needed the English translation.

One further similarity between fact and fiction can only have been (if not mere coincidence) a literary memory. In his *Memoirs* Siegfried Sassoon describes rather poetically the bursting of a shell in the air:

> One of our shrapnel shells, whizzing over to the enemy lines, bursts with a hollow crash. Against the clear morning sky a cloud of dark smoke expands and drifts away. Slowly its dingy wrestling vapours take the form of a hooded giant with clumsy expostulating arms. Then, with a gradual gesture of acquiescence, it lolls sideways, falling over into the attitude of a swimmer on his side. And so it dissolves into nothingness. (Sassoon, *Fox-Hunting Man,* "At the Front")

Readers of Tolkien might well once again recall the death of Saruman:

> To the dismay of those that stood by, about the body of Saruman a grey mist gathered, and rising slowly to a great height like smoke from a fire, as a pale shrouded figure it loomed over the Hill. For a moment it wavered, looking to the West; but out of the West came a cold wind, and it bent away, and with a sigh dissolved into nothing.
>
> Frodo looked down at the body with pity and horror, and as he looked it seemed that long years of death were suddenly revealed in it, and it shrank, and the shrivelled face became rags of skin upon a hideous skull. (*LotR* VI.8.1020)

Note the "hooded giant" / "pale shrouded figure," the "expostulating arms" turning to "acquiescence," like Saruman wavering and looking to the West, as if for hope of forgiveness, which does not come; and of course in both cases, the dissolving into nothing.

Direct borrowing cannot be proven, but it looks at least plausible. One might conclude, much more generally, that the influence of World War 1 *literature* on Tolkien is as likely as the influence of his experiences of war themselves: though the one would naturally be modified by the other.

Heroism in Tolkien

One result, either of Tolkien's own experience, or of his reactions to the post-war literary responses, shows itself in a strange contradiction. On the one hand, Tolkien is very generally regarded as "the father of heroic fantasy". The claim is not exactly true, since there was before him a British tradition of literary fantasy (E.R. Eddison, Lord Dunsany), and contemporary with him a strong tradition of American heroic fantasy springing from the pulp magazines (Robert E. Howard, Fritz Leiber, Lyon Sprague de Camp, Jack Vance, etc.). Nevertheless, Tolkien did act as a model and a trailblazer for later writers, to which many of them (George R.R. Martin, Michael Swanwick, etc.) have testified.

Yet the strange thing is that Tolkien was very reluctant to use the word "hero", or any of its derivatives, in his fiction. In *The Silmarillion* – packed though it is with heroes of traditional type – the word is never used once. In *The Hobbit* it occurs only five times, always qualified: characteristic is what Gandalf says right at the start, in ch. 1: dragons are not to be slain, "not without a mighty Warrior, even a Hero. I tried to find one; but warriors are busy fighting one another in distant lands, and in this neighbourhood heroes are scarce, or simply not to be found" (1.30). Other occurrences are either negative, or located far in the past.[23] *The Lord of the Rings* continues the pattern: six uses (in 525,000 words), two of them located in the far past, one immediately rejected ("Samwise the Strong, Hero of the Age" VI.1.901), and two in the diminished modern meaning of "central character of a story" ("Gollum! [...] Would you like to be the hero?" IV.8.713) Only once is the word used seriously, when Gandalf rejects Bilbo's offer to take the Ring to Mordor – "only a small part is played in great deeds by any hero. You need not bow! Though the word was meant [...]" (II.2.270) – and it seems clear that Bilbo at least wonders how it can possibly apply to him.[24]

23 In "A Short Rest", referring to Elrond, we are told that in those days "there were still some people who had both elves and heroes of the north for ancestors" (3.61); in "Inside Information", we are told "dwarves are not heroes" (12.225); in "The Return Journey", Bilbo congratulates himself on being "not yet one of the fallen heroes" (18.299).

24 Apart from the passages just quoted, Helm's Deep is called after "a hero of old wars" (*LotR* III.7.528); Sam asks twice whether Gollum could be a "hero", or a villain (*LotR* IV.8.713); Elros and Elrond are of the line of "heroic chieftains of the Edain" (*LotR* App.A 1034). The first and last of these are placed in the far past; the middle and the ones quoted above are rejected or diminished. Bilbo is the only character present in *LotR* to be seriously called a hero, and Bilbo's reaction to it seems to be disbelieving.

It is not as if Tolkien rejected the very idea of heroes' existence. As noted above, in his 1936 *Beowulf* lecture he mentions "men who have heard of heroes and indeed even seen them," clearly referring to his own experience. He accepted heroes as fact, he portrayed them in fiction, but he consistently shied away from the word: an apparent and surprising contradiction.

The whole question of the twentieth-century redefinition of the hero indeed deserves much greater and wider attention, but in Tolkien's case the motivation seems clear. World War I had left British society, at least, "traumatised". Many families, probably most of them, had heroes of their own to celebrate – in the case of the authors of this paper, an ancestor who broke the Hindenburg Line with the North Staffordshire Regiment on 29th September 1918 (JB), an uncle who stormed the Mole at Zeebrugge from H.M.S. Iris on St George's Day, 23rd April 1918 (TAS). But no memory of them could be kept without simultaneous awareness of the price paid for heroism. The kind of triumphant celebration one finds in the Victorian novels of, say, G.A. Henty, was not possible any more. It was not that heroism had been discredited, but it was certainly nuanced, and very often ironised.

Also, but not so often, rethought. Alumni of King Edward's are celebrated in the School Song – itself a product of Victorian triumphalism – with the words, "these have plucked the bays of battle, those have won the scholar's crown," and if Tolkien is the shining example of the latter, the shining example of the former was Field Marshal Sir William Slim. Not only were the two men almost exact contemporaries (Slim was five months the elder), and co-evals at King Edward's, they were also both Catholics – not at all common in Birmingham in those days – and both (if briefly) attended St Philip's Catholic Grammar School in Edgbaston. They must have known each other from the age of ten.

Slim was a hero by anyone's standards. Serving with the Royal Warwickshire Regiment, he was badly wounded at Gallipoli – where the Lancashire Fusiliers won five of their Victoria Crosses on the same day – but returned to service in time to be wounded again in Mesopotamia. In the Second World War, by this time a general, he was badly wounded again fighting in Africa, but recovered to lead the invasions of Iraq and Iran, and then to defeat the attempted Japanese invasion of India and go on to reconquer Burma. Slim, however, had rather unexpected views on heroism, born of personal experience. John Masters, cited already in this article, records an occasion when a speech by Slim made a deep impression on a body of professional soldiers not normally inclined to take much notice of generals' pep-talks. What Slim said was that the dominant feeling on a modern battlefield was loneliness – no drums and trumpets, no serried ranks, no colours waving – and that officers' duty was to prepare their men for it (Masters 4.42). Later on Slim commented that physical courage was one thing, moral courage was another. His Japanese opponents, he felt, failed for lack of it (Slim 23.537). They did not dare to confess failure to their Emperor and would not change their plans, even when these no longer had any hope of success.

Tolkien may not have read what Slim eventually wrote, though I have no doubt (TAS) that he followed Slim's career with close attention. But he came independently to similar conclusions. On loneliness, one should note how Bilbo's heroic moments almost invariably come on his own, in the dark – Gollum, the spiders, Smaug's tunnel, and the bold decision first to hand over the Arkenstone and then to return to face the infuriated dwarves: while the last is as good an example of moral courage as one could hope for.

Tolkien's major achievement, one could argue, was in fact to create a new-style image of heroism for an uncertain and dispirited age, in his hobbits, so clearly – as Tolkien indeed said with regard to Sam Gamgee (qtd. in Carpenter 89) – possessing the virtues of the unmilitary, civilian soldier of the conscript armies of two world wars: not aggression but doggedness, "seeing it through" from a sense of duty, refusing to be daunted even when things seemed hopeless.

Around this, though, one should recognise his creation of a whole spectrum of heroic styles, ancient and modern, often working through contrasts and comparisons: Théoden and Denethor, Boromir and Faramir, Boromir and Aragorn, Faramir and Éomer, Éowyn and Arwen, Túrin and Beren, Bilbo and Frodo, Frodo and Sam, Pippin and Merry, Legolas and Gimli. In them one may see a compilation of attitudes drawn from ancient literature and contemporary life, at once a revival and a discovery.

Not the least of Tolkien's achievements, one might also say, was to spark a gallery of similar approaches from scores of later writers. A "Literary History of Heroism" has yet to be written – and in literary circles the topic remains unpopular – but the decisive moment in it, as far as modern times are concerned, remains the life and work of Tolkien, itself a blending of scholarship and reality: the finest flower of literature to grow from the muddy and corpse-strewn fields of France and Flanders.

Bibliography

BOND, Brian and Simon ROBBINS (eds.). *Staff Officer: The Diaries of Walter Guinness (First Lord Moyne) 1914-1918*. London: Leo Cooper, 1987.

BRATMAN, David. "In Search of the Shire: Tolkien and the Counties of England". *Mallorn* 37 (December 1999): 5-13.

BRIDGWATER, Douglas (ed.). *The Road to Yozgad: My War 1914-19*. Privately printed, 2013.

BUCHAN, John. *The Battle of the Somme*. London: Nelson, 1917. Vol 16 of *Nelson's History of the War*. 24 vols. 1915-1919.

CARPENTER, Humphrey. *J.R.R. Tolkien: A Biography*. [1977]. Boston: Houghton Mifflin pb. edn., 2000.

11th Battalion Lancashire Fusiliers War Diary. The National Archive. Public Records Office War Office 95/2246.

FORESTER, C.S. *The General*. [1936]. Annapolis, MD: The Nautical & Aviation Publishing Company of America, 1982.

GARTH, John. *Tolkien and the Great War: The Threshold of Middle-earth*. London: HarperCollins, 2003.

GRAVES, Robert. *Good-bye to All That*. [1929]. London: Penguin, 1960.

HALL, Brian N. *Communications and British Operations on the Western Front, 1914-1918*. Cambridge: Cambridge University Press, 2017.

JÜNGER, Ernst. *Storm of Steel*. [1920] trans. Michael Hofmann. London: Penguin, 2003.

LEERSEN, Joep. *National Thought in Europe: A Cultural History*. Amsterdam: Amsterdam University Press, 2006.

MACKAY, Andrew and Amy WARBURTON. *"Made of the Right Stuff": The History of the 11th Battalion Lancashire Fusiliers 1914-18*. Privately printed, no date.

MASTERS, John. *The Road Past Mandalay.* [1961]. London: Companion Book Club, 1963.

PRIOR, Robin, and Trevor WILSON, *Command on the Western Front: The Military Career of Sir Henry Rawlinson 1914-18.* Oxford: Blackwell, 1992.

SASSOON, Siegfried. *The Complete Memoirs of George Sherston.* [1937]. London: Reprint Society, 1940.

"School Song." *Old Edwardians Website.* www.oldeds.kes.org.uk/school-song.html.

SCULL, Christina and Wayne G. HAMMOND. *The J.R.R. Tolkien Companion and Guide: Chronology.* London: HarperCollins, 2006.

SLIM, Field-Marshal Sir William. *Defeat into Victory.* [1956]. New York City, NY: Cooper Square, 2000.

TOLKIEN, J.R.R. "*Beowulf*: The Monsters and the Critics." In *The Monsters and the Critics and Other Essays.* London: HarperCollins, 1997, 5-48.

The Book of Lost Tales. Part Two. Ed. Christopher Tolkien. Boston, MA: Houghton Mifflin Co., 1984.

The Hobbit. [1937] 2nd edition. Boston: Houghton Mifflin, 1966.

The Letters of J.R.R. Tolkien. Ed. Humphrey Carpenter. London: George Allen & Unwin, 1981.

The Lord of the Rings. [1954-5]. 50th Anniversary edition. Boston, MA: Houghton Mifflin, 2004.

TOUT, Ken. *Tanks, Advance!* [1987] London: Grafton, 1989.

25th Division War Diary. The National Archive. Public Records Office War Office 95/2222.

Glenn E. Peterson

Strategic Blunders in the First Age Great Battles: Tolkien's Commentary on World War I

In *Tolkien and The Great War*, author John Garth draws a comparison between the Battle of Unnumbered Tears and the Battle of the Somme (Garth 266). While noting that tactical differences exist between the two battles, Garth makes the point that both had long-term disastrous impacts due to errors made by those in charge of the Elvish and British sides. Both battles marked major turning points in their respective wars. However, when considering many of the other battles that occur during the First Age, strategic errors are made by the Elves repeatedly. Fëanor's solo charge during the Battle-under-Stars and Turgon's refusal to take the threat to Gondolin seriously are examples of this phenomena. But these are not the only examples. Many of the First Age Great Battles are reflective of Tolkien's experience both as a soldier and as an observer during World War I (hereafter WWI) and influenced the development of his First Age legendarium.

Tolkien's personal experience with World War I was short but brutal. The war broke out in August of 1914 when he was still at Oxford, and while he enrolled in the Officers Training Corp shortly thereafter, he delayed actual enlistment until June of 1915. He departed England a year later in June of 1916 and participated in the Battle of the Somme in the French countryside as it began on July 1. In October, he became afflicted with trench fever from lice and the following month was sent back to England to recuperate. The Battle of the Somme would effectively come to an end later that month. While Tolkien's entire tour of duty on foreign soil lasted less than six months, those were a difficult six months. In the Somme, there were over 1,000,000 casualties between the British and French on one side and the Germans on the other, with approximately 150,000 dead for each including over 19,000 dead British on the first day alone, all for a net gain of a few miles of territory. Aside from the excessive general losses, Tolkien had personally lost two of his three best friends (one, Rob Gilson, due to a shell burst on the first day of the Somme, and the second, G.B. Smith, due to gangrene a few days after it was over). The war itself did not end until November of 1918 with the Treaty of Versailles being signed in June of 1919. Although he had difficulty recovering from the trench fever and was in and out of various hospitals for several years, Tolkien served in various home guard duties until being decommissioned in late 1919.

While this was a difficult time for him due to the war and his illness, it was also a very productive time creatively. Tolkien wrote the first draft of "Kortirion among the Trees" in 1915 and the main components of *The Book of Lost Tales* was in rough draft form by 1919-1920 (*LT* I 25). The greater part of his early legendarium was written contemporaneously with World War I. But this was not Tolkien's only exposure to the various battles of WWI. Prior to his deployment, he would have read and heard about the war; it would have been inescapable in English society at the time.

The Silmarillion describes five named Great Battles occurring during the First Age: the First Battle, Dagor-nuin-Giliath, Dagor Aglareb (which began the Siege of Angband), Dagor Bragollach (which ended the Siege of Angband), and the Nirnaeth Arnoediad. In the development of the legendarium, these five battles remained fairly constant in their presence. The "Earliest Silmarillion" and the *Quenta Noldorinwa* refer to the Dagor-nuin-Giliath as the First Battle (under varying names), but this and the other three later battles were in existence from the earliest drafts of the legendarium (*SME* 22). By the time the Annals of Beleriand and Quenta Silmarillion were written, the four initial Great Battles had been shifted in number and a separate named First Battle had emerged (*LR* 263).

The origins of the wars and these five battles will be the focus here. In particular, a general comparison will be made between these battles and select main battles of WWI to show the commonalities and how the real-world battles helped shape Tolkien's development of the First Age legendarium. This is not to say that there is a one-to-one correspondence between the Great Battles of the First Age and the Great Battles in WWI, but that war in Tolkien's imaginary subcreation was heavily influenced in a thematic sense by significant engagements of WWI. Several dominant themes will be compared: origins, demoralization, bad decision making, prolonged stalemate, new technologies, and lack of cooperation amongst allies. But before examining Tolkien's depiction of his First Age leaders and their decisions, let us consider his concept of the ideal leader, Aragorn, and compare that to a subject for which he is most known academically, *Beowulf.* The focus is specifically on a comparison between the *ofermod* as shown by Beowulf in his fight with the dragon ("ofermod" here meaning "overmastering pride" although a consensus definition has not been reached, Shippey (227)) and, as an antithesis, Aragorn and The Fellowship's final fight with Sauron (their own dragon) and the strategy employed in the final major battle in the War of the Ring.

Beowulf and Aragorn: Two different types of kings

In Beowulf's fight with the dragon, he is an old king. Once the dragon burns down a portion of the countryside, Beowulf gathers a group of retainers about him and goes to the dragon's lair to kill it. However, once there, he orders his retainers to stay behind while he engages in personal combat with the beast. Beowulf's kinsman Wigláf, seeing his lord in trouble, speaks directly to the retainers exhorting them to help. Therefore, the fight takes place in full view of Wigláf and the retainers. However, none of the other retainers follow Wigláf into battle. Together, Beowulf and Wigláf defeat the dragon but at the cost of Beowulf's life. Logically, if Beowulf cannot defeat the dragon by himself, but Beowulf and Wigláf together are (barely) able to win, then Beowulf plus Wigláf plus the other retainers would also be able to defeat the dragon, possibly without loss of any of their lives. But Beowulf eschews this option and chooses to make the attempt by himself. The retainers are not there to help in the fight but are rather brought along as an audiencc to witness Beowulf's glory. Also, Beowulf has an iron shield made for him prior to the conflict, but no iron shields were made for his retainers. Beowulf, from the outset, apparently planned to fight the dragon by himself, and his pride results in his downfall.

Compare this to the Fellowship's approach to fighting Sauron after the Battle of the Pelennor Fields. In *The Lord of the Rings*, Gandalf states,

> We must push Sauron to his last throw. We must call out his hidden strength so that he empties his land. We must march out to meet him at once. We must make ourselves the bait, though his jaws should close on us. He will take that

> bait, in hope and in greed, for he will think that in such rashness he sees the pride of the new Ringlord: and he will say: 'So! he pushes out his neck too soon and too far. Let him come on, and behold I will have him in a trap from which he cannot escape. there I will crush him, and what he has taken in his insolence shall be mine again for ever.' (*LotR* V.9.880)

This is followed by Imrahil's statement during the march through Ithilien to the Black Gates regarding the heralds' cries: "Say not *The Lords of Gondor*. Say *The King Elessar*. For that is true, even though he has not yet sat upon the throne; and it will give the Enemy more thought, if the heralds use that name" (*LotR* V.10.886).

The Fellowship is trying to bait Sauron into focusing on them and thereby divert attention away from Frodo and Sam's effort to destroy the Ring. The key element to the success of this strategy is the anticipation that Sauron will believe that Aragorn is engaging in *ofermod*. And Sauron has good reason for believing this: Númenór was cast down due to the pride of Ar-Pharazôn at Sauron's instigation, Sauron seduced the Ringwraiths (three of which were Númenóreans) in their pride, and Isildur fell due to his. Sauron's past successes when dealing with the overmastering pride of the Númenóreans have set him up for assuming Aragorn and The Fellowship will follow in those footsteps, and it is this assumption that they use to secure Sauron's failure in this final battle.

Aragorn thus serves as the counterpoint to the *ofermod* of Beowulf. Consider the similarities: both stories are concerned with fighting a great supernatural evil, that evil is a threat to the realms for which the two kings are responsible, and both involve small companies on a mission. But whereas Beowulf did not avail himself of the assistance of his company and ordered them to stay behind, Aragorn relies upon it. Indeed, the whole point of the assault on the Black Gates is to provide an opportunity for one of his fellows to achieve a success that Aragorn himself cannot. Beowulf attacks foolishly for his own glory when he could have used his company to assure success, while Aragorn only appears to act foolishly while actually sacrificing himself for the chance that others will succeed. Another key difference is that Aragorn humbles himself by listening to divine guidance in the form of the Maia Gandalf while Beowulf relies only upon his own wisdom. Aragorn recognizes that while he may be king, he is not the final authority in the world.

Beowulf's focus is on himself and his own glory; Aragorn's focus is on everyone else and their victory. Specifically, it is Aragorn's overmastering of the overmastering pride through his recognition of Sauron's weakness, his ability to let himself be the bait, and his reliance on his associates to succeed that provides for the final defeat of Sauron. Beowulf has none of these characteristics. While Beowulf is an example of a great warrior but a not-so-great king, Aragorn is both a great warrior and a great king. Given Tolkien's extensive knowledge of Beowulf and related epics and the effect of pride in their downfall, he is showing the difference between the self-oriented (albeit virtuous) paganistic kingship of Beowulf and the monotheistic pre-Christian ideal of self-sacrificial kingship of Aragorn. He is trying to rescue the concept of heroism from the self-interested pursuit of glory and transform it into a higher form of heroism consistent with his own Christian beliefs. According to Tolkien, good leaders control their pride and do not place their own interests ahead of those they lead.

But the character of Aragorn is a late development in Tolkien's legendarium. The writing of *The Lord of the Rings* did not begin until twenty years after WWI when Tolkien was in his 40s, and the character of Aragorn as a Númenórean king in hiding did not appear until several years after that (*SD* 121). If Aragorn is Tolkien's attempt to depict a good king, and Beowulf is an example of a poor king, then Tolkien is clearly not putting forth the notion that all kings are good nor that all kings are bad. His view is more nuanced than that. But what is there to say about Tolkien's First Age leaders?

Origins of the War(s)

The impetus for the Noldorian rebellion that led to the First Age wars in Beleriand was Morgoth's theft of the Silmarils and the death of Finwë, father of Fëanor. But while later discussion between the Elves emphasized the reclamation of the stolen Silmarils as the stated goal of the rebellion, in fact, the death of Fëanor's father had equal importance in giving birth to the Exile. In Tolkien's earliest depictions of the legendarium, the death of Fëanor's father is even more important than the jewels: "And this was the meaning of Manwë, saying that the death of Bruithwir would be the root of the greatest evil, for it was that slaying that most inflamed both Gods and

Elves" (*LT I* 148; Bruithwir being an early name for Finwë). The importance of Finwë's death is carried all through the legendarium until *The Silmarillion* itself is finally published. Here it is stated that Fëanor "ran from the Ring of Doom, and fled into the night; for his father was dearer to him than the Light of Valinor or the peerless works of his hands; and who among sons, of Elves or of Men, have held their fathers of greater worth?" (*S* 66). At least initially, his father mattered more to Fëanor than the Silmarils. His speech shortly thereafter to the Noldor quotes his desire for vengeance on Morgoth for both the theft and the murder: "Vengeance calls me hence, but even were it otherwise I would not dwell longer in the same land with the kin of my father's slayer and of the thief of my treasure" (*S* 69).

Immediately thereafter, Fëanor uses Finwë's death to inspire the other Noldor to action: "Yet I am not the only valiant in this valiant people. And have ye not all lost your King?" (*S* 69). He does not mention the Silmarils in his attempt to motivate, just the death of the King. However, later in the same speech, he does speak of the gems: "But when we have conquered and have regained the Silmarils, then we and we alone shall be lords of the unsullied Light [...]" (*S* 70). So while he promises the Silmarils as a reward to the other Noldor, he does not use them as a cause.

And a desire for vengeance for a fallen king would make more sense as a society-wide motivation for war than the Silmarils alone. The Silmarils were stated as being only revealed during certain ceremonies in Valinor and could only be seen by Fëanor and his sons at other times (*S* 56). So why would the Noldor population forsake Valinor for gems that they could only see from a distance once a year and never hold or even come physically close to themselves? After the Noldor arrival in Beleriand, they became a symbolic embodiment of all that Morgoth had taken from them, but prior to that, other motivations are in play.

Tolkien's experience observing the start of WWI with the assassination of Archduke Ferdinand echoes Finwë's assassination. The Archduke's death triggers the start of the conflict in the same way that Finwë's death triggers the rebellion of the Noldor. As Tolkien would have personally observed, the sudden death of a leader could cause a cascade effect in the psychology of many people to take action that otherwise appears foolish.

There is another reason for the war other than vengeance for a lost leader and reclamation of the Silmarils: desire for gain. Fëanor's speech to the Noldor contains promises of brutal war with Morgoth but also a pledge that the Noldor would be able to establish realms for themselves if they followed him away from Valinor. He even promises that the Noldor will replace the Vala as the dominant masters of Middle-earth: "But when we have conquered and have regained the Silmarils, then we and we alone shall be lords of the unsullied Light, and masters of the bliss and beauty of Arda. No other race shall oust us!" (*S* 70). Similarly, many of the participants in WWI believed it would be a short war with commensurate cost but that the aftermath would yield new colonies to rule. In the nineteenth century, many of the larger countries had established colonies throughout the world and these all fed into the wealth of many European states. This led to a general competition between the European powers to claim as many foreign territories as possible. The desire for overseas possessions drove both the Noldor and the European countries into war.

Alliances also play a role in both conflicts. In WWI, after the assassination of Archduke Ferdinand (heir to the Austria-Hungary throne) by a Serbian nationalist, Austria-Hungary declared war on Serbia. Russia, a cultural ally of Serbia, then declared war on Austria-Hungary. Germany, a member of the Triple Alliance with Austria-Hungary, declared war on Russia. And then France. France and Britain (members of the Triple Entente with Russia) responded with declarations of war themselves. In the case of WWI, the alliances were formal treaties between countries, but in Middle-earth, these alliances were informal and family-oriented, but no less binding or complex. While some of the Elves were eager to go, others followed only reluctantly due to ties with their kin. For example, Fingolfin was slow to agree, but went out of a sense of duty to his people and because he did not trust Fëanor to lead them well (*S* 71). Finarfin also did not wish to go and turned back after the Kinslaying although his children continued on due to their relationship with their cousins, the children of Fingolfin (*S* 75). These family/kin relationships led many to go to war even though they personally had doubts about the endeavor.

Nationalism in the form of the Elves' fear of Men and their feelings of racial superiority also play a role. Fëanor directly states that the Noldor should get to Beleriand before Men appear in order to take what is rightfully theirs. After the Noldor arrive in Beleriand, they talk down to the Sindar and hold them as "lesser" Elves. These feelings of nationalism also play a role in how the Noldor and Sindar act towards each other once all are in Beleriand. Tolkien himself was a nationalist but more in terms of patriotism: he was proud of his English heritage and believed that citizens should be proud of their country, but he applied that principle to citizens of other countries, not just his own. Even living through two wars with Germany, he did not consider the Germans as inferior and admired several of their "national" characteristics (*Letters* 55).

The importance of physical objects like the Silmarils is unique to Tolkien's world, but a murdered leader, promises of realms to rule (imperialism), feelings of racial superiority (nationalism), and being bound by alliances were powerful motivating factors in both the origin of WWI and the First Age war. Tolkien would have seen first-hand how the death of one person can start a chain of events leading to wholesale war as countries that had no proverbial dog-in-the-fight were drawn into a conflict due to formal alliances, feelings of being better than even their allies, and greed for ever-larger possessions.

Demoralization: The First Battle and the inadvertent cost of the Battle of Verdun

The First Battle occurred after Morgoth re-entered Middle-earth following the theft of the Silmarils but prior to the arrival of the Noldor from Valinor. Morgoth's motivation in initiating this assault was likely an attempt to destroy the Beleriand Elves and establish dominance before the inevitable response came from the Valar for the destruction of the Two Trees. He attacked in a two-pronged assault, and while Morgoth's forces won in the sparsely populated western regions of Beleriand, the Elves won in the east. The victory in the east was brought about by a combination of Thingol's Sindar forces and Denethor's Nandor army. However, while victory in the east was achieved, there was a very high cost for the Elves: Denethor, king of the Nandor, and many of his folk were killed. The reason for the high losses were avoidable:

> But the victory of the Elves was dear-bought. For those of Ossiriand were light-armed, and no match for the Orcs, who were shod with iron and iron-shielded and bore great spears with broad blades; and Denethor was cut off and

> surrounded upon the hill of Amon Ereb. There he fell and all his nearest kin about him [...]. After the battle some returned to Ossiriand, and their tidings filled the remnant of their people with great fear, so that thereafter they came never forth in open war, but kept themselves by wariness and secrecy [...]. (*S* 83)

There was a noticeable difference in the level of armaments used by the Orcs on one hand and the Nandor on the other. Metal-based technology was available to the Nandor; the dwarves had steel and iron as did the Sindar, so the lack of heavy armaments was by choice. The Nandor's lighter arms would be appropriate for a woodlands-based conflict where stealth and accuracy were paramount, but not proper for an open-plains battle where brute force is the more valuable commodity. They failed to recognize both the capability of their foes and the challenge of the expected terrain and adjust accordingly; as a result they were decimated in open combat. The reasons for their lack of proper preparation are not discussed by Tolkien, but the consequences are. While the First Battle was a victory in the east; in the aftermath the Nandor removed themselves to Ossiriand and fought only in a defensive mode for the rest of the war. They were lost to the Eldar as an active participant.

Now consider Verdun in WWI. It was a very long battle taking almost the entire year of 1916. There was an initial German success in gaining some territory, but France eventually retook the lost ground towards the end of the year. The casualties were horrific with over 1,000,000 combined dead or wounded. But key to relating Verdun to the First Battle is that Verdun had a long-term influence on French national consciousness which led to a debilitating effect on the French ability to take aggressive action. After Verdun, the British had to take the lead in the west. This is similar to the Nandor's response to the loss of Denethor; they withdrew from active offensive action leaving the Sindar, and eventually the Noldor, to be the primary participants on the Elven side. Having been called up to active duty in the summer of 1916 and being part of the Somme offensive partially designed to take pressure off the French at Verdun, Tolkien would have been very much aware of Verdun and what was taking place there. While recuperating in the hospital the following year, he certainly would have been aware of the French loss of aggression as the British assumed an ever-larger role in directing the course of the war.

Bad decision making: The Second Battle and command overconfidence in the Somme and Ypres

The Second Battle (Dagor-nuin-Giliath, Battle-under-stars) occurred when the Fëanorean component of the Noldor Exiles arrived in Beleriand and was attacked by Morgoth's army in an attempt to destroy them before they could ally with the Sindar. The Fingolfian component had been left behind purposefully in the Helcaraxë; this was a gross tactical (and diplomatic) error on Fëanor's part as he had divided the Noldor forces and left his followers vulnerable to attack. But Morgoth's attack failed and the Orcs retreated to Angband followed in hot pursuit by the Noldor. Fëanor outpaced his army in the pursuit (further splitting his forces), and, once over-exposed, was subject to an Orc/ Balrog counterattack that led to his death. The Noldor had won the day, but at the cost of their overall commander. Fëanor left behind a demoralized and politically divided force.

Fëanor seems to embody the concept of *ofermod* (overweening pride) but there is a difference between the tactical *ofermod* that Tolkien explicitly disapproves in Beorhtnoth and the strategic *ofermod* to which Fëanor falls prey. At the Battle of Maldon, Duke Beorhtnoth allowed the invading Vikings time without interference to assemble their troops in defensive array rather than engaging them when they were vulnerable (*HBBS* 4). This was an instantaneous response to a particular tactical situation and led to his defeat. However, the mistake that Fëanor made was not an instantaneous response. The distance between the bridges of Menegroth and Angband is roughly a hundred and fifty leagues, or 450 miles (*S* 82), and if the scale in Fonstadf's *Atlas* is assumed correct (28), then Fëanor's charge across Ard-galen was approximately 250-300 miles in length. If that is taken as a rough estimate and a horse can travel approximately 40 miles per day over easy terrain (Rossabi), then the pursuit across the Ard-galen plain took anywhere from several days to a week. Fëanor and his immediate compatriots in the charge had plenty of time to consider what they were doing, and they did it anyway. This is more than simply getting carried away emotionally in anticipation of battle; this was a serious inability to recognize the larger strategic situation.

Fëanor's strategic *ofermod* would be reminiscent of the behavior of General Sir Douglas Haig, the British commander throughout much of WWI. According to some WWI scholars, Haig possessed little imagination and was very stubborn in his insistence on repeating the same slow press tactics at the Somme in 1916 (with over 400,000 casualties) as at 3rd Ypres (Passchendaele) a year later in 1917 (with over 250,000 casualties) (Fussell 12-13). Critics of his also point to his belief as late as 1926 that cavalry, even in the presence of modern artillery and tank warfare, was, and would continue to be, the most important component of the army on the battlefield.

Tolkien's personal experience at the Somme under the command of General Haig would have had a demoralizing effect on his faith in authority. He saw the same leader making the same mistakes resulting in the same mass casualties, and yet Haig remained in his position until the end of the war. Tolkien does seem to gain a sense of justice through his writings: in the real-world, Haig survives and dies a natural death years after his troops, but Fëanor pays the price for his flaws and does not survive for long in Exile.

Stalemate: The Third Battle and the beginning of trench warfare at the First Battle of the Marne

The initial attack in the Third Battle (Dagor Aglareb, The Glorious Battle) was committed by Morgoth against Dorthonion with smaller bands sent to the east and west of the mountains with the express purpose of diverting potential elvish support away. However, Dorthonion successfully resisted the main attack and counterattacks by Fingolfin and Maedhros from the west and east respectively were made to great effect. While in the First and Second Battles the Elves made strategic errors, in the Third Battle it was Morgoth's turn to err. He attempted a center attack directly against a stronghold of the Elves but made minimal efforts to protect his flanks. He had sent out smaller forces to the east and west to conduct guerrilla warfare and create general mayhem. But there does not seem to have been a strategic plan to these assaults other than causing disruption. These minor attacks were countered and the failures of those minimal attacks turned into opportunities for the Elves to mount large scale counter-offensives against the central Orc army resulting in advances all the way to Angband. This was a clear victory for the Elves, but an incomplete one as they did not have the forces to destroy Thangorodrim. The end result was a stalemate that lasted for four centuries. The Siege of Angband had begun.

This is similar to what happened in the early months of WWI where the Germans launched an assault on France in the hopes of defeating them before fully engaging with France's ally Russia. The German plan was to defeat one foe before engaging with the second. However, the German offensive stalled, and the First Battle of the Marne of September 1914 was the French and British response to the German attack, with the final outcome being a partial German retreat. This battle still favored mobile cavalry attack like many of the mid to late 1800's cavalry wars (e.g., the Crimean War and the Boer Wars), and so played into the notion that while this Great War may be large, it would behave in the traditional sense. But while artillery had been used in warfare for centuries, industrial developments beginning in the 1850s had vastly improved its durability, range, delivery power, and accuracy. In 1897, the French developed the long-barrel recoil which allowed for rapid re-firing without having to reposition the gun after each shot. Still, there had not been a major battle fought on European soil since the 1850's Crimean War so while artillery development had proceeded, no armies had faced the full and prolonged effects of these new developments prior to the First Battle of the Marne. In the aftermath of the battle, soldiers began to dig trenches to protect themselves from the onslaught. This began the trench system and set the stage for a long drawn out war.

Tolkien was in Oxford when the war broke out in 1914 but this battle would have been foremost in his mind as he contemplated enlistment. His notes indicate that he felt pressure to enlist as early as 1914 when his closest TCBS colleagues were enlisting but delayed due to a desire to finish his schoolwork (Garth 50). With Marne being one of the first major battles fought by the British and such a momentous enlistment decision hanging in the balance, Tolkien would have been paying close attention. His personal experience in the trenches at the Somme would have cemented in his mind the nature of siege warfare.

New technologies: The Fourth Battle and fighting the last war

The Fourth Battle (Dagor Bragollach; Battle of Sudden Flame) ended the Siege of Angband with a surprise assault by Morgoth involving overwhelming numbers and new "technology". Caught by surprise, the Elves were routed and lost the immediate territory of Ard-galen. However, Morgoth did not try to conquer all at once. He was content with the gains made in the Fourth Battle: the capture of Dorthonion and much of the eastern region, and stopped without overextending himself. This has a parallel with the later stage WWI Allied strategy of "bite and hold" where the Allies would advance, then wait and regroup, and then advance again. This was a marked improvement on the early war Haig strategy of being constantly on the offensive until exhausted troops could fight no more.

New technologies were also employed by Morgoth in the Dagor Bragollach: dragons and Balrogs. The Elves believed that Morgoth was stagnant during the Siege and so had not anticipated these new weapons. They had encountered Glaurung in a younger weaker form but did not anticipate what he would become once fully mature. They also had encountered Balrogs prior to the Fourth Battle (Fëanor was killed by them), but had not faced them in open warfare in significant numbers. This assumption that their current strength was sufficient because it had been in the past and failing to predict their enemy would change tactics is a classic example of generals fighting the last war rather than the current one.

Similarly, in WWI, artillery has already been mentioned, but radio and air reconnaissance were also introduced at the First Battle of the Marne. Additional new weapons systems were developed during the war, most notably flamethrowers, poison gas, and tanks. Flamethrowers were first used by Germans in 1914 against the French as a test but then in 1915 against the British on a wider basis. The first use of flamethrowers by the British was also at the Somme although in a very limited manner. The first use of poison gas was by Germans on the western front at the Second Battle of Ypres in April of 1915 with reports being made in the Daily Mirror the following month. Tanks were not used in great numbers until late in the war although the British did use 32 tanks in the Somme offensive (where Tolkien was stationed) to little effect. Churchill believed that tanks were best used in large numbers and with the element of surprise (Havardi 76-79).

Tolkien seems to have agreed with him when devising the Fourth Battle. In that case, the dragons and Balrogs were used as part of a surprise mobile attack and in large enough numbers to overwhelm the defenders. Tolkien would have seen both the effects and the consequences of the new flamethrowers in person and embodied them in his Balrogs and dragons. It is not known if Tolkien had any direct experience with poison gas, but he enlisted only a month after the first use of poison gas was reported. All these new technologies were not abstract entities for Tolkien; he had personal experience with several of them which would have influenced his understanding of war as he wrote on the First Age.

Lack of coordination: The Fifth Battle and distrust between the Allies

The Fifth Battle (Nirnaeth Arnoediad, Battle of Unnumbered Tears) was a major disaster for the Elven forces and is covered extensively in Garth. But rather than examine the particular tactics of the battle itself, the focus here is on the behavior of the Elvish allies and the lack of coordination in the order of battle that led to the debacle. The Union of Maedhros was initially established to coordinate an attack on Morgoth's forces after his victory in the Fourth Battle. However, due to past misdeeds and poor diplomacy, neither Nargothrond nor Doriath added much to the effort. Nargothrond because they had adopted a defensive posture and had decided to keep themselves safe through stealth; Doriath due to the Fëanorians' demand to surrender the Silmaril in Thingol's possession which he refused to do. The resulting force was divided into east and west components: the western force under Fingon's command consisting of Elves and Men (who eventually became the Númenóreans) and the eastern force under Maedhros. Maedhros' forces also included Men (two tribes of Easterlings) and Dwarves. But given the differences in capability and lack of shared history, those different ethnic forces were not incorporated in an effective manner and were managed as separate entities. Furthermore, while

Fingon and Maedhros were ostensibly cooperating, they were too far apart to enable effective coordination. The "Allies" did not trust each other enough to surrender their individual commands to a single authority or integrate their forces to fight as a single entity. Most of the Elvish "Allies" did not wish to be led by the Fëanorians and so loss of coordination became an issue.

Tolkien's description of the Union of Maedhros reflects the Allied forces in WWI; Britain, France, and Russia were ostensibly allies, but they each maintained their own command and were loath to integrate their forces into a single command under a central leader. It is understandable that Russia would maintain a separate command structure being located by itself on the Eastern Front, but British and French troops were both stationed in the trenches in the West, and still could not integrate. This was a problem throughout the war. Once the United States entered the war, the American general Pershing also caused unnecessary casualties for his forces by not integrating the much more experienced French troops with his inexperienced new arrivals. However, real-world leaders learned from this and the issue was rectified during World War II, where one individual, Eisenhower, was made supreme military commander over all Allied forces.

The Overall Campaign

At a higher level and when viewing both wars in a broader context, the Elves failed to follow Sun Tzu's basic maxim on war: "Know the enemy and know yourself; in a hundred battles you will never be in peril" (Sun Tzu 84). The Elves did not understand themselves very well being carried along by emotion (jealousy, *ofermod*, etc.), over-estimating their capabilities, and not facing their weaknesses. They similarly did not understand the Enemy they were facing: after many centuries of living in direct contact with the Valar, the Noldor at least should have understood that they are lesser beings who had no hope of conquering one of the two greatest Valar. They continually underestimated Morgoth's resources and his very nature. They understood neither themselves nor their enemy and were only saved by last minute outside intervention in the War of Wrath.

This echoes WWI. Both the Triple Entente and the Triple Alliance believed at the outset that the war would be short, each side believed it would be a glorious victory with little cost in time, men or materiel, and eventually the Entente Allies were saved (or at the least greatly assisted) by intervention from an outside source. In general concept (and direct equations should be viewed with caution), if Morgoth's forces are assumed to have the place of the WWI Germans (the "kalimban" barbarians of the early Qenya Lexicon), then the Sindar and Nandor represent the continental forces (French, Russian, etc.) while the British occupy the place of the Exiled Noldor, with the Fëanorians being the gung-ho pro-war party and Fingolfin's larger host representing more cautious participants (like Tolkien). Finally, the Americans occupy the place of Eönwë and the forces of the Valar. When the United States joined the Allies in 1917, the German defeat became logistically inevitable.

In terms of specific battles, the First Battle is a partial victory, but with Denethor's death, the will of the Green Elves is broken for fighting in any way other than defensively. The Second Battle is a success, but costs the main leadership due to foolhardiness (*ofermod*). The Third Battle is an unqualified immediate success, but Angband is not taken, the enemy remains, and a stalemate ensues. The Fourth Battle is a major loss due to new strategy and new technologies being employed by Morgoth against the unprepared Elves. And the Fifth Battle is a disaster for the Elves due to poor coordination and unwillingness to work together for the common good, but provides the impetus for the final intervention of the Valar. Similarly in WWI, Verdun causes the French to largely withdraw from offensive action. Passchendaele and the Somme demoralize the British forces due to command errors and a dogged determination to continue pushing without regards to the consequences to the troops. Trench warfare begins as a result of the Marne. Finally, diplomatic considerations inhibit the ability of the Allies from truly coordinating their activities.

It is not just the Somme that influenced Tolkien's writing. While the Somme was something he personally participated in and so likely had the most profound effect on him, all of the major battles of WWI would have been witnessed by him through media either before his own involvement or afterwards during his recovery. Many of his writings of the First Age reflect this. The overall tenor of the WWI Great Battles is reflected in the Great Battles of the First

Age: demoralization, bad command decisions, inconclusive stalemate, lack of adjustments to new technologies, and political infighting.

Tolkien is an author of his time. When he is writing about the First Age wars, he is writing about his own experience. This is not to say that there is an equation occurring in the manner of an allegory (fictional character A = real life person B, or fictional event C = real life event D), but that he was influenced by what he lived through and witnessed around him.

Bibliography

FONSTAD, Karen Wynn. *The Atlas of Middle-Earth*. rev. ed. Boston, MA: Houghton Mifflin, 1991.

FUSSELL, Paul. *The Great War and Modern Memory*. Oxford University Press, 2013.

GARTH, John. *Tolkien and the Great War: The Threshold of Middle-Earth*. Boston, MA: Houghton Mifflin, 2003.

HAVARDI, Jeremy. *The Greatest Briton: Essays on Winston Churchill's Life and Political Philosophy*. London: Shepheard-Walwyn, 2010.

ROSSABI, Morris. "All the Khan's Horses." *Natural History* 103.10 (1994): 48.

SHIPPEY, Thomas A. "Boar and Badger: An Old English Heroic Antithesis." *Leeds Studies in English* 16(1985): 220-39.

SUN Tzu. *The Art of War*. Trans. Samuel Griffith. London: Oxford University Press, 1971.

"10 Significant Battles of the First World War." *British Imperial War Museum*. 2017, http://www.iwm.org.uk/history/10-significant-battles-of-the-first-world-war. 21 June 2018.

TOLKIEN, J.R.R. *Beowulf*. London: Houghton Mifflin, 2014.

"The Homecoming of Beorhtnoth Beorhthelm's Son." *The Tolkien Reader*. New York City, NY: Ballantine Books, 1966, 3-24.

The Letters of J.R.R. Tolkien. Ed. Humphrey Carpenter, with the assistance of Christopher Tolkien. Boston, MA: Houghton Mifflin, 1981.

The Lord of the Rings. 50th Anniversary edition. Boston, MA: Houghton Mifflin, 2004.

The Lost Road and Other Writings. (The History of Middle-earth 5). Ed. Christopher Tolkien. London: Harper-Collins, 2002.

Sauron Defeated. (The History of Middle-earth 9). Ed. Christopher Tolkien. London: Harper-Collins, 2002.

The Shaping of Middle-earth. (The History of Middle-earth 4). Ed. Christopher Tolkien. London: Harper-Collins, 2002.

The Silmarillion. Ed. Christopher Tolkien. London: Harper Collins Publishers, 2007.

Annika Röttinger

The Great War in Middle-earth – or: Where to Find Modern Warfare in *The Lord of the Rings*

> The gasping pools were choked with ash and crawling muds, sickly white and grey, as if the mountains had vomited the filth of their entrails upon the lands about. High mounds of crushed and powdered rock, great cones of earth fire-blasted and poison-stained, stood like an obscene graveyard in endless rows, slowly revealed in the reluctant light. (*LotR* IV.2.631)

What reads like a description of the battlefields in northern France during the Great War is in fact a scene from John Ronald Reuel Tolkien's fantasy epic *The Lord of the Rings*. During the Great War, Tolkien served on the British side in the Battle of the Somme in 1916. Most of his friends did not survive the war and the horror of the trench warfare left its mark on Tolkien for the rest of his life. The destruction of a peaceful world by 'evil' and loss through death were to become the core themes of his literary work. This article examines how the experiences of the young Tolkien in the Great War affected his major work, *The Lord of the Rings*.

Those who read *The Lord of the Rings* with scientific curiosity will find approaches to interpretation in all areas of academic research, be it philosophy, botany, theology or history. Reading the epic as a historian, one will notice the many links to the Great War. They are rarely direct juxtapositions, but rather individual moments and images, conveyed feelings, and the unspoken between the lines that are reminiscent of the war.

Tolkien's aversion to biographical interpretations of his works becomes very clear in his letters; in one, for example, he says "I object to the contemporary trend in criticism, with its excessive interest in the details of the lives of authors and artists. They only distract attention from an author's works [...] and end, as one now often sees, in becoming the main interest" (*Letters* 288). Considering the frequency of such arguments in his correspondence, one realises how parallels were already being drawn during his lifetime between his experiences and his literary work – obviously much to his displeasure. For the scientific approach to his work, however, it is essential to consider the biography of its author. In spite of Tolkien's opinion, I think that it by no means distracts attention from the work, but rather directs a more sensitive focus to it and enables a multi-layered exploration. After all, Tolkien himself could not deny the influence of his experiences on his literary work, and said in his Foreword to *The Lord of the Rings*: "An author cannot of course remain wholly unaffected by his experience, but the ways in which a story-germ uses the soil of experience are extremely complex, and attempts to define the process are at best guesses from evidence that is inadequate and ambiguous" (*LotR* Foreword.xxiv).

I intend to look at *The Lord of the Rings* through the lens of *applicability*, as suggested by Tolkien (Foreword.xxiv). This principle allows his sub-creation to be applied to real structures, without forming simple and insufficient allegories: "I think that many confuse 'applicability' with 'allegory'; but the one resides in the freedom of the reader, and the other in the purposed domination of the author" (Foreword.xxiv). Every person is influenced and shaped by the circumstances and the time in which he lives and grows up; both the author, whose personal experiences can flow into his work, and the reader, who looks at the story through the lens of his own time. Tolkien's experiences on the Western Front in 1916 can be found in *The Lord of the Rings*, but only if one knows what to look for or if one intensively examines the subject of the Great War. The element of applicability is so subtly and sensitively implemented that it offers the reader a more complex level of observation.

By taking up structures and elements from the primary world, the sub-creation becomes more credible and coherent. These models are closely linked to the author's experiences and views: "I take my models like anyone else – from such 'life' as I know" (*Letters* 235). The same happens to Tolkien's war and other life experiences. His fictional world in *The Lord of the Rings* has a narrative density that can be traced back to the influences of the primary world. His friend, C.S. Lewis, who had also served on the Western Front, reviewed *The Lord of the Rings* and wrote about the War of the Ring:

> This war has the very quality of the war my generation knew. It is all there: the endless, unintelligible movement, the sinister quiet of the front, when 'everything is now ready', the flying civilians, the lively, vivid friendships, the background of something like despair and the merry foreground, and such

heaven-sent windfalls as a *cache* of choice tobacco 'salvaged' from a ruin. (Lewis 88, emphasis in the original)

With this he could have unintentionally encouraged the search for allegories by fans (and scholars) instead of preventing them, as was probably his intention. Tolkien himself, too, underlined the importance of his war experiences for his novel: "One has indeed personally to come under the shadow of war to feel fully its oppression; but as the years go by it seems now often forgotten that to be caught in youth by 1914 was no less hideous an experience than to be involved in 1939 and the following years" (Foreword.xi).

Where and how to find the Great War in Middle-earth?

In order to find Tolkien's Great War experiences in *The Lord of The Rings*, I have divided the above mentioned 'moments' that are reminiscent of the war into three categories, which I will examine in more detail below.

Visual descriptions

The destruction of nature by industrialisation already concerned Tolkien in his childhood. The destruction of nature by the war, which he had experienced as a young man, must have been an even more drastic experience for him. So it is not surprising that the clearest element of the Great War in *The Lord of the Rings* is a destroyed landscape. Christoph Nübel, a German military historian, describes the landscape on the Western Front: "The war landscape here was a vast area of infinite destruction. It no longer had any of the usual landscape features and seemed completely extinct. The gas in the atmosphere additionally underlined its hostile character" (Nübel 305, my translation).

In Tolkien's main work, Frodo Baggins and Samwise (Sam) Gamgee cross the Dead Marshes on their way to Mordor together with Gollum. It is an inhospitable, marshy land that is difficult to pass. A long time ago a great battle had taken place there. While passing through, the three companions come across the ghostly remains of the many warriors who died in that battle. In its description, the Dead Marshes are very reminiscent of the war landscape at the Somme:

> On either side and in front wide fens and mires now lay, stretching away southward and eastward into the dim half-light. Mists curled and smoked from dark and noisome pools. The reek of them hung stifling in the still air. Far away, now almost due south, the mountain-walls of Mordor loomed, like a black bar of rugged clouds floating above a dangerous fog-bound sea. (*LotR* IV.2.625)

The no man's land between the trenches may have left a very similar impression: a rutted, muddy land, where impact holes filled with rainwater, creating numerous puddles and pools. Fog, created by the smoke from the guns, hung over a foul-smelling swamp. In *The Lord of the Rings* Frodo, Sam, and Gollum come across the faces of the dead lying in the water. This sight could be found in the Somme's no man's land as well. The bodies of the fallen soldiers could usually not be salvaged and buried. Thus, their corpses remained there and decayed very fast in the humid soil. Soldiers who were hit by shells did not leave bodies behind that could have been buried. Their remains penetrated the earth much faster. The heavy autumn rains of 1916 contributed furthermore to the marshy landscape that would later inspire the Dead Marshes.

> There was a faint hiss, a noisome smell went up, the lights flickered and danced and swirled. For a moment the water below [Sam] looked like some window, glazed with grimy glass, through which he was peering. Wrenching his hands out of the bog, he sprang back with a cry. 'There are dead things, dead faces in the water,' he said with horror. 'Dead faces!' [...]
>
> [Frodo:] 'They lie in all the pools, pale faces, deep deep under the dark water. I saw them: grim faces and evil, and noble faces and sad. Many faces proud and fair, and weeds in their silver hair. But all foul, all rotting, all dead.' (*LotR* IV.2.627-628)

At the Somme, the young Tolkien had been confronted with a similarly terrible picture several times. Comparing this striking passage with Humphrey Carpenter's description of what Tolkien witnessed at the front, the applicability becomes even clearer:

> Worst of all were the dead men, for corpses lay in every corner, horribly torn by the shells. Those that still had faces stared with dreadful eyes. Beyond the trenches no-man's-land was littered with bloated and decaying bodies. All around was desolation. Grass and corn had vanished into a sea of mud. Trees, stripped of leaf and branch, stood as mere mutilated and blackened trunks. Tolkien never forgot what he called the 'animal horror' of trench warfare. (Carpenter 117-118)

This was perhaps Tolkien's first encounter with so many decomposing and bloated bodies, when his battalion marched to Usna Hill and the following morning to the front at La Boisselle on 14th July 1916. There they found many dead soldiers who had fallen victim to the Battle of the Somme that had started on the 1st of July. The stench from the trenches on the frontline could already be smelled from far away, just like the Dead Marshes. The faces staring 'with dreadful eyes' is something else that later became a part of the marshlands in Middle-earth. The following dialogue follows directly on Frodo's above quoted statement:

> Frodo hid his eyes in his hands. 'I know not who they are; but I thought I saw there Men and Elves, and Orcs beside them.'
>
> 'Yes, yes,' said Gollum. 'All dead, all rotten. Elves and Men and Orcs. The Dead Marshes. There was a great battle long ago [...]. They fought on the plain for days and months at the Black Gates. But the Marshes have grown since then, swallowed up the graves; always creeping, creeping.' (IV.2.628)

Death does not distinguish between good and evil, as implied by Gollum's statement. Here, too, a long time ago, a great battle had taken place which had raged for several months, similar to its possible model, the Battle of the Somme. In the no man's and of the Somme, German soldiers lay next to British, Irish, French and many others, just as in the Dead Marshes elves lay next to humans and orcs. The swampy area at the Somme has changed since 1918; it has become green again. The large war cemeteries, which today characterise the landscape along the Somme, usually contain single and predominantly anonymous gravestones or crosses, but they are only symbolic: the dead are rarely, as in civilian cemeteries, directly under the respective gravestone. In this respect, nature has also 'swallowed' the graves of the fallen in reality, as Gollum calls it. Perhaps Tolkien may have thought of the burial of his friends Rob Gilson and Geoffrey B. Smith while writing this passage, as their graves have also lost all individuality and dignity.

When Boromir dies in *The Lord of the Rings*, it is very important to his companions to give him a proper burial. They have very little time, but they do not want to leave his body between his enemies. "'First we must tend the fallen,' said Legolas. 'We cannot leave him lying like carrion among these foul Orcs.' [...] 'We have not the time or the tools to bury our comrade fitly, or to raise a mound over him'" (*LotR* III.1.414-415). So they decide on a ship burial for their fallen 'comrade' – note the term!

The many unburied dead intensify the horror of the unnatural landscape even more – in the Dead Marshes as well as at the Somme. The destruction of nature brought about by mankind and the misuse of technology and progress for the purpose of destruction are further core topics in *The Lord of the Rings*. Tolkien wrote in a letter in 1960: "Personally I do not think that either war (and of course not the atomic bomb) had any influence upon either the plot or the manner of its unfolding. Perhaps in landscape. The Dead Marshes and the approaches to the Morannon owe something to Northern France after the Battle of the Somme" (*Letters* 303). Here again, Tolkien's dislike of simple allegories becomes apparent. Five years after the publication of *The Lord of the Rings* he had to face more and more questions and discussions about possible comparisons. In this quote he at least gives one possibility concerning the Dead Marshes and the foreland to Mordor. But just in the next sentence he states: "They owe more to William Morris and his Huns and Romans, as in *The House of the Wolfings* or *The Roots of the Mountains*" (*Letters* 303). He thus relativises his previous statement and shows that a direct comparison is not that simple.

Another example of the applicable visual correspondence with the conditions on the Western Front is the abandoned city of Osgiliath. It is the last defense between Minas Tirith and the enemy in Mordor. In between there is a wasteland, also called 'Noman-lands' (*LotR* IV.2.631). Osgiliath is captured and liberated several times. The city belongs to Ithilien, a province of Gondor. It is defended by the rangers of Faramir, who says about Osgiliath: "So do we ever watch the shores nigh Osgiliath, which our enemies now partly hold, and issue from it to harry our lands" (*LotR* IV.5.666).

Those who return to Ithilien from battles or explorations feel the relief of not being that close to the 'front' anymore. Yet there is a constant awareness here of how close the enemy has already come. Osgiliath and other places are little more than ruins and their inhabitants have long since fled or died. Ithilien is now used as a base against the enemy and offers several places of refuge. Henneth Annûn is the largest base and serves as both a command centre and a retreat where soldiers can gather their strength before returning to battle. This description fits Osgiliath as well as Rubempré or Bouzincourt: abandoned places in the hinterland of the front, of which only ruins remain, that served the commanders as a retreat and also as a command centre. Places where the immediate proximity of war was perceptible and audible: the noise of the artillery, the buzzing and screeching of the grenades being fired as well as their impact, the whistling that signaled an attack, the rattling of the machine guns, the noise of planes and tanks as well as the cries of the soldiers. Despite the background noise, which in such places might have been somewhat (but not much) muffled, they were relatively outside the danger zone, so that soldiers could recover in a quieter and perhaps more natural landscape, at least for a short time.

Dagorlad, the battle plain just to the north of the gates of Mordor, and Mordor itself are both wastelands in which nothing fertile will ever grow again: "a land defiled, diseased beyond all healing – unless the Great Seas should enter in and wash it with oblivion" (*LotR* IV.2.631-632). Only the sea could cleanse this place, but even then the land, like Atlantis or Númenor, would be lost forever. For the hobbits, a dead country like Mordor is even more horrible than the Dead Marshes in which between all the dead faces there was at least a touch of nature:

> Frodo looked round in horror. Dreadful as the Dead Marshes had been, and the arid moors of the Noman-lands, more loathsome far was the country that the crawling day now slowly unveiled to his shrinking eyes. Even to the Mere of Dead Faces some haggard phantom of green spring would come; but here neither spring nor summer would ever come again. Here nothing lived, not even the leprous growths that feed on rottenness. (*LotR* IV.2.631)

In this passage Tolkien conveys in a very poignant language what will happen to the world (and to nature) if evil prevails. It is not difficult to recognise his own experiences of war:

> The gasping pools were choked with ash and crawling muds, sickly white and grey, as if the mountains had vomited the filth of their entrails upon the lands about. High mounds of crushed and powdered rock, great cones of earth fire-blasted and poison-stained, stood like an obscene graveyard in endless rows, slowly revealed in the reluctant light. (IV.2.631)

This representation of the Dead Marshes, with which I introduced this paper, could also be a description of the landscape at the Somme in 1916. In particular, the "great cones of earth fire-blasted and poison-stained" are more reminiscent of the impact holes of grenades and artillery than of ground formations in

Mordor. The fear of poison gas attacks in the Great War remained the same among the soldiers on both sides. Also the "gasping pools [...] choked with ash" and the "crawling muds, sickly white and grey" would have been an everyday sight at the frontline. In Mordor, everything was cleared for the purpose of industrialisation and war; nature was irretrievably destroyed. This fate would also have befallen Fangorn Forest if Saruman had not been stopped in his preparations for war in Isengard. Especially for a nature lover and a sensitive mind like Tolkien, the battlefields at the Somme must have left a similar impression to the one that Isengard and Mordor do on the reader: a landscape so devastated and rutted by the war that it seems impossible to imagine that anything could ever grow there again. For both hobbits, as well as for Tolkien himself, evil shows itself in the form of environmental destruction. To describe this destroyed landscape, he used the language and images of war, industrialisation, and urbanisation.

Emotional impressions

Even more intense, but less tangible, are the emotional impressions in the story, which strongly recall the Great War and the time after it. These impressions are most clearly manifested in the characters of Frodo and Sam. They are the only members of the fellowship who cross the Dead Marshes and Mordor. They have the most difficult task: the destruction of the One Ring in Mount Doom. A constant feeling of threat and imminent doom accompanies the two hobbits and thus also the reader. If they fail in their quest (one could perhaps say 'duty to their fatherland'), the freedom of the entire world is at stake. As they walk through the dead landscape of Mordor, both are physically ill and show symptoms similar to those of the Great War soldiers, as well as hunger and great thirst: "'Water, water!' muttered Sam. He had stinted himself, and in his parched mouth his tongue seemed thick and swollen; but for all his care they now had very little left, perhaps half his bottle, and maybe there were still days to go" (*LotR* VI.3.936).

The air in Mordor is filled with ash clouds and smoke, breathing is difficult, and there is a heavy, bitter stench, as of decaying corpses. The other companions, each acting in their own storyline, are also affected by this growing threat.

Before the battle for Helm's Deep there is a long wait for the Rohirrim, while the mighty enemy army is getting closer and closer. The men in the fortress can't see their enemy, but they can hear their approach. Occasionally a lightning bolt illuminates the landscape in front of them and they see the overpowering enemy for a short moment. They do not know if they will survive the night:

> It was now past midnight. The sky was utterly dark, and the stillness of the heavy air foreboded storm. Suddenly the clouds were seared by a blinding flash. Branched lightning smote down upon the eastward hills. For a staring moment the watchers on the walls saw all the space between them and the Dike lit with white light. (*LotR* III.7.532)

This scene could as well have occurred in a trench: the anxiety and the waiting, the poor visibility, and, at the same time, the knowledge that the enemy is nearby until a sudden flash of light, perhaps triggered by shellfire, brightens the landscape for too short a moment. The Rohirrim may have won the Battle of Helm's Deep, but it's clear that this victory, like any other, is only temporary – a 'breather' in the War of the Ring. Again, it shows how important it was for Tolkien that the dead receive a burial in his literary work. In the morning after the battle for Helm's Deep, the Rohirrim build two burial mounds for their dead and bury the bodies according to their origin in Rohan: one for the Westfold men and one for the men of the East Dales. Háma, captain of the king's guard of Théoden, is buried in his own grave (*LotR* III.8.545).

One thing that defines the modern warfare of the Great War is the emotional and psychological stress soldiers were constantly under. In Middle-earth, there is also an equivalent. Psychologically, the most terrible weapon of the enemy is the undead Nazgûl, whose shrill screams spread terror and despair among Gondor's soldiers (*LotR* V.4.808-809, 823). As soon as the soldiers hear the screeching, they are paralysed with shock and even the bravest of them can no longer fight:

> The Nazgûl came again, and as their Dark Lord now grew and put forth his strength, so their voices, which uttered only his will and his malice, were filled with evil and horror. Ever they circled above the City, like vultures that expect their fill of doomed men's flesh. Out of sight and shot they flew, and yet were ever present, and their deadly voices rent the air. More unbearable they became, not less, at each new cry. At length even the stout-hearted would fling themselves to the ground as the hidden menace passed over them, or they would stand, letting their weapons fall from nerveless hands while into their

> minds a blackness came, and they thought no more of war; but only of hiding and of crawling, and of death. (*LotR* V.4.823)

Soldiers on both sides of the front showed a similar reaction to falling, screeching grenades. Paul Ettighofer, a veteran of Verdun, writes:

> The bursting of the mines drowned out the long, dull, booming howling of the invisible grenades. It roars around, it smashes into the day, it is mean and malicious and causes nausea or insanity in the brain. It faints people and paralyzes all decisiveness. You live in this chaos of noise and you can't think. You get drunk from shaking your head and chest, drunk from the roar of the material battle. (Ettighofer 58, my translation)

Both descriptions are very similar. Gondor's soldiers too clearly show a kind of war neurosis. They can only think of hiding, of getting themselves to safety (even crawling), and they think of death, no longer of their orders, as if everything had become indifferent. Their hands are 'unnerved' or 'nerveless'; they have lost their nerves (*LotR* V.4.823).

Political and social level

Mechanised warfare is the most striking comparison between the Great War and the War of the Ring in *The Lord of the Rings*. The enemy fights with unprecedented technologies and mass-produced weapons and armor in an army that is both progressive and numerically superior. Tolkien pushes the mechanised warfare in his work to the extreme. The soldiers themselves, the orcs, have been bred for war and know neither fear nor pain. They are "fundamentally a race of 'rational incarnate' creatures, though horribly corrupted" (*Letters* 190); genetically engineered beings held as slaves by evil. Saruman leads the industrialisation of Middle-earth, roots out entire forests, and has joined evil to gain even more power. Nature itself, in the form of the Ents, the tree shepherds of Fangorn Forest, rebels against the industry that made war possible. The Ents destroy the wall around Isengard and another natural force, the River Isen released by the Ents, destroys Saruman's machinery. Here another element related to the Great War can be found. The Ent Treebeard reflects like a young soldier about the entry into the war: "Of course, it is likely enough, my friends [...] that we are going to our doom: the last march of the Ents. But if we stayed at home and did nothing, doom would find us anyway, sooner or later" (*LotR* III.4.486).

When the water breaks in over Isengard, the underground "factory halls" are flooded and destroyed. Even though it is not explicitly described, it can be assumed that not all orcs have been withdrawn from Isengard before to fight in Helm's Deep. Rather, many would have been left behind to continue the production of weapons and armour. These orcs will have drowned in the flooding water. This picture in turn evokes the description of wounded soldiers who drowned in grenade funnels during the Third Battle of Flanders in Ypres. Due to the low groundwater level, the impact craters filled up very quickly in heavy rain and the ground became a swampy mud. Anyone who was injured, looking for shelter from artillery fire in one of those holes, or slipped, was usually unable to escape and eventually drowned in the rising water. The Dead Marshes can also be found in this picture.

The battle over Minas Tirith on the Pelennor Fields is the largest battle in the War of the Ring. Different armies of the free peoples of Middle-earth fight against the army of Sauron, which is superior in numbers. During the battle, Minas Tirith is under siege, which is described very vividly. The ground around the city is covered with debris and corpses and the orcs are beginning to dig trenches around Minas Tirith out of bowshot:

> Busy as ants hurrying orcs were digging, digging lines of deep trenches in a huge ring, just out of bowshot from the walls; and as the trenches were made each was filled with fire, though how it was kindled or fed, by art or devilry, none could see. All day the labour went forward, while the men of Minas Tirith looked on, unable to hinder it. And as each length of trench was completed, they could see great wains approaching; and soon yet more companies of the enemy were swiftly setting up, each behind the cover of a trench, great engines for the casting of missiles. (*LotR* V.4.822)

The orcs have "machines", siege towers and projectiles that can ignite fire behind the city walls, and catapults with which they throw the severed heads of fallen Gondorian soldiers into the city (822-823). Terms like 'missiles', 'engines', or 'trenches' are more reminiscent of a modern, mechanised war than a medieval-like battle in a fantasy epic. This applies to the general language of this chapter as well. During the battle Pippin says: "The Lord has given me leave" (827) – he is 'on leave' from the front, so to speak – there is a "great assault" (828), and the narrator mentions "companies" (V.1.170, for example) more than once. The quotation above also mentions trenches filled with fire, of which nobody is able to explain how they are kindled. A German soldier wrote in January 1916 in a letter to his parents:

> The [French] trenches were splashed with a burning liquid. From our battery observatory, one could observe very well. Everything was covered in black steam and smoke, through which from time to time one saw fiery rays shoot. [...] The newspaper does not say, of course, that it was a fire attack, nor does the French report, of course, say anything about it. (Ebert 130, my translation)

It is not clear whether Tolkien had ever seen or heard of such a flame attack as it is described here. However, the similarity of the descriptions is very astonishing. The siege technique used by Sauron's army ranges from medieval to ancient. It has catapults, projectiles, siege towers and a large battering ram (*LotR* V.4.828-829). But the tactics and the way they are used are more similar to modern warfare than an archaic one. The deadly projectiles mentioned in the quote, fired behind the trenches, immediately evoke artillery guns. It is a clear example of Tolkien's applicability: he tells of a terrible war, consciously or unconsciously processing his own experiences, and places it in a fantastic and archaic secondary world.

What remains at the end of the story, both for the reader and for the characters, is a feeling of loss. At the end of the Third Age, the elves leave Middle-earth and with them much knowledge and culture are forgotten and irretrievably lost. The certainty remains that the world has changed completely within a very short time as a result of the events in the war and that society has been forced into completely new patterns. This was also true in 1918, when millions of young men were dead who could have contributed to society, economy, and culture. Life was no longer the same: an age had passed, a new one had dawned. The end of the war not only brought relief and joy, but also terrible loss and great sorrow – in England as well as in Middle-earth.

When Frodo and Sam return to the Shire after the destruction of the Ring, they have to solve one last conflict together with their companions Merry and Pippin. Saruman has subjugated the Shire and must be defeated. In this respect, their home is saved twice: by destroying the One Ring and by defeating Saruman. But it is lost to the war veteran Frodo.

> 'But,' said Sam, and tears started in his eyes, 'I thought you were going to enjoy the Shire, too, for many years, after all you have done.'

> [Frodo:] 'So I thought too, once. But I have been too deeply hurt, Sam. I tried to save the Shire, and it has been saved, but not for me. It must often be so, Sam, when things are in danger: some one has to give them up, lose them, so that others may keep them.' (*LotR* VI.9.1029)

Tolkien wrote in an undated letter, probably in 1956, "I think that 'victors' never can enjoy 'victory' – not in the terms that they envisaged; and in so far as they fought for something *to be enjoyed by themselves* (whether acquisition or mere preservation) the less satisfactory will 'victory' seem" (*Letters* 235, emphasis in the original). Just like Frodo finds no peace for himself, many veterans despaired after their return. War neuroses, trauma, depression, and suicide were part of everyday life in the 1920s. The inability to talk about what they had experienced and the lack of treatment for (new) mental illness in many cases led to the isolation of the soldiers from society. Frodo as well withdraws more and more from social life. He is often sick, and his wounds never heal completely. He is plagued by nightmares and hallucinations – he cannot get rid of his war trauma. In contrast to Frodo, Sam manages to leave his war experiences behind him (Hooker 132-133). He finds joy in the Shire and is happy and grateful to be home again. Sam starts his own family and rises from a simple gardener to mayor of the Shire. In a way, he is very similar to Tolkien, who felt most attached to the Hobbits of all of Middle-earth's peoples:

> I am in fact a *Hobbit* (in all but size). I like gardens, trees and unmechanized farmlands; I smoke a pipe, and like good plain food [...]; I like, and even dare to wear in these dull days, ornamental waistcoats. I am fond of mushrooms (out of a field); have a very simple sense of humour (which even my appreciative critics find tiresome); I go to bed late and get up late (when possible). I do not travel much. (*Letters* 288-289, emphasis in original)

Like Sam, Tolkien returned to his wife and started a family with four children, developed professionally and eventually became famous. On the other hand, he is not like the hobbit, because Sam symbolises the simple soldier, the British Tommy, for whom Tolkien had great respect. In June 1941 he wrote in one of many letters to his son Michael, who at that time served as a soldier in the British air force during the Second World War: "I suffered once what you are going through, if rather differently: because I was very inefficient and unmilitary (and we are alike only in sharing a deep sympathy and feeling for the 'tommy', especially the plain soldier from the agricultural counties)" (*Letters* 54).

Michael Livingston argues that Tolkien himself is most clearly reflected in Frodo's character and his non-healing (spiritual) wounds (Livingston 20-21). In my opinion, Tolkien's social environment, his starting a family, and his general mindset contradict this. Without wanting to draw comparisons and allegories with Tolkien's life, in the characters of Sam and Frodo, Tolkien combines both sides of the homecoming from war. One respect in which Tolkien actually seems more similar to Frodo than Sam is his social status. Sam doesn't just stand for the simple Tommy, but personifies the classic batman, the officer's servant. Stamina and tenacity, limited imagination, narrow-mindedness and stubborn optimism, courage and indestructibility as character traits as well as the tasks during the mission speak for it: Sam takes care of Frodo's things, rations the food, cares for Frodo's physical and psychological well-being and encourages and reinforces him again and again. He defends and saves his master (or 'officer') many times (Hooker 125, 127-128). Tolkien himself wrote "My 'Sam Gamgee' is indeed a reflexion of the English soldier, of the privates and batmen I knew in the 1914 war, and recognised as so far superior to myself" (Carpenter 114).

Frodo, on the other hand, fills the role of the officer. As the Ring-bearer, he is the leader of the fellowship, he must decide where to go and which paths to take. When the fellowship breaks, Frodo and Sam move on alone. Now the relationship between the officer and the batman becomes even clearer. Like many soldiers, Frodo feels the burden of the whole world on his shoulders and asks why it came to him, of all people, at the beginning (*LotR* I.2.51). He wishes it hadn't happened during his lifetime, but in the course of the story he accepts his destiny and grows with it: "I feel that as long as the Shire lies behind, safe and comfortable, I shall find wandering more bearable: I shall know that somewhere there is a firm foothold, even if my feet cannot stand there again" (*LotR* I.2.62).

This must have happened to many volunteers who, after their initial enthusiasm for war, had to experience the shocking disillusionment of the reality of war. It may have been a comfort to them that their family and home were safe and that it was worth the effort. Frodo, too, is only a 'small man' who bears an excessive burden for the common good and who recognises the appreciation for his homeland and his ordinary, simple life too late.

What is striking is that Sam's role as batman is emphasised more when Frodo and Sam are in great danger. For example, when Frodo is held as a prisoner by the orcs in the tower of Cirith Ungol in Mordor. Sam saves him and puts himself in grave danger. But it is his duty, whatever happens, and so he fulfills it (*LotR* VI.1.901). And as the two hobbits master the last and most dangerous stage of their journey, through Mordor and to Mount Doom, Sam takes the lead as Frodo becomes too weak: "'So that was the job I felt I had to do when I started,' thought Sam: 'to help Mr. Frodo to the last step and then die with him? Well, if that is the job then I must do it'" (*LotR* VI.3.934).

Sam accepts his own death because he will die together with Frodo in fulfilling his mission. The next moment, his dwindling hope and acceptance of his own death turn into new strength and iron will. With a new sense of responsibility, Sam realises that Mordor is a land rutted by craters, in whose 'grenade funnels', one might almost say, they can find shelter. With this determination he convinces Frodo to go on. In the end, Sam carries his master when he can no longer walk himself, thus ensuring that the mission can be completed successfully (*LotR* VI.3.940-941). Sam is the real hero of the story and thus exemplifies Tolkien's respect for the simple soldier.

When Sauron is finally defeated, Saruman flees to the peaceful and secluded Shire to continue to wield his power there. The returning hobbits organise the resistance and Saruman is finally defeated. During the scouring of the Shire, another characteristic of the traumatised war survivor is revealed in Frodo: He is determined to prevent anyone from being killed and refuses to take part in the fighting himself. Even Saruman, who is responsible for the destruction and suffering and who tries to kill Frodo, is spared (*LotR* VI.8.1005, 1018-20). Merry then says to him, "But if there are many of these ruffians, [...] it will certainly mean fighting. You won't rescue [...] the Shire, just by being shocked and sad, my dear Frodo" (1006).

The expression "being shocked" is conspicuous and immediately reminds the reader of "shell shock" in this context. Before, in Ithilien, at the celebrations in honour of him and Sam, Frodo hesitates to put on a ceremonial sword (*LotR* IV.4.954-955). Further signs of post-traumatic stress disorder can be seen in Frodo until his departure at the end of the story. The most impressive scene is probably this one: "On the thirteenth of that month Farmer Cotton found Frodo lying on his bed; he was clutching a white gem that hung on a chain about his neck and he seemed half in a dream. 'It is gone forever,' he said, 'and now all is dark and empty'" (*LotR* VI.9.1024).

It doesn't become clear exactly what 'it' is that Frodo has lost forever. At first one might think of the One Ring, because he holds Arwen's Evenstar just as he had held the corrupting ring. But 'it' could also symbolise innocence or hope (Livingston 18). Or the lost intimacy, the feeling of belonging to a big whole or the joy over being home. Whatever it is, without it everything is "dark and empty." This passage has a certain resemblance to Frodo's statement on the slopes of Mount Doom, shortly before the destruction of the Ring: "I am naked in the dark, Sam, and there is no veil between me and the wheel of fire. I begin to see it even with my waking eyes, and all else fades" (*LotR* VI.3.938).

Like many traumatised soldiers of the Great War, Frodo has lost his sense of taste and misses parts of his memory. He can no longer remember what exactly happened, only the moment itself is perceptible. On the way back home, however, the memory turns into torture. At the Ford of the Bruinen, where Frodo had barely escaped the Nazgûl at the beginning of the journey, he is reminded of his injury by the ringwraiths on Weathertop. The wound hurts and the memory weighs heavily on him – exactly one year has passed to the day – and Gandalf explains that some wounds will never heal completely. Frodo realizes "There is no real going back. Though I may come to the Shire, it will not seem the same; for I shall not be the same. I am wounded with knife, sting, and tooth, and a long burden. Where shall I find rest?" (*LotR* VI.7.989). Frodo finds no peace and leaves Middle-earth at the end of the story. He leaves all his possessions to his faithful friend Sam, who not only provided for Frodo before and during the war, but also afterwards.

Friendship and comradeship are the guiding topics of Tolkien's work. The special friendship between Frodo and Sam is also the camaraderie of two soldiers who together fought for their lives. The hobbits Merry and Pippin as well as Legolas and Gimli also embody such camaraderie motifs, although there is no difference in rank among them. Joseph Loconte thematically describes this in his book *A Hobbit, a Wardrobe, and a Great War*: "[A]s veterans of this conflict, Tolkien and Lewis chose to remember not only its horrors and sorrows: they wanted to recall the courage, sacrifice, and the friendship that made it endurable" (Loconte 170).

The loss of his closest friends during the war accompanied Tolkien throughout his life. Not only his most important friends of the TCBS, but also many fellow students and acquaintances had signed up for military service and never returned from the trenches. When Tolkien wrote in 1965 "By 1918 all but one of my close friends were dead" (*LotR* Foreword.xxiv), he probably meant even more friends than Rob Gilson and Geoffrey B. Smith. Maybe that's why the friendship with C.S. Lewis was so important to Tolkien; Lewis had also served on the front lines and could understand Tolkien in a way that probably only very few could. In 1916, G.B. Smith wrote to Tolkien:

> I do pray for you at all times and in all places [...], and may you survive, and we survive the fiery trial of these events without loss of our powers or our determination. So shall all things be for good. Meanwhile trust God and keep your powder dry, and be assured that to three other men you are more than their own selves. (qtd. in Garth, *Great War* 145)

Due to the early loss of his parents and Father Francis's later ban on continuing to meet with Edith, Tolkien turned more to his male friends and it can be said that they were a kind of a family substitute in some ways.

It is often speculated whether the orcs in Tolkien's work are a parallel to German soldiers (Croft 47-50). It doesn't really matter whether we are talking about the First or the Second World War. If one imagines a war scene in which the enemy comes through the smoke as a grey mass, silhouette-like and threatening, one can certainly see the inspiration for the orcs. Imagine gas masks that rob any human characteristic from a face and that distort language, as incomprehensible as it may have sounded before, even more strangely. Modris Eksteins writes:

> For many, gas took the war into the realm of the unreal, the make-believe. When men donned their masks they lost all sign of humanity, and with their long snouts, large glass eyes, and slow movements, they became figures of fantasy, closer in their angular features to the creations of Picasso and Braque than to soldiers of tradition. (Eksteins 163)

This is another example of how the element of applicability can be applied to Tolkien's work. At a time when many Englishmen had their German surnames anglicized – the most famous of them being George V – Tolkien had great respect for the German nation (Garth, *Great War* 42). More than 20 years later and one year after the publication of *The Hobbit*, Tolkien received an inquiry in 1938 from Rütten & Loening Publishers in Potsdam, who wanted to translate *The Hobbit*. For the translation, however, proof of Tolkien's Aryan origin was necessary, which Tolkien refused (*Letters* 37-38). This is one of the reasons why it took so long for the book to be published in German. Tolkien prepared two possible reply letters, only one of which remains, so it must be assumed that the other (possibly milder) letter was sent. The remaining draft, however, provides much information about Tolkien's attitude to the 'German cultural heritage':

> I have been accustomed, nonetheless, to regard my German name with pride, and continued to do so throughout the period of the late regrettable war, in which I served in the English army. I cannot, however, forbear to comment, that if impertinent and irrelevant inquiries of this sort are to become the rule in matters of literature, then the time is not far distant when a German name will no longer be a source of pride. (*Letters* 37-38)

In 1941 Tolkien wrote a letter to his son Michael to air his anger towards Nazi Germany:

> I have spent most of my life, since I was your age, studying Germanic matters (in the general sense that includes England and Scandinavia). There is a great deal more force (and truth) than ignorant people imagine in the 'Germanic' ideal. I was much attracted to it as an undergraduate (when Hitler was, I suppose, dabbling in paint, and had not heard of it). [...] I suppose I know better than most what is the truth about this 'Nordic' nonsense. (*Letters* 55)

And because this 'Germanic ideal' from the quote above was so important to him, he cherished a personal grudge against Adolf Hitler and National Socialism, who had so corrupted this ideal:

> Anyway, I have in this War a burning private grudge – which would probably make me a better soldier at 49 than I was at 22: against that ruddy little ignoramus Adolf Hitler [...]. Ruining, perverting, misapplying, and making for ever accursed, that noble northern spirit, a supreme contribution to Europe, which I have ever loved, and tried to present in its true light. (*Letters* 55-56)

In an interview with *Sunday Times Magazine* in 1967, in which he was explicitly asked for a confrontation of orcs and Germans, Tolkien said very clearly, "I've never had those sort of feelings about the Germans. I'm very anti that kind of thing" (qtd. in Garth, *Great War* 219).

A certain influence on the concept of the enemy drawn in *The Lord of the Rings* can be seen (Croft 47-50). However, it is limited to exactly that – the influence on the concept of an enemy – and it does not represent an allegory to a certain ethnic group. So, one could also see the adversarial Germans as a 'model' for the Haradrim who were enemies of Gondor. Like the German Empire, Harad is a strong country, whose inhabitants are not essentially evil, but have been led into war by their leaders. They used the old enmity between Harad and Gondor to further fuel hatred and warfare.

In Ithilien, Sam, who repeatedly acts as an identification figure for the reader, experiences for the first time a battle between humans. A Haradrim dies and falls to the ground in front of Sam. The hobbit reflects on the similarity of the young man with himself and his own situation. He wonders whether he was really evil or whether unfortunate circumstances had brought him into this hostile situation: "[Sam] wondered what the man's name was and where he came from; and if he was really evil of heart, or what lies or threats had led him on the long march from his home; and if he would not really rather have stayed there in peace" (*LotR* IV.4.661).

This may reflect Tolkien's own experiences with the death of enemy soldiers, most of them at his age. He may have seen many of them in the no man's land at the Somme or in conquered trenches. It also shows that Tolkien did not construct a Manichaean world view in his work. The categories 'good' and 'evil' are relative and 'the good' are not all consistently good. One example is Boromir, who is influenced by the Ring and tries to steal it from Frodo. Frodo also falls for the Ring at the end. Likewise, as the above quote shows, the ones fighting for 'evil' are perhaps just soldiers on one side of the war. It is a story about war and as such, two sides are inevitably at war with each other. One side is 'the good side' from their own perspective, as opposed to their enemies fighting on the 'side of evil'. For Tolkien it mattered and made a difference who the leaders of each side were and what their intentions looked like (*Letters* 82). Tolkien also used the term 'Orc' (as well as 'Orkishness') in his everyday language for people who did evil or were evil in his eyes (*Letters* 64, 78, 82,

111, 246). From cutting down forests for industry to fascism, this term could encompass many kinds of 'malice'. Conversely, Tolkien also used terms like 'Hobbit' or 'Hobbitry' for the goodness in human beings (*Letters* 78, 170, 288-289). In 1944, Tolkien wrote a letter to his youngest son Christopher, who at the time was in pilot training with the British Air Force in South Africa:

> For we are attempting to conquer Sauron with the Ring. And we shall (it seems) succeed. But the penalty is, as you will know, to breed new Saurons, and slowly turn Men and Elves into Orcs. Not that in real life things are as clear cut as in a story, and we started out with a great many Orcs on our side . . . . . Well, there you are: a hobbit amongst the Urukhai. Keep up your hobbitry in heart, and think that all stories feel like that when you are *in* them. You are inside a very great story! (*Letters* 78, emphasis in the original)

This excerpt shows how Tolkien used terms and characters from his secondary world as metaphors in the primary world to describe facts or express his opinion. Tolkien's own attitude to war is probably best illustrated by Faramir's oft-quoted statement: "War must be, while we defend our lives against a destroyer who would devour all; but I do not love the bright sword for its sharpness, nor the arrow for its swiftness, nor the warrior for his glory. I love only that which they defend" (*LotR* IV.5.672). Faramir is an exception among men and, with his views on war and his chosen tactics, represents a modern commander rather than an archaic one. Both in Gondor and Rohan, war is almost glorified. Especially for the Rohirrim it is the honorable and glorious that characterises war and even into the hopeless Battle on the Pelennor Fields they ride with belligerence (*LotR* V.5.870f). When the world is threatened by evil and the freedom of the individual is threatened, war is sometimes inevitable. Tolkien does not glorify war itself, but idealises a non-mechanical and non-technical type of warfare (Croft 25).

A man of his time?

An anti-modern traditionalist who conservatively defends himself against any kind of industrial progress and therefore flees from reality – this is a common cliché about J.R.R. Tolkien. Despite his childhood experiences, when he was first confronted with the consequences of industrialisation, and his traumatic experiences during the Great War, Tolkien was a man anchored in the present. This is shown not least by his ability to come to terms with the experiences of the Great War. If one wants to classify J.R.R. Tolkien in the time in which he lived, one encounters some controversies. Tom Shippey calls him the "author of the century" (Shippey) and thus clearly places him in the context of the 20th century. In the meantime, numerous other researchers locate Tolkien in modernism or post-modernism (see ex. Honegger and Weinreich, Hiley, Nicolay). Brian Rosebury, for example, sees *The Lord of the Rings* as the last work of Great War literature, published 40 years after the war (Rosebury 126). On the other hand, scholars argue that Tolkien was a romanticist (see ex. Eilmann, Reilly, Veldman). They see him as an uprooted man of his time, who is more likely to fit into the 19th century. Tolkien's nostalgic view of a pre-industrial past speaks for Romanticism, but it is this almost wistful view of an irretrievably lost past that distinguishes Modernism from other literary genres (Flieger 11, 16).

If one compares Tolkien's works with those of other war veterans, such as Robert Graves's *Goodbye to All That*, Siegfried Sassoon's *Memoirs of an Infantry Officer*, or Erich Maria Remarque's *All Quiet on the Western Front*, it is striking that Tolkien does not reproduce his experiences directly, but instead incorporates them into his fantastic narrative in epic form. In addition, the ironic tone that expresses the disillusionment and senselessness of war is characteristic for other Great War authors. Tolkien completely lacks this irony – or cynicism. One reason for this could be his deeply rooted faith, which always gave him support (Nicolay 92f.). The experiences and 'models' of these authors are similar, but the literary processing of their memories is very different. Among the writers who served in the Great War and are classified as fantastic, such as A.A. Milne or H.G. Wells, Tolkien's work can best be compared with that of his friend C.S. Lewis. Like Tolkien, Lewis served on the Western Front in the Somme region and later wrote successful fantasy novels (Loconte xiii-xiv). In this comparison, it must be borne in mind that both writers knew each other well and influenced and supported each other not least through their literary circle, the 'Inklings'.

The Lord of the Rings is a narrative written with the insight and experience of a war survivor who knows the worries and fears of veterans. Tolkien's work shows not only the experience of war and how it changes one's own character, but also both sides of homecoming (Garth, *Great War* 51). Where Sam can detach from his experience and start a family, Frodo withdraws more and more from society and shows clear symptoms of a post-traumatic stress disorder. War is not only a feature of Tolkien's literary work, but also of his entire life. Tolkien did not witness the Second Boer War (1899-1902) first-hand himself as a child, as the family had already returned to England in 1896, but he would have perceived the after-effects of the war and the reputation of its generals in British society. He experienced the uncertain and rearming period until 1914 in the form of participation in the King Edward's Cadet Corps, King Edward's Horse, and later the Officers' Training Corps (Garth, "Tolkien at Fifteen"). His experiences in the Great War (1914-1918), in which he served himself, have already been worked out, as well as his experiences as a father during the Second World War (1939-1945), in which two of his sons fought. After all, he lived in later years until his death in the Cold War (1947-1989), whose uncertain atmosphere should not be underestimated. Other conflicts, such as the Spanish Civil War (1936-1939) or the Vietnam War (1955-1975), may have had less impact on Tolkien's personal life, but may have been present in his everyday life through media coverage and the many protests and demonstrations. At least with regard to the situation in Spain, Tolkien's letters offer an insight into his thoughts (*Letters* 95-96). War is one of the central *topoi* in *The Lord of the Rings*, as in Tolkien's literary oeuvre, and gives the secondary world a structure. The described ages of Middle-earth each end with a great, decisive war that changes the world (Hiley, "Problem of Closure" 174).

In conclusion, it can be said that J.R.R. Tolkien's traumatic experiences on the Western Front in 1916 are reflected in his literary masterpiece, *The Lord of the Rings,* in epic form. Despite his great personal loss, his work has no cynical tone, which distinguishes Tolkien from other writers who took part in the war. The literary reappraisal of his experiences is neither allegorical nor escapist, but rather a way of expressing and conveying his own war experiences, whether consciously or unconsciously. Thus, in *The Lord of the Rings* very clear references to the Great War can be drawn, even though Tolkien rejected the biographical interpretation of his works. The fact that his life experience has been incorporated into his work is emphasised by a letter to his publisher in which he wrote

"But forgive me! It is written in my life-blood, such as it is, thick or thin; and I can no other. I fear it must stand or fall as it substantially is" (*Letters* 122).

However, I cannot agree with Tolkien's statement "This story is not about JRRT at all" (*Letters* 239) in view of the references worked out here.

Bibliography

Carpenter, Humphrey. *J.R.R. Tolkien: A Biography.* Boston and New York: Houghton Mifflin, 2000.

Croft, Janet Brennan (ed.). *Baptism of Fire: The Birth of the Modern British Fantastic in World War I.* Altadena, CA: Mythopoeic Press, 2015.

War and the Works of J.R.R. Tolkien. Contributions to the Study of Science Fiction and Fantasy 106. Westport, CT and London: Praeger, 2004.

Ebert, Jens (ed.). *Vom Augusterlebnis zur Novemberrevolution: Briefe aus dem Weltkrieg 1914-1918.* Göttingen: Wallstein, 2014.

Eksteins, Modris. *Rites of Spring: The Great War and the Birth of the Modern Age.* Boston, MA: Houghton Mifflin, 1989.

Ettighofer, Paul. *Verdun: Das große Gericht 1936.* Augsburg: Universitas, 1996.

Eilmann, Julian. *J.R.R. Tolkien: Romanticist and Poet.* Cormarë Series 36. Zurich and Jena: Walking Tree Publishers, 2017.

Flieger, Verlyn. *A Question of Time: J.R.R. Tolkien's Road to Faërie.* Kent, OH: The Kent State University Press, 2000.

Garth, John. *Tolkien and the Great War: The Threshold of Middle-earth.* London: HarperCollins, 2003.

"Tolkien at fifteen, a warrior-to-be". https://johngarth.wordpress.com/2014/03/05/tolkien-at-fifteen-a-warrior-to-be/. 5 March 2014.

Hiley, Margaret. *The Loss and the Silence: Aspects of Modernism in the Works of C.S. Lewis, J.R.R. Tolkien, and Charles Williams.* Cormarë Series 22. Zurich and Jena: Walking Tree Publishers, 2011.

"The Problem of Closure: War and Narrative in *The Lord of the Rings.*" *Gewalt, Konflikt und Krieg bei Tolkien. Hither Shore* 6. Ed. Thomas Fornet-Ponse. Düsseldorf: Scriptorium Oxoniae, 2009, 168-179.

Honegger, Thomas and Frank Weinreich (eds.). *Tolkien and Modernity 1.* Cormarë Series 9. Zurich and Jena: Walking Tree Publishers, 2006.

Tolkien and Modernity 2. Cormarë Series 10. Zurich and Jena: Walking Tree Publishers, 2006.

Hooker, Mark T. "Frodo's Batman." *Tolkien Studies* 1 (2004): 125-136.

Lewis, C.S. "Tolkien's *The Lord of the Rings.*" *On Stories and Other Essays on Literature.* Ed. Walter Hooper. New York City, NY: Harcourt Brace Jovanivich, 1982, 83-90.

Livingston, Michael. "The Shell-shocked Hobbit. The First World War and Tolkien's Trauma of the Ring." *Baptism of Fire. The Birth of the Modern British Fantastic in World War I.* Ed. Janet Brennan Croft. Altadena, CA: Mythopoeic Press, 2015, 9-22.

Loconte, Joseph. *A Hobbit, a Wardrobe, and a Great War: How J.R.R. Tolkien and C.S. Lewis Rediscovered Faith, Friendship, and Heroism in the Cataclysm of 1914-1918.* Nashville: Thomas Nelson, 2015.

Nicolay, Theresa Freda. *Tolkien and the Modernists. Literary responses to the dark new days of the 20th century.* Jefferson, NC: McFarland, 2014.

Nübel, Christoph. *Durchhalten und Überleben an der Westfront: Raum und Körper im Ersten Weltkrieg.* Zeitalter der Weltkriege 10. Paderborn: Verlag Ferdinand Schöningh, 2014.

Reilly, R. *Romantic Religion. A Study of Owen Barfield, C.S Lewis, Charles Williams, J.R.R. Tolkien.* Great Barrington, MA: Lindisfarne Books, 2006.

Rosebury, Brian. *Tolkien: A Cultural Phenomenon.* New York City, NY: Palgrave Macmillan, 2003.

Shippey, Tom. *J.R.R. Tolkien: Author of the Century.* London: HarperCollins, 2001.

Tolkien, J.R.R. *The Letters of J.R.R. Tolkien.* Ed. Humphrey Carpenter, with the assistance of Christopher Tolkien. London: George Allen and Unwin, 1981; London: HarperCollins, 1995.

The Lord of the Rings. 50th Anniversary edition. Boston, MA: Houghton Mifflin, 2004.

Rosebury, Brian. *Tolkien. A Critical Assessment.* Hampshire: Palgrave Macmillan, 2002.

Veldman, Meredith. *Fantasy, the Bomb, and the Greening of Britain: Romantic Protest 1945-1980.* Cambridge: Cambridge University Press, 1994.

Tal Tovy

Aspects of Total War in *The Hobbit* and *The Lord of the Rings*

A wide variety of factors influenced the writing of Tolkien's masterpieces. Numerous studies have noted Tolkien's experiences as a young junior officer on the Western Front during the First World War, and some have dealt with them in great detail.[1] The horror of war, the futility of trench warfare, the routine of bombing and sniping, the diseases and pests, the ravages of the weather, the loss of brothers in arms, and over and above everything else, the death of his close friends from the TCBS group. All had an influence on Tolkien as he approached the writing of *The Hobbit*, and the effects of his experiences continue to reverberate throughout the pages of *The Lord of the Rings*. The effect of this war on Tolkien and his writing is beyond doubt (Carpenter 80-86; Jones 47-48). Nevertheless, this chapter argues that these books were written within a broader historical context, caused by the fundamental transformation in the character of war as it became 'Total War', which Tolkien indeed experienced both as an individual, but also as part of a collective belonging to Western civilization. Furthermore, it is important to remember that Tolkien began writing his books in a climate of increasing political radicalism in Europe, as the politics of the 1920s and 1930s drew their inspiration from the legacy of the First World War. The vast structure of 19th century civilization was buried in the trenches of the Western Front, Eric Hobsbawm writes, adding that the 20th century cannot be understood (and it is possible to argue that neither can the beginning of the 21st century) without understanding the First World War, and that Western civilization continued to live and think in terms that were influenced by that war (Hobsbawm 22).

During the 19th century the nature of war changed, from limited wars between European houses of royalty to total war between nations and peoples. War ceased to be a caprice of rulers in their pursuit of dynastic ambitions and imperial

1 See in particular the comprehensive book by Janet Brennan Croft, *War and the Works of J.R.R. Tolkien*. Westport: Praeger, 2004.

honor, aims that characterized, for example, the wars waged by Louis XIV or the various wars of succession in the 18th century. War became an ideological battle of survival, as demonstrated in the American Revolution and the wars of the French Revolution. It was quite clear to the people in both revolutions that if Europe's imperial armies would emerge victorious, the gains of the revolution would be lost in their entirety.[2] War became a matter of life and death for entire collectives. In the second half of the 19th century, the ideological essence of war was combined with dramatic technological changes that increased the firepower of the various means of war and thus their lethality (Wawre 137-139; Murray 250-251). But perhaps the most dramatic change in the nature of warfare and its management in the 20th century derived from the introduction of the aerial dimension, which expanded the scale and scope of war and turned it into total war (Buckley 1-4).

The aim of this chapter is to show how the conception of total war is manifested in the pages of *The Hobbit* and *The Lord of the Rings* and to argue that this broad historical context must be understood in order to gain further insight regarding the factors that influenced Tolkien's writing. In other words, there is no doubt that Tolkien's experience in the First World War must be understood; however, I believe that it is part of a context that is larger than the mere fact that this war and certainly the Second World War were radical cases of the phenomenon of total war. Actually, the manifestations of total war, which emerged from the First World War, changed the worldview of those that survived the horrors of the war. One must particularly emphasize the phenomenon of the home front becoming a legitimate target in the waging of war, as it became militarily possible to make it a target by using the air power that the various countries in the conflict acquired during the war.

This is the place to note that when an author writes he relies, among other things, on readers having a basic understanding of the world of concepts he is using, so that the work will be comprehensible. In other words, a literary work can be viewed as an attempt by the author to communicate with the readers.

---

2 See the Survey in Howard (54-93). Howard reviews the transition from wars waged by the standing armies of the European royal houses to the revolutionary wars in which the masses began to participate. The survey locates the phenomenon of war in a broad historical context and shows how political and social changes had a crucial influence on the change in the character of war.

Nevertheless, there will always be cultural differences between the author and his audience, and that is certainly the case if the work is translated into other languages and read years after it was written. Therefore, one reader's interpretation is not necessarily that which the author was intending. These cultural differences between author and readers have been termed "intentional fallacy" by William Wimsatt and Monroe Beardsley, who argued that the intent of the author is not necessarily significant in attempting to understand the intention of the work.[3] As this is the case, my training as a military historian has led me to read *The Hobbit* and *The Lord of the Rings* in light of the phenomenon of total war, to which Tolkien and his generation were exposed during the First World War.

Thus, the essence of total war is at the center of this chapter. The first part will examine the phenomenon of total war and its military and social manifestations in the years that are relevant to Tolkien's writing. This examination is essential as it locates Tolkien's works in the cultural context that affected his generation in all areas of life. The second part of this chapter will demonstrate the manifestation of total war in *The Hobbit* and *The Lord of the Rings*, with an emphasis on the dimension of aerial war.

Total war

Total war in the modern era is a historic innovation expressed in the expansion of the scope of war, due to two main factors. The first factor was the enlistment of the entire nation, which provided a larger amount of manpower for waging war. This actually is the factor that created the ideological dimension of total war. Indeed, enlistment was enforced legally through universal draft laws, but the basis for enlistment was patriotic and derived from the desire to protect the unique national and cultural attributes of each country.[4] Notably, not every country adopted conscription – Britain, for instance, did not – but the conception penetrated deeply as an approach that turned war into a matter concerning the people and not only the ruler.

---

3 The term first appeared in the paper by Wimsatt and Beardsley 468-488.
4 On the subject of total war see Beckett 1-21; Buckley 12-20.

The second factor was the industrial revolution, which not only provided improved, more lethal means of war but also, and more importantly, the ability to mass produce them. Tolkien provides us with one manifestation of this in his description of the Orcs' weapons workshops. Mass production as a critical factor in waging modern war caused a major transformation in the character of war.[5] This due to the fact that damaging a nation's industrial ability assumed direct strategic importance. And since the industrial complexes were inevitably located in and around urban areas, the home front became a legitimate target. Furthermore, most of the manpower available for enlistment or for supporting the war efforts, in Western Europe, came from the urban areas, a fact that heightened the importance of crippling the urban front.[6] Thus, war ceased to be merely a military engagement along clearly delineated fronts; instead, it became (or at least attempted to become) a battle that ranged across the entire area of the participating nations, and since the home front became a source of power and a target, the distinction between battle front and home front and between military and civilian was blurred; The rear became front, the home front (Tallett 158-168; Purseigle 45-68).

Some have argued that total war can be identified as far back as the French Revolution (Broers 247-268; Black, 1-11). Other historians claim that it was the American Civil War that more clearly demonstrated the characteristics of total war. If we argue that damaging the home front had military significance, then General Sherman's march toward Atlanta and Savannah can be identified as such. Sherman and his commending officer, General Grant, believed that the war would end only after the Union had destroyed the South's economic capabilities. Such destruction would be of strategic importance but would also strike a stunning psychological blow to the population of the South. General Sherman implemented the scorched earth principle, ordering his forces to confiscate food from the residents of the South that lived adjacent to the routes taken by his forces. Food that could not be taken was destroyed along with the farm animals and the industrial infrastructure of Georgia. A similar trend can be seen in General Phillip Sheridan's campaign in the Shenandoah Valley

5 Regarding this context, see Wawro 45-68; Showalter 73-93.

6 One must remember that in the middle of the 19th century, Europe (and the United States) experienced swift processes of urbanization and industrialization, which heightened the economic importance of urban regions compared to rural areas.

in September 1864 (Janda 7-26). Thus, we can argue that the confiscation of food was based not only on logistical concerns owing to the fact that Sherman's Army was traveling without a supply convoy, but also served as a mechanism to destroy the South's civilian infrastructure and thereby bring about a military collapse at the front.[7]

Although researchers disagree about the identification of the first total war, all agree that the First World War was indeed such a war.[8] The war created a total engagement since war or defeat directly affected the global status and future of each nation. As war became such a fateful endeavor – a veritable existential struggle – a social and cultural climate emerged that defined war as a crusade whereby the enemy must be totally destroyed. This could be accomplished by harnessing all of the nation's resources, including manpower, the economy, industry, technology, science, and even art. This social climate, meaning war as a crusade, was established gradually in the final decades of the 19th century and the beginning of the 20th and reached its peak in the weeks following the assassination of the heir to the Austro-Hungarian throne.

Militarily, the First World War quickly became a static war, particularly on the Western Front (Thomson 558-564).[9] The war plans of the various countries (except for Britain) forecast a quick and decisive attack. However, it turned out that defense is many times stronger than attack, as predicted by Jan Bloch in his book, *Is War Now Impossible?* (1899).[10] The armies of France, Britain, and Germany sought ways to break the stalemate at the front, leading to the

---

7 Nevertheless, it is important to note that despite the radical manifestations seen during the Civil War, Europe viewed it as an internal American affair, of no importance beyond the confines of the United States and of no military significance to Europe. Further, one must recall that every civil war is by nature more total and violent, as it contains the fundamental conditions of an all-out ideological battle to the death (whether religious, ethnic, or political).

8 See the discussion in DeGroot 262-281. See also Chickering 35-53.

9 For a general and exhaustive review of the war on the Western Front, see Prior 204-233.

10 The book from 1899 is an abbreviated Russian-to-English translation of the six-volume tome published a year prior. By analyzing several wars that occurred throughout the second half of the 19th century, Bloch describes a linear process beginning with the dramatic progress in military technology that occurred throughout the second half of the 19th century (smokeless gun powder, improved cannon and guns, and machine guns). This progress provided the entrenched soldier with an advantage over the assaulting soldier. Bloch argued that the inferiority of the assaulting soldiers would put an end to the quick attacks and decisive victories, and that armies would aim to prevent themselves from being outflanked by the enemy and would therefore dig in and lengthen the front lines. As lengthy front lines would have to be held for a lengthy period of time, this would lead to nations enlisting armies of millions, with war turning into an apocalyptic clash between industrial forces. On Bloch's theory, see Gat 109-112; Echevarria 43-45.

development of a long line of lethal means of war, such as chemical agents, increased utilization of airplanes, the emergence of the tank, and the enlistment of millions of soldiers to hold the lengthy front lines. But more than anything else, the Western Front saw the creation of the quintessential symbol of the war – trench warfare – which was one of the factors that influenced Tolkien's writing (Travers 213-226). Furthermore, trench warfare and the conscription of millions of soldiers were the prominent military manifestation of the First World War as a total war.

In order to support the war effort, the participating European countries recruited all their human and material resources, with the civilian population experiencing firsthand the horrors of war, more than in any other prior war on the Continent. This was due to the occupation of large areas and the economic war waged by the Entente Powers against Germany *vis à vis* the unlimited submarine warfare that Germany waged against England. This economic war, along with the need to supply the troops and the war, led to food rationing, damage to infrastructure, and a decline in the standard of living. But one of the most important phenomena of the First World War, which had a dramatic effect on the British population, was the aerial attacks on the home front. This was a self-fulfilling prophecy.[11]

In 1898 Ferdinand von Zeppelin began to construct his first airship in Germany. Despite a series of mishaps and disasters in the years before the First World War, the airships made their mark on the history of aviation and the developer of the airship, Zeppelin, became a "brand" name. Britain followed Germany's achievements with concern. In July 1908, the *Daily Mail* published a lengthy article claiming that Germany was building a force of 3,500 airships capable of transferring hundreds of thousand of soldiers across the Channel within half an hour. One must keep in mind that at this time, Imperial Germany had also initiated a naval arms race, which was perceived in Britain as a threat to its command of the seas. The report in the *Daily Mail* garnered much public attention and the impression in Britain was

11 A large body of literature has focused on Germany's aerial bombing of Britain's cities during WWI. For examples, see Castle; Cross; Fegan. One of the issues common to this literature is the moral and psychological effect on the British civilian population. Beyond this literature, the aerial bombings are also an important part of the historical development of air power and of course of the general literature on WWI.

that times were changing to its disadvantage (Fegan 9-14). Accounts of the German airships and the dangers posed by them continued to preoccupy Britain's newspapers in the years before the war, and to a greater extent after the attacks by the German zeppelins on cities in Belgium, such as Liège and Antwerp, during the first weeks of the war.[12]

The British fear of the airships was unrelated to Belgium's fate; rather, it derived from concern that the German attacks would spread to the cities of England. Although the activity of the zeppelins in the months following the attacks on Belgium was negligible, London was well aware of their potential as a weapon of terror, and Britain's press continued to be engrossed in this threat. And indeed it came. In the night between 19-20 of January 1915, Germany conducted an aerial attack on the east coast of England and in June 1915 began a series of bombings of London itself (Biddle 20-25). In 1801, in a letter to the Board of Admiralty, Admiral John Jervis made a famous remark. He wrote that "I do not say [...] that the French will not come. I say only they will not come by sea" (qtd. in Andidora 3). The Germans found the way and in English consciousness, Britain ceased to be an island whose defense was based on the historical, unshaken superiority of the Royal Navy. This mental achievement outweighed by far the actual loss of life and property, certainly when compared to the number of casualties at the front (Budiansky 90-95).[13] The aerial attacks were first and foremost a weapon of terror, meant to disrupt routine life on the home front and undermine the fighting spirit of the civilians, following years of blackouts, huddling in shelters, and watching the appearance of the zeppelins every night, later followed by the Gotha G.IV airplanes that replaced them (Biddle 29-35).[14]

After the war, targeting the enemy home front using air power in order to defeat it became a legitimate military strategy. This conception was expressed most prominently in Giulio Douhet's military theory, formulated at the beginning of the 1920s.[15] Simply put and to summarize his two basic principles,

---

12 Regarding the coverage by the British press, see: Budiansky 41-42. As for the development of the zeppelins and their initial usage, see Morrow 3-10.

13 Throughout the entire war, the Germans conducted 51 aerial strikes, in which a total of 200 tons of explosives were dropped, causing the deaths of several hundreds of civilians.

14 It is important to keep in mind that during the war, Britain, too, began to bomb Germany's cities.

15 Douhet's theory was examined using the following sources: MacIsaac 629-636; Meilinger, *Airwar* 7-30; Meilinger, "Giulio Douhet" 1-34; Stephens 33-43; Boyne 110-118.

Douhet stated that an aerial force must be built based on strategic bombers whose mission would be to bomb the industrial and population centers of the enemy. This in order to decide the next war and avoid static, exhausting trench warfare. His argument, as put forth in *The Command of the Air* (*Il Dominio dell'Aria*, 1921), was that the morale of the population would collapse following the strategic bombings and that the capacity for industrial production would be fatally wounded following the strikes on the industrial complexes. These trends would bring the war to its conclusion, with victory going to the side that succeeded in securing aerial control.

There is no doubt that Douhet's theory clearly supported the concept of total war as a mechanism that must be brought to bear in the next war. But the central manifesto regarding total war in the years between the two world wars was Erich Ludendorff's book, *The Total War* (*Der Totale Krieg*), published in 1935. Ludendorff argued that the character of modern war had changed, as the French Revolution had liberated the power of the people, causing a national awakening and popular enthusiasm. He identified the roots of total war in the French Revolution and stated that the clear, practical manifestation of the characteristics of modern war, meaning total war, had occurred during the First World War. In this war, Ludendorff writes, not only armies were involved, but entire nations. Not only soldiers at the front suffered, but also the population on the home front. This due to the impressive development in the ability of the air force to shift the war far beyond the traditional front lines, economic warfare, and the restrictions that the warring nations themselves placed on civilian society in order to supply what was needed to continue the war effort.[16]

Manifestations of total war prior to the First World War can also be found in the realm of literature – fictional, not only in theoretical military writings. Indeed, the First World War radicalized the anti-romantic trends against positivism, which had begun toward the end of the 19th century. By this I mean the increasing doubts in the optimistic faith regarding the power of swift progress in science and technology to bring about improvement in various areas such as

16 For a discussion of Ludendorff's conception of total war, see Speier 306-321; Chickering 151-196.

morality, education, welfare, and society in general.[17] Thus, for instance, the books by Jules Verne may be seen as representing faith in progress, while the morbid books by H. G. Wells, both fiction and non-fiction, represent the pessimist current, based on the possible, destructive implementation of advanced technologies (Echevarria 24-26). In his impressive book, *Anticipations of the Reaction of Mechanical and Scientific Progress upon Human Life and Thought* (1902), Wells describes the future of Western civilization based on accelerated industrialization and urbanization and a global economy. In his view, the destructive potential of modern technology threatened to put an end to civilization if countries continued to be hostile toward each other. In a chapter dealing with war in the 20th century (ch. 6), Wells analyzes war based on Bloch's forecasts. He too thought that the swift acceleration in the intensity of firepower would cause a tactical and strategic military stagnation, which would lead to the collapse of the world economy, hunger, epidemics, and the complete breakdown of the warring societies.[18]

With Tolkien, too, we can find a negative attitude toward technology as assisting in the production of weaponry that is ever more lethal. This is how he describes the technological skills of the Goblins:

> They make no beautiful things, but they make many clever ones. [...] Hammers, axes, swords, daggers, pickaxes, tongs, and also instruments of torture, they make very well [...]. It is not unlikely that they invented some of the machines that have troubled the world, especially the ingenious devices for killing large numbers of people at once, for wheels and engines and explosives always delighted them [...]. (*Hobbit* 4.73)

To Bloch's analysis Wells added the struggle between airplanes for aerial control, and several years later he published the novel *The War in the Air* (1908) in which he, in fact, predicted the brutal, strategic aerial bombings of the Second World War. The book is actually a severe warning issued in the context of increasing international tensions. The book describes how airships and airplanes of the great powers cross oceans and continents in a global war, in order to strike at the heart of the enemy's country and centers of population and industry

17 One must keep in mind that toward the end of the 19th century a cultural current emerged, representing a pessimistic approach, arguing that Western civilization was declining. It was called *Fin de Siècle* and contrasted (and perhaps even defied) the great optimism of *La Belle Époque* (the Beautiful Era).

18 For a comprehensive discussion of Wells's apocalyptic and dystopian view, see Kumar 168-223.

(Echevarria 84-88).[19] In the wake of this war and the damage to the home front, Wells once more describes the collapse of advanced, modern civilization. This actually is a constant formula that will recur in later books that he published: the rise of modern civilization and its collapse in destructive wars that cause plagues and anarchy as in medieval times (as Wells saw them). From a historical perspective, we can argue that Wells's apocalyptic vision was realized, but Wells's contemporaries also awaited the Armageddon that the flying machines of the next war would deliver (Biddle 11-20).

Tolkien and Total War

The First World War was a watershed in European history.[20] From a quantitative point of view, the Second World War exceeds its predecessor on almost every measure; there is no doubt about that. But from the psychological-consciousness aspect, the first exceeds the second. Throughout the 19th century, Europe experienced a series of social and scientific revolutions that created optimism and generally speaking, the standard of living of Europeans (mainly in Western Europe) improved significantly. The First World War broke out after nearly a hundred years of relative stability in Europe. From the Congress of Vienna (1815) to the German invasion of Belgium, which marked the beginning of the war (4 August 1914), Europe enjoyed a century without major wars; a hundred years of (relative) peace, progress, and optimism (*La Belle Époque*) (MacMillan 10-17). Although wars did occur in Europe, such as the wars for the unification of Germany, they were limited geographically and did not draw in the rest of Europe's nations, as in the years of the war with Napoleon.[21] Other wars were waged on the outskirts of Europe (e.g., the Crimean War), but most wars occurred far beyond the Continent itself (the Mexican-American War, the Spanish-American War, and the Russo-Japanese War). Although it is true that at times political tensions were heightened, especially due to the race for empire, the major European powers (Russia, England, Austro-Hungary, France, and Germany) were not drawn into a general conflict among themselves. Furthermore, from the conclusion of the war between Germany and France (1870-1871), it

19 For more on the subject of air war in popular culture, see Corum 101-102.
20 See the discussion in Bell 129-148.
21 On the characteristics of war in the 19th century, see Murray 219-248; Frevert 417-43.

seemed that Europe was at peace. The four years of World War I put an end not only to Europe's stability but also to its old order.

The collective memory of the First World War was formed in the trenches of the Western Front, and to this day it is called 'The Great War'. This, even though numerically, the Second World War exceeded it on almost every measure, as mentioned. One reason was the enormous loss of life relative to the size of the population; for instance, France lost 20% of all males of military age. If we include the wounded and disabled, the *gueules cassés* ('broken faces'), then two-thirds of France's soldiers were casualties. Britain lost an entire generation, mostly from the upper classes (Jones 44-45). A quarter of all students from the exclusive universities of Cambridge and Oxford, which at the conclusion of their studies were supposed to lead the empire upon which the sun never sets, were killed. The meat grinder of the Western Front killed off these men, who as gentlemen were supposed to serve as exemplary models for British society and promote its imperial status. "Already behind him among the goblin dead lay [...] many a fair elf that should have lived yet long ages merrily in the wood" (*Hobbit* 17.296), Tolkien writes, describing the aftermath of the Battle of the Five Armies. It is difficult to avoid the comparison to accounts from the fighting in the Battle of the Somme, in which Tolkien himself participated (Garth 161-168).[22]

With the stagnation at the front and the need for enlisting millions of soldiers and for supporting the war effort, the belligerents were forced to harness all their national resources, including public opinion, to the war effort. In democratic countries severe restrictions were placed on liberal principles. Politicians had to formulate a challenge *vis à vis* the murderous intents (as they saw them) to destroy the national values of their country, such as Russian barbarism versus Germanic superiority, the democracy and the liberalism of England and France

22 The battle of the Somme began on 1 July 1916 with an infantry assault preceded by several days of heavy artillery bombardment of the German lines. It ended in the middle of November 1916, without the French and English managing to break the German lines and advancing significantly. Three and a half months of fighting and over half a million killed and all the British and French had to show for it was a gain of several kilometers. In the first day of fighting the British Army lost twenty thousand soldiers; twice that number were injured. That day is still the largest loss in a single day that the British Army has ever suffered. For a review of the Battle of the Somme, see Murray 294-295; Stevenson 168-171. Regarding the Somme in Britain's collective memory, see Bond 194-208.

versus the absolute-autocratic rule of Germany. Thus, in his War Message to Congress (3 February 1917), President Wilson stated the following:

> "[...] there can be no assured security for the democratic Governments of the world. We are now about to accept gauge of battle with this natural foe to liberty and shall, if necessary, spend the whole force of the nation to check and nullify its pretensions and its power. We are glad, now that we see the facts with no veil of false pretence about them, to fight thus for the ultimate peace of the world and for the liberation of its peoples [...]." (Wilson)

The aims of the war were defined as total: a complete victory over the enemy. This determination was defined in the Second World War in the concept of "unconditional surrender". In this political climate, there was no place for compromise. It was an absurd goal that led to the continuation of the grinding and bloodletting on the Western Front and caused the downfall of both defeated and victors, except for the United States. Four empires ceased to exist and many of the countries that were established on their ruins were pushed into the arms of political revolution and radicalism: communism, Nazism, fascism. France and Britain, which emerged victorious only due to the unlimited material resources of the United States, were exhausted by the war. France suffered an unprecedented demographic blow, and Britain's economy was mortally damaged due to the exploitation of most of its resources (Roberts 319-321). All the political mechanisms fashioned after the war, meaning the redrawing of Europe's map, were intended primarily as a method of curbing Soviet communism and preventing the reconstruction of German militarism. Therefore, the post-war climate was uncompromising, into the 1930s.

Tolkien published *The Hobbit* and began writing *The Lord of the Rings* in the years prior to the Second World War, finishing it after the conclusion of the war. But in various letters he argues that these books were not an allegory. In a letter from 1956, Tolkien wrote: "There is *no* 'allegory', moral, political or contemporary in the work [*LotR*] at all" (*Letters* 232, italics in original).[23] However, in the introduction to *The Lord of the Rings*, Tolkien wrote something that may support the main argument of this chapter. He wrote that the major part of the chapters of *The Lord of the Rings* was written before 1939 and that these chapters shaped the rest of the book. Another example is his letter to Stanley

---

23 See also *Letters*, nos. 34 (41), 109 (119-123), and 131 (143-161).

Unwin, from 13 October 1938. Tolkien writes: "The darkness of the present days [Sudeten crisis?] has had some effect on it" (41), alluding to the chapters of *The Hobbit*'s sequel which he had begun writing. Thus we can conclude that the political climate on the eve of the war, when those living at the time felt the storm clouds gathering once again over the Continent, affected Tolkien as well, vis à vis the political, and later the military aggressiveness, of Germany, Italy (and before that, Japan).[24] Work on *The Lord of the Rings* continued after the Second World War, as the West substituted the fascist, Nazi enemy with an old-new enemy, communism.

Janet Brennan Croft argues that the reality of the Second World War can be clearly discerned in Tolkien's writing, if only due to the fact that his son, Christopher, participated in this war. There is no doubt, Croft continues, that Tolkien was deeply affected by the momentous events of the 1930s and the war years (Croft 57-72). Furthermore, from his letters it is apparent that Tolkien's preoccupation with the world of fantasy did not prevent him from being involved in the real world around him, and he was clearly sensitive to the various social processes and political trends occurring in Europe in the years in which he wrote his books (Neiberg 82-104).[25]

Returning to one of the most basic definitions of total war as a fight to the death, we can identify Tolkien's description of the Battle of the Five Armies as a total event. The hatred of the goblins for the dwarves has turned into a blazing fire. The dwarves, elves, and men unite as "the goblins were the foes of all" (*Hobbit* 17.293). Notably, prior to the formation of the three-sided coalition, the parties were preparing to battle each other. But in the face of the threat from the goblins, all the other disputes were set aside. Reading the section about the Battle of the Five Armies, it is clear that the goblins and their allies, the wolves, intended to destroy the armies they were facing, which would allow them to take over the lands they desired.

The conception of total war, with its main characteristics, appears clearly in *The Lord of the Rings*. The atmosphere in the trilogy is darker than in *The Hobbit*,

---

24 Regarding political radicalization in the 1930s, see Rudhart 140-145; Roberts 504-520; Bell 107-116; Diehl 97-112.

25 Tolkien is known to have read the *Daily Telegraph* each morning (*Letters* 367).

particularly because the plot winds its way amidst an existential struggle with enormously powerful forces of darkness. Every battle in this epic is a matter of life and death, and there is no possibility of surrender, as it would mean certain destruction or enslavement, which is perceived as being even worse than death. War is forced upon the nations and peoples of Middle-earth and therefore it is a defensive and just war. They do not want it, but they have no choice; they must make a stand and fight. War is for survival and not for the conquest of territories or for booty, wealth and glory.

In my opinion, Tolkien does not glorify war in his books.[26] It is still terrible, and his heroes strive to avoid it. Nonetheless, they do not balk at going out and fighting to defend the principles that are important to them. Besides the race of the hobbits, the other races – humans, dwarves, elves, and, of course, their enemies – are all warriors skilled in the use of various weapons, and even though the history of Middle-earth abounds with wars (similar to Europe's history), the wars in *The Hobbit* and *The Lord of the Rings* are described as being imposed upon these races by an external enemy. This argument corresponds with the statement made by the British philosopher, Bertrand Russell, that war was always a great evil, but in some particularly extreme circumstances, it may be the lesser of two evils. This was to argue in favor of all-out war against Nazism, since the victory of this murderous ideology meant the end of democracy and liberalism (Russell 7-13). In this spirit we can understand, too, the wars in *The Lord of the Rings*, and especially the wars against the armies of Saruman and Sauron. These were wars against the forces of darkness whose desire was to destroy or enslave the cultures of Middle-earth and the free spirit of its inhabitants.

We can similarly argue that England was not eager to embark upon war, neither in 1914 nor in the years prior to 1939. Suffice us to recall the pictures of British Prime Minister Neville Chamberlain upon his return, alighting from the plane that brought him back from Munich (30 September 1938). He immediately issued his notorious declaration that he had brought "peace for our time," waving the piece of paper signed by Hitler. This agreement was lauded enthusiastically in Britain and the world; Chamberlain reached peaks of popularity at home and was received by King George VI as a victor. Less than a year later another

26 See also the discussion in Croft 6-8.

terrible war broke out in Europe. England did not desire this war, but when it was imposed upon her she fought valiantly, rejecting Hitler's proposals for compromise after the conquest of France, and in fact served as a beacon of freedom and hope for the nations under Nazi occupation.

The Fellowship of the Ring was formed for one sole purpose: the destruction of the Ring and the elimination of the global threat, in the trilogy's terms, which meant destroying Sauron and saving the peoples of Middle-earth. This was an unnatural fellowship, whose journey and final battle (the Battle of the Morannon or the Battle of the Black Gate) are in fact imposed upon it, by the very nature of the mission they took upon themselves. Although, as mentioned above, Tolkien opposed political allegories, we cannot ignore the historiographic approach that views Hitler as the instigator of the Second World War in Europe. There are almost no historians who cast doubt on his responsibility and aggressive policy in the second half of the 1930s. Further, the policies adopted by Britain, France, and the Soviet Union were aimed, above all, at preventing or at least postponing the outbreak of the next war.

Even if the origins of the Nazi aggression (and to a large extent that of Japan and Italy also) are to be found in the outcomes of the First World War, in the 1930s political forces emerged in the radical right that aimed to use military force to shatter what they viewed as the unreasonable and unjust status quo established in the Versailles Treaty. Even if we do accept Tolkien's rejection of an analogy between the fantasy of *The Lord of the Rings* and the political reality in 1930s Europe, it is still a fact that the political radicalization and aggression of Japan, Italy, and Germany accompanied Tolkien's life. Consequently Tolkien, along with dozens of millions throughout Europe, lived in a political atmosphere that was edging toward another awful war. At the time, people envisioned swarms of airplanes dropping their lethal cargos on Europe's peaceful cities, as had already occurred in China and Spain, and the nightmare of masses of soldiers walking blindly among clouds of chemical agents, returned to stalk them.

Tolkien's "Aerial Dimension"

As mentioned, from Britain's point of view, one of the unique new aspects of this war, along with exceptionally heavy losses and submarine warfare, was Germany's strategic bombing of England. But air power was also of military value on the battlefields of the various fronts, where it was wielded tactically in missions such as observation, directing artillery, and bombing forces in the immediate vicinity of the front. Tolkien gave this role to the Great Eagles, but his attitude toward them is tentative. Certainly, both in *The Hobbit* and *The Lord of the Rings*, the eagles rescue the heroes of the story, saving Bilbo and the dwarves, arriving in the nick of time in the Battle of the Five Armies, the battle at the Black Gate, and the rescue of Gandalf. Nonetheless, in *The Hobbit*, Tolkien relates to us that these eagles were descendants of an ancient race from the northern mountains, while the rest of the eagles "are not kindly birds. Some are cowardly and cruel" (*Hobbit* 6.114). In a letter written by Tolkien in 1958 he stated that "The Eagles are a dangerous 'machine'. I have used them sparingly, and that is the absolute limit of their credibility or usefulness" (*Letters* 271). The eagles are not part of the plot and Tolkien uses them as agents of eucatastrophe.[27] In any case, the Great Eagles appear as "military support" to the heroes of the story, comparable to the support role of the various air forces in the First World War.[28]

A "strategic air power" does appear in Tolkien's books, in the form of the dragon and the flying creatures that the Nazgûl ride during the siege of Gondor. We can argue that flying creatures, and particularly dragons, appear too in the Nordic and Germanic mythologies (such as *Beowulf*) that greatly influenced Tolkien's writing.[29] But I believe that in *The Hobbit* and *The Lord of the Rings* Tolkien took this one step further by positioning the flying creatures as weapons that terrorize the civilian population – just like

27 This is a term coined by Tolkien in a lecture he gave in 1939 and which was published in 1947 under the title "On Fairy-stories". According to a letter he wrote to his son Christopher (*Letters* 100), the term refers to the creation of a sudden happy turn in a story. The term is similar to the concept of *deus ex machina*, meaning the insertion of an additional element that does not logically follow from the plot, in order to solve problems in the story and arrive at a happy end.

28 Jeff LaSala examines the appearance and actions of the eagles in *The Hobbit* and *The Lord of the Rings* and calls them Tolkien's Special Forces. This is a fascinating insight, testifying to the contemporary interpretations that can be applied to literary works, including Tolkien's.

29 Tolkien described *Beowulf* as one of the "most valued sources" for *The Hobbit* (*Letters* 31). Tolkien may also have been inspired by the talking dragon Fafnir of the Völsunga Saga.

the zeppelins and later the Gotha bombers in the First World War. I think there are two clear examples of this. The first is Smaug's attack on the lake city, Esgaroth. Previously, we are told that the same dragon had destroyed the dwarf kingdom and the city of Dale. The description of the dragon's attack on the city (Chapter 14: "Fire and Water") is similar to the descriptions of the zeppelin attacks on London. Most of the residents of the city are in their homes and even those in the streets fail to identify the approaching threat. Smaug strikes the city again and again, destroying its houses, "and still no arrow hindered Smaug or hurt him" (*Hobbit* 14.260). Further along, we are told that the dragon's attack will swiftly burn the city and that it has been years since he has enjoyed the destruction of a city (261).

The second example is the description of the flying creatures that the Nazgûl ride during the siege of Gondor, as described through the eyes of Pippin: "like shadows of untimely night [...] five birdlike forms, horrible as carrion-fowl yet greater than eagles, cruel as death" (*LotR* V.4.809). The description further indicates that this is a weapon of terror and intimidation, meant to induce the inhabitants of the city to surrender. Thus, in fact, Tolkien is in agreement with the very same military theoreticians who had argued that air power can decide a war on its own by terrorizing the civilian population. Even if Tolkien was not familiar with Douhet's books or with professional military writings, the public discussion held in Britain and particularly Stanley Baldwin's famous saying that "the bomber will always get through," leave no room for doubt that Tolkien was well aware of this discussion.[30] But if there is a doubt, let us not forget that *The Lord of the Rings* was written by Tolkien during the Second World War, in which England's cities, and particularly London, suffered aerial bombings throughout almost the entire war.

Conclusion

The main argument of this chapter has been that the essence of Total War had an influence on Tolkien's writing, along with many other significant influences.

30 From an essay published by Baldwin in the *Times* on 11 November 1932. See also Middlemas and Barnes 735. Regarding the belief in the absolute power of air forces in the years prior to the war, see Black 131-133.

This argument is not based on a historical perspective, but on an analysis of the feelings of those living at the time, as expressed in the press and culture of the time, including popular culture. Tolkien was a man of the 19th century. Indeed, he was born at the turn of the century but he was raised and educated in distinctly 19th century institutions. The First World War, as Hosbawm has stated, brought about the collapse – directly witnessed by Tolkien – of the enormous structure of 19th century culture. This collapse derived not only from the events of the war but also, if not more, from the dramatic events that followed it, which included the Spanish Flu that killed millions (even more than the war itself), economic crises, and the rise of radical political ideologies that continued to shock the societies of Europe in the decades after the war. Europeans lived with the constant sense that another great war was only a matter of time.

It is possible that Tolkien aimed to leave his works in the realm of fantasy literature and through their plots to instruct the young generation as to values such as ethical behavior, friendship, sacrifice, etc. Also, even if an analogy between Tolkien's books and the political, military, and social reality in the years in which he wrote them seems inevitable, we must keep in mind that there is a type of dialog between author and reader and that there are always differences between the two. It is possible that readers in the years after the publication of the trilogy did make an analogy with the years of the Second World War or (perhaps) with the post-war confrontation between the great powers, i.e., the Cold War. It is also possible that those who have been exposed to this epic after 9/11 may identify Osama Bin Laden with the figure of Sauron, his armies analogous to the armed militias of radical Islam organizations. This, especially in the climate of a total war between cultures, is evident particularly in the rhetoric of the various radical Islamic organizations.

It is impossible to ignore the historical fact that Tolkien wrote and worked in a specific cultural climate, with its numerous manifestations. Total war, expressed most distinctly in the First World War, continued to accompany Europeans well into the 1920s and 1930s. The political escalation and military aggression of the second half of the 1930s reminded Europe of the horrors of the Great War. Just as many others in the arts were affected, one way or the other, by the events prior to the Second World War, the war itself, and the onset of the Cold

War, there is no doubt that Tolkien was affected as well. The shadow of total war was too dark and heavy to ignore, and remains so to this day.

Bibliography

ANDIDORA, Ronald. *Iron Admirals: Naval Leadership in the Twentieth Century.* Westport, CT: Greenwood Press, 2000.

BECKETT, Ian F.W. "Total War." *Warfare in the Twentieth Century: Theory and Practice.* Eds. Colin McInnes and G.D. Sheffield. London: Unwin Hyman, 1988, 1-21.

BELL, Philip. "The Great War and Its Impact." *Themes in Modern European History, 1890-1945.* Ed. Paul Hayes. London and New York: Routledge, 1992, 129-148.

BELL, P.M.H. *Twentieth-Century Europe: Unity and Division.* London: Hodder Arnold, 2006.

BIDDLE, Tami Davis. *Rhetoric and Reality in Air Warfare: The Evolution of British and American Ideas about Strategic Bombing, 1914-1945.* Princeton: Princeton University Press, 2001.

BLACK, Jeremy. *The Age of Total War, 1860-1945.* Westport, CT: Praeger, 2006.

Avoiding Armageddon: From the Great War to the Fall of France, 1918-1940. London: Bloomsbury, 2012.

BOND, Brian. "The Somme in British History." *War in the Age of Technology: Myriad Faces of Modern Armed Conflict.* Eds. Geoffrey Jensen and Andrew Wiest. New York City, NY: New York University Press, 2001, 194-210.

BOYNE, Walter J. *The Influence of Air Power upon History.* Gretna: Pelican, 2003.

BROERS, Michael. "The Concept of Total War in the Revolutionary–Napoleonic Period." *War in History* 15 (2008): 247-268.

BUCKLEY, John. *Air Power in the Age of Total War.* Bloomington, IN: Indiana University Press, 1999.

BUDIANSKY, Stephen. *Air Power.* New York City, NY: Penguin, 2004.

CARPENTER, Humphrey. *Tolkien: A Biography.* Boston, MA: Houghton Mifflin Company, 1977.

CASTLE, H.G. *Fire over England: The German Air Raids of World War I.* London: Secker & Warburg, 1982.

CHICKERING, Roger. "Sore Loser: Ludendorff's Total War." *The Shadows of Total War: Europe, East Asia, and the United States, 1919-1939.* Eds. Roger Chickering and Stig Förster. Cambridge: Cambridge University Press, 2003, 151-196.

"World War I and the Theory of Total War." *Great War, Total War: Combat and Mobilization on the Western Front, 1914-1918.* Eds. Roger Chickering and Stig Förster. Cambridge: Cambridge University Press, 2000, 35-53.

CORUM, James. *The Luftwaffe: Creating the Operational Air War, 1918-1940.* Lawrence, KS: Kansas University Press, 1997.

CROFT, Janet Brennan. *War and the Works of J.R.R. Tolkien.* Westport, CT: Praeger, 2004.

CROSS, Wilbur. *Zeppelins of World War I.* London: I.B. Tauris, 1991.

DEGROOT, Gerard J. "The First World War as Total War." *A Companion to Modern European History, 1871-1945.* Ed. Martin Pugh. Cambridge, MA: Blackwell, 1997, 262-281.

DIEHL, James M. "No More Peace: The Militarization of Politics." *The Shadows of Total War: Europe, East Asia, and the United States, 1919-1939*, Eds. Roger Chickering and Stig Förster. Cambridge: Cambridge University Press, 2003, 97-112.

ECHEVARRIA, Antulio J. *Imagining Future War: The West's Technological Revolution and Visions of War to Come 1880-1914.* Westport, CT: Praeger, 2007.

FEGAN, Thomas. *The "Baby Killers": Germans Air Raids on Britain in the First World War.* Barnsley: Pen & Sword Military, 2012.

FREVERT, Ute. "War." *A Companion to Nineteenth-Century Europe, 1789-1914.* Ed. Stefan Berger. Malden, MA: Blackwell, 2006, 417-443.

GARTH, John. *Tolkien and the Great War: The Threshold of Middle-Earth.* Boston, MA: Houghton Mifflin Company, 2004.

GAT, Azar. *The Development of Military Thought: The Nineteenth Century.* Oxford: Clarendon, 1992.

HOBSBAWM, Eric. *Age of Extremes: The Short Twentieth Century, 1914-1991.* London: Abacus, 1995.

HOWARD, Michael. *War in European History.* Oxford: Oxford University Press, 1976.

JANDA, Lance. "Shutting the Gates of Mercy: The American Origins of Total War, 1860-1880." *Journal of Military History* 59 (1995): 7-26.

Jones, Leslie A. *J.R.R. Tolkien: A Biography*. Westport, CT: Greenwood Press, 2003.

Kane, Thomas M. *Strategy: Key Thinkers*. Cambridge: Polity, 2013.

Kumar, Krishan. *Utopia and Anti-Utopia in Modern Times*. Oxford: Blackwell, 1987.

LaSala, Jeff. "The Eagles of Middle-earth: Tolkien's Special Ops." *Tor.com*. 21 Dec 2016. https://www.tor.com/2016/12/21/tolkien-eagles-manwes-special-ops/. 23 January 2019.

MacIsaac, David. "Voices from the Central Blue: The Air Power Theorists." *Makers of Modern Strategy: From Machiavelli to the Nuclear Age*. Ed. Peter Paret. Princeton, NJ: Princeton University Press, 1986, 624-647.

MacMillan, Margaret. *The War that Ended Peace: The Road to 1914*. New York City, NY: Random House, 2013.

Meilinger, Phillip S. *Airwar: Theory and Practice*. London: Frank Cass, 2003.

"Giulio Douhet and the Origins of Airpower Theory." *The Paths of Heaven: The Evolution of Airpower Theory*. Ed. Philip S. Meilinger. Maxwell AFB AL: Air University Press, 1997, 1-34.

Middlemas, Keith and John Barnes. *Baldwin: A Biography*. London: Weidenfeld and Nicolson, 1969.

Morrow, John H. "The First World War, 1914-1919." *A History of Air Warfare*. Ed. John A. Olsen. Washington D.C.: Potomac Books, 2010, 3-25.

Murray, Williamson A. "The Industrialization of War, 1815-1871." *The Cambridge History of Warfare* Ed. Geoffrey Parker. Cambridge: Cambridge University Press, 2005, 219-248.

"Towards World War 1871-1914." *The Cambridge History of Warfare*. Ed. Geoffrey Parker. Cambridge: Cambridge University Press, 2005, 249-277.

"The West at War." *The Cambridge History of Warfare*. Ed. Geoffrey Parker. Cambridge: Cambridge University Press, 2005, 294-295.

Neiberg, Michael S. *Warfare and Society in Europe: 1898 to the Present*. London and New York City, NY: Routledge, 2004.

Prior, Robin. "The Western Front." *The Cambridge History of the First World War (vol. 1): Global War*. Ed. Jay Winter. Cambridge: Cambridge University Press, 2014, 204-233.

PURSEIGLE, Pierre. "Home Front: The Mobilization of Resources for Total War." *The Cambridge History of War (vol. 4): War and the Modern World.* Eds. Roger Chickering, Dennis Showalter and Hans van de Ven. Cambridge: Cambridge University Press, 2012, 45-68.

ROBERTS, J.M. *Europe 1880-1945.* New York City, NY: Longman, 1989.

RUDHART, Alexander. *Twentieth Century Europe.* Englewood Cliffs, NJ: Prentice-Hall, 1986.

RUSSELL, Bertrand. "The Future of Pacifism." *The American Scholar* 13 (1943): 7-13.

SHOWALTER, Dennis E. "Mass Warfare and the Impact of Technology." *Great War, Total War: Combat and Mobilization on the Western Front, 1914-1918.* Eds. Roger Chickering and Stig Förster. Cambridge: Cambridge University Press, 2000, 73-93.

SPEIER, Hans. "Ludendorff: The German Concept of Total War." *Makers of Modern Strategy: Military Thought from Machiavelli to Hitler.* Ed. Edward M. Earle. Princeton, NJ: Princeton University Press, 1943, 306-321.

STEPHENS, Alan. "The True Believers: Airpower between the Wars." *The War in the Air 1914-1994.* Ed. Alan Stephens. Maxwell AFB AL: Air University Press, 2001, 29-68.

STEVENSON, David. *1914-1918: The History of the First World War.* London: Penguin, 2005.

TALLETT, Frank. "World War One: Conduct and Consequences." *Themes in Modern European History 1890-1945.* Eds. Nicholas Atkin and Michael Biddiss. London and New York City, NY: Routledge, 2009, 146-180.

THOMSON, David. *Europe Since Napoleon.* London: Pelican, 1966.

TOLKIEN, J.R.R. *The Hobbit, or, There and Back Again.* Boston, MA: Houghton Mifflin, 1966.

The Letters of J.R.R. Tolkien: A Selection. 1st Houghton Mifflin pbk. edition. Eds. Humphrey Carpenter and Christopher Tolkien.Boston, MA: Houghton Mifflin, 2000.

The Lord of the Rings. 50th Anniversary edition. Boston, MA: Houghton Mifflin, 2004.

TRAVERS, Tim. "The War in the Trenches." *A Companion to Europe, 1900-1945.* Ed. Gordon Martel. Malden, MA: Blackwell, 2006, 213-226.

WAWRO, Geoffrey. "War, Technology, and Industrial Change." *The Cambridge History of War (vol. 4): War and the Modern World.* Eds. Roger Chickering, Dennis Showalter, and Hans van de Ven. Cambridge: Cambridge University Press, 2012, 45-68

Warfare and Society in Europe, 1792-1914. London and New York City, NY: Routledge, 2004.

WILSON, Woodrow. "Joint Address to Congress Leading to a Declaration of War Against Germany." 2 Apr 1917. https://www.ourdocuments.gov/doc.php?flash=false&doc=61. 23 January 2019.

WIMSATT, William K. and Monroe C. BEARDSLEY. "The Intentional Fallacy." *The Sewanee Review* 54.3 (1946): 468-488.

Section II:

Biography: The Personal Becomes Art

John Rosegrant

Fault Lines Beneath the Crack

It is illuminating to unpack Tolkien's well-known statement in his letter of 12 August 1916 to G.B. Smith, about his reaction to the battlefield death of fellow TCBS member Rob Gilson:

> So far my chief impression is that something has gone crack. I feel just the same to both of you [Smith and the other surviving TCBS member, Christopher Wiseman] – nearer if anything and very much in need of you – I am hungry and lonely of course – but I don't feel a member of a little complete body now. I honestly feel that the TCBS has ended [...]. (*Letters* 10)

This is a very powerful statement of distress – but distress at what, exactly? By writing "*something* has gone crack" [italics added], Tolkien, an extremely skilled wordsmith not prone to vagueness, indicated uncertainty about just what was troubling him. Judging from the end of the quoted passage the "something" surely includes the TCBS, but if that were all it included then why did Tolkien not express himself along the lines of, "The TCBS has gone crack," or why did he not employ a word like "coterie" that Wiseman found fitting in his subsequent letter quoted below (Garth 184)?

A crack in the TCBS is apparently the meaning Smith and Wiseman responded to in Tolkien's statement. An incensed Smith wrote that when he and Tolkien next met, "I am not quite sure whether I shall shake you by the hand or take you by the throat ..." (quoted in Garth 179) and

> 'As to the winnowing of the TCBS,' he said, 'I really do not care two straws. It only refers to its executive capacity ...' The group was spiritual in character, 'an influence on the state of being', and as such it transcended mortality; it was 'as permanently inseparable as Thor and his hammer'. The influence, he said, was 'a tradition, which forty years from now will still be as strong to us (if we are alive, and if we are not) as it is today ...' (Garth 180)

And Wiseman

> was baffled by Tolkien's assertion that he no longer felt part of a 'little complete body', and went on: 'Speaking for myself I know that I belong to a coterie of three. [...] Now this coterie is for me quite sufficient. It is the TCBS. [...] I as yet see no reason to doubt that there is an achievement for our striving and a prize for our winning provided we are willing to pay the price. I cannot see that the TCBS is altered.' (Garth 184)

Another meaning of Tolkien's "something" can be gleaned by considering other words in his statement, and seeing how they contrast with Smith and Wiseman's language. Tolkien refers to the TCBS not as a coterie, or any similar word such as "club", "set", or "circle", but as "a little complete body". Tolkien implicates his own body with his statement that he is hungry as well as lonely. And the word "crack" conjures a physical break in something, as well as an immediate auditory experience such as gunfire makes. Perhaps without consciously intending it, Tolkien has associated his feelings about the death of his friend to the bodily insults of war. This vivid, immediate, body-oriented language is quite different from the abstract language of Smith and Wiseman quoted above, utilizing words such as "executive capacity", "spiritual", "state of being", "tradition", "achievement", and "prize". Smith's metaphor of the inseparability of Thor and his hammer makes the point even clearer, because it insists not on the intactness of an actual body but of a relationship between body and object. I propose that Tolkien wrote "*something* has gone crack" because he experienced Gilson's death not only in terms of the interpersonal loss of a beloved member of an intense social group, with all the creative and spiritual implications focused on by Smith and Wiseman, but also as a blow to his body-self.

In this chapter I intend to develop these thoughts in two interrelated directions. First, although it is clear that the trauma of World War I affected Tolkien strongly, these effects can only be understood clearly if we take into consideration the psychological vulnerabilities that Tolkien brought into the war. As the reactions of the remaining TCBS members to Gilson's death indicate, trauma affects different people in different ways: unlike Tolkien, Smith and Wiseman did not invoke the body and they vehemently denied as well that any crack had taken place in the social, creative, and spiritual realms. Second, the most important specific vulnerabilities that Tolkien brought into the war were those I have indicated above as forming his reaction to Gilson's death: vulnerabilities to emotional loss and physical ailment. The crack of World War I exacerbated pre-existing fault lines in Tolkien's interpersonal relationship schemas and his body-self.

Psychological Effects of Trauma

A brief discussion of the general psychological effects of trauma will be helpful before exploring Tolkien's personal reaction to the trauma of World War I. Traumatic events are ones that overwhelm the victim's ability to cope with them and assimilate them into his/her ongoing sense of self. This happens because the quantity of aversive stimulation is too much to handle (Freud) and/or because the victim must totally devote him/herself to managing and surviving the external event (Krystal; Oliner, *Psychic Reality*). In either of these situations self-continuity is disrupted. Traumatic events include *shock trauma*, such as abrupt exposure to death, physical injury, or sexual violence (American Psychiatric Association; Lingiardi and McWilliams) and *cumulative* or *strain trauma*, in which repeated experiences of less shocking stressors cumulatively have traumatic effect.

Certain reactions are common after experiencing traumatic events (American Psychiatric Association; Lingiardi and McWilliams). These include: repetitive re-experiencing of the event in thought, fantasy, dream, or action; avoidance of reminders of the event; somatic symptoms including illness, irritability, and sleep disturbance; affective states such as rage, terror, shame, or emotional numbing; and cognitive symptoms such as constant rumination about the event or, in an opposite manner, being unable to remember or think about the event.[1]

All of these reactions are manifestations of the victim's ongoing but failing effort to heal from the trauma and find meaning in it by integrating it with the pre-existing self (Auerhahn and Laub; Krystal; Oliner, *External Reality, Psychic Reality*) This effort to process the trauma continually fails because the trauma is too painful to think about and feel at a tolerable level of arousal, so it is *desym-*

1 The formal diagnosis of Post-Traumatic Stress Disorder (American Psychiatric Association) is based on several arbitrary cut-off points in the above symptoms that actually exist on a continuum rather than categorically, so considering a trauma victim's particular stress reactions is more meaningful than trying to decide whether they do or do not qualify formally as Post-Traumatic Stress Disorder.

bolized – rendered unavailable for conscious verbal reflection (Bucci; Freedman and Lavender; Lasky). As a result, the trauma either is repeatedly re-experienced without becoming more tolerable (such as in flashbacks or traumatic dreams), or is split off from verbal and affective processing and therefore expressed in ways that are hidden from conscious awareness (such as in somatic symptoms, emotional numbing, and dissociation). These dynamic processes do not necessarily, or even usually, mean that the trauma is absent from conscious memory, although that can occur. Rather, desymbolization means that even if consciously remembered and spoken about, the full horror of the trauma is not tolerable in conscious thought and feeling and so cannot be put into words.

As I describe at length below, somatization appears to have been a major avenue for Tolkien to express traumatic experience, so I will briefly elaborate here on why the body is a common location for trauma symptoms. Infants primarily relate to the world via their bodies. They explore by touching things and putting them into their mouths, they express distress by crying and wriggling or thrashing their bodies, and they are comforted by being held. They of course do not yet have words, and their feelings are inchoate states of arousal rather than clearly delineated emotions. With appropriate caretaking, infants and toddlers gradually learn language and develop the ability to recognize and name specific emotions, but these higher-order symbol systems do not eliminate the body as a locus of self-expression, and it remains available as an avenue to express emotions too painful to put into words (Bucci). When experience is of traumatic intensity so that words cannot effectively symbolize it, a psychic message of warning bypasses language and goes instead straight to the body (McDougall).

The typical traumatic reactions described above build upon, and are intertwined with, the pre-traumatic personality. Whether one is traumatized by a particular event, and how severe the trauma is if it occurs, depends on the pre-existing strengths and vulnerabilities of the experiencing person (Lingiardi and McWilliams). This is apparent for example from the fact that some but not all soldiers experience trauma symptoms after battle, and those who are traumatized may experience different specific symptoms at different intensities. More importantly for the understanding of Tolkien that I am developing here, post-traumatic symptoms may not only result from the trauma but also express individual personal meanings resulting from earlier life history (Adams-Silvan and Silvan; Oliner, *Psychic Reality*; Renik; Sugarman). Moses gives examples of a soldier who repetitively relived his killing of an enemy soldier and eventually recognized that this repetition was partly motivated by childhood guilt over angry feelings, and another soldier whose guilt about the battlefield deaths of his buddies was linked to his guilt about the earlier deaths of family members. From my own practice I mention the not uncommon examples of young women and men who find their first sexual experiences traumatic, even if consensually desired, because they stir up childhood memories of parental misattunement and abuse.

Pre-Existing Fault Lines in Tolkien's Psyche

It is widely understood that the war had a major impact on Tolkien's writing. From the more general to the more particular, we have studies exploring how Tolkien shared the modernist concern with trying to find a way to express the culture-changing horror of the war, however different from the modernists his solution was (Garth; Hiley; Honegger and Weinreich; Shippey, *Road, Author*; Weinreich and Honegger); Croft's exploration of themes in Tolkien's work that are congruent with themes of the war; studies of traumatic reactions experienced by Frodo (Livingston; Smol) and Túrin (Sinex); and manifest one-to-one similarities, such as the tank-like mechanical dragons in "The Fall of Gondolin" (*LT* II), or the similarity acknowledged by Tolkien (*Letters* 303) between the Dead Marshes and the Somme battlefield.

On one level these effects of the war can be understood as Tolkien using his monumental creative talent to integrate and find meaning in his war experiences. I wish to explore the effects of the war on a more personal level by examining Tolkien's pre-war suffering from emotional loss, and his susceptibility to physical ailments particularly at times of stress, and then examining how the traumatic exacerbation of these vulnerabilities by World War I shaped Tolkien's later life and writings.

The young Tolkien's most obvious emotional losses, of course, were due to his orphaning. Tolkien's mother Mabel died of diabetes on 14 November 1904, when he was twelve years and ten months old. It is clear from Tolkien's letters that he was intensely grieved by her death ("I remember [...] when I was not yet thirteen after the death of my mother [...] vainly waving a hand at the sky saying 'it is so empty and cold'" [*Letters* 416]; "When I think of my mother's death [...] worn out with persecution, poverty, and, largely consequent, disease, in the effort to hand on to us small boys the Faith [...] I find it very hard and bitter, when my children stray away" [*Letters,* 353-4]). Carpenter (*Biography* 39) reports that Tolkien's personality changed after his mother's death so that from then on he was subject to dark, despairing moods.

Tolkien's reaction to his father's death is less apparent from available records. His father had died 15 February 1896, when Tolkien was three years and one month old, and it is likely that the conscious impact of this death on Tolkien was ameliorated by his young age, and by the fact that he with his mother and brother had already traveled away from his father ten months earlier. Conscious thoughts, feelings, and needs for his father at this age were probably much less than for his mother at age twelve.

However, it is important here to take note of Tolkien's Atlantis dream:

> [...] I have what some might call an Atlantis complex. [...] I mean the terrible recurrent dream (beginning with memory) of the Great Wave, towering up, and coming in ineluctably over the trees and green fields. (I bequeathed it to Faramir.) I don't think I have had it since I wrote the 'Downfall of Númenor' as the last of the legends of the First and Second Age. (*Letters* 213),

and

> In sleep I had the dreadful dream of the ineluctable Wave, either coming out of the quiet sea, or coming in towering over the green inlands. It still occurs occasionally, though now exorcized by writing about it. It always ends by surrender, and I awake gasping out of deep water. (*Letters* 347)

Several aspects of these descriptions show that this was a traumatic dream: it was "terrible" and "dreadful", it consisted of being inexorably overwhelmed and appears to have involved actual motoric gasping for breath during awakening, and it was repetitive and unchanging until Tolkien was able to creatively transform it in his legendarium.

Tolkien also noted that the Atlantis dream had been part of his life "beginning with memory". This indicates that Tolkien had traumatic experience long before the death of his mother, and thus suggests that his father's death had a greater impact than was consciously apparent. I have previously discussed the likelihood that the death of Tolkien's father impacted him with guilt and anxiety about hubris that significantly affected his later writing (Rosegrant, "Wave").

Could the Atlantis dream also signify other early trauma in addition to the death of his father? Bunting (*Finding Tolkien, 1904*) has hypothesized that Tolkien's mother was physically and emotionally abusive, even attacking him and his brother murderously in the year before her death (*Finding Tolkien*) and that the resulting insecurity in their relationship intensified the trauma of her death so that Tolkien had ten- and twenty-year anniversary reactions. Although Bunting's focus on the psychological significance of Tolkien's pre-war life is valuable, I think her conclusions extend beyond what is tenable, and currently available records do not support the view of Tolkien's mother as abusive (Rosegrant, "Comment"). However, examination of a number of songs in Tolkien's legendarium indicates that he had unusual sensitivity to themes of early mother-child separation and reunion, and this may indicate that he experienced "strain trauma" – repeated small painful separation experiences that have a powerful cumulative effect – in relation to his mother (Rosegrant, "Mother Music").

Evidence of the youthful Tolkien's vulnerability to physical ailments, particularly correlated with times of stress, is found in Carpenter (*Biography*) and Scull and Hammond (*Chronology*). The infant Tolkien is reported (vaguely) to have suffered from the heat, so much so that it was bad for his health and was a prominent reason given for his being taken back to England late in his third year. After what appears to have been an idyllic period living in the small village of Sarehole and being taught at home by his mother, Tolkien at age eight began attending the autumn term at King Edward's School, and in September his family moved to the city, which Tolkien remembered as "dreadful" (qtd. in Carpenter, *Biography* 25). In his first term he frequently missed school due to illness; the timing of these illnesses suggests that they were influenced by the stress of new school and new home.

When Tolkien was twelve both he and his brother were seriously ill with measles and whooping cough at a time that corresponded with the beginning of their mother's fatal illness. Mabel reported in a letter of Christmas 1903 that she had a "lingering illness", and she was formally diagnosed with diabetes in April 1904. The boys became sick in January 1904, and appear to have been affected until at least late May, since Mabel commented in a late June letter that the boys now looked very much healthier than they had a month previously. Although it is unremarkable that the Tolkien boys contracted these diseases, which were common in children in the early twentieth century, the duration of their illnesses was unusually long; measles typically lasts one week or less, and whooping cough typically about seven weeks, with cases lasting three months or more being at the extreme of the range (Merck). The unusually long duration of these illnesses, together with their co-occurrence with Mabel's sickness, suggests that they were influenced by the stress of his mother's illness.

Tolkien had numerous milder ailments prior to the war: When he was seventeen he decided to be "ferocious" on the school rugby team, and during games he badly damaged his tongue and his nose. During the summer of that year he accidentally cut his hand on a knife. At age twenty-one Tolkien injured his foot (it is unclear how this happened or how severe it was). Later that year, and again just after turning twenty-two, Tolkien was briefly ill.

To summarize this section, Tolkien entered the war with two prominent areas of psychological vulnerability developed in his earlier life. First, he was highly sensitized to the pain of emotional loss, certainly from the deaths of his parents, and possibly from strain trauma in his early relationship with his mother. Second, Tolkien was vulnerable to physical ailments, and this vulnerability was probably exacerbated by experiences of stress.

Cracks of War

Tolkien's war experience landed blows precisely on the two areas of sensitivity I have described: he was struck hard with interpersonal loss and physical sickness. That Tolkien suffered greatly from interpersonal loss is obvious from his reactions to the deaths of his friends; this was central to his feeling that "something has gone crack," and see also his statement in the Foreword to *The Lord of the Rings*: "One has indeed personally to come under the shadow of war to feel fully its oppression; but as the years go by it seems now often forgotten that to be caught in youth by 1914 was no less hideous an experience than to be involved in 1939 and the following years. By 1918 all but one of my close friends were dead" (xxiv). There is no need to belabor the point.

Tolkien's physical illness incurred during the war merits more examination. On 27 October 1916, about six weeks after writing that "something has gone crack" – six weeks filled with military operations documented by Garth and Scull and Hammond (*Chronology*) – Tolkien reported sick with a fever of 103 degrees. He was diagnosed with trench fever and sent back to England. I have summarized his subsequent career as a patient in the below table. All information is drawn from Garth and Scull and Hammond (*Chronology*), with the exception of the asterisked entries drawn from Carpenter (*Biography*). Although it is always risky to give a diagnosis more than one hundred years after the fact, the pattern of illness documented by these sources strongly indicates that Tolkien's physical suffering was in part caused by traumatic emotions expressed via the body.

DATE	MEDICAL STATUS	MILITARY STATUS
27 October 1916	103 degree fever; diagnosed with Trench Fever	Sent back to England
2 December 1916	Fever abated one week previously, but still has pain and weakness	Unfit for service six more weeks.
23 January 1917	Improved, but had two slight returns of fever and still has pain and weakness	Unfit for general service for two more months
28 March 1917	Improving but still has pains	Unfit for general service for one more month
April 1917*		Fails examination that would have qualified him for non-combat posting in England*
1 June 1917		Declared fit for general duty; posted in England
July 1917		Fails examination that would have qualified him for non-combat posting in England

* This information taken from Carpenter (*Biography*). It probably refers to the same event that Garth places two months later, in July. Garth's dating is most likely more accurate.

Mid-August 1917	Hospitalized for fever	
16 October 1917	Discharged from hospital, still weak and in pain	Unfit for general duty for one month
16 November 1917	Slowly recovering; has had one slight bout of fever	Unfit for general duty for two months
19 January 1918	Slowly recovering; has had two slight attacks of fever	Unfit for general duty for one month
19 February 1918	Slowly improving; weak and needs hardening	Unfit for general duty
Late February-early March 1918	Five days influenza	
19 March 1918	Improving but still needs hardening	Unfit for general duty
10 April 1918		Declared fit for general duty; posted in England
29 June 1918	Contracts gastritis	
By 12 July 1918	Hospitalized	
17 July 1918		Unfit to serve in any capacity for one month
Late July-August 1918	Loses nearly 28 pounds in hospital	
4 September 1918		Unfit in any category for two months
11 September 1918	Transferred to convalescent hospital	
1 October 1918		Authorized for sedentary employment only
14 October 1918		Unfit for any duty other than sedentary employment for six months
11 November 1918		Armistice signed
14 February 1919		Fit only for sedentary employment
7 June 1919		Unfit for general service
8 July 1919		Discharged from military service

4 September 1919		Awarded temporary retired pay until 6 December; can then re-apply
11 November 1919	Still some disability	Awarded maximum disability pay and directed to hostel for treatment; does not seek said treatment

After 11 November 1919, Scull and Hammond (*Chronology*) document no physical ailments until March 1922 – twenty-seven months later – when Tolkien suffered from influenza.

Several dates in the above table are particularly worth highlighting because they indicate the probable contribution of unverbalizable emotional trauma to Tolkien's ailments. First is the sheer length of his suffering from trench fever and its sequelae, for a total of nearly eighteen months from 27 October 1916 to 10 April 1918. Typical duration of trench fever is five or six days, with one to eight recurrences of fever at five- or six-day intervals occurring in about half the cases, and relapses occurring up to ten years after the initial infection (Merck). The duration of Tolkien's case, though not unheard of, was an outlier by these standards. Second is the occurrence after the sequelae of trench fever had abated of a new severe symptom, gastritis, resulting in the overall duration of Tolkien's disability being long enough to prevent his return to combat. Third is the fact that symptoms continued long enough for Tolkien to be awarded full disability pay, after which he apparently returned to health quickly enough that he did not undergo the treatment recommended when disability pay was awarded. It is also important to note that Tolkien had two additional hospitalizations after the initial one, indicating renewed severity of symptoms, and that both re-hospitalizations occurred when he was at increased risk of being sent back into combat: The first re-hospitalization, lasting about two months, began in August 2017 after Tolkien had been declared fit for general duty in June and then probably in July had failed an examination that would have qualified him for non-combat duty in England. The second re-hospitalization, from mid-July to mid-September 1918, occurred after Tolkien had been declared fit for general duty on 10 April.

The above data make a strong case that Tolkien's illness during World War I in part resulted from the emotional trauma of his service on the Somme, and from anxiety about the possibility of return to combat, that were expressed through his body because they could not be otherwise symbolized.[2]

The Fault Lines Stay Open

If war trauma exacerbated psychological vulnerabilities to emotional loss and physical illness that Tolkien had developed in earlier life, we would expect these areas of vulnerability to remain powerful for him in later life. A first indication that this was so is the lifelong sadness that Tolkien felt about the wartime deaths of his friends (Tolkien, John and Priscilla 41). In this section I examine evidence of ongoing vulnerability to loss and illness in Tolkien's life, and in the subsequent section I examine the ways in which he expressed this vulnerability in his fiction.

As Tolkien himself commented in the first of the following excerpts from his letters, records often do not record deeply personal and private emotions. This limitation in understanding Tolkien's emotional life is compounded by the fact that a portion of his letters and personal papers remains unavailable to the public. Nevertheless, what is available gives a picture of Tolkien as a man deeply sensitive to loss.

In a letter of 11 July 1972 to his son Christopher about Tolkien's wife Edith who had died on 29 November 1971, Tolkien wrote,

> [S]omeone close in heart to me should know something about things that records do not record: the dreadful sufferings of our childhoods, from which we rescued one another, but could not wholly heal the wounds that later often proved disabling; the sufferings that we endured after our love began – all of which (over and above our personal weaknesses) might help to make pardonable, or understandable, the lapses and darknesses which at times marred our lives – and to explain how these never touched our depths nor dimmed our memories of our youthful love. (*Letters* 421)

---

2 This is in no way to suggest that Tolkien was malingering or consciously shirking duty. Military doctors examined him regularly and documented definitely that he was suffering from genuine and severe physical ailments. The misconception that trauma symptoms expressed through the body are "all in the head" results from a false dichotomy between mind and body.

And in a letter of 24 January 1972 to his son Michael, Tolkien wrote,

> […] I still often find myself thinking 'I must tell E about this' – and then suddenly I feel like a castaway left on a barren island under a heedless sky after the loss of a great ship. I remember trying to tell Marjorie Incledon this feeling, when I was not yet thirteen after the death of my mother (Nov. 9, 1904), and vainly waving a hand at the sky saying 'it is so empty and cold'. And again I remember after the death of Fr Francis my 'second father' (at 77 in 1934), saying to C.S. Lewis: 'I feel like a lost survivor into a new alien world after the real world has passed away.' But of course these griefs however poignant (especially the first) came in youth with life and work still unfolding. In 1904 we (H[illary] & I) had the sudden miraculous appearance of Fr Francis' love and care and humor – and only 5 years later […] I met the Lúthien Tinúviel of my own personal romance […]. And in 1934 she was still with me […]. But now she has gone before Beren, leaving him indeed one-handed […]. (*Letters* 416-417)

These letters are replete with the pain of loss of love, pain so intense that Tolkien experienced derealization ("a lost survivor into a new alien world after the real world has passed away") and alienation from all relationships, both with people ("a castaway", "a lost survivor") and with the world as a whole ("on a barren island under a heedless sky," "it is so empty and so cold"). It seems clear that whether or not the "dreadful sufferings of our childhoods" included other things, primary in Tolkien's mind as he wrote those words were his and Edith's orphaning. This is shown not only by the fact that Tolkien is writing directly about the pain caused by loss, but also because only a new deep primary love relationship had been able to partly heal the pain: "trying to tell Marjorie Incledon" seems not to have been enough; the love of "second father" Father Francis, and then the Lúthien of his own personal romance, were much more soothing.

But even Lúthien's (Edith's) love "could not wholly heal the wounds that later proved disabling," or prevent "the lapses and darknesses that at times marred [their] lives." So in these letters Tolkien was describing intense suffering from emotional loss beginning well before the war and continuing throughout his life after the war, only partially smoothed over by love relationships.

A final point I wish to make about these letters is that Tolkien metaphorically described his pain at emotional loss as bodily impairment. He and Edith "could not wholly heal the *wounds* that later proved disabling," and "now she has gone before Beren, leaving him indeed *one-handed*" [italics added].

Tolkien again used a metaphor of body impairment to describe his pain at the death of C.S. Lewis. Tolkien's deep friendship with Lewis is attested in a variety of sources (Carpenter, *Biography, Inklings;* Kilby) and Tolkien himself wrote "C.S.L. was my closest friend from about 1927 to about 1940, and remained very dear to me" (*Letters* 349). Despite their later partial estrangement, Tolkien wrote on 26 November 1963, four days after Lewis's death, "So far I have felt the normal feelings of a man my age – like an old tree that is losing all its leaves one by one: this feels like *an axe-blow near the roots*" [italics added] (*Letters* 341).

Therefore, although bodily metaphors for emotional suffering at times of loss are far from unique to Tolkien, they appear to have had a special valence for him. He employed such metaphors in response to both Edith's and Lewis's death, and whereas *wounds* is a conventional metaphor, *one-handed* and *an axe-blow near the roots* are personal coinings. It is likely that somatic metaphors were charged with personal meaning for Tolkien because of his regular acquaintance with physical suffering.

The best summary of Tolkien's ongoing physical sufferings after the war is Scull and Hammond's (*Reader's Guide*) entry under "Health" (1.483-487). As they report, "A remarkable number of the letters Tolkien wrote contain comments on his [poor] health" (1.483), and "Tolkien used a variety of names to describe the physical pains he suffered as he advanced in years, and it is not always clear how he applied them" (1.485). Such names included fibrositis, lumbago, arthritis, rheumatism, and simply "pain". Doctors could not always identify causes for his complaints; for example, gastric pains that Tolkien began to suffer in 1969 were never medically explained.

Scull and Hammond tellingly quote Rayner Unwin's thoughts on Tolkien's health as follows:

> It is difficult to judge [...] to what extent his unspecific complaints [...] disguised some specific illness or were, at least in part, a defence against his failure to achieve some rashly-promised goal. [...] [H]e did suffer a great number of much more specific illnesses and accidents [...]. [H]is catalogue of physical woes grew year by year. [...] There was no particular pattern to these ailments. Sometimes the

> less specific complaints seem to have been associated with worry, but for the most part they were far from psychosomatic. [...] I might have suspected that he was protesting too much [...] to be taken entirely seriously. [...] I now believe that [...] he was more liable than most men to minor ailments *and less able to cope with the distractions they caused* [...]. (*Reader's Guide* 1.483-484, italics added)

The takeaway from all this seems to be that after the war Tolkien was plagued both by more specific, diagnosable physical ailments and by more nonspecific, vague physical ailments than most people, and that furthermore he was less able to cope with these ailments when they did occur. Although sometimes the ailments were associated with specific stressors, and Unwin respectfully and tentatively hazarded the term "psychosomatic", more often there were no obvious stressors.

This pattern of symptoms is consistent with the idea that Tolkien had difficulty symbolizing painful feelings, and that his body had become readily available for expressing these desymbolized emotions. In combination with his history of physical suffering discussed above, this suggests that early in life, probably in response to orphaning, Tolkien developed a propensity to express trauma through his body, that this propensity was kindled to much greater strength by war trauma, and that for the remainder of his life Tolkien suffered in his body unprocessed psychological pain.

Emotional Loss and Physical Debility in Tolkien's Fiction

Tolkien's sensitivity to loss during his adult life is even clearer in his fiction than in the biographical detail available to us. It is widely understood that loss is a major theme in Tolkien's writings. "[...] the sustained and grieved sense of loss, of which death is but one form [...] floods through the history of Middle-earth" (Senior 173); "the many quick-moving scenes [...] are secondary to the sense the book conveys of things slipping into – or already become part of – an irrecoverable past" (Hannon 37); "Tolkien's whole marvelous, intricate structure has been reared to be destroyed, that we may regret it" (Parker 609). This pervasive sense of loss in his writings may be understood as way to express and integrate the trauma of the war intertwined with the earlier trauma of Tolkien's life. As Brogan stated about Tolkien's legendarium, "It was therapy for a mind wounded in war, and before that by deep sorrow in childhood and young manhood" (358). That is not all that it was, as Brogan also acknowledged, but it was an important part (Rosegrant, "Dialogue").

The connection between Tolkien's personal trauma and his fiction will become clearer by moving from his general fictional theme of loss to focus specifically on depictions of loss of love as it is affected by and affects war and battle. Physical debility does not have a general presence in Tolkien's writings equivalent to that of loss, but it does play a significant role in Tolkien's depiction of war and battle, not only in the obvious form of a result of fighting, but also as something that precedes and helps to explain the course of battle. Tolkien explored the interweaving of war with loss of love and physical disability in his depiction of several characters that I examine below.

Kullervo/Túrin

Although Tolkien elaborated much of his legendarium over a long period of time during and after the war, the story of Kullervo/Túrin is unique in that he produced a version prior to the war as well as after, allowing us to see how he expressed in his pre-war years themes that he continued to develop post-war.

"The Story of Kullervo", which Tolkien based on the Swedish traditional "Kalevala", is rife with separation and loss beginning on the very first page, when a swan is deprived of two of her younglings (who become two important men) by an eagle and a hawk. Kullervo is born after his father is killed, so that his "mother's heart is dead within" (7) – so one parent was actually dead and the other emotionally dead. Kullervo is emotionally abused ("for lack of their mother's care the children were reared in crooked fashion, for ill cradle rocking meted to infants by fosterers in thralldom: and bitterness do they suck from breasts of those that bore them not" 8) and physically abused as his step-father tries to kill him by drowning, burning, and hanging. Although Tolkien did not finish the story his notes show that he intended to end with the melodramatically heightened episode of love that is lost because the love itself was illicit: Kullervo learns that his lover was his unknown sister and that she has killed herself upon discovering the incest; he proceeds to commit suicide himself.

Bunting (*1904*) and Flieger have discussed the personal significance for Tolkien of this story. He was infatuated with the *Kalevala* when he encountered it, and more particularly by the story of Kullervo since this small section of the *Kalevala* is the part from which he developed his own story (Bunting *1904*). Tolkien's "Kullervo" describes the character's childhood abuse more sensitively and with more detail than the original *Kalevala*, and Bunting concluded that this indicated that Tolkien had been abused himself. Flieger avoided such literal extrapolation and proposed that Tolkien's fascination with the story and with Kullervo's emotional pain resulted from Tolkien's orphaning, pointing out that he first included and then deleted these lines from the original *Kalevala*: "I was small and lost my [mother-deleted] father / I was young (weak) and lost my mother" (*Kullervo* 143).

Flieger pointed out that another alteration Tolkien imposed on the original *Kalevala* material was that in the original the central character was handsome, but in Tolkien's version he was "ill favoured and crooked, broad and illknit and knotty" (20). The word "crooked" had already appeared in the description of the loveless fashion of Kullervo's upbringing (quoted above); Kullervo's physical crookedness was of a kind with his upbringing, suggesting that Tolkien was depicting physical debility to symbolize the consequences of loveless upbringing.

Tolkien continued to rework this story after the war, with Kullervo becoming the character Túrin Turambar. Although the final version of this story (*Children of Húrin*) is much more literarily sophisticated and novelistic, and drops most of the wild fantasy, it too culminates in the tragedy of incestuous love resulting in suicide. Physical debility also remains central in the later story and even though it results realistically from war (Sinex) rather than metaphorically from lack of love in childhood, the themes of physical debility and loss of love are tragically wound together in the triangle of Gwindor, Finduilas, and Túrin. The elf maiden Finduilas loved the elf Gwindor, but when Gwindor returned maimed from battle, and then Túrin arrived, healthy, beautiful, and commanding, Finduilas shifted her love to Túrin, who however was never aware that she loved him other than as a sister would. Gwindor died broken-hearted in battle, asking Túrin to protect Finduilas, but after orcs bore her away Túrin failed to rescue her because the dragon Glaurung had bewildered him.

Taken together, the stories of Kullervo and Túrin demonstrate the consistent importance for Tolkien of themes of loss of love and of physical debility, originating before the war and continuing after. After the war Tolkien worked these themes into scenes of war and its effects, but he did not essentially alter them. This is consistent with the idea that Tolkien's war trauma built upon and integrated pre-existing childhood trauma.

Faramir and Éowyn

Tolkien stated that Faramir was the character in *The Lord of the Rings* most like himself (*Letters* 232). The genuineness and depth of this identification allowed Tolkien to take one step in the process of healing himself of his traumatic dream of the Great Wave by bequeathing it to Faramir (*Letters* 213, quoted above). Because of this identification we can expect Tolkien to have attributed to Faramir trauma reactions especially similar to his own, and indeed we see in the story of Faramir and Éowyn that battle wounds were compounded by loss of love that was experienced as bodily ailment, and that final healing required new love.

Both Faramir and Éowyn were borne to the Houses of Healing after the Battle of the Pelennor Fields, afflicted near to death with ailments that were compounded of the physical and the emotional: battle wounds and loss of love. When Aragorn ministered to Faramir, he commented, "He is nearly spent. […] But this comes not from the [physical] wound. See! That is healing." Imrahil's subsequent comment emphasizes that the physical wound was relatively unimportant: "[T]he wound was not deep or vital. How then do you read the matter?" And Aragorn replied, "Weariness, grief for his father's mood, a wound, and over all the Black Breath" (*LotR* V.8.864).

Although Aragorn placed less etiological importance on grief than on the Black Breath, the grief he alluded to was Faramir's distress over being so far below his brother in his father's esteem that his father appeared willing for him to die, distress so acute that Gandalf had feared it would make Faramir suicidal. Denethor had bemoaned not having a captain of Boromir's quality in the thick of battle, and Faramir said, "'Since you are robbed of Boromir, I will go and do what I can in his stead – if you command it.' 'I do so,' said Denethor. […] Gandalf it was that last spoke to Faramir ere he rode east. 'Do not throw your life away rashly or in bitterness,' he said. [...] 'Your father loves you, Faramir, and will remember it ere the end'" (*LotR* V.4.816-817).

As Aragorn ministered to Éowyn it became clear that her wounds too were more emotional than physical, that she was primarily wounded by loss of love. After commenting that her physical wounds were well-tended, Aragorn wondered out loud about her emotional state. Beginning with "I know not how I should speak of her," he compared her as he first encountered her to a shapely lily that is hard as steel or perhaps turned to ice, about to die, and then said, "Her malady begins far back before this day, does it not, Éomer?" Aragorn, Éomer, and Gandalf then discussed Éowyn's hopeless love for Aragorn, and Gandalf elaborated that even before she met Aragorn, "[S]he was doomed to wait upon an old man [Théoden], whom she loved as a father, and watch him falling into a mean dishonoured dotage." Aragorn concluded with, "I have, maybe, the power to heal her body. [...] But to what she will awake: hope, or forgetfulness, or despair, I do not know. And if to despair, then she will die, unless other healing comes which I cannot bring" (*LotR* V.8.866-867).

The other healing to which Aragorn refers is love, and it comes in the form of Faramir. Faramir does not go to the Field of Cormallen to celebrate the destruction of the Ring because as Steward his job is to remain in Minas Tirith. Éowyn does not go because although healed of her physical wounds she still is burdened with grief. Aware that she loved and may still love Aragorn, Faramir declares his love for her. Éowyn replies, "I wished to be loved by another [...] but I desire no man's pity." Faramir explains that his feeling for her is not pity and again declares his love. "Then the heart of Éowyn changed, or else at last she understood it. And suddenly her winter passed, and the sun shone on her" (*LotR* V.5.964).

Gorlim and Meglin

In Gorlim, from the story of Beren and Lúthien (*S*), and Meglin, from the Fall of Gondolin (*LT II*), Tolkien depicted a different and in part opposite entanglement of loss of love with wartime trauma: rather than love eventually healing wartime wounds, loss of love in these stories leads to betrayal and wartime death. Gorlim was one of a small band of warriors led by Beren's father Barahir fighting against Morgoth's troops. Lonely and weary of battle and hiding, Gorlim sometimes stole away to his old home in search of his wife, and one day hallucinated a vision of her. (This is an interesting depiction of a traumatic stress reaction.) He returned to search for her and was captured and brought before Sauron, who promised to unite him with his wife if he would betray Barahir. Gorlim complied, and Sauron informed him that he had created the vision of the wife to seduce Gorlim and proceeded to have Gorlim killed. Barahir and all his men then were slain with the exception of Beren, who was away when the attack took place.

Meglin coveted the hand of Idril, daughter of Turgon King of Gondolin. Meglin is described (in a manner that Tolkien never used for elves as he later developed them) as follows: "Less fair was he than most of this goodly folk, swart and of none too kindly mood [...] and whispers there were that he had orc blood [...]" (*LT II* 165). Tolkien thus worked physical fault into the tale, although in milder form than that suffered by Kullervo or Gwindor. Idril had no liking for Meglin and instead wedded the heroic man Tuor. Meglin was later captured by orcs and betrayed the secrets of Gondolin, with possession of Idril one of his promised rewards. Similar to what happened to Barahir and his men but on grander scale, Gondolin was destroyed after a mighty battle. Tuor slew Meglin and escaped together with Idril, their son Eärendil, and a few others.

Frodo

In Frodo, Tolkien gave his clearest depiction of someone suffering stress reactions subsequent to trauma. Livingston diagnosed Frodo with Post-Traumatic Stress Disorder because of the following symptoms: after the Ring was destroyed Frodo became strongly avoidant of additional violence, initially demonstrated when he did not wish to wear a sword for the feast in his honor to be held in Ithilien, and demonstrated more dramatically as he repeatedly tried to prevent violence during the Scouring of the Shire, even though Merry stated and events proved that violence was necessary to defeat Sharkey and his ruffians. Frodo even tried to restrain violence against Sharkey after Sharkey attempted to stab him (although he was unable to prevent Wormtongues's fatal attack). Additionally, Frodo manifested a series of anniversary reactions to trauma during which he was struck with mixtures of physical and emotional pain: on the homeward journey on the anniversary of being stabbed by the Nazgûl, when they reached the Ford of Bruinen where he had almost succumbed to the wound; on the anniversary of being attacked by Shelob; and then again on the second anniversary of these two events.

Frodo's sufferings on these anniversaries mingle physical and emotional pain that resonate with Tolkien's own mingled sufferings of physical pain and pain of loss. The site of Frodo's physical injury hurts on the anniversary of the Weathertop attack, but as he describes to Gandalf he also knows that he has lost his home: "There is no real going back. Though I may come to the Shire, it will not seem the same; for I shall not be the same. I am wounded with knife, sting, and tooth, and a long burden. Where shall I find rest?" (*LotR* VI.7.989). And when Frodo is found on the first anniversary of Shelob's attack, he is muttering, "It is gone forever [...] and now all is dark and empty" (*LotR* VI.9.1024). As Livingston pointed out, although "It" is generally thought to refer to the Ring, this is not explicit; Livingston wonders if "It" might also refer to loss of innocence or hope (17-18). Whether or not "It" points to loss of innocence and hope, the vagueness of "*It* is gone forever" [italics added] serves to emphasize loss rather than a specific thing lost.

We learn more about Frodo's trauma reaction in the poem "The Sea-Bell". In the Preface to *The Adventures of Tom Bombadil* it is reported that someone scrawled on the copy of this poem in the Red Book *Frodos Dreme*, and Croft (20) pointed out that it depicts a form of shell-shock, so we may consider "The Sea-Bell" to be a depiction of a post-traumatic dream. The narrator of the poem steps into a boat and is borne to Faerie. All was lovely there, but everyone fled him and left him alone:

> But whenever I came it was ever the same:
> the feet fled, and all was still;
> never a greeting, only the fleeting
> pipes, voices, horns on the hill.

The narrator declares himself King and demands a response, but is struck down

> to the ground falling, on my hands crawling
> with eyes blind and my back bent.

He finds his boat and is borne back to the normal world, where

> ragged I walk. To myself I talk;
> for still they speak not, men that I meet.

To Croft's recognition of this as shell-shock we can add that it shows mingled physical suffering and emotional loss, Tolkien's twin trauma themes.

Smol expounded on how Frodo's mingled bodily suffering and emotional loss are manifested not only in his specific post-traumatic reactions but in his ongoing traumas as he endures them throughout his quest. Using Kristeva's concept of *abjection*, Smol explored how Frodo's sufferings put him on the edge of losing both his sense of self and his connection to others. Kristeva described the abject as that which must be expelled from the self in order to maintain a coherent sense of self: "what is abject [...] is radically excluded and draws me toward the place where meaning collapses" (2); and abjection is caused by "what disturbs identity, system, order [...] The in-between, the ambiguous, the composite." (4). Specimens include thoughts about foulness, pollution, rotting corpses, and horror. Yet even though expelled the abject may be experienced as fascinating so that one is drawn to relate to it or even own and identify with it, in which case one becomes abject oneself and alienated from validating relationships.

Smol discussed how Frodo's response to the corpses – quintessential abjects according to Kristeva – in the Dead Marshes shows him attracted to abjection that begins to lead to the loss of his coherent self: whereas Sam responds to the sight of the corpses with horror, he finds Frodo "standing lost in thought, looking at the pale lights. His hands hung stiff at his sides; water and slime were dripping from them" (*LotR* IV.2.627) – showing that Frodo had tried to reach the corpses. When Sam wonders who they were, Frodo gives his answer "in a dreamlike voice" (628) This allusion to an altered state of consciousness points to the destabilization of Frodo's identity.

Smol further explicated Frodo's mingled bodily and emotional loss by exploring his identification/disidentification with Gollum. Gollum is a figure of abjection in that he is horrible and animal-like, an eater of disgusting uncooked food, even suspected by Sam of eating corpses, and as pointed out by Nagy because his language is regressed from civilized speech – even the name "Gollum" is onomatopoeic with rude swallowing. In trying to reconstitute Gollum as Sméagol, Frodo is trying to protect himself from the process that he is succumbing to under the influence of the Ring: becoming like Gollum an abject, cut off from all human relationships.

Frodo's final loss, of course, is of the Shire, and his friends, and especially Sam, as he sails from the Grey Havens. In his farewell he says, "I have been too deeply hurt, Sam. I tried to save the Shire, and it has been saved, but not for me. It must often be so, Sam, when things are in danger: some one has to give them up, lose them, so that others may keep them" (*LotR* VI.9.1029). Frodo's loss of human connection is emphasized by his contrast with Sam who marries, has many children, and as mayor plays an important role in the larger Shire community.

Thus we see that several times in his fiction, when Tolkien most directly addressed war trauma, he depicted it as the intermingling of his two psychological vulnerabilities that he brought to the war and which then were intensified by the war: physical pain intermingled with emotional loss. Tolkien appears to have struggled all his life to find words to symbolize his trauma. And so it is fitting to close with Frodo saying goodbye to Sam in language that could serve as almost a direct rejoinder to "something has gone crack": "Do not be too sad, Sam. You cannot always be torn in two" (*LotR* VI.9.1029).

Bibliography

ADAMS-SILVAN, Abby and Mark SILVAN. "'A Dream is the Fulfillment of a Wish': Traumatic Dream, Repetition Compulsion, and the Pleasure Principle." *International Journal of Psychoanalysis* 71 (1990): 513-522.

AMERICAN PSYCHIATRIC ASSOCIATION. *Diagnostic and Statistical Manual of Mental Disorders.* 5th ed. Washington, D.C.: American Psychiatric Association Publishing, 2013.

AUERHAHN, Nanette and Dori LAUB. "Annihilation and Restoration: Post-Traumatic Memory as Pathway and Obstacle to Recovery." *International Review of Psychoanalysis* 11 (1984): 327-344.

BROGAN, Hugh. "Tolkien's Great War." *Children and Their Books.* Eds. Gillian Avery and Julia Briggs. Oxford: Clarendon 1989, 351-368.

Bucci, Wilma. *Psychoanalysis and Cognitive Science.* New York City, NY: Guilford, 1997.

Bunting, Nancy. "Finding Tolkien in his Stories." *Lembas Katern* 2016: 73-86.

"1904: Tolkien, Trauma, and its Anniversaries." *Mythlore* 34 (2015): 59-81.

Carpenter, Humphrey. *The Inklings.* London: Harper Collins, 2006.

J.R.R. Tolkien: A Biography. Boston, MA: Houghton Mifflin, 2000.

Croft, Janet. *War and the Works of J.R.R. Tolkien.* Westport, CT: Praeger, 2004.

Flieger, Verlyn. "Tolkien, *Kalevala*, and 'The Story of Kullervo.'" The Story of Kullervo *by J.R.R. Tolkien.* Ed. Verlyn Flieger. Boston, MA: Houghton Mifflin, 2019, 133-163.

Freedman, N. and Joan Lavender. "On Desymbolization: The Concept and Observations on Anorexia and Bulimia." *Psychoanalysis and Contemporary Thought* 25 (2002), 165-199.

Freud, Sigmund. "Beyond the Pleasure Principle." *The Standard Edition of the Complete Psychological Works of Sigmund Freud*, volume 18, 1-64. Ed. James Strachey. London: Hogarth, 1955.

Garth, John. *Tolkien and the Great War.* Boston, MA: Houghton Mifflin, 2003.

Hannon, Patrice. "*The Lord of the Rings* as Elegy." *Mythlore* 24.2 (2004): 36-42.

Hiley, Margaret. *The Loss and the Silence.* Zurich and Jena: Walking Tree Publishers, 2011.

Honegger, Thomas and Frank Weinreich (eds.). *Tolkien and Modernity 2.* Zurich: Walking Tree Publishers, 2006.

Kilby, Clyde S. *Tolkien and the Silmarillion.* Wheaton, IL: Harold Shaw, 1976.

Kristeva, Julia. *Powers of Horror.* New York City, NY: Columbia University Press, 1982.

Krystal, Henry. "Trauma and the Stimulus Barrier." *Psychoanalytic Inquiry* 5 (1985): 131-161.

Lasky, Richard (ed.). *Symbolization and Desymbolization: Essays in Honor of Norbert Freedman.* New York City, NY: Karnac, 2002.

Lingiardi, Vittorio and Nancy McWilliams. *Psychodynamic Diagnostic Manual,* 2nd Ed. New York City, NY: Guilford, 2017.

Livingston, Michael. "The Shell-Shocked Hobbit: The First World War and Tolkien's Trauma of the Ring." *Mythlore* 25 (2006): 77-92.

McDougall, Joyce. *Theaters of the Body.* New York City, NY: W.W. Norton, 1989.

Merck Manual for the Professional, 2019. www.merckmanuals.com/professional.

Moses, Rafael. "Adult Psychic Trauma: The Question of Early Predisposition and Some Detailed Mechanisms." *International Journal of Psychoanalysis* 59 (1978): 353-363.

Nagy, Gergely. "The 'Lost' Subject of Middle-Earth: The Constitution of the Subject in the Figure of Gollum in *The Lord of the Rings*." *Tolkien Studies* 3 (2006): 57-79.

Oliner, Marion. "External Reality: The Elusive Dimension of Psychoanalysis." *The Psychoanalytic Quarterly* 65 (1996): 267-300.

Psychic Reality in Context. London: Karnac, 2012.

Parker, Douglass. "Hwaet, We Holbytla..." *Hudson Review* 9 (1957): 598-609.

Renik, Owen. "Typical Examination Dreams, 'Superego Dreams,' and Traumatic Dreams." *Psychoanalytic Quarterly* 50 (1981): 159-189.

Rosegrant, John. "A Comment on '1904: Tolkien, Trauma, and its Anniversaries'. *Mythlore* 34 (2016): 167-170.

"From the Ineluctable Wave to the Realization of Imagined Wonder: Tolkien's Transformation of Psychic Pain into Art." *Mythlore* 35 (2017): 133-151.

"Mother Music." *Tolkien Studies*, in press.

"Tolkien's Dialogue Between Enchantment and Loss." *Mythlore* 33 (2015): 127-138.

Scull, Christina and Wayne G. Hammond. *The J.R.R. Tolkien Companion and Guide: Chronology*. Rev. ed. London: Harper Collins, 2017.

The J.R.R. Tolkien Companion and Guide: Reader's Guide. Rev. Ed. London: Harper Collins, 2017. 2 vols.

Senior, W.A. "Loss Eternal in J.R.R. Tolkien's Middle-Earth." *J.R.R. Tolkien and His Literary Resonances: Views of Middle-Earth*. Eds. George Clark and Daniel Timmons. Westport, CT: Greenwood, 2000, 173-182.

Shippey, Tom. *J.R.R. Tolkien: Author of the Century*. Boston, MA: Houghton Mifflin, 2000.

The Road to Middle-Earth. Boston, MA: Houghton Mifflin, 2003.

Sinex, Margaret. "Wounded by War: Men's Bodies in the Prose Tradition of *The Children of Húrin*." *Baptism of Fire*. Ed. Janet Brennan Croft. Altadena, CA: Mythopoeic Press, 2015, 38-59.

Smol, Anna. "Frodo's Body: Liminality and the Experience of War." *The Body in Tolkien's Legendarium.* Ed. Christopher Vaccaro. Jefferson, NC: McFarland, 2013.

Sugarman, Alan. "The Use of Play to Promote Insightfulness in the Analysis of Children Suffering from Cumulative Trauma." *Psychoanalytic Quarterly* 77 (2008): 799-833.

Tolkien, John and Priscilla Tolkien. *The Tolkien Family Album.* Boston, MA: Houghton-Mifflin, 1992.

Tolkien, J.R.R. *The Adventures of Tom Bombadil and other verses from the Red Book.* London: George Allen & Unwin, 1962.

The Book of Lost Tales, Part Two. (The History of Middle-Earth 2). Ed. Christopher Tolkien. New York City, NY: Ballantine, 1984.

The Children of Húrin. Ed. Christopher Tolkien. Boston, MA: Houghton Mifflin, 2008.

The Letters of J.R.R. Tolkien. Ed. Humphrey Carpenter, with the assistance of Christopher Tolkien. Boston, MA: Houghton Mifflin, 1981.

The Lord of the Rings. 50th Anniversary edition. Boston, MA: Houghton-Mifflin, 2004.

The Silmarillion. Ed. Christopher Tolkien. Boston, MA: Houghton Mifflin, 1977.

The Story of Kullervo. Ed. Verlyn Flieger. Boston, MA: Mariner Books, 2017.

Weinreich, Frank and Thomas Honegger (eds.). *Tolkien and Modernity 1.* Zurich: Walking Tree Publishers, 2006.

Michael Flowers

Tolkien in East Yorkshire, 1917-18: A Hemlock Glade, Two Towers, The Houses of Healing and a Beacon

Lordynges, ther is in Yorkshire, as I gesse,
A merssshy contree called Holdernesse [...]
Chaucer, "The Summoner's Tale"

Dr Stuart Lee has recently reconstructed as much of the 'lost' television interviews Tolkien gave in March 1968 for the BBC film *Tolkien in Oxford,* as is possible more than half a century after the event. Towards the end of the reconstruction the interviewer asks "about places in Tolkien's fictions that are linked to Oxford." Rather surprisingly, Tolkien did not mention somewhere like the Radcliffe Camera or Addison's Walk, or one of the colleges. The first location he mentioned was far from Oxford. Outside of Oxford it may have been expected that he would initially think of Sarehole Mill, or Cannock Chase, or the village of Great Haywood in Staffordshire. However, Tolkien replied that there was "nothing which is highly derivative", but then he added "... mostly places fairly remote from here. Like a little place on the extreme Yorkshire east coast called Roos, r-double o-s" (162). This placing of Roos first among all other locations highlights the importance of Roos in particular, and East Yorkshire in general, to Tolkien as an inspiration for his legendarium.

Although Tolkien's eighteen months in East Yorkshire have been examined previously, it is the contention of this paper that there are reasons why earlier accounts provide only a partial picture. Humphrey Carpenter is very sketchy on Tolkien's residence in the area, and at the time his biography was written Tolkien's war record was not yet available for inspection, so his account has since been proved to include some chronological errors. For instance, Carpenter dated Edith Tolkien's inspirational dance among the 'hemlocks' to the painful period after her first child's birth, but anyone with a basic knowledge of natural history and Edith's medical condition would rule out the possibility of it taking place during the winter of 1917-18 (95-98). John Garth in his *Tolkien and the Great War* corrected Carpenter's guesswork, and undertook considerable original research when he was examining Tolkien's period in Holderness, but has admitted that he only spent one day on the ground visiting East Yorkshire's Tolkien locations.[1] Of course his work was also more broadly focussed on the whole of Tolkien's Great War experience than a specific look at Tolkien's time in Holderness. In contrast, Phil Mathison knows Holderness intimately, but he has confided that he has not read any fiction written by Tolkien.[2] This approach means that aspects of Tolkien's fiction which appear to have been directly inspired by East Yorkshire locations have been neglected. The following account comes from the viewpoint of a reader with a deeper knowledge of Tolkien's fiction than Mathison, coupled with an attempt to follow Tolkien's actual footsteps in more detail than was possible for either Garth or Carpenter.[3]

Holderness is still a forgotten, hidden, and neglected part of the country in 2019, as it was when Tolkien was stationed there just over a century ago, but he would have been aware of its existence before he arrived. Tolkien had studied Chaucer at both school and university, so he would have known the above lines, which are the first two from "The Summoner's Tale" in Chaucer's epic work, *The Canterbury Tales* (Chaucer 129). This is almost certainly the earliest reference to Holderness in English Literature. Since Chaucer's time extensive drainage of Holderness has been undertaken, so when Tolkien arrived it was no longer quite the "mersshy contree" of Chaucer's time. Many readers of biographies of Tolkien probably have a fairly accurate image of Oxford in their minds, and Birmingham is also quite a well-known English city. However, East Yorkshire is virtually unknown in comparison. Holderness would have been a relatively sparsely inhabited area between the only large city of Kingston-upon-Hull and the sea. The roads were unmetalled at that time, which meant that travelling away from the rail network was slow and uncomfortable. Tolkien would have been able to travel by rail from Hull to Hornsea, and from Hull to Withernsea, but there was no rail link between these two coastal towns which were to be significant locations for Tolkien while he remained in East Yorkshire. Holderness was (and still is) a relatively flat

1 Garth, John. Personal communication to author, 12 Sep. 2014.
2 Mathison, Phil. Personal communication to author, 7 Oct. 2014.
3 Photographs of the locations mentioned in this article, and some of the personalities involved, can be found by visiting some of the panels on the right-hand side of Michael Flowers' blog: eybirdwatching.blogspot.com.

country with big skies, very little substantial woodland, and was predominantly an area where cereal crops were produced.

Once Tolkien was stationed in East Yorkshire, he was living for the first time in his life in an area in which an extremely high proportion of the surviving place-names are Scandinavian or Anglian in origin. This would have appealed to the philologist in Tolkien. Locations with which Tolkien became acquainted in East Yorkshire include Thirtle Bridge, the army camp in which he was based. Thirtle derives from the Old Norse of Thorkell, which is a shortened form of Thorketil. The first element comes from the Norse God Thor, and the second, "ketill", is from cauldron ("Last Name: Thirtle"). Danthorpe, which is a few miles north-west of Roos, means village of the Danes (Kent 57), and Hilston, which is even closer to Roos, means Hildof's farm (Kent 50). Hildof is believed to be a Scandinavian and Anglian hybrid. Finally, Frodingham south-east of Roos is derived from "the settlement of Froda's people" (Allison 85). Tom Shippey explained in *The Road to Middle-earth* that "Frodo" is an English form of [the] original Froda. Shippey points out the parallels between Froda, a character mentioned in passing in *Beowulf*, and Tolkien's protagonist (Shippey, 232-7). However, the proximity of Frodingham to Roos, and Tolkien's known interest in Yorkshire place-names in particular, indicates that he may well have also been thinking about this name associated with an historical Froda, and a place he knew during the Great War, when he was writing *The Lord of the Rings* nearly thirty years later. Tolkien would urge us "not to desire to see the bones of the ox" from which the soup has been boiled (*OFS* 39), but it is a possible ingredient, so is included here. The name Roos itself is unusual in that it has Celtic origins, but this will be examined later.

Of course, Tolkien originated in the West Midlands where smaller divisions of counties were referred to as *hundreds*, which date from the late Saxon period. However, Holderness was a division of the East Riding of Yorkshire that was known as a *wapentake* until quite late into the nineteenth-century. This is a term used in several other northern counties. It was this word Tolkien appropriated for his "weapontake", which he transformed from its original meaning to refer to the mustering of armed warriors in Rohan. It should be pointed out that the Old Norse equivalent of the word also had three distinct other meanings which Tolkien would have encountered (Hammond and Scull 528). However, what cannot be disputed is that Tolkien modelled the four farthings of the Shire on the divisions in Yorkshire of the three 'thridings', or what have become known as 'the Ridings' (32).

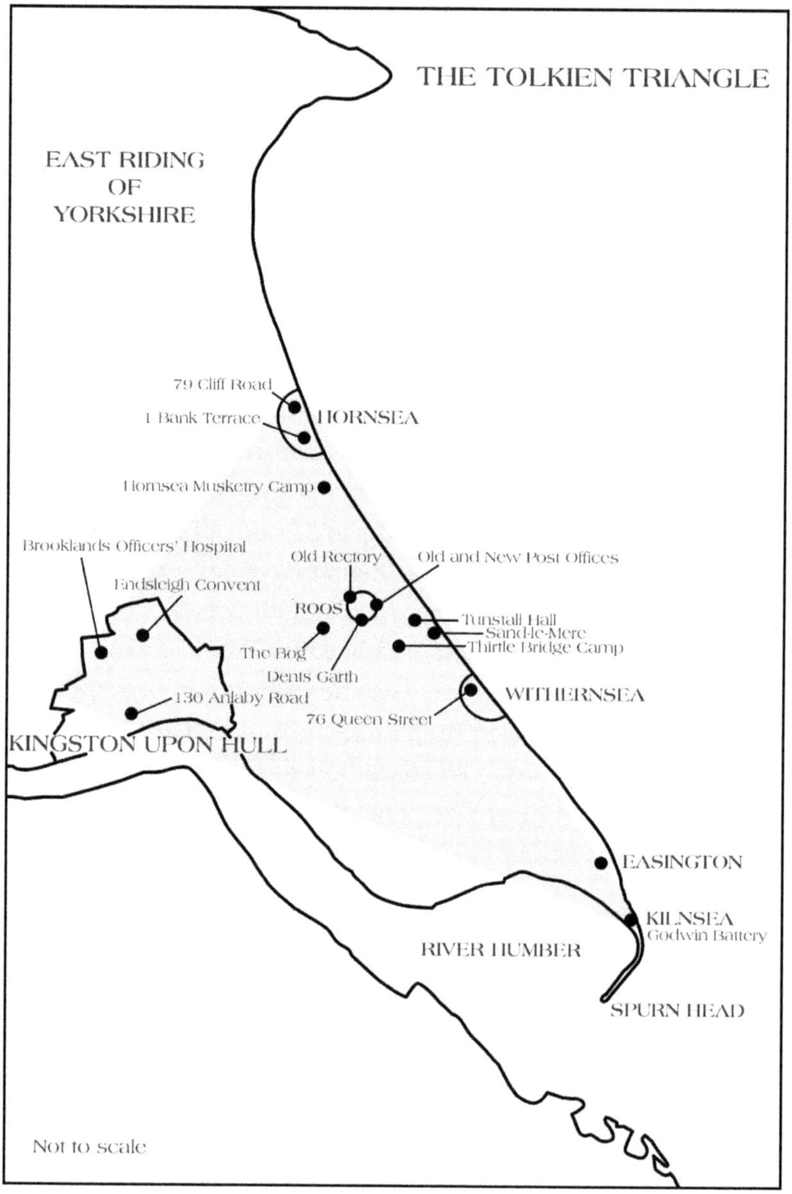

Phil Mathison: The Tolkien Triangle

Hornsea

In 1916 Tolkien participated in the "animal horror" (*Letters* 72) of the Battle of the Somme as a signaller for the 13th Lancashire Fusiliers, but contracted trench fever, and was invalided home on 9 November 1916 (Scull and Hammond, *Chronology* 102). He was hospitalised at Edgbaston (Birmingham) from which he travelled on occasion to Great Haywood (Staffordshire) to see Edith, but at the end of February 1917 he was transferred to Harrogate, and after a medical examination was ordered to join the 3rd Reserve Battalion of the Lancashire Fusiliers at Thirtle Bridge, near Withernsea (Garth 234). Tolkien was sent to East Yorkshire for "hardening", and with the ultimate intention that he would be passed fit to participate on the front line again. Tolkien actually arrived in Hornsea by train from Hull on 19 April 1917 (Mathison, *Tolkien in East Yorkshire* 34). Hornsea is a coastal resort sixteen miles from the city of Hull. Tolkien seems to have spent some time initially at the fifty-two-acre Hornsea Musketry Camp, which was based at the small hamlet of Rolston nearly one mile to the south of Hornsea (Mathison, *Tolkien in East Yorkshire* 54). Tolkien would have received consolidation of firearms training here. Edith, with her cousin Jennie Grove, took lodgings close to the station in Hornsea by 5 May 1917, presumably to be close to him.

Hornsea is perhaps the most picturesque location at which Tolkien stayed in East Yorkshire. This is largely provided by the natural wonder which is the tree-lined Hornsea Mere – the largest natural freshwater lake in Yorkshire. Hornsea Mere belonged to the Roman Catholic Strickland-Constable family, whose seat of Wassand Hall lies on the western fringes of the Mere. Margaret Strickland-Constable, the wife of the incumbent at that time, would later be in charge of the Brooklands hospital in which Tolkien would subsequently be a patient. Her diaries offer glimpses of life at an Officers' Hospital, but are also an invaluable record of various Zeppelin raids on the east coast during the war, and inexperienced English pilots ditching their planes in the mere (Chichester-Constable). Incidentally, the suffix 'sea' in East Yorkshire locations, such as Hornsea, Skipsea, Withernsea, and Kilnsea, does not refer to their proximity to the sea, but to their freshwater lakes or inland seas which were left behind after the last Ice Age. Over recent centuries most of these have either been swallowed up by the eroding coastline, or have silted up, and only the largest at Hornsea was present in 1917 and is still present today.

When Tolkien was transferred permanently from the Musketry Camp thirteen miles south-east to Thirtle Bridge, Edith moved out of her lodgings in Hornsea. Phil Mathison has discovered that her final letter from there was dated 1 June 1917 (*Tolkien in East Yorkshire* 34). The next surviving envelope was sent from her Withernsea lodgings on 12 July 1917. For the intervening nearly six weeks her residence is unknown, and as there is no extant correspondence, the suggestion is that for this brief period the Tolkiens did not need to correspond. "The Horns of Ulmo", rewritten about this time from the earlier "Sea Chant of an Elder Day", includes a note that its "[p]resent shape [was] due to rewriting and adding [an] intro[duction] [...] in a lonely house near Roos, Holderness [...] Spring 1917" (*SME* 215). As Tolkien's residence in other locations in spring 1917 may be inferred by the survival of envelopes addressed to him by Edith, it seems highly likely that during the period 1 June to around 12 July 1917 the Tolkiens were either living together or were in close proximity somewhere in the Roos area.

Roos

The leaves were long, the grass was green,
The hemlock-umbels tall and fair,
And in the glade a light was seen
Of stars in shadow shimmering.
(*LotR* I.11.191)

Tolkien mentions Roos three times in his published *Letters*. On the first occasion in 1955 he informed his American publishers: "The kernel of the mythology, the matter of *Lúthien Tinúviel* and *Beren*, arose from a small woodland glade filled with 'hemlocks' (or other white umbellifers) *near* [my emphasis] Roos on the Holderness peninsula – to which I occasionally went when free from regimental duties while in the Humber Garrison in 1918 [*sic*]" (*Letters* 221). His 1964 letter to Christopher Bretherton gives a largely similar account (*Letters* 345) as does his 1972 epistle to his youngest son, Christopher, after Edith's death. However, there is one subtle difference, because in the final "Roos" letter Tolkien informs his son that the woodland glade was "*at* Roos" [my emphasis] (*Letters* 420). Tolkien may have been slightly more precise with words in correspondence with Christopher. There are a few possible candidates in the Roos area, but John Garth identified the wooded area of Dents Garth near All Saints' Church in Roos as the correct location (Garth 238). Dents Garth is on the extreme south-east edge of the village, from which it would have been possible to see Thirtle Bridge, where Tolkien was stationed several times while in the area.

According to a popular wild flower guide, "many other umbellifers are loosely referred to as hemlock" (Blamey, Fitter, and Fitter 180), and Tolkien's letter quoted above indicates this was precisely the case with him. Rather surprisingly, the linguistically precise Tolkien was vague about this particular subject. However, Christopher Tolkien explained his father "regarded the restriction of a vernacular name to this or that species within a large group of plants not easily distinguishable to the eye as the pedantry of popularising botanists – who ought to content themselves with the Linnean names" (Garth 238). He evidently called all similar umbellifers 'hemlocks', and what was good enough for him was also good enough for his story of tragic lovers.

John Garth identified Tolkien's 'hemlocks' as Queen Anne's Lace or cow parsley (238), and Dinah Hazell in her *Plants of Middle-earth* concurs (54). The most recent reference work on this subject also believes cow parsley is the "more likely" species Tolkien encountered (Judd and Judd 185). It may be possible to estimate the date of Edith's dance by comparing the flowering period of cow parsley at Roos in the springs of 2014-2018 and extrapolating that back to 1917. In 2014 the white umbels began to open in sheltered spots around 1 May, and by 10 May it was a fine spectacle – it remained in this condition for most of the rest of the month. However, in Dents Garth, the supposed site of Edith's dance in Roos, the flowering was definitely beginning to look tired and faded in most places of the woodland by 27 May. Heavy rain both on and subsequent to that date ensured it did not survive into June. It is unlikely that Tolkien would have commented favourably on the beauty of the whiteness of the 'hemlocks' if it had already begun to fade, so at a first glance a date in June seems rather unlikely. However, in 2018 after a very cold February and March the umbels didn't really begin to flower until 10 May, and they were largely intact at the end of May. Similarly, in late May 2015 the flowers were still in excellent condition at the end of May.

The earliest-surviving "Tale of Tinúviel" mentions that Beren and Tinúvel met "on a time of June" (*LTII* 10; *B&L* 41), and as it is in prose there was no reason for Tolkien to alter the month for it to scan or rhyme in verse. It would therefore seem almost certain that the real-life inspiration also took place in June 1917. The clues from the natural world such as the chestnut blossom and the main flowering dates of cow parsley both suggest an earlier date in the month, so the most probable time for the dance would be quite early in June before the cow parsley faded completely, and the chestnut blossom had begun to die back – the first ten days of June are the most likely.

Anyone with a classical education in the early twentieth century would have been aware that Socrates was sentenced to death, and was poisoned by a fatal drink of hemlock. Socrates, despite the urging of his friends, accepted the court's decision and nobly drank the fatal dose whilst still discoursing to his disciples. Hemlock is therefore associated from ancient times with a story of noble self-sacrifice, and it seems highly appropriate that Tolkien utilised the name hemlock at the very commencement of his great story of love and self-sacrifice. It appears Tolkien selected the name 'hemlock', either from a lack of precise botanical knowledge of the exact species he saw, or because he felt that that word fitted best within his story.

Cow parsley must be the species Tolkien intended as the "great misty growth of [...] white umbels [...] were like a cloud about the boles of the trees" (*LTII* 10; *B&L* 41). However, unless further documentary evidence becomes available the absolute certainty of the identification of the woodland will have to remain conjectural, nevertheless there are several striking local landmarks, which would seem to support the identification. Dents Garth and Roos churchyard contain beech, horse chestnut, and all the other tree and plant species mentioned in the various versions of the encounter between Beren and Lúthien. The only exception is a mature elm tree – Beren leans on a young elm in the earliest surviving version of the text (*LTII* 11; *B&L* 42) – but mature examples of this species were probably lost in the devastating effects of the Dutch Elm disease of the 1970s and 1980s. A sapling, probably growing from a sucker of one of the original trees, was found just south of the church car park in 2015. The continued presence of an active rookery in Dents Garth indicates the previous presence of elms in the woodland, as traditionally this is the tree species in which these corvids prefer to nest. This evidence is bolstered by the nearest property to the church, which in Tolkien's time, as now, was simply called "The Elms" with "Elm Farm" the adjacent property to the north.

About five metres away from the cow parsley in the churchyard is a railed off area, which contains a damp subterranean staircase surmounted by an escutcheon depicting the palm of a hand above three circular features containing wavy lines, which represents water. This is the heraldic device of the Sykes family (the hand denotes a baronet), who commissioned the exterior stairs down to the crypt probably during the restoration of the church in 1842. Of course, in Tolkien's mythology Beren had to make the much more perilous journey down to Melko's underground fortress of Angamandi (later Angband), and his heraldic device, drawn by Tolkien much later, features a disembodied hand, because his hand clasping a Silmaril was lost to the ravening wolf Karkaras (later Carcharoth).

A further plausible link to Tolkien's fiction is a three-trunked tree, which is the nearest tree to the church, to the south-east between the church and the entrance in the southern exterior churchyard wall. In the earliest-surviving version of Tolkien's story, Tinúviel [Lúthien] is imprisoned by her father Tinwelint (later Thingol) in Hírilorn, a mighty Beech tree: "so deeply cloven was her bole that it seemed as if three shafts sprang from the ground together and they were of like size, round and straight, and their grey rind was smooth as silk, unbroken by branch or twig for a very great height above men's heads" (*LTII* 18, *B&L* 53). John Garth remarked that the "three-trunked tree does seem such a specific and seemingly random detail to have [been] included in the story" ("Comment"), so the finding of such a tree actually in Roos near the genesis of the tale is suggestive. This tree is over one-hundred-and-fifty feet in height in Roos churchyard, and would certainly have been there in Tolkien's time. It has some similarities to his description, including the cloven bole, the three shafts of equal size, the grey bark, and branches above the height of men, although now there are also some more recent younger lower twigs. The fairly smooth bark is now partly obscured by ivy stems, but crucially this tree is a lime, or more poetically a linden-tree, not a beech. The tree adjacent to this lime tree is a beech. Of course in the poem about Beren and Lúthien in *The Fellowship of the Ring*, the original version of which dates back to around 1919, (Hammond and Scull 172), Tinúviel's feet are described as "light as leaf on lindentree." The leaves of both the beech and the lime are at their freshest green when the cow parsley is in bloom.

On the southern side of the church car park is a meagre unimpressive waterway heading south out of the village. This is very difficult to see in the summer as it is concealed by the heavy undergrowth, and as it is often a mere trickle it is very easy to ignore. It only becomes slightly more visible in the winter. In Tolkien's forest of Neldoreth in which the tree Hírilorn grows is a river called Esgalduin. By no stretch of the imagination could the tiny Roos Beck be classified as a river, but the hidden aspect of the beck may have more significance. In Tolkien's tale there was no tiny hidden stream, but the far more majestic river Esgalduin, which flowed through Neldoreth. The 'esgal' element in Esgalduin means 'screen' or 'hiding', and Esgalduin actually translates as "River under veil" (*S* 329, 358), so as unlikely as it sounds Roos Beck may have been part of the 'cauldron of soup' in the back of Tolkien's mind when he created the far more magical River Esgalduin.

In All Saints' church is an item of high-quality but now foxed framed calligraphy on one of the walls. It post-dates Tolkien's time in the area, but it is of interesting local historical value, and it contains etymological information which would have interested him. It reveals that the original spelling of the village name was Ros, and that the name is unusual in the area as being of Celtic origin and means either marsh or moorland. Tolkien had a known interest in Yorkshire place-names, so he may have researched this information himself. After the Norman Conquest the name of the village was utilised by major landowners, so in c.1158 a Robert de Ros took the title of Baron of Helmsley (Kent 88). The editors of *Parma Eldalamberon* 11 examined the meaning of *ros*, and their suggested derivations include the Welsh *rhôs,* which means 'moor, heath or plain'; or the Breton word *ros*, which means 'hillock', and the Irish word *ros*, which means 'promontory' (Gilson et al, 6n7). This latter definition may have some significance because in notes about the conclusion of *The Book of Lost Tales* in the Faring Forth, Tol Eressëa was to be "uprooted and dragged near to the Great Lands, nigh to the promontory of Rôs," which was to be followed by the "Battle of Rôs" in which the Elves were to be defeated (*LT II* 283). Christopher Tolkien proposed that Rôs may be Brittany (ibid.), but the editors of *Parma Eldalamberon* postulated that "the promontory of Rôs may have been suggested to Tolkien by Roos" (Gilson et al 6n7). It could be argued that Roos, which is slightly higher than some of the immediately surrounding area, lies at the head of the promontory of Holderness, which dribbles away to the elongated sand spit of Spurn Point.

Tolkien clearly had a romantic experience in Roos, which remained with him all his life until the event was even obliquely memorialised on his own gravestone. In the more immediate aftermath of Edith's dance he worked on his Goldogrin vocabularies and grammar and even invented a meaning for 'rôs', with an exceedingly romantic flavour: "embrace" (Gilson et al 66). However, this may have been an extremely temporary definition. It is known that in due course 'rôs' evolved in the etymologies to be equivalent to "foam, spindrift, [and] spray" (*S* 441). This later definition of 'rôs' could actually be an oblique reference to the hemlocks because 'foam' is an effective synonym for Tolkien's own 'cloud-like' or 'mist'.

Tolkien's linguistic invention may also have attempted to memorialise Dents Garth in another respect. Lúthien's father's realm was named Doriath and in the etymologies, Doriath is also known as Garthurian, meaning fenced realm (*LR* 358).[4] However, it should also be emphasized that 'garth' is not a particularly rare Northern word, and Tolkien would have encountered it before. In *The Lord of the Rings* 'garth' is used on a couple of occasions by Treebeard. Towards the end of the narrative Treebeard renames the area around Isengard as "The Treegarth of Orthanc" (VI.6.979), and earlier when singing of the entwives, their part of the song mentions spring returning to "garth and field" (III.4.477). In Tolkien's writing 'garth' clearly has positive connotations, as of course Dents Garth did in Tolkien's remembrance of his past life with Edith.

In the early period of Tolkien's writings he often utilised real-life locations with changes of name to fit his secondary world. For instance, it is now generally accepted that Kortirion is Warwick and Great Haywood became Tavrobel in *The Book of Lost Tales*, and that "Great Haywood is recognizable [...]. At the

4 I am indebted to John Garth for drawing Garthurian to my attention ("Re: Roos Extra").

place where the rivers Trent and Sow meet, the grey stone of Essex Bridge, with its fourteen arches, leaps the 'joining waters' to Shugborough Hall, the 'House of the Hundred Chimneys' on the far side" (McIlwaine 212). These examples illustrate it is possible that he also may have utilised some of the Roos landmarks to provide firm foundations in the physical world with which to anchor the emerging mythological narrative of Beren and Lúthien. The 'hemlocks', the three-trunked tree, the heraldic hand, the elm trees and a single beech next to a 'linden-tree', the concealed appearance of Roos Beck, all within fifty metres of Dents Garth, may seem insignificant or coincidental in isolation; but taken in conjunction with each other and combined with his positive use of the word *garth*, Dents Garth does seem to be the most likely venue for the location for Edith's dance, and therefore the inspiration for the meeting of Beren and Lúthien in the legendarium.

Mathison believes that Tolkien's clue on the MS of "The Horns of Ulmo" that it was rewritten "in a lonely house near Roos" (*SME* 215) refers to Tolkien's billet at Thirtle Bridge Camp, but the linguistically-precise Tolkien would never have described a location at which over one thousand five hundred men were stationed as "a lonely house near Roos." On balance he was probably based away from the camp and in a house not adjacent to other dwellings, but not too far from Roos. One possibility is a building on the outskirts of Halsham, a village less than two miles from Roos, which had a few isolated buildings at that time, as it does now. It is a much smaller village, and more strung-out than the comparably more tightly-knit Roos.

Halsham

Even if Tolkien wasn't actually living in Halsham, it is likely he would have been drawn to the village in his free time, as it is a fairly short walk of about two miles from Roos across the fields. The strength of Tolkien's Roman Catholic faith must never be underestimated. According to the *Victoria County History*, there "is little evidence of Roman Catholicism" in Roos (Kent 93), but Halsham is quite a different matter. In medieval times Halsham was the seat of the Constable family, and after the Reformation the family remained loyal to their Roman Catholic faith, and they kept links to the parish even when they moved to their impressive new Elizabethan Hall on the Burton Constable estate. Halsham had some recusants in 1595-6, and between eight to sixteen in the 1660s and 1670s. As late as the eighteenth century eight Roman Catholics were still living in the village (Allison 39). There is still visible evidence of the faith in Halsham. The most striking reminder is the mausoleum of the Constable family. This was constructed between 1792 and 1802, and it had been restored as recently as c. 1900 (Allison 32). It has marked similarities to Sauron's temple in Númenor, as it is described in the *Notion Club Papers*.[5] When Lowdham sees the Radcliffe Camera in Oxford he is reminded of Sauron's temple, which apart from the blackened colouration perhaps better fits the description of Halsham Mausoleum rather than the Radcliffe Camera. However, in Tolkien's fiction the dimensions have become truly monumental: "it was in the form of a circle at the base, and the walls were fifty feet in thickness, and the width of their base was five hundred feet across the centre, and they rose from the ground five hundred feet, and they were crowned with a mighty dome; and it was wrought all of silver, but the silver was turned black" (*SD* 367). Tolkien had utilised the Radcliffe Camera library when he studied for his degree in Oxford, and at that time it was black from industrial soot, so if he saw the Halsham Mausoleum he would have been immediately reminded of the Oxford building. When he returned to Oxford after the war he was almost in the same position as Lowdham, as he was confronted with the sooty Radcliffe Camera, and would no doubt remember the Halsham equivalent, although that was of course almost pristine in comparison. In an earlier Old English version of a text a further relevant aspect to Halsham appears: "it was built in the midst of the town [...] on the high hill which before was undefiled but now became a heathen fane" (*SD* 384). As mentioned earlier Halsham is a small settlement not a town, but the mausoleum was built on the highest point of land in Halsham. When it was being constructed, evidence was discovered of a possible prehistoric burial site. Would Tolkien have disapproved of ancient remains being disturbed to construct a Roman Catholic monument to the dead, to such an extent that he would consider it a heathen fane? A clue as to Tolkien's possible stance may be gathered from a letter in which he discussed the Númenóreans of Gondor's "great interest in ancestry and in tombs," which he declared was "proud, peculiar, and

---

5 I am obliged to Charles Noad for mentioning the similarity to Sauron's temple in Númenor ("Re: Halsham Mausoleum").

archaic" (*Letters* 281). The implication is that he disapproved of lavish funerary monuments, and he went on to have a simple grave himself.

The original order for Tolkien's posting to Holderness was made on 27 November 1916 from the headquarters of the Lancashire Fusiliers, which at that time was actually in Halsham (Mathison, *Tolkien in East Yorkshire* 12). However, by the time Tolkien had arrived only a few months later the HQ had been moved to Tunstall, which was more convenient for Thirtle Bridge Camp (56). Nevertheless, it is entirely possible that the military maintained some presence in the village. The most likely building in Halsham for the HQ is the oldest residence, now known as Halsham House (1584), but previously it was a former almshouse and school. Halsham House, is immediately south-west of the mausoleum, and has a strange small alcove built into the side of an exterior wall, possibly present at the time of original construction, which contains a small statue. On closer examination this proves to be a figure of the Virgin Mary. The Catholic credentials of Halsham are plain to see after a little investigation, but whether this or a similar statue was present when Tolkien was in the area is probably a question which may never be answered. At an exhibition at Burton Constable in 2014 an information panel stated that during the Great War the Constable family encouraged Roman Catholic soldiers to join them at mass (Reynolds). At the present time it is not known where Tolkien worshipped while in Holderness.

Thirtle Bridge

After the idyllic period near Roos, it is believed Tolkien had his first lengthy stint at Thirtle Bridge Camp, which is approximately 1¼ miles south-east of Roos. Rather confusingly, Tolkien was based at Thirtle Bridge at various times during his eighteen months in Holderness. On some detailed old maps Thirtle Bridge is marked, but there were no buildings in that area before the Great War, it was simply a bridge over the Tunstall drain on the road to Withernsea. The nearest place of habitation before the war was an isolated farmhouse at Renish. However, for the duration of hostilities a temporary camp was installed on the higher ground above Thirtle Bridge catering for 1,500 men (Garth 234). A rough idea of what was present at Thirtle Bridge during Tolkien's time may be gleaned from a local paper which advertised the auctioning off of "the whole of the existing hutments" of both Thirtle Bridge and the smaller Dimlington site, which consisted of: "about 40 sectional wooden huts of various sizes, 50 armstrong sectional canvas huts, bath houses, cook houses, several brick buildings, cooking ranges, boilers, a No. 5.0 Bno independent boiler and connections, and 1.25 inch iron piping" (*Yorkshire Post*, 2 Aug 1919, 3). Today very little survives of the camp. However, the southernmost section of the present Mona House is believed to incorporate the Officer's mess and the footprint of the former cookhouse survives as a corrugated barn. The bridge over the drain has a dedicated keystone bearing the date 1833, so the bridge looks very much as it would have in Tolkien's time, although some red bricks higher than the dated stone are probably 1950s in date.

Thirtle Bridge was an army camp, and Tolkien was there at a time of war, but when not actually engaged in repelling Zeppelin attacks or involved in physical activity time hung heavy on the hands of the "inmates". The only known surviving letters written at Thirtle Bridge from an independent source describe duties at the camp as "tedious, and boredom was rife" (Mathison, *Tolkien in East Yorkshire* 64). This implies that Tolkien would certainly have had time to mull over his emerging mythology, and even to have managed to write. This is confirmed by his Gnomish Lexicon which is dated Withernsea 1917. At no known period did Tolkien live in Withernsea, so the use of it here translates to the nearby camp of Thirtle Bridge. Tolkien's handwritten note accompanying a contemporary photograph shows that Withernsea was synonymous with Thirtle Bridge for Tolkien. The Tolkien Estate have confirmed that a photograph of Tolkien in an army hut published on page 38 of *The Tolkien Family Album* is accompanied by Tolkien's handwriting which says: "Self in Hux's and my cubicle, Withernsea [Thirtle Bridge] 1917" (Blackburn, "Tolkien in Staffordshire"). "Hux" must refer to Tolkien's long-time comrade and friend Leslie Risdon Huxtable, with whom he had also shared quarters on Cannock Chase. Huxtable was another signalling officer, and was believed to have been trained to be Tolkien's deputy at one time, ready to take over if anything happened to Tolkien. Ironically, he was injured in an explosion, and he returned to England before Tolkien. Garth mentions him as being based at Tunstall Hall after receiving an injury in France, and he was present at the Minden Dinner with Tolkien on 1 August 1917 (Garth 235, 239).

Withernsea

When Tolkien was based at Thirtle Bridge, Edith moved into lodgings in Withernsea three miles to the south-east. It is known she was installed there by 12 July 1917 (Mathison, *Tolkien in East Yorkshire* 54). Phil Mathison discovered that Edith's lodgings in Withernsea were at 76 Queen Street on the corner of Queen Street and Hull Road, which is now the Lifeboat Café. The back of this property may still be seen from the top of Withernsea Lighthouse. John Garth has shown that Withernsea had a temporary significance in Tolkien's developing mythology. In a Gnomish lexicon he was compiling he wrote under the title and the name of Eriol, the mariner, the words "Tol Withernon (and many places besides), 1917" (Garth 236). Eriol is significant because in some respects he can be seen as a self-portrait, and in early versions of the legendarium his arrival in Eressëa provides the framing-story of *The Book of Lost Tales*. Unfortunately for East Yorkshire, Tol Withernon (almost certainly inspired by Withernsea) was never mentioned again in any writings, which have been published so far.

Edith's lodgings at 76 Queen Street are about two hundred yards away from Withernsea's only monolithic structure, the lighthouse completed in 1894. The lighthouse is one hundred and twenty-seven feet high (39m) and is at least three times the height of any of the surrounding buildings. The lighthouse is a striking structure in what is an otherwise unremarkable town made even more so by being painted brilliant white. The lighthouse is unusual in being built well inland from the sea ("About the Lighthouse"), and Edith's lodgings were slightly nearer to the lighthouse than the sea. Today the white tower is surrounded by domestic dwellings, but in 1917 the adjacent area was much less cluttered, as contemporaneous postcards show. Since completion it has always dominated the surrounding town and countryside.

When the light was working the beam could be seen for a radius of seventeen miles, but even unlit as it is today, the lighthouse as a structure may still be observed from the southern edge of Roos. The road leaving Roos undulates slightly, so in the hollows the lighthouse is lost to sight, but it comes back into view again as soon as height is regained. The lighthouse would have been visible to Tolkien from the Thirtle Bridge camp as long as the sightlines were not blocked by the temporary camp buildings.

Shortly after the outbreak of war the *Hull Daily Mail* reported that Withernsea lighthouse had been in darkness for a fortnight (19 Sep 1914, 3), so when Tolkien was in Holderness three years later the light would still have been doused for most of the time. However, the beam was permitted to glow again during the Second World War if a special convoy needed escorting through the hazardous shallows off the Yorkshire coast. The evidence is lacking for the Great War, but the Withernsea Museum assumes that the situation would have been almost identical during the earlier conflict (Simpson).

Although Tolkien explicitly states in his interview with Denys Gueroult that he did not think in symbols ("BBC Interview"), when he caught sight of the brilliant white lighthouse from anywhere in Holderness after 12 July 1917, surely he would be reminded of Edith, especially while she was lodged virtually at the lighthouse's foot? Indeed, it seems highly probable that even after Edith left for Cheltenham that this striking white structure would still remind Tolkien of his wife's former sojourn in the town.

There is only one direct route Tolkien could have used from Thirtle Bridge to Withernsea when he wished to visit his wife or when he needed to catch a train to Hull for monthly medical examinations, and that is the twisting, undulating road now known as the B1242. For over a mile after leaving the camp there would hardly have been a single man-made structure visible between Thirtle Bridge and Withernsea in what was, and still is, a completely rural landscape. However, 1¼ miles south-east of Thirtle Bridge on the edge of a small settlement called Waxholme is a hill, on the summit of which is a ruined mill, variously called Withernsea Mill, Waxholme Mill, Owthorne Mill, and more often simply the Black Mill.

The mill last ground corn in 1892, and its sails were removed in 1904. In 1917 the black-painted windmill was still at its full height of approximately sixty feet, and was being used as a watch-tower by the army (Chapman and Chapman 30). It can safely be assumed that on the summit guns were mounted as a defence against low-flying Zeppelins or potential invaders on foot from the beach at Waxholme. Only a few years ago the family who own the mill discovered a box of Great War ammunition in its foundations (Mathison, "Re: Tolkien Seminar"). As the road from Thirtle Bridge approaches the mill it dips into a deep depression, so the final ascent to the mill becomes quite steep, and the black mill on the summit would have loomed larger than if it had been approached on the level. A century later the badly ruined mill is just a presence on a hazardous bend, but in 1917 and 1918 as a contemporary newspaper report makes clear, the whole coastal road running from Easington through Withernsea, up to Hornsea and finishing in Skipsea was under military control (*Hull Daily Mail*, 29 Apr 1916, 2), so there would have been a series of road blocks at significant junctions, and one of the most prominent was at this point (*Hull Daily Mail*, 6 Dec 1917, 4). Tolkien stated in his 1972 letter to his youngest son that he was "for a brief time in command of an outpost of the Humber Garrison in 1917" (*Letters* 420); the finding of the ammunition adds weight to the theory that the Black Mill was an outpost of the Humber Garrison, but further evidence would have to come to light before it could be proved conclusively that this was the outpost Tolkien mentioned.

From the Black Mill it is possible to see both the white spike of Withernsea lighthouse over a mile distant in a south-easterly direction, but also a quite different white structure about 1½ miles away to the south-west. The latter was new when Tolkien was in the area – the gleaming white water-tower at Rimswell was completed in 1916. Although it is clear that Tolkien would have seen and journeyed past many of these white and black towers during his war service, there is absolutely no similarity between the white tower at Rimswell and any of the white towers in his fiction.

Brooklands Officers' Hospital

While Edith was still lodging beneath the shadow of the white tower of Withernsea Lighthouse, by 13 August 1917 her husband had a recurrence of trench fever and was sent to the first of the two hospitals or "Houses of Healing" he would become acquainted with in East Yorkshire: Brooklands Officers' Hospital on Cottingham Road in Hull. This ten-week stay was the first of two long stints lasting in total for nearly eighteen weeks at this convalescent home, and his time spent there was extremely productive. In the first instance he was able to spend long periods working on the building-blocks of his emerging language, known at the time as Goldogrin. There have been many writers who have attempted to follow Tolkien in writing fantasy narratives, but none of them have matched his care in creating grammars and languages. His fiction was "*fundamentally linguistic* in inspiration" (*Letters* 219, italics in original), the language, as he often attested – words or names came first – and stories followed afterwards. In addition to the time spent on the foundation of his lexicons, vocabularies, and grammars Tolkien also wrote down for the first time the earliest versions of two stories which he continued to write, rework, and re-imagine for almost the whole of his writing life: "The Tale of Tinúviel" and "The Tale of Turambar". The central importance of Lúthien Tinúviel is exemplified by his placing of the fictional name Lúthien under his wife's name on their gravestone more than half a century later. In addition to what were to become major works in his legendarium, he is known to have composed at least two new poems at Brooklands: "The Companions of the Rose" and "The Grey Bridge of Tavrobel" (Scull and Hammond, *Reader's Guide* 2.1455). In August 1917 he explained to Christopher Wiseman that the former was the only poem he had written so far that year (Garth 231, 240). This seems to have spurred him on as "Sea-Song of an Elder Day" was rewritten between 31 August and 2 September and retitled "The Horns of Ulmo", and a little later he also revised "The Mermaid's Flute" (Scull and Hammond, *Chronology* 109).

Brooklands was operated by Margaret Strickland-Constable (née Pakenham), who was actually the commandant, not the matron as stated by some earlier researchers. She was proficient in German, French, Swedish, Danish, and Norwegian, and she is thought to have worked for the censor department during the war. Her knowledge of these languages would have provided a little common ground between her and Tolkien on her brief visits to the hospital. However, in his second long stay at Brooklands Tolkien was said to have learnt a little Russian and improved his Spanish and Italian – not languages in which Strickland-Constable excelled. Margaret Strickland-Constable was soon to be a war widow, as her husband killed himself in a London hotel on his return from the front in December 1917.

Brooklands was only officially opened as a hospital for officers as late as 31 July 1917 by Major General Sir Stanley von Donop (*Hull Daily Mail*, 1 Aug 1917, 2). Recent research has revealed that almost all of the personnel associated with Brooklands mentioned in a newspaper article written to mark its opening were Roman Catholics. It is not known if Tolkien's faith helped him to gain a place here, as this was the only hospital for officers in the immediate area. On completion accommodation was provided for only seventeen patients, and on the opening day three were installed (*Hull Daily Mail*, 1 Aug 1917, 2), to be joined by Tolkien only a fortnight later (Garth 236). Brooklands enjoyed a good reputation amongst local officers, as an overheard comment by Margaret's brother, which Strickland-Constable proudly included in her diary, implies: "What you want to do is arrange to have a good crash, so as to get sent to Brooklands" (Chichester-Constable). Likewise, Tolkien found the surroundings congenial, and surviving ordnance survey maps from 1910 show that the substantial grounds contained several mature trees. The map also shows that the conservatory was there as early as 1910, which must have been another boon for the invalids. Only the western half of the detached building including the conservatory was utilised as the hospital; the remainder was a private dwelling known as the Cedars, named after the large tree in its garden. Cottingham Road itself was at that time a fairly quiet leafy-lined thoroughfare, and opposite it on the other side of the road was the recently-founded municipal college, later the Hull University campus, but in 1917 that area consisted mainly of large open fields.

As mentioned earlier Strickland-Constable's diaries for the time survive, and although she does not refer to Tolkien by name we do know that he was in Brooklands for the second long period when the Zeppelin raid of 6 August 1918 took place in Hull. She mentions two majors with neurasthenia who hid under their beds when the bombardment took place, but the remainder, including Tolkien, were said to be "quite calm" (Chichester-Constable). This second summer Tolkien was hospitalised at Brooklands was probably the longest period free from distractions he would enjoy for the remainder of his life. There is no evidence that Edith, their first child, John, nor Jennie Grove moved up north again to be near Tolkien once she left for Cheltenham around the third week of August 1917. Once he returned to Oxford, and later academic duties, his spare time for working on his language-creation would have been severely curtailed by both work commitments and the demands of his ever-increasing family. The almost two months at Brooklands in the summer of 1918 gave him a real opportunity for constructing the strong foundations of language creation and for time spent on writing some of the central narratives of what would become *The Book of Lost Tales.*

Although Tolkien shared some of his time at Brooklands with an officer friend, and was able to produce some good work on his emerging mythology, it seems the diet there could have been a lot more nutritious. On 11 October 1918, a month to the day after Tolkien left Brooklands for the final time, Colonel Easton wrote to the local newspaper asking for presents of game (presumably birds like pheasant, and possibly meat like venison) to be donated to the institution, which he pointed out was the only officers' hospital in Hull and the surrounding district (*Hull Daily Mail,* 12 Oct 1918, 2). A medical report notes Tolkien lost two stone in weight after his attack of gastritis and during his second stay at Brooklands, so some of this weight loss may have been due to insufficiently nutritious food. Tolkien's emaciated frame around this time can be easily gauged by examining the photograph published in *The Tolkien Family Album* (41). This likeness depicts a very thin uniformed Tolkien on a seashore with Edith. When Phil Mathison wrote his book, he assumed that this was taken at Hornsea (*Tolkien in East Yorkshire* 35). However, the Tolkien Estate revealed that on the back of the photograph Tolkien had added the following words: "Withernsea/July (?)/1917./ taken by L.R. Huxtable" (Blackburn, "Tolkien in East Yorkshire").

Easington

On the 16 October 1917 Tolkien was discharged from Brooklands for the first time and he initially returned to Thirtle Bridge. However, by 16 November he had already been transferred to the 9th Battalion, Royal Defence Corps, and they were based ten miles further south down the coast at Easington. There are only a few clues as to where Tolkien lived or what he worked on at this time. One of the manuscripts of what became "The Song of Eriol" includes a later note, which says "Easington, 1917-18" (Mathison, *Tolkien in East Yorkshire* 91). In addition, a note on a manuscript of "Elf Alone" (formerly entitled "The Lonely Harebell") explains it was written at a "farmhouse near Easington" (91). One of the largest landowners in the area was a Robert Walker who owned a substantial property, called "The Tower" in Easington, which has changed very little since 1918 (88). Walker, who left diaries which have been examined, is known to have rented out some of his properties to army personnel, but it is not known for certain if one of these was Tolkien. On a modern Ordnance Survey map there are only a handful of farms and farmhouses in the Easington area, bounded as it is on one side by the sea, and on the other by the proximity of the Humber estuary, so theoretically it should be possible to determine exactly where Tolkien lived during the winter of 1917 to 1918.

As a man steeped in history, Tolkien was almost certainly aware that at the time of the *Domesday Book* most of the land around Easington, indeed the whole of Holderness, which was not owned by the church, belonged to the Earl of Holderness, a certain Drogo (English 7). It is rather surprising that he would choose Frodo's father's name from a hated Norman overlord if Tolkien "felt that his true culture had been crushed and forgotten" (Garth 52) by the Norman Conquest. Whether Tolkien recalled this name when he was writing *The Lord of the Rings* and selecting a name for Frodo's father is debatable. However, East Yorkshire contains both North and South **Frod**ingham, and was controlled by Earl Drogo, so there does appear to be at the least a tenuous link between these two members of the Baggins family in the landscape of the East Riding.

Kilnsea

When trench fever or other illnesses returned over the winter of 1917-18 he was sent another two miles further south to Kilnsea for treatment at the hospital at the Godwin Battery (Mathison, *Tolkien in East Yorkshire* 90). This "House of Healing" was very different from the other in the quiet leafy suburbs of Hull. At that time it was approximately 250 yards from the sea, and, it being winter, some of Tolkien's visits must have coincided with pounding waves. Tolkien as far as his memory went back could remember a "terrible recurrent dream" of a "Great Wave, towering up, and coming in ineluctably over the trees and green fields" (*Letters* 213). Although Tolkien's nightmare predated his internment in Kilnsea hospital, it was probably intensified by his proximity to what had until relatively recently been called the German Ocean. The Godwin Battery hospital, as is evident from contemporary aerial photographs, was built very close to North Marsh Lane, and at the southern end of the lane about 550 feet away from the hospital is the Blue Bell public house, which had a very clear proof embedded in its side of the destructive power of the sea. The plaque states that the inn was built in 1847, and at that time was 534 yards from the sea. When Tolkien was there in early 1918 he would have been able to estimate, should he have wanted to, that the inn was already much closer to the sea.

As Tolkien made clear in his interview with Denys Gueroult he was always "historically minded" ("BBC Interview"), and he would no doubt have heard of examples of the destruction of historical artefacts. The tower of Old Kilnsea church was finally swallowed up by the sea in 1831 (Crowther 176, plate 3), and in 1818 an old ornate medieval cross was removed inland to safety (plate 1). This cross is thought to have either commemorated the landing of the future Henry IV at Raverspurn in 1399, or the return of King Edward IV from exile in 1471. Photographs survive of Easington being almost submerged by severe flooding in 1906, and it is likely this most recent inundation would have been brought to Tolkien's attention. The recurrent great wave dream continued to haunt Tolkien until he managed to exorcise it from his system by writing the "Downfall of Númenor" in the 1930s (*Letters* 213). John Garth has shown that the storm poem "Sea Chant of an Elder Day" became more violent in the rewriting in Holderness, and Tolkien's proximity to destructive seas may have had an effect on his subsequent maritime writing.

In Hammond and Scull's *The Lord of the Rings: A Reader's Companion* when Tolkien mentions the Beacons of Gondor, which were lit to summon aid from Rohan, the authors quite rightly note that "almost every English man, woman, and child would immediately think of the beacons lit in 1588 to warn of the approach of the Spanish Armada" (509). The authors go on to mention earlier beacons in antiquity, but they fail to refer to Tolkien's personal association with a beacon during the Great War. The Kilnsea Beacon was originally erected in Napoleonic times and was constructed of wood, but when Tolkien was in Holderness it had been moved westwards from its earlier location on a hill, because otherwise it would have been lost to the sea many years earlier. By 1917 the wooden beacon had been replaced by a very distinctive metal structure. The Kilnsea Beacon during the Great War was situated north of the Godwin Battery, but nearer the battery than Easington. It was finally dismantled in the

Second World War, as it was thought to be a too readily identified landmark for enemy planes (Crowther 136).

When Tolkien was with the Humber Garrison, he travelled to Dunstable to sit a signalling course exam in the second half of July 1917. It is possible that Tolkien's duties as a signalling officer may have been connected with one of the most striking surviving remnants of the Great War in the area. In 1916 an Acoustic Sound Mirror was erected at Kilnsea to listen out for approaching aircraft (Crowther 89), which at that time effectively meant Zeppelins, as German planes were unable to travel across the North Sea to Yorkshire. The sound was focussed by the concave dish to the "collector's head" mounted on the metal pipe still visible in 2019, on which was attached a rudimentary microphone. Wires from this led down into a trench in which an operator with headphones would listen for approaching aircraft, and would provide an early warning – actually of only four minutes. We will probably never know if Tolkien was one of these "listeners" but even if not, when he was in the Kilnsea area he could not have failed to see this monumental concrete structure. As a trained signalling officer, he must have been aware of how this structure operated and was utilised.

Kilnsea is the southernmost inhabited village in that part of East Yorkshire, and marks the end of Tolkien's known physical association with Holderness. Admittedly, Tolkien only spent eighteen months in East Yorkshire, but these were crucial in the development of his emerging mythology. The dance of Edith in the "hemlock glade" signifies both an idyllic period in his married life, and simultaneously an inspirational turning point in his mythological world-building. Additionally, it also symbolises a return to a much-needed calmer period of recovery after the ravages of surviving the Somme. Arguably, just as crucial were the nearly twenty weeks of recuperation over two summers spent in Brooklands Officer's Hospital. This gave him the invaluable concentrated time to build up and construct his complex vocabularies and grammars of Goldogrin languages; compose new poems or rework older examples, and write the earliest versions of "The Tale of Tinúviel" and "The Tale of Turumbar". These two "Great Tales" of his legendarium were to stay with him for the remainder of his life, but their dissemination to a wider and very appreciative public was more than half a century in the future. Indeed, the fullest narratives of both of these stories were only published posthumously. On 11 September

1918 Tolkien was transferred to the Savoy Convalescent Hospital in Blackpool, and by early November he had recovered enough to accept work on the *New English Dictionary* in Oxford (Scull and Hammond, *Chronology* 113-4). The armistice was signed on 11 November 1918, by which time Tolkien had resumed his married family life and commenced his long academic career in Oxford.

Appendix: Tolkien in East Yorkshire Chronology[6]

1917

19 April	Tolkien posted to Hornsea Musketry Camp. He joins 3rd Reserve Battalion.
1 May	Tolkien attends a medical board examination. Tolkien spends some time at Hornsea Musketry camp.
5 May	Edith lodging at 1 Bank Terrace, Hornsea on this date. Tolkien posted to Thirtle Bridge, but is actually based at Hornsea Musketry Camp.
12 May	Tolkien declared fit for home service.
c. 1-10 June	Edith Tolkien dances in a glade of Cow Parsley at or near Roos.
1 June	Tolkien found fit for general service during a medical board examination. Edith still at 1 Bank Terrace, Hornsea.
2 June	Edith leaves 1 Bank Terrace, Hornsea.
2 Jun-11 July	Tolkien may have been able to lodge with Edith for 6 weeks near Roos when put in charge of an outpost.
12 July	Edith lodging at 76 Queen Street, Withernsea by this date.
13 July	Tolkien at 'Waverley', Cliff Road, Hornsea, on route for Dunstable.
14-21 July	Tolkien sits a signalling exam at Dunstable.
31 July	Brooklands Officers' Hospital opens with 3 patients.

6 This chronology was constructed by using dates from Scull and Hammond, Garth, Mathison, plus my own research in the Chichester-Constable diaries and local newspapers.

1 August	Tolkien attends annual Minden Day dinner at Thirtle Bridge or Tunstall Hall?
13 August	Tolkien admitted to Brooklands Officers' Hospital by this date.
21-4 August	Edith leaves Withernsea for Cheltenham sometime about this date.
22 August	Zeppelin raid on Hedon, but there are no casualties.
Late August	Tolkien admits to C. Wiseman he has only written 1 poem so far in 1917: "The Companions of the Rose".
25 September	Zeppelin raid on Hull.
16 October	Tolkien leaves Brooklands Officers' Hospital for Thirtle Bridge.
16 November	Tolkien attends a medical board examination. His address is 9th Royal Defence Corps, Withernsea. He still requires some indoor hospital treatment. John Francis Reuel Tolkien born in Cheltenham.
19 November	Tolkien's address is 9th Royal Defence Corps, Kilnsea.
24 November	Tolkien promoted to Lieutenant.

1918

19 January	Tolkien attends a medical board examination and is still based with 9th Royal Defence corps at Easington.
19 February	Tolkien attends a medical board examination.
10 March	Zeppelin raid on Hull; a woman died of shock 2 days later.
19 March	Tolkien attends a medical board examination. 9th Royal Defence corps is disbanded and Tolkien is to be based at Thirtle Bridge.
10 April	Medical board decides Tolkien fit for general service.
10-28 June	Tolkien at Penkridge Camp and Brocton Camp, Cannock Chase.
29 June	Tolkien succumbs to gastritis at Brocton Camp.

12 July	Tolkien back at Brooklands Officers' Hospital by this date. He develops his Qenya and Goldogrin lexicons and brushes up his Italian and Spanish.
26 July	Tolkien ordered to embark for Boulogne, even though still in hospital.
4 September	Tolkien attends a medical board examination and is considered 100% disabled after losing 2 stones in weight.
11 September	Tolkien is released from Brooklands Officers' Hospital and transferred to Blackpool Savoy Convalescent Hospital.
19 November	Tolkien is in Oxford on this date.

Bibliography

"About the Lighthouse." Withernsea Lighthouse Museum. 2016. www.withernsea lighthouse.co.uk/about-the-lighthouse/. 7 Jan 2018.

ALLISON, K.J. (ed.). *A History of the County of York, East Riding, Vol. V. Holderness: Southern Part.* Oxford: Oxford University Press, 1984.

BLACKBURN, Cathleen. "Re: J.R.R. Tolkien in Staffordshire." E-mail to Scott Whitehouse. 9 April 2015.

"Re: Tolkien in East Yorkshire." E-mail to Phil Mathison. 17 Nov. 2015.

CARPENTER, Humphrey. *J.R.R. Tolkien: A Biography.* London: George Allen & Unwin, 1977.

CHAPMAN, Maeve and Ben CHAPMAN (eds.). *The Archive Photographs Series: Withernsea.* Stroud: Chalford, 1996.

CHAUCER, Geoffrey. *The Riverside Chaucer.* Ed. F.N. Robinson. 3rd ed. Oxford: Oxford University Press, 1987.

CHICHESTER-CONSTABLE, Margaret. *Diaries.* Beverley, The Treasure House, DDST/NA1640.

CROWTHER, Jan. *The People Along the Sand: The Spurn Peninsula and Kilnsea, A History, 1800-2000.* Andover: Phillimore, 2006.

ENGLISH, Barbara. *The Lords of Holderness, 1086-1260: A Study in Feudal Society.* Hull: Hull University Press, 1991.

BLAMEY, Marjorie, Richard FITTER and Alastair FITTER. *Wild Flowers of Britain & Ireland.* London: A & C Black, 2003.

GARTH, John. [Comment], comment on Tolkien Society Facebook Group Page, 29 May 2015. https://m.facebook.com/groups/6522796067?view=permalink&id=10153240175736068&_rdr. 7 Jan. 2019.

"Re: Roos Extra." E-mail to author. 16 Sep 2016.

Tolkien and the Great War: The Threshold of Middle-earth. London: HarperCollins, 2003.

GILSON, Christopher, Carl F. HOSTETTER, Patrick WYNNE and Arden SMITH (eds.). *Parma Eldalamberon* 11. Walnut Creek, CA: Elvish Linguistic Fellowship, 1995.

HAMMOND, Wayne G. and Christina SCULL. *The Lord of the Rings: A Reader's Companion*. London: HarperCollins, 2014.

HAZEL, Dinah. *The Plants of Middle-earth: Botany and Sub-creation*. Kent, OH: Kent State University Press, 2006.

Hull Daily Mail, 19 Sep 1914. "Paul Pry." Our Holderness Letter. www.britishnewspaperarchive.co.uk/viewer/bl/0000324/19140919/035/0003. 14 April 2019.

Hull Daily Mail, 29 Apr 1916. "Paul Pry." Our Holderness Letter. www.britishnewspaperarchive.co.uk/viewer/bl/0000324/19160429/004/0002. 14 April 2019.

Hull Daily Mail, 1 Aug 1917. Hospital for Officers. www.britishnewspaperarchive.co.uk/viewer/bl/0000324/19170801/007/0002. 14 April 2019.

Hull Daily Mail, 6 Dec 1917. "Our own correspondent." Withernsea Council. Lead pipes and the Water Supply. www.britishnewspaperarchive.co.uk/viewer/bl/0000324/19171206/042/0004. 14 April 2019.

Hull Daily Mail, 12 Oct 1918. Brooklands Officers' Hospital, To the editor. www.britishnewspaperarchive.co.uk/viewer/bl/0000324/19181012/011/0002. 14 April 2019.

JUDD, Walter and Graham JUDD. *Flora of Middle-earth: Plants of J.R.R. Tolkien's Legendarium*. Oxford: Oxford University Press, 2017.

KENT, G.H.R. (ed.). *A History of the County of York, East Riding, Vol. VII. Holderness: Middle and North Divisions*. Oxford: Oxford University Press, 2002.

"Last Name: Thirtle." *Surname DB: The Internet Surname Database*. 2017. www.surnamedb.com/Surname/Thirtle. 7 Jan. 2019.

LEE, Stuart D. "'Tolkien in Oxford' (BBC, 1968): A Reconstruction." *Tolkien Studies* 15, 2018. 115-176.

MCILWAINE, Catherine. *Tolkien: Maker of Middle-earth*. Oxford: Bodleian Library, 2018.

MABEY, Richard. *Flora Britannica*. London: Sinclair Stevenson, 1996.

MATHISON, Phil. "Re: Tolkien Seminar – Phil M." E-mail to the author, 5 Jul. 2015.

Tolkien in East Yorkshire, 1917-1918: An Illustrated Tour. Newport: Dead Good, 2015.

NOAD, Charles. "Re: Halsham Mausoleum." E-mail to author. 2 May 2015.

REYNOLDS, Pat. "Re: Burton Constable." E-mail to author. 5 Aug 2015.

SCULL, Christina and Wayne G. HAMMOND. *The J.R.R. Tolkien Companion and Guide: Chronology.* 2nd ed. London: HarperCollins, 2017.

The J.R.R. Tolkien Companion and Guide: Reader's Guide. 2nd ed. London: HarperCollins, 2017. 2nd vol.

SHIPPEY, Tom. *The Road to Middle-earth.* 3rd ed. London: HarperCollins, 2005.

SIMPSON, Tony. "Re: Withernsea Lighthouse." E-mail to the author. 24 Feb. 2015.

TOLKIEN, John and Priscilla TOLKIEN. *The Tolkien Family Album.* London: HarperCollins, 1992.

TOLKIEN, J.R.R. "BBC Interview." Denys Gueroult, interviewer. 26 Nov. 1964. www.realmofhistory.com/2017/10/28/rare-extended-edition-tolkien-bbc-interview/. 14 April 2019.

Beren and Lúthien. Ed. Christopher Tolkien. London: HarperCollins, 2017.

The Book of Lost Tales, Part Two (The History of Middle-earth 2). Ed. Christopher Tolkien. George Allen & Unwin, 1984.

The Lays of Beleriand (The History of Middle-earth 3). Ed. Christopher Tolkien. London: George Allen & Unwin, 1985.

The Letters of J.R.R. Tolkien: A Selection. Eds. Carpenter, Humphrey and Christopher Tolkien. 1st Houghton Mifflin pbk. ed. Boston, MA: Houghton Mifflin, 2000.

The Lord of the Rings. 50th Anniversary edition. Boston, MA: Houghton Mifflin: 2004.

The Lost Road (The History of Middle-earth 5). Ed. Christopher Tolkien. London: Unwin Hyman, 1987.

"On Fairy-Stories." Tolkien on Fairy-Stories. Eds. Anderson Douglas A. and Verlyn Flieger. London: HarperCollins, 2008, 27-84.

Sauron Defeated (The History of Middle-earth 9). Ed. Christopher Tolkien. London: HarperCollins, 1992.

The Shaping of Middle-earth (The History of Middle-earth 4). Ed. Christopher Tolkien. London: George Allen & Unwin, 1986.

The Silmarillion. Ed. Christopher Tolkien. London: George Allen & Unwin, 1977.

Yorkshire Post, 2 Aug 1919. https://www.britishnewspaperarchive.co.uk/viewer/bl/0000687/19190802/086/0003. 14 April 2019.

Wilhelm Kuehs

Two Poets at War: J.R.R. Tolkien and Ernst Jünger in the Battle of the Somme, a Semiotic Approach

At the front: about the authors

On 6 October 1914 Ernst Jünger, 19 years old at that time, enlisted at the *Ersatzbattalion* of the *Fusilier-Regiment* 73 (Schwilk 93) and was ready to go to war. Pretty much at the same time J.R.R. Tolkien, 22 years old, stayed on the Phoenix Farm of his aunt Jane Neave waiting for the Michaelmas Term to begin and working on a poem called *The Voyage of Éarendel the Evening Star* (Scull and Hammond 54; *LT* II 267f). This was the germ of his legendarium and the beginning of the attempt to write "a body of more or less connected legend [...] which I could dedicate simply to: to England" (*Letters* 144). So this autumn of 1914, right at the beginning of the Great War was an important time for both poets. They came to themselves so to say, Tolkien to mythology, Jünger to war.

When Tolkien arrived in France and approached the frontier in Mid-June 1916 (Scull and Hammond 81), Jünger had already been at war two years, had been wounded several times and was eager to get the Iron Cross (Schwilk 123). Following the two poets through the battle of the Somme from June to late October reveals patterns of behavior which point to cultural patterns of thinking about and dealing with war. While Ernst Jünger tried to be a war hero of mythological dimension, Tolkien tried to survive, mourned his dead friends, and was not especially ambitious to win himself a reputation as a warrior. What he really thought about war – he told his son Michael in a letter in October 1940 – was that he saw his time in the army as a mere waste of time (*Letters* 46).

On 28 October 1916 J.R.R. Tolkien was brought to the hospital of Gazaincourt suffering from "trench fever". He was no longer fit to serve in the army (Scull and Hammond 94). Ernst Jünger on the other hand ended his wartime in autumn of 1918 with the highest military decoration possible: the Pour le Mérite (Schwilk 196). Up to this time he had written an enormous war diary containing sixteen booklets. This would be the source of his first novel "*In Stahlgewittern*" (*Storm of Steel*).

Tolkien had no such diary but he was also writing and thinking about literature while he was in reserve and even when he reached the trenches. His idea of creating fairy stories goes back to the time before the war, looming now in the unconscious waiting for the nighttime or a moment of leisure to reappear and become a poem. Later Tolkien would claim that "Escape is one of the main functions of fairy-stories" (*OFS* 69) and so it is no surprise that there is no mention on war in the poems Tolkien wrote at the front (Croft 17).

But as Tom Shippey has it, war changed everything and traumatized a whole generation (Shippey xxx). Tolkien and Jünger are just two of hundreds of poets who would deal with their wartime experience: landscapes of decaying bodies of men and horses, devastating bombing through night and day, comrades shot and wounded, dying and neglected. This first war of the 20th century was a new kind of war. Ernst Jünger wrote in his essay "Der Kampf als inneres Erleben" ("Fight as an Inner Experience") that the machines were like a huge non-personal wave of destruction which laid waste to whole landscapes, but he also said that, behind this overwhelming force, human will and power were at work (Jünger, "Kampf" 106). This was a new experience for the soldiers. They not only had to fight man against man but man against machines. The use of poison gas, of tanks and explosive agents, converted fighting to an unimaginable nightmare.

In this maelstrom of blood and gore something evil crept into the fairy world, or should we say, Tolkien started to see behind the veil that romantic writers and collectors like Andrew Lang had woven and espy a shadow in the background? He had seen as many other soldiers in combat that there were forces that could extinguish mankind. So the question of the origin of evil arises (Shippey ix). As always, Tolkien tried do give an answer through a tale. One of the first stories he began after coming home from war was the tale of *Tuor and the Fall of Gondolin* (Garth 38). In this tale Tolkien for the first time talked about war, and he gave us a description of the gathering of Melko's army, which astonishingly resembles accounts from the battle at the Somme.

> Then on a time Melko assembled all his most cunning smiths and sorcerers, and of iron and flame they wrought a host of monsters such as have only at

> that time been seen and shall not again be till the Great End. Some were all of iron so cunningly linked that they might flow like slow rivers of metal or coil themselves around and above all obstacles before them, and these were filled in their innermost depths with the grimmest of the Orcs with scimitars and spears; others of bronze and copper were given hearts and spirits of blazing fire, and they blasted all that stood before them with the terror of their snorting or trampled whatso escaped the ardour of their breath; yet others were creatures of pure flame that writhed like ropes of molten metal, and they brought to ruin whatever fabric they came nigh, and iron and stone melted before them and became as water, and upon them rode the Balrogs in hundreds; and these were the most dire of all those monsters which Melko devised against Gondolin. (*LT* II 170)

Jünger's narration of a moment in combat sounds pretty much alike.

> At once the hurricane broke loose. A curtain of flames was let down, followed by a sudden impetuous tumult such as was never heard, a raging thunder that swallowed up the reports even of the heaviest guns in its tremendous reverberations and made the earth tremble. This gigantic roar of annihilation from countless guns behind us was so terrific that, compared with it, all preceding battles were child's-play. What we had not dared to hope came true. The enemy artillery was silenced, put out of action by one giant blow. We could not stay any longer in the dugouts. We got out on to the top and looked with wonder at the wall of fire towering over the English lines and the swaying blood-red clouds that hung above it. (Jünger, *Storm* 250)

When reading these descriptions of war, knowing that both Tolkien and Jünger saw combat in 1916, we could take this as a striking evidence that both poets are affected by war in the same way. But this would be entirely wrong.

Life and literature

Between life and literature there is a gap filled with semiosis. We don't really know how life affects literature, all we know is that there must be a connection, and this connection has to be in the form of an abduction.

Even the tiniest glimpse, the beginning of any process of realization, has the form of an abduction. This is so, because there is no direct way from ontological reality to our consciousness. Our organs of perception are affected by something Charles Sanders Peirce called the dynamic object. It has an impact on our mind and sets semiosis in action (Peirce, *Semiotic* 197). Through this first step of realization of primary indexicality, the immediate object emerges in our mind. "Primary indexicality occurs when, amid the thick stuff of the sensations that bombard us, we suddenly select something that we set against that general background and decide we want to speak about it [...]" (Eco, *Kant* 14). At this moment, perception emerges from the state of Firstness to what Peirce called Secondness, which means we are now in a dualistic relation to the immediate object (CP 8.328).[1] In a further state of perception we get into Thirdness and begin to integrate the representation of the immediate object into a web of meaning which we call the encyclopedia.

This is a very cursory view of the process of perception from bottom up, but things are quite complicated when we take a look the other way round. There are cultural patterns implied in our mind which are responsible for selecting aspects of the immediate object we can call the ground. The cultural patterns in our mind constantly search for likenesses and analogies, and when they find them in the ground of the immediate object they produce primary iconism (Eco, *Kant* 100ff.).

So this is a bottom-down effect which can partially explain why different people will have different experiences of the same event. This is particularly important for our inquiry in at least two ways. It shows that there is not only a gap between perception and meaning regarding one single person but there are also semiotic gaps between different persons, between two authors as well as between authors and readers and not to forget between different readers.

So when we start the quest of comparing Tolkien's and Jünger's writing regarding their war experience we are heading for the perilous realm of semiotics. A lot of traps with dragons inside waiting for us and we have to be careful not to lose our way.

Literature and meaning

"As for any meaning or 'message', it has in the intention of the author none" (*LotR*, Foreword.xxiii). This often quoted passage from the Foreword of the *The Lord of the Rings* is generally read as a statement against allegoric interpre-

1 The standard citation style for the *Collected Papers of Charles Sanders Peirce* is by volume and paragraph.

tation. This reading is valid for sure. But from a semiotics point of view, there are further layers of possible meanings.

Tolkien raises the question of potential and favored meanings of a text. Usually we tend to ask: What does the author mean? This question arises from years and years of literature lessons in school. It seems that teachers and a lot of literature scientists incline towards the idea that literature is a kind of riddle posed to the reader by the author. This view is not altogether false but it blocks the exploration of other perspectives. Umberto Eco states three possible intentional points of view in regard of a text: the intention of the author (*intentio auctoris*), the intention of the reader (*intentio lectoris*) and the intention of the text (*intentio operis*) (Eco, *Limits* 58).

This kind of view is a starting point for several insights. First of all we can come to the conclusion that the intention of the author, his interpretation of the text so to speak, has no privileged status and that literature is not only a riddle-game. What is written is written and the semiotic reader has to try to find a balance between the strands of meaning which are offered by the text as a strategy of creating sense and the intention of the reader who will bring his own encyclopedia to the text.

But the case is not entirely lost. The text tends to produce what we call an ideal or model reader. This model reader is no real person but a strategy of the text. For example, the text suggests a special kind of encyclopedia competence as for example in a medieval romance. Usually we will find no explanations of the concept of chivalric love there. So the knowledge about chivalric love is a competence of the model reader (Eco, *Role of the Reader* 7).

The linear manifestation of the text in itself holds potential meanings. The cooperation of the reader opens the systems of codes and in this way the text will become a matter of interpretation. Speaking with Eco, there are open and closed text. Open texts tend to invite the reader to let their interpretive skills loose, to see the text as an invitation for adventure. James Joyce's *Finnegans Wake* seems to be an example to the extreme (Eco, *Limits* 148). *Finnegans Wake* is a rhizome in itself, and so a picture of the network of the cultural interconnections of patterns and strands. Through this structure it evokes a search for meaning always opaque and meandering.

When we look at our sample of texts we have a corpus of average open texts in Tolkien's legendarium and a corpus of quite closed texts in Jünger's wartime writings. This openness and closedness of the text regards the production of the model reader as a strategy of reading as only one indication towards the ideological structures. We will see that Jünger's texts try to close down the reading to codes of fascism and heroic masculinity while Tolkien's texts give the opportunity to set a vast varieties of codes into action.

Being at war:

Personal accounts of war

Unfortunately, the letters between Tolkien and his fiancée Edith Bratt between 1913 and 1918 were nearly totally omitted from the published collection of letters (*Letters* 1), so we only have a few personal accounts of Tolkien from this time. But even those hints show that Tolkien was not an eager soldier. In a letter to Edith Bratt from March 1916 he confessed that he got bored reading military lecture notes and instead longed to work on his invented language (*Letters* 8).

In August 1916 Tolkien saw combat. On 8 to 9 August four men in his immediate neighborhood were killed, four more were wounded. He also learned that one of his close friends had died fighting. In a letter from 12 August he wrote to Geoffrey Smith: "So far my chief impression is that something has gone crack. [...] I am hungry and lonely of course" (*Letters* 10). So he grieved for his lost friend and for losing the comfort of the company he and his friends had during college.

Later on, in WW II, Tolkien wrote to his son Michael on 9 June 1941 (*Letters* 55). His view on war has not altered at all. He saw himself as "very inefficient and unmilitary" (*Letters* 54). And in another letter to his son Christopher in 1943 he said "[I]f I was of military age, I should, I fancy, be grousing away in a fighting service, and willing to go to the bitter end" (*Letters* 65).

The message is easy to grasp and consistent over the years. War seems to be necessary sometimes, but it is nothing to be proud of and nothing a man wants to attend. More directly Tolkien expresses it in another letter to Christopher Tolkien in 1944: "The utter stupid waste of war, not only material but moral and spiritual, is so staggering to those who have to endure it. And always was (despite the poets), and always will be (despite the propagandists) – not of course that it has not is and will be necessary to face it in an evil world" (*Letters* 75).

In the case of Ernst Jünger it is much more difficult to say what we have to see as a private encounter and what was written for publication. But fortunately there is not much difference between his war diary and his novel *Storm of Steel* in reference to ideological codes and meanings.

Before going into the battle at the Somme (22 July 1916) Jünger wrote in his diary: "Lecturing with a platoon, quite according to the motto three-fourths will perish but always ahead with brave courage!" (Jünger, *Kriegstagebuch* 165).[2] In October 1916 Jünger was waiting for his mission to begin. Under fire he was checking lists of soldiers and found someone he knew from Berlin. This was no friend of his, but a man who has done Jünger wrong, and so he looked for the list of dead soldiers. Jünger could not find his name and wrote: "Sadly not, bad weeds grow tall [...]" (Jünger, *Kriegstagebuch* 190).[3]

An entry from 18 May 1916 in the war diary is quite typical for Jünger's attitude. In these three small passages he states that he saw someone dying and a little pig was shot in his buttocks. On the same day Jünger noted that he was searching beetles for his collection (Jünger, *Kriegstagebuch* 106). Jünger was a very enthusiastic hobby entomologist. There are several species named after Jünger (Schöning 1), and since 1985 the land of Baden Württemberg gives an award on entomology in Jünger's name every three years.

This disturbing nearness of human suffering and high interest in insects we can find in all of Jünger's war diaries. One of the most unsettling passages Jünger wrote during World War II when he was in Vincennes, Paris. He was in charge of commanding a firing squad executing a deserter. In this entry in

2 "Hielt noch Unterricht mit einem Zug, so ungefähr mit dem Motto ¾ werden wohl draufgehn, aber immer mit frohem Mut!" All translations from Jünger are my own.

3 "Leider nicht. Unkraut vergeht schlecht [...]."

his diary Jünger entwined his precise observation of the environment, especially the meat flies waiting for the dead body, and his cold description of the actions necessary to kill somebody (Jünger, *Strahlungen* I 45ff.).

Why are Jünger's war diaries so disquieting? It is a rather simple aesthetic concept which we can find here and in most of Jünger's novels and essays. He applied the same moral codes to human beings and insects by describing both in the same somber and cold way. His observations are at any time highly accurate and aloof regardless of the subject. Form and substance are in correlation, and so we can identify what Umberto Eco called the ideolect of a work or corpus of works (Eco, *Semiotics* 272). Eco said that in this ideolect we can find the strategy of the generation of a text. It is the core of the work and from there on we can explore the other levels of meaning, the meandering of sense and the connections to other cultural entities.

War as a frame of experience

The concept of framework was first introduced by Gregory Bateson to explain the difference between play and ritual from a psychological point of view. He said: "The first step in defining a psychological frame might be to say that it is (or delimits) a class or set of messages (or meaningful actions)" (Bateson 186). So we have, as a participant of society, a bundle of codes at hand to distinguish play from ritual, or in our case, war from peace. We can recognize this by using specific sets of codes which are suitable for war.

Usually we have to deal with an overcoded abduction when facing a well-known situation like war (Eco, *Sign* 206). We are familiar with all the possible social acts inside such a frame and we know the important differences from other frames. So everybody knows that killing is not as strictly prohibited in war than in peace. We can even say that the social meta-code of war orders soldiers to kill and that there are only few exceptions of this order. In the official code of traditional warfare it was allowed to kill every man of the enemy but it was forbidden to kill children and women. But underneath this more or less official code there was always a subcode of violence which permits killing, rape and enslavery of all the people available. These two codes are in a constant antagonism when fighting starts, so we are in need of a kind of rule of war. Since the 19th century there were a series of efforts to codify a set of rules about the conduct of war, first written down as the Hague Convention of 1899. It provides us with a set of rules, a framework regarding the behavior of soldiers.

So we can say the Hague Convention is a kind of primary social framework (Goffman 21f.). This frame organizes the meaning and the possible action. It lets us expect a particular kind of experience (Goffman 345). But in World War I a reorganization of the frame took place and this was experienced as a breaking of the frames and a change of codes which Goffman calls downkeying the frame (Goffman 359). Suddenly both Tolkien and Jünger were confronted by a frame for which there were no proper codes at hand. We will look at this reorganization of the frame especially in regard of the soldier.

The making of the hobbit as a warrior

What Tolkien experiences as a crack (*Letters* 10) might be this change of codes. Suddenly he found himself in a slightly other kind of frame than expected. And the frame kept altering. There was nothing left of the courtesy of Arthurian romance (*SGGK* 3) or the "northern heroic spirit" (*HBBS* 22). This kind of war was ultimately new and Tolkien as well as Jünger struggled to find a new set of codes to deal with the situation.

Umberto Eco would call this process the creating of a meta-abduction.

> It consists in deciding as to whether the possible universe outlined by our first-level abductions is the same as the universe of our experience. In over- and undercoded abductions, this meta-level of inference is not compulsory, since we get the law from a storage of already checked actual world experience. In other words, we are entitled by common world knowledge to think that, provided the law is the suitable one, it already holds in the world of our experience. In creative abductions we do not have this kind of certainty. We are making a complete "fair guess" not only about the nature of the result (its cause) but also about the nature of the encyclopedia (so that, if the new law results in being verified, our discovery leads to a change of paradigm). (Eco, *Sign* 207)

The First World War was such new kind of experience. A war of mass killings, of gas attacks, tanks, and air fights. The soldier was no longer important as a possible hero. He became part of the material of war. Tolkien saw this change of paradigm at least when writing to his son Michael in 1941. His sympathy for the "plain soldier from the agricultural counties" (*Letters* 54) seems a bit nostalgic in the onset of World War II.

This plain soldier was in some respect the prototype of the hobbit as a warrior. Sam Gamgee, so Tolkien said, was "indeed a reflexion of the English soldier" (qtd. in Carpenter 81). Janet Brennan Croft has stated that in Sam but also in Merry and Pippin we can detect some qualities which Tolkien called "the northern heroic spirit" (Croft 20). Essentially to this attitude is that personal pride could never beat out love and loyalty (*HBBS* 22). When Merry and Pippin return to the Shire they have grown not only from the elixir Treebeard gave them but in being a responsible part of society (Croft 91-92).

Looking at Tolkien's war experience and his personal comments on his work we can trace the development of his construction of the hobbit as a warrior. His observations and his encounters with soldiers on the front have established a new framework of war.

Tolkien tried a meta-abduction and rearranged parts of his encyclopedia of war and came to a slightly different concept of the soldier as from a traditional point of view. We can witness this struggle on many levels. As we have seen in his letters, Tolkien tried to reassure himself and his sons that fighting against evil was an important task for every man. In his lectures on Beowulf he explored what he called the "northern heroic spirit", and in his novel he shows a manifold view of how war can be used as a frame of action.

The making of the Orcs

Ernst Jünger also felt this dramatic change of the framework of war. In his novel *Storm of Steel* he used aesthetic techniques of expressionism to grasp his experiences as we have seen above. He tried to establish a new set of codes for war to save the idea of the heroic fighter apart from the war of machines.

In Jünger's essays we can observe a meta-abduction regarding the paradigm of war. In *Die totale Mobilmachung* (*Total Mobilization*), Jünger tried to combine his admiration of war and technical progress. The modern war as a war of machines diminishes the individuum only to give him rebirth as a new war hero. War is not a task of individuals and their merits but an industrial process in which the warrior becomes a kind of war-worker (Jünger, *Mobilmachung* 130). Total mobilization means that everybody will be a part of the army. And so war is no longer an aristocratic game but a characteristic of the national democratic state (Jünger, *Mobilmachung* 129).

Here starts a new mythology of war. What Joseph Campbell called "creative mythology" and what we know as mythopoiesis is here in full swing and we can witness the genesis of a new kind of hero.

Jünger seems to suggest that the old kinds of war-heroes like Achilles or Beowulf are obsolete in this new war of machines. They are replaced by workers of war. But this is not the whole story. The war of machines is a quest which will transform the old hero. But this old hero is at the same time the model for the new superman soldier. The Battle of the Somme, the storm of steel, is a night-sea journey to transform and give rebirth to the mythological superman soldier (Campbell, *Hero* 95).

C.G. Jung showed the same development in a deep-psychological analysis of the alchemical process. The *Rosarium Philosophorum*, an alchemical tractate from the 17th century, describes in its sixth chapter the death of the queen and the king and their purification inside of their grave. At the end the queen and the king are resurrected as a hermaphroditic being of ultimate strength (Jung 104ff.).

This quite strange description is the pattern of death and rebirth of the hero to which Jünger refers. In "Der Kampf als inneres Erleben" he celebrates in an expressionistic furor the birth of this new hero. "War is a great school and the new human will be of our kind" (Jünger, "Kampf" 77).[4] This new human is to be thought of in reference to Friedrich Nietzsche's "Übermensch" (Superman), a thoroughly transformed human being, destroyed in war and rebuilt in fight.

The new hero of war is the *Landsknecht* (lansquenet) ("Kampf" 60). Jünger leaves no doubt what these lansquenets are for. They are killers. "Life means killing" (45)[5] wrote Jünger in 1922, and "That is war [...] the want of the blood, for

4 "Der Krieg ist eine große Schule, und der neue Mensch wird von unserem Schlage sein."
5 "Leben heißt töten."

the joy of celebration and ceremony" (51).[6] For Jünger, war is the fulfillment of being. Combat is a kind of intoxication which leads to higher consciousness like a shamanistic experience (65).

In a preface to *Storm of Steel* Jünger's rhetoric rose to a crescendo of glorification of war (Jünger, "Vorwort" 10), but in his military writing he is aware of the problem of the plain soldier in a war dominated by mechanical artillery (Jünger, *Technik* 23).

Reading this and keeping Jünger's personal attitude in mind, it is easy to come to the conclusion that Jünger was a warmonger, one who tried to prolong military conflict. He himself was enlisted after the war as an officer and made himself a name as one of the prominent right-wing publicists of his time. His recreating of the soldier as a superhero was one of the main influences on the Nazis in forming a kind of secret order of supermen called the SS.

As a reader of Tolkien, one has surely another association. What Jünger described is nothing but the ideal of an Orc army. Born to kill, hungry for blood and without mercy, Orcs are the prototype of the warrior superman Jünger had in mind. Of course Jünger didn't know anything about Orcs when writing this. The influence may have gone the other way around.

Whether Tolkien knew about Jünger, we don't know. It is likely that he heard about his novel *Storm of Steel*, and we can take it for granted that Tolkien was well aware of the unwillingness of the Germans to accept their defeat and of the rhetoric of war in the *Weimarer Republik*. He surely observed that the German soldiers established clubs and formed paramilitary units commanded by political leaders. So Germany at the time was ultimately a militaristic society.

Britain was also militaristic, but politically rather than in its essence. Soldiers came home from war, traumatized for sure, but the majority were happy to be alive and at home, and tried to re-establish their former lives and go back to their work and their families, just as Tolkien and his peers did. Still, the imperialistic politics of Britain produced conflicts in every part of the world;

6 "Das ist der Krieg [...] Das ist nur das Bedürfnis des Blutes nach Festfreuden und Feierlichkeiten."

throughout the second half of the 19th century Britain was more or less constantly at war, and was in conflict with Russia about Crimea, involved in the war in Afghanistan, and dealt with insurrections in India and elsewhere. But there had to have been some kind of difference in cultural patterns about war and peace between Britain and Germany. In no other way can we explain the different attitude of German and British society. Each of these ways depended not on the individuals but on the culture. German and Britain culture provided two entirely different frames of post-war reality. This evolves from two different ways to deal with the experience of the Great War.

Everybody had to cope with a situation where most of the usual codes of war were no longer valid. A meta-abduction was in need. A meta-abduction is in every case a rearrangement of material of an encyclopedia already at hand. In Germany as well as in Britain the prewar society was deeply rooted in militarism. The middle class as well as the aristocracy oriented themselves towards military carriers. To become an officer was a possibility to climb in the social hierarchy, to rise from the bourgeoisie to nobility for example.

In Tolkien and in Jünger we have not only two eminent writers of their time but also two exemplary live designs. Tolkien felt fortunate to go back to university and marry his beloved Edith. Jünger never really came to terms with his war experience and compensated for this by glorifying war. What was it, that lead these two poets to these entirely opposite decisions?

One explanation lies in a denial of war in everyday life in the British society. Lawton A. Brewer claims that in the Victorian era, war was seen as necessary for the better of the British empire, but these wars were not seen as fights between equal enemics. The Social Darwinistic consensus in society, the conviction of the superiority of the English race, transformed these wars in mere police actions. The war as a determining part of British society was suppressed into a collective unconsciousness (Brewer 43). There was a narration of the so-called Victorian interlude as a time of peace. Historians and novelists painted a picture of the glory of the empire (Brewer 37f) and only few such as Joseph Conrad focused on the disturbing and terrible aspects of colonialism. In Britain we can observe an ongoing mythopoiesis about war and peace and the self-perception of a nation beginning far back in the age of discovery. In semiotic terms this can be seen as a second-order semiological system (Barthes 113). The language-object, as Barthes called it, in this example the experience of war as combat, is extinguished as such and superimposed by a meta-language which nourishes the ideological realm of society. Barthes called this semiotic construction a myth.

I am not entirely in agreement with Barthes about these terms. What Barthes shows as a second-order semiological system I like to call an artificial myth, to distinguish it from a genuine myth which evolves without a conscious effort inside a society. Artificial myths are part of invented tradition (Trevor-Roper 1). They are always introduced into societies through rather few but influential individuals and peer groups. For example, as Hugh Trevor-Roper demonstrates, the tradition of wearing a kilt as part of Scottish self-concept is an invention of the 19th century established through commercial interests (Trevor-Roper 15ff.).

The artificial myth of the relative peace of the Victorian era was an instrument of political indoctrination. The British were exceptionally successful at creating a narrative of the just war they were fighting. This narrative was transposed from colonialism to Europe in the advance of the Great War. Tolkien accepted this narration for himself as a soldier and adapted it for his artificial mythology. As Croft shows, just war is one of the major concepts of Tolkien's ideological sphere (Croft 138).

Like every war, a just war needs an enemy, and this enemy was right at hand. The war society in which Jünger lived and which he helped to create is not entirely strange to the readers of Tolkien. It is the society of Orcs. Claiming this is not an analogy (which Tolkien abhorred) but an application of a cultural pattern. The similarities between German society after the Great War and the society of Orcs reaches deep.

The problem of evil and specially the problem of evil people is a subject Tolkien dealt with from the very beginning. When thinking about the Orcs or Goblins as the significant doers of evil deeds and as servants of Melkor and Sauron, Tolkien steps back from the idea of the ultimate evil. This gnostic heresy he was never in danger of agreeing with. There is no moral black or white, good and evil in Tolkien's legendarium. On every level the moral clarity is broken and distorted. This is because Tolkien believed in a catholic worldview, in which being inside the created world means to be away from God, from the only and whole good. So this earth is in need of salvation as Middle-earth is also.

The Orcs therefore are not creatures of utter evil. As we see in *The Silmarillion*, they were Elves at first. They were ensnared by Melkor, "were put [...] in prison, and by slow arts of cruelty were corrupted and enslaved; and thus did Melkor breed the hideous race of the Orcs [...]" (*S* 50). The evilest race of Middle-earth was born out of the noblest. Nobody is safe in this broken world and each of us is in danger to fall into traps of evil.

Tolkien saw the Germans as people of great virtue, as brave and full of possibilities. He saw the Germans under the spell of a madman who corrupted the roots of this culture. The roots, Tolkien knew it, are the mythological pattern, the mythological stories from which a culture takes its self-perception. When these roots are twisted and distorted, the branches and leaves are also poisoned.

Out of a perverted mythology there has to arise a perverted society. Tolkien saw this very clearly in 1941 in a letter to his son Michael:

> Yet I suppose I know better than most what is the truth about this 'Nordic' nonsense. Anyway, I have in this War a burning private grudge [...] against that ruddy little ignoramus Adolf Hitler [...]. Ruining, perverting, misapplying, and making for ever accursed, that noble northern spirit, a supreme contribution to Europe, which I have ever loved, and tried to present in its true light. (*Letters* 55-56)

Two strategies of mythopoesis

At least since Horkheimer and Adorno we are aware that myth has not ceased to exist through enlightenment. As ever before the narration of life tends to take the form of a succession of adventures (Horkheimer and Adorno 55). The effort of enlightenment to extinguish myth as a method of explanation has produced nothing but myths by itself (Horkheimer and Adorno 18). It is not possible to escape myth as a form of narration. This is so because of the biological process of perception of humans. In the process of perception, we start an unconscious act of abduction which leads to the creation of cultural patterns and the invocation of archetypal structure in our mind. The mythical worldview is a deep-rooted characteristic of being human. War is an experience humankind lived with since the end of the Neolithic age at least. When matriarchy crumbled and the first warrior societies established their empires, war became a constant part of life.

The cultural patterns inside the framework of war were to some extent constant until the Great War. Combat since the ancient time has been either a matter of duel or a battle between two armies fought mostly by infantry and cavalry. Machines like catapults or the like were used to some extent, but never overpowered human forces. Fighting in World War I was an utterly different experience than fighting in, for example, the Crimean War in the 1850s or the Balkan Wars at the beginning of the 20th century.

In the unfolding of World War I, the use of tanks destroyed the strategies of cavalry. Mortars disturbed all classical plans of deployment. When in 1915 the German army started to use poison gas, this was the beginning of modern chemical warfare.

The patterns of heroism were destroyed in this modern conduct of war. As we have seen, Tolkien and Jünger were facing the same challenge. The patterns of heroism in war had to be recreated.

Tolkien and Jünger took very different ways in fulfilling their tasks. We have seen that Jünger tried to reestablish a pattern of anti-heroism with one or two twists. His hero is modeled in the fashion of an ancient war hero like Achilles in the *Illiad*. A man drunken from his wrath lets loose the terrors of war without any regard for his comrades or his enemy. Another mythological pattern for this kind of warrior might be the Nordic berserk. Dressed in bearskin, biting his shield and whirling his sword, he fights without mercy even against gods built out of steel.

Taking Jünger's political and ideological efforts into account, it is obvious that the *intentio auctoris* was to narrow down the possible codes for his texts to fascism and masculinity. The texts in themselves also intend the use of fascistic codes. As Klaus Theweleit's analysis of Ernst Jünger shows, everything in this huge corpus of texts pushes the reader to the cultural patterns of the new human being of fascistic theories (Theweleit 210). It is very difficult to find a crack in these codes and it is hard to establish a reading aside from fascism. Even Jünger's writings about insects cannot be read as an innocent longing for nature. This idyllic descriptions of butterflies and beetles are too often embedded in scenes of cruelty and death.

On the other hand, Tolkien solved the problem of the heroic by recreating not one but a vast amount of possible cultural patterns. As a usual way of dealing with mythology, Tolkien took parts of ancient stories and transformed them in his own special way to make them suitable for our time. What Tolkien achieved is not only a "mythology for England" (*Letters* 144) but nothing less than a mythology for Europe. He accomplished this task by intermingling mythological stories from ancient Greece with the heroic songs of Finland and transformed all these through the experience of war and technical progress.

The heroic for sure is one of the major themes of Tolkien's work, and he offers several possible implementations. Boromir as well as Húrin are tragic heroes. The bitter faith of Húrin enslaved by Melkor resembles the concept of the absurd hero of Camus (Mitchell 87). Bilbo seemed to be a comical hero at first glance, a trickster, but as we look deeper into his life and adventures he turns out to follow a very old heroic pattern. He, as well as Frodo, are the heroes who developed from weaklings to a strong but unlikely force of salvation. In this cultural pattern of heroism we can find what Tolkien called the eucatastrophe (*OFS* 78). This function of *Dramatis Personae*, as Vladimir Propp puts it, came late in the succession of tales and changes everything. But before we will talk about this special kind of hero, we have to take a look at some of the others.

The type of hero favored by Jünger, Tolkien abhorred. He himself may have favored the perspective of Faramir (Croft 101; *Letters* 232) who said: "War must be, while we defend our lives against a destroyer who would devour all; but I do not love the bright sword for its sharpness [...]" (*LotR* IV.5.672). In this we can even trace a last melancholic shadow of the great knights of Arthurian romance. Tolkien showed us this chivalry not only in Aragorn but also in his poem *The Fall of Arthur*, where he takes us to the long-sunken realm of gallant heroes and enchanted landscapes. In this text particularly we can begin to recognize how Tolkien saw and observed humankind. Man and woman are always vulnerable and even when they try to be strong and keen life will break them.

It seems to me that this is the base of Tolkien's *conditio humana*. In many of his letters he mentioned his conviction that the world we live in is in need of salvation. This is the religious undertone we should be aware of in Tolkien's writing. He saw man as a sinner in a world full of war, hatred, and misery. Man himself is not able to overcome this state of being by himself. He needs the helping hand of God or at least of an angel, which is nothing but an emanation of God's power in Christian terms, so to speak. A hero can only be a hero in the *Imitatio Christi* – the imitation of Christ. And this means in a Christian society not only to be a monk, a nun or a priest. In every position in life we have the possibilities to orientate our life towards the gospel.

One figure in Tolkien's legendarium particularly exemplifies this cultural pattern of the *Imitatio Christi*. Frodo shies away from violence as a method of ending a conflict and finds a way to bring the eucatastrophe to Middle-earth. His course as a hero began quite unimpressively by leaving the Shire in a kind of Huckleberry Finn-type adventure. But soon it became a grim journey through utmost danger, and Frodo learned about war and killing. Even he himself fought and thought about killing Gollum. Through the long walk to Mordor and the loss of all hope, he is transformed. He grows to be a new kind of hero, one without any fighting merits, without killing and looting the enemy. He is a spiritual hero.

There were cultural patterns of such heroes before Tolkien for sure. One may think about Francis of Assisi for an example, who was perhaps Tolkien's archetype for Frodo when we take into regard that Chesterton, as one of the major Catholic writers of England, wrote about Francis and admired him, and Tolkien followed Chesteron's writing (*Letters* 92). But Tolkien was not naive. He never thought that Frodo's way could be the solution in a world like ours. War against Mordor was inevitable for Frodo and Sam to find a way to the Crack of Doom.

Social background and cultural patterns

The question of how two poets so alike in experience and social background came to such different philosophical and literary conclusions about war and the cultural pattern of being a hero is not easy to answer.

Tolkien and Jünger more or less had the same social origin. Both were born in a middle-class family. Tolkien's father died early but his mother was able to send Tolkien to grammar school until he began to win scholarships, and he managed to be successful in his university career.

Ernst Jünger was born into a family of teachers and academics (Kiesel 31f.). He had a rebellious youth, struggled in school, and ran away to the Foreign Legion in 1913 (Schwilk 81). His engagement as a soldier in the First World War and his success, his medals, his awards was the first time in his life in which he felt self-assured. So maybe this was the actual reason for Jünger's enthusiasm for being a warrior and a killer. But that seems to me to be too simple an answer. Ernst Jünger was an intelligent young man. After the war he studied and read a lot. So he basically should have been able to create a multi-perspective similar to Tolkien's. But he decided to become a fascist and a warmonger.

Maybe the answer lies not mainly in personal or psychological circumstances but in the broader social surroundings, the culture in which an individual in respect of his social stratum develops, what we can call the "habitus" (Bourdieu 277f.). The habitus is a set of possibilities in acting and thinking which are inherited from the social stratum in which one is educated. This is a framework inside of the social framework. Jünger, inheriting the habitus of the German bourgeoisie of the 19th century, was not in possession of the same codes as Tolkien. Jünger in particular had no easy access to the codes of Catholic moral theory. Raised in a secular family with a Protestant background, pity seemed not a desirable virtue first hand. When we take in account that German culture emphasized militarism far more than British society, then we have a hint of what was the cause of Jünger's development as a poet and soldier.

This argument gains validity when we look at the interwar situation in Germany and Britain. The habitus of the German man was centered around militarism. After the war politics was nothing but a prolonging war with other means. So combat was a normal instrument of political struggle. Paramilitary units dominated the streets and politicians used them to enforce their agendas. In Britain this was entirely different. Outside of ideological disagreements, civil war was not an option.

These differences in the political culture and habitus of middle-class families in England and Germany might not be the only cause of Tolkien's and Jünger's differing worldviews, but there we can at least locate one factor in how each of them reconstructed the cultural pattern of heroism after the Great War. And this can lead us to a deeper understanding of the history of the 20th century.

Bibliography

BARTHES, Roland. *Mythologies.* New York City, NY: Noonday Press, 1991.

BATESON, Gregory. *Steps to an Ecology of Mind.* San Francisco, CA: Chandler, 1972.

BOURDIEU, Pierre. *Die feinen Unterschiede: Kritik der gesellschaftlichen Urteilskraft.* Frankfurt am Main: Suhrkamp, 1987.

BREWER, Lawton A. "Collective Memory and Empire: George Gissing and the Unconscious of War." *Between Memory and Mythology: The Construction of Memory of Modern Wars.* Ed. Natalia Starostina. Newcastle-Upon-Tyne: Cambridge Scholars Publishing, 2015, 37-52.

CAMPBELL, Joseph. *Creative Mythology: The Masks of God IV.* London: Penguin/Arkana, 1991.

The Hero With a Thousand Faces. London: Harper Collins/Fontana, 1993.

CAMUS, Albert. *Der Mythos des Sisyphos.* Reinbek bei Hamburg: Rowohlt, 1999.

CARPENTER, Humphrey. *J.R.R. Tolkien: A Biography.* Boston, MA: Houghton Mifflin, 2000.

CHESTERTON, G.K. *Francis of Assisi.* London: Hodder & Stoghton, 1923.

CROFT, Janet Brennan. *War and the Works of J.R.R. Tolkien.* Westport, CT: Praeger, 2004.

ECO, Umberto. "Horns, Hooves, Insteps: Some Hypotheses on Three Types of Abduction." *The Sign of Three: Dupin, Holmes, Peirce.* Eds. Umberto Eco and Thomas A. Sebeok. Bloomington, IN: Indiana University Press, 1983, 198-220.

Kant and the Platypus. Boston, MA: Mariner Books/Houghton Mifflin Harcourt, 2000.

Limits of Interpretation. Bloomington, IN: Indiana University Press, 1994.

Role of the Reader. Bloomington, IN: Indiana University Press, 1979.

A Theory of Semiotics. Bloomington, IN: Indiana University Press, 1976.

GARTH, John. *Tolkien and the Great War.* London: Harper Collins, 2003.

GOFFMAN, Erving. *Frame Analysis.* Boston, MA: Northeastern University Press, 1986.

HORKHEIMER, Max and Theodor W. ADORNO. *Dialektik der Aufklärung.* Frankfurt am Main: Fischer, 1988.

JUNG, C.G. *Die Psychologie der Übertragung.* München: dtv Verlagsgesellschaft, 1973

JÜNGER, Ernst. "Der Kampf als inneres Erlebnis." *Werke – Essays I.* Ed. Ernst Jünger. Stuttgart: Klett Cotta, 1960, 11-108.

Kriegstagebuch 1914 -1918. Ed. Helmuth Kiesel. Stuttgart: Klett Cotta, 2010.

Storm of Steel. New York City, NY: Howard Fertig, 1996.

Strahlungen I Das erste Pariser Tagebuch/Kaukasische Auszeichnungen. München: dtv Verlagsgesellschaft, 1964.

"Die Technik in der Zukunftsschlacht." *Politische Publizistik.* Ed. Sven Olav Berggötz. Stuttgart: Klett Cotta, 2001, 23-26.

"Die totale Mobilmachung." *Werke – Essays I.* Ed. Ernst Jünger. Stuttgart: Klett Cotta, 1960. 123-148. "Vorwort In Stallgewittern Hannover 1920." *Politische Publizistik.* Ed. Sven Olav Berggötz. Stuttgart: Klett Cotta, 2001, 9-13.

KIESEL, Helmut. *Ernst Jünger: Die Biographie.* München: Siedler, 2007.

MITCHELL, Jesse. "Master of Doom by Doom Mastered: Heroism, Fate, and Death in *The Children of Húrin.*" *Mythlore* 29.1/2 (2010): 87-114.

PEIRCE, Charles Sanders. *Collected Papers of Charles Sanders Peirce,* vols. 1-6. Eds. Charles Hartshorne and Paul Weiss. Cambridge, MA.: Harvard University Press, 1931-1958. 8 vols.

PEIRCE, Charles S. and Victoria WELBY-GREGORY. *Semiotic and Significs: The Correspondence between C.S. Peirce and Victoria Lady Welby.* Eds. Charles S. Hardwick and James Cook. Bloomington, IN: Indiana University Press, 1977.

PROPP, Vladimir. *Morphology of the Folktale.* Austin, TX: University of Texas Press, 2008.

SCHWILK, Helmut. *Ernst Jünger – Ein Jahrhundertleben – Die Biografie.* München, Zürich: Piper, 2007.

SCULL, Christina and Wayne G. HAMMOND. *The J.R.R. Tolkien Companion and Guide: Chronology.* London: Harper Collins, 2009.

SHIPPEY, Tom. *J.R.R. Tolkien: Author of the Century.* London: Harper Collins, 2000.

THEWELEIT, Klaus. *Männerphantasien 2 Männerkörper zur Psychoanalyse des weißen Terrors*. Reinbek bei Hamburg: Rowohlt, 1982.

TOLKIEN, J.R.R. *The Book of Lost Tales: Part Two* (The History of Middle-Earth Volume 2). Ed. Christopher Tolkien. London: Harper Collins, 2002.

The Children of Húrin. Ed. Christopher Tolkien. London: Harper Collins, 2007.

The Fall of Arthur. Ed. Christopher Tolkien. London: Harper Collins, 2013.

"The Homecoming of Beorhtnoth Beorhthelm's Son." *The Tolkien Reader*. New York City, NY: Ballantine, 1966, 1-24.

The Letters of J.R.R. Tolkien. Ed. Humphrey Carpenter and Christopher Tolkien. London: Allen & Unwin, 1990.

The Lord of the Rings. 50th Anniversary edition. Boston, MA: Houghton Mifflin, 2004.

The Silmarillion. Ed. Christopher Tolkien. London: George Allen and Unwin, 1977.

Sir Gawain and the Green Knight, Pearl, and Sir Orfeo. Ed. Christopher Tolkien. London: Harper Collins, 2006.

Tolkien On Fairy-stories. Eds. Verlyn Flieger and Douglas A. Anderson. London: Harper Collins, 2014.

TREVOR-ROPER, Hugh. "The Invention of Tradition: The Highland Tradition of Scotland." *The Invention of Tradition*. Eds. Eric Hobsbawm and Terence Ranger. Cambridge: Cambridge University Press, 1983, 15-42.

Section III:

Roots of Major Themes of the Legendarium in the Great War

John Garth

Revenants and Angels: Tolkien, Machen, and Mons

Twin myths

Towards the end of September 1914, just eight weeks after the outbreak of the Great War, two myths were born. One had nothing ostensibly to do with the current war, or indeed any war: a poem by an utterly unknown young writer about a mariner who sails off the edge of the world and becomes a celestial object. As he put pen to paper on 24 September and wrote "The Voyage of Éarendel the Evening Star" (Scull and Hammond 61), the 22-year-old J.R.R. Tolkien created the very first element in what was to become his incomparably rich and compelling Middle-earth mythology.

The other myth born that week had everything to do with the sudden war. On 29 September, the *London Evening News* published a short story called "The Bowmen", by Arthur Machen, 54 years old and long established as a writer of popular fiction with a supernatural flavour. Set during the British Army's desperate retreat from Mons, Belgium, a month earlier, it describes the plight of 1,000 soldiers in the rear guard, facing likely annihilation. Miraculously, St George, the patron saint of England, comes to their aid with English longbowmen from the Battle of Agincourt five centuries earlier. The German attackers at Mons fall to a rain of ghostly medieval arrows, leaving 10,000 dead with no visible wounds. The British soldiers of 1914 watch bewildered, but escape to fight another day.

Machen modestly declared his tale "an indifferent piece of work" ("Introduction", *The Bowmen* 11), and in normal circumstances it would surely have been forgotten as quickly as yesterday's newspapers. Instead, the winds of war fanned its reputation in the most extraordinary way. Soon his story was caught up in the controversy over a legend that sprang to life in the following months. It was said that an angel, or many angels, had appeared and held off the German advance so the British could extricate themselves from this hellish corner.

There are analogues for "The Bowmen" and the Angels of Mons in Tolkien's work: revenants and angels who appear in time of war and intervene to aid the weak against the strong, the defender against the invader, good against evil, and the medieval against the quasi-modern. There are also older epic and legendary analogues for both Machen's and Tolkien's stories of supernatural intervention. I will reserve for a later study the question of direct reference or influence. Here, I will use Machen's story and its resultant myth simply as a closely contemporary measure of Tolkien's aims and achievements in the revenant elements of his legendarium prior to *The Lord of the Rings*.

Machen's ambition was small: to entertain and uplift newspaper readers in September 1914. Tolkien's was much greater: "to make a body of more or less connected legend" which he could dedicate to England (*Letters* 144) – often characterised as a wish to create "a mythology for England." Neither writer aimed for his imaginings to be mistaken for something that really happened. Yet each writer in his way exceeded his ambitions. Machen's story birthed a legend which a vocal (and apparently significant) proportion of his compatriots actually believed. Tolkien's "mythology for England" became largely unmoored from English history and culture, acquiring fairly global appeal in the process. His work succeeds superlatively in inviting readers to experience his stories *as if* they are true. Were Tolkien's legendarium and the Bowmen/Angels stories, born at the same time, vivified by similar contemporary imaginative needs? Do the ingredients that made the Angels of Mons a focus of impassioned belief also help to explain Tolkien's extraordinary power of commanding what he called "secondary belief"? Was he solely aiming at achieving "secondary belief", or did he want any of the revenant elements in his legendarium to provoke doubt and disbelief, as the Angels of Mons legend often did?

Scope

"The Bowmen" and the Mons legend usefully determine the scope of this survey and history of Tolkien's supernatural interventions. The short story and the legend both feature epiphanies, that is, miraculous manifestations by supernatural beings, in aid of people who otherwise look set to lose a battle and perhaps a war. "The Bowmen" features the reappearance of mortals who have died, whether as ghosts (the archers) or as a sanctified being (St George); revenants in the etymological sense of beings who come back. Such sanctified former mortals are the Christian equivalent of the classical demigods translated to the night sky as stars or constellations, such as Castor and Pollux. Quite distinct in nature are the angels of the Mons legend. These were never mortals; they come from the ranks of the eternal divine. Notably, they seem to come from the lowest ranks of the traditional angelological hierarchy: not the archangels but the *angeloi* ('messengers') who traditionally have most dealings with humankind.

These categories overlap almost perfectly with interventions that Tolkien himself would term supernatural. Although he called it "a dangerous and difficult word in any of its senses, looser or stricter," his own practical interpretation of *supernatural* can be grasped easily enough. In his essay 'On Fairy-stories' he writes that "to fairies it can hardly be applied, unless *super* is taken merely as a superlative prefix. For it is man who is, in contrast to fairies, supernatural [...] whereas they are natural, far more natural than he. Such is their doom" (*OFS* 28). He means that fairies, however long they might live, can only exist within the world; whereas after we mortals have died, our immortal souls leave this world for heaven or elsewhere.

Supernatural interventions in Tolkien's legendarium, therefore, are those conducted within the world by beings who essentially belong beyond it. We should consider two kinds of revenants: mortals who have passed from ordinary life into a sanctified existence (equivalent to St George or to figures in classical myth immortalised as demigods or celestial bodies); and mortals who have died and have not been sanctified (equivalent to the Agincourt archers at Mons). For the purposes of this paper, I will not consider divine creatures from before Time.

Young Tolkien

Tolkien's interest in stories of supernatural intervention in battle predates Machen's tale by several years. It was an important aspect of the kind of story he liked most, "heroic legend on the brink of fairy-tale and history, of which there is far too little in the world [...] for my appetite" (*Letters* 144). The interface between the supernatural and the real in 'heroic legend' is exactly where such interventions most often occur.

In Tolkien's most formative and intense early friendship, he and Christopher Wiseman had called themselves "the Great Twin Brethren". It was a reference to Castor and Pollux (Greek Polydeuces), the inseparable divine twins known as the Dioscuri; who, after transformation into the two brightest stars in the constellation Gemini, reappeared at the Battle of Lake Regillus in the 5th century BC to help save Rome from the Tarquins.[1] The epithet comes from Lord Macaulay's "The Battle of Lake Regillus", passages of which were learnt by rote at Tolkien's school by boys competing in the annual prize recital (Burns 15).

Doubtless Tolkien was familiar with well-known instances where more recent history and the supernatural mingle: how the pagan Emperor Constantine saw a cross in the sky before winning the Battle of Milvian Bridge outside Rome in 312 AD, and converted to Christianity; how, in William of Malmesbury's account, saints George and Demetrius saved besieged Crusaders from a Saracen onslaught at Antioch in 1098; how Joan of Arc turned the wind in favour of boats bringing provisions to besieged Orléans in 1429; how a phantom army appeared aloft at the English Civil War's 1642 Battle of Edgehill and turned its outcome against the king. Introducing "The Battle of Lake Regillus", Macaulay notes how St James was said to have appeared on a grey horse at the head of Cortes's conquistador forces in Mexico (108).

As for ghosts, Tolkien was already sufficiently interested before the war to propose two motions about them in debates at Exeter College, Oxford. Whether in earnest or not, he made the case in 1913 that "This House believes in ghosts." His 15 June 1912 proposal "That a belief in ghosts is essential to the welfare of a people" (Garth, *Tolkien at Exeter* 15; Scull and Hammond 40), seems to foreshadow his wish that England should have a folklore to compare with Finland's *Kalevala*,[2] and his own ambition to compose a mythology dedicated to his own country (*Letters* 144).

1 I am grateful to Jessica Yates for alerting me to the origin of this epithet.
2 "The Kalevala", typescript draft from the immediate post-war years, *Kullervo* 105.

Machen's 'The Bowmen'

Tolkien was surely aware of Machen's tale of ghostly revenants at Mons sooner or later. Odds are good that he read "The Bowmen" at some point – it was reprinted widely during the war.[3] The plot would surely have piqued his curiosity, whatever he might have thought of the execution. Stories with bows and arrows had been a Tolkien favourite from childhood onwards (*OFS* 55), followed by the medievalism of William Morris and, just when Machen's story was becoming famous, by the supernatural in its broadest sense.

The direct inspiration for Machen's story was strictly contemporary. On 9 August, five days after Germany had invaded Belgium, the British Army sent 80,000 men to try to halt the advance. This was virtually all Britain's defensive strength, but on Sunday 23 August near Mons in Belgium it was overwhelmed by a German force four times its size. The British retreated almost 250 miles non-stop in two weeks. For the first week, there was a news blackout and newspapers peddled vague but patriotic guesswork. However, on Sunday 30 August *The Times* and the *Weekly Dispatch* broke the silence. The *Dispatch* report, under the headlines "Tidal Wave of German Troops – Need for the Country to Grasp the Danger" (Clarke 95), inspired sympathetic agonies in Machen.

Machen was also tapping consciously into two pre-existing narrative inspirations.

> First of all, all ages and nations have cherished the thought that spiritual hosts may come to the help of earthly arms, that gods and heroes and saints have descended from their high immortal places to fight for their worshippers and clients. Then Kipling's story of the ghostly Indian regiment got in my head and got mixed with the mediævalism that is always there [...]. (Machen, *The Bowmen*, 11)[4]

The result was a story of obliterating odds and claustrophobic terror that suddenly lifts in a moment of fantastic release:

> For as the Latin scholar uttered his invocation he felt something between a shudder and an electric shock pass through his body. The roar of the battle died down in his ears to a gentle murmur; instead of it, he says, he heard a great voice and a shout louder than a thunder-peal crying, "Array, array, array!"

---

3 When the story was anthologised in 1915 (with the subtitle *The Angels of Mons* more prominent than the title) its first impression of 50,000 copies was almost sold out within days. An expanded second edition appeared by the end of that year and world sales topped 100,000 (Clarke 158).

4 Rudyard Kipling's story is "The Lost Legion" (*Strand Magazine* and *New York Sun*, May 1892).

> His heart grew hot as a burning coal, it grew cold as ice within him, as it seemed to him that a tumult of voices answered to his summons. He heard, or seemed to hear, thousands shouting: "St. George! St. George!" [...]
>
> And as the soldier heard these voices he saw before him, beyond the trench, a long line of shapes, with a shining about them. They were like men who drew the bow, and with another shout, their cloud of arrows flew singing and tingling through the air towards the German hosts. (Machen, *The Bowmen*, 34-35)

Angels of Mons

In the Great War, the idea of supernatural intervention had wings. From 1915 it cannot be doubted that Tolkien knew about the Angels of Mons; and some interest must be presumed in a mind stirred in youth by "the Great Twin Brethren". That year, via print and word of mouth, everyone heard about it.

Debate raged over whether the Mons vision was real, a mass hallucination, or mere retrospective rumour sparked by Machen's September 1914 short story. It "reached an almost unbelievable array of people through whatever media were available" (Bleiler 2). Soldiers of the Somme, in which Tolkien fought in 1916, were trained by veterans of Mons, and by this means "the Angel of Mons" became for them "a catch-all phrase for a range of miraculous escapes from danger that were attributed to supernatural or divine forces" (195), according to historian David Clarke, to whose insightful 2004 account, *The Angel of Mons: Phantom Soldiers and Ghostly Guardians*, I am indebted.

Clarke argues that the news about the retreat from Mons had been so dire that it had "predisposed sections of society towards a belief that the British Expeditionary Force had only survived defeat *as a result of a miracle*" (89; his italics). "The Bowmen" delivered what such people sought. Machen had used the ghostly time-slip motif in previous stories, and there were ample precedents for crafting fiction to read like reportage; but *Evening News* readers knew him as a reporter (99-101). Soon numerous parish magazines were reprinting the story. Machen, asked by a Roman Catholic priest for the sources of his report, replied that "The Bowmen" was plain fiction, but was informed by the priest that he must be mistaken because it was obviously true (105). From the spring of 1915, in newspapers, pamphlets, books and gossip, soldiers and nurses who had been at Mons were quoted (almost always anonymously) as eyewitnesses to a divine vision of some sort. There were paintings and postcards showing the Angels of Mons; there were pieces of music inspired by it.

"Wild tarradiddles"

A thoroughly perplexed Machen, in the teeth of seemingly heartfelt claims from patriotic eyewitnesses, desperately tried to point out that actually his story had predated any rumours of angels. One article in the *Occult Review* of May 1915 caught his attention with its reference to "a row of shining beings," which he was sure derived from his own reference in "The Bowmen" to "a long line of shapes with a shining about them" (Sinnett, qtd. in Clarke 112-13).

The controversy made Machen's story famous. "It was as if I had touched the button and set in action a terrific, complicated mechanism of rumours that pretended to be the sworn truth, of gossip that posed as evidence, of wild tarradiddles that good men most firmly believed," he said (qtd. in Clarke 107). One of his articles ran under the headline "No escape from 'The Bowmen': My sympathy with Frankenstein" (Clarke 146).

Strict rationalists, such as C.S. Lewis's fearsomely sceptical private tutor W.T. Kirkpatrick, were considerably exercised. Young Lewis mischievously wrote home to his father, "the real subject to get him on just now is the Mons angels. You should drop him a cue in your next letter: you know – 'a man was telling me the other day that he had seen with his own eyes' or something of the kind" (Lewis, *Collected Letters* I.151).

Machen's own protests fell largely on deaf ears, or were actively dismissed. Some actually insisted Machen had written "The Bowmen" *because* he had heard the rumours of angels. Even a respected public figure such as G.K. Chesterton could characterise Machen's story as being "in line with many popular rumours" (166) rather than as their originator.

"Quickened to full life by war"

The legend of the Angels of Mons, in the view of Clarke, was the product of three influences: literary invention (by Machen); propaganda and lies (by promoters of the legend); and the backdrop of ancient tradition and folklore. It all added up to a "cauldron of belief and invention" (242). His words echo Tolkien's from *On Fairy-stories*: "Speaking of the history of stories and especially of fairy-stories we may say that the Pot of Soup, the Cauldron of Story, has always been boiling, and to it have continually been added new bits, dainty and undainty" (*OFS* 44-45).

Contemporaries and historians agree that the Great War was a period when new bits were thrown into the Cauldron of Story in unaccustomed quantities. Speaking of the Mons retreat, Chesterton wrote in 1915, "In that blackness began to grow strange emotions, long unfamiliar to our blood. Those six dark days are as full of legends as the six centuries of the Dark Ages" (165). During the war, French infantryman Marc Bloch witnessed "a prodigious renewal of oral tradition, the ancient mother of myths and legends" (qtd. in Clarke 12). Fussell, in his cultural survey *The Great War and Modern Memory*, writes: "the Great War seems especially fertile in rumor and legend. It was as if the general human impulse to make fictions had been dramatically unleashed by the novelty, immensity, and grotesqueness of the proceedings" (117).

The literary inventiveness of Machen and Tolkien in September 1914, the transformation of Machen's story into full-blown legend during the next years, and the simultaneous growth of Tolkien's legendarium, all bear out the power of war to make the imagination fertile. It does not fully elucidate Tolkien's later statement that for him "a real taste for fairy-stories was wakened by philology on the threshold of manhood, and quickened to full life by war" (*OFS* 56), but it does demonstrate that his transformation into a mythopoeic writer was part of a much wider phenomenon. Far more readily than in peacetime, during the Great War it was possible to stray into Faërie, defined as a world where wonders and the supernatural become as visible or palpable as reality.

St George

St George predominated in early accounts of the Mons vision, echoing Machen's story. An influential account by nurse Phyllis Campbell in the *Occult Review* begins with a wounded Lancashire Fusilier asking her for a picture of St George to confirm that this was whom he had seen. He is backed up by another soldier. "They both *knew* it was St George. Hadn't they seen him with his sword on every 'quid' they'd ever had?" (qtd. in Clarke 141).[5]

England's patron saint had been on the gold sovereign since 1817, depicted by Italian artist Benedetto Pistrucci as a naked horseman in the cloak and helm of a Greek soldier, riding triumphant over a fallen dragon. St George was said to have been a Greek soldier in the Roman army in the reign of Diocletian (284-305) and to have been martyred for refusing to recant his Christian faith. In the Anglo-Saxon Ælfric's *Lives of the Saints*, many attempts were made to torture and execute George, which only succeeded when he crossed himself and assented to be killed (Ælfric 306-19). His martyrdom became eclipsed by the story, popularised in *The Golden Legend* printed by William Caxton in 1483, of his dragon-slaying, which shows marked similarities with the myth of how Perseus rescued Andromeda from a sea-monster. In a 1938 lecture on dragons, Tolkien theorised that the slaying of "the symbolic dragon [...] a symbol of actual *evil*: a visible shape as it were of the Devil" was attached to St George because he "was probably a soldier, an officer in the army, so that this way of representing his sanctity may have seemed specially appropriate."[6]

Although the version of the Mons legend that ultimately dominated featured angels, the one that featured Saint George and his archers persisted, especially in the Catholic channels perhaps most likely to have reached Tolkien (Clarke 129). The Catholic *Universe*, quoting an unnamed Catholic officer, described a group of men making a desperate sortie with cries of "St George for England!" and then becoming conscious of "a large company of men with bows and arrows going along with them, and even leading them on against the enemy's

5 Campbell says other eyewitnesses included "officers of high rank, a Roman Catholic priest, and English and French soldiers" (qtd. in Clarke 141).
6 Bodleian Tolkien A 61, fols. 123-24.

trenches." A German prisoner asked them afterwards "who was the officer on a great white horse who led them?" (qtd. in Clarke 114).

In the Great War, every side thought it was in the right and many had their own stories of divine intervention. Russians saw St Michael the Archangel, the Virgin Mary, the infant Christ; the French saw Joan of Arc and St Michael (Clarke 65, 138). The editor of the *Occult Review* wondered "whether St Michael and St George were different interpretations, according to nationality, of the same apparition" (qtd. in Clarke 138). As Clarke notes, iconographically the two were similar: holy warrior who defeat highly symbolic dragons; symbolising Lucifer in the case of the Archangel Michael.

The eternal war

To many of Tolkien's compatriots, British efforts were divinely sanctioned, and for some it was not a significantly greater step to believe that they might also be divinely aided: that the Angels of Mons were a sign of God's wrath at atrocities by German soldiers in Belgium and France. In the *Occult Review*, Campbell said there were

> saints and angels fighting on this common earth, with common mortal men, against one devilish foe to all humanity. [...] The cries of mothers and little children, the suffering of crucified fathers and carbonized sons and brothers, the tortures of nuns and virgins, and violated wives and daughters, have all gone up in torment and dragged at the Ruler of the Universe for aid, and aid has come. (qtd. in Clarke 143)

Signs that Tolkien saw Germans as barbaric monsters around this time vanish after his return from the trenches (Garth, *Tolkien and the Great War* 218). More nuanced and probably more enduring was his 1916 opinion that the war was "for all the evil of our own side with large view good against evil" (*Letters* 10). The "large view" was the cosmic one. He wrote in 1944: "In real (exterior) life men are on both sides: which means a motley alliance of orcs, beasts, demons, plain naturally honest men, and angels" (*Letters* 82). The "real (exterior)" world was paralleled by an ideal (interior) or cosmic one in which honest men and angels were properly divided from orcs, beasts and demons. Against this backdrop, he accepted as a Catholic that the First World War was merely "back to normal" (*Letters* 393); and when the Second World War ended he said "Wars are always lost, and The War always goes on" (116). Such convictions shaped his fiction, in which earthly conflicts are an aspect of an eternal divine conflict: "an actual conscious reaction" against claims that the 1914-18 war would be "the war to end all wars." ("BBC Interview"). His stories of angelic or ghostly intervention emerge from this matrix: just as evil seems set to triumph in the world, aid may come from beyond.

Eärendel de-sanctified

Yet in the early years of his work on his legendarium, there is a near-absence of the kind of divine intervention seen in "The Battle of Lake Regillus", "The Bowmen" or the Mons legend, where supernatural beings suddenly appear during battle to help or inspire the righteous.

Considering how Machen's bowmen were transmogrified into Angels of Mons, it is ironic that in creating his 1914 Éarendel, Tolkien turned an angel into a non-angel. In the lines from the Anglo-Saxon poem *Crist I* which inspired him, *Éarendel* is the morning star, *engla beorhtast* ("brightest of angels"), allegorically portending the advent of Christ as Venus portends the sunrise. But in June Tolkien had been reading a book of Germanic philology which hypothesised the pre-Christian Germanic hero underlying Éarendel and various Norse and German legendary figures with related names, all linked either with stars or sea.[7] It was this ur-hero Tolkien was trying to imagine in 1914, so he specifically stripped away the Christian, angelic aspects to create his star-mariner.

It has not been asked why Tolkien made his Éarendel the evening star rather than the morning star of *Crist*. Astronomical as well as philological considerations may help explain this, and much more. From early August, Tolkien spent about a fortnight in Cornwall, on the Lizard peninsula, which gives uninterrupted views westward over the Atlantic. On clear evenings just as the sun set, Venus appeared above the sea, the brightest object in the western sky,

7 Symons 62-63. See also Garth, "The Road from Adaptation to Invention" 14.

and sinking exactly due west into the waves after an hour and a half.[8] In the poem, likewise, Éarendel appears above "the Ocean's cup," speeds away "from Westerland" and travels "Down the sunlit breath of Day's fiery death." It would seem that for Tolkien, Venus in the west had been something to contemplate as war erupted far behind him in the east.

Accordingly, his poem looks away from war where Machen's story looks towards it. Far from sharing Machen's aim of inspiring communal courage against the enemy, Tolkien's aims seem to have been to experiment in myth-making; to celebrate a self-consciously individual quest for beauty; and hence, indeed, to map a trajectory away from service for his country in the war. Resisting enormous peer pressure to enlist in the Army at this point, Tolkien had determined to complete his Oxford degree. As I have argued in *Tolkien and the Great War* (45-47), "The Voyage of Éarendel the Evening Star" is a narrative to suit his predicament. As the planet Venus, the adventurer follows a wayward path contrary to that of the fixed stars, defying regimentation. Éarendel is aware of the sorrows of "the folk of earth," but only as he leaves them behind (*LT II* 269).[9]

When Tolkien built a legendarium around this first hero, the imagined world soon became a world at war, and in the 1917 battle story "The Fall of Gondolin" Eärendel's birth is "the fulfilment [...] of the desire of the Valar and the hope of the Eldalië [Elves]," as if Tolkien had some special role for him (*LT II* 165). "The Fall of Gondolin" had mapped the growth of Eärendel's father, Tuor, from self-indulgent wanderer (and wonderer) to emissary bearing the sea-god Ulmo's message to the city of Gondolin to prepare for war; so we might reasonably expect even more of the prodigal son.

8 Tolkien's letters show the visit spanned at least 5-16 August. The moon, full on 6 August, was low on the opposite horizon. I used Stellarium software and thank Andrew McMurry for further advice. Often cloudy or overcast at first, the weather improved considerably, apart from a thunderstorm on the night of 14-15 August (monthly weather report of the Meteorological Office, August 1914, Met Office website).

9 If we accept that the volunteer-fever of 1914 coloured Tolkien's first mythological poem in this way, it can be seen to share a point of origin with "The Bowmen". The news articles about the retreat from Mons that inspired Machen to write, by stressing both the courage and the terrible vulnerability of the retreating British, were also what inspired the biggest surge of volunteers at Army recruiting offices – a third of a million men on 3 September alone, and almost a million in all by the end of the year (Clarke 88).

Yet Tolkien's notes for the never-written "great tale of Eärendel" (*LT II* 242) suggest a very personal odyssey for the mariner. He sails west only to seek Tuor or his own wife Elwing. Reaching the city of Kôr, he finds its Elves have marched off to aid their war-beleaguered cousins. Eventually, shining from the dust of gems on the streets of Kôr, he soars into the sky, apparently still in search of Elwing. He seems cursed, like a celestial Flying Dutchman, to endless lonely wandering. The broad shape of his actions were set, but they remained empty of the significance Tolkien would later give them, having as yet no relation to the fictional war.[10] His defeat of the Spider of Night – never fully recounted but suggesting a symbolic conquest over despair – gives the only glimmer of what Eärendel would come to represent.

Perhaps a sense of irony and disenchantment, so widespread culturally after the Great War, restrains this early version of Eärendel. Perhaps the star-mariner simply could not yet escape from his origins as a representation of personal longing, facing away from war. For many years after Tolkien abandoned *The Book of Lost Tales*, at any rate, Eärendel remained disconnected from war and simultaneously free of most marks of divinity. His big moment took a long time coming.

The dead that live

Glimmers of the kind of divine role Eärendel lacks first appear in the early "Tale of Tinúviel", the story closest to Tolkien's heart, inspired by a moment when his wife Edith danced in a spring glade the year after the Somme. Tinúviel is half-divine; her lover Beren is touched with sanctity through her and through the daring recovery from Melko of one of the stolen Silmarils, three jewels preserving "holy" light (*LT II* 34). When Beren dies of wounds, Tinúviel's grief sways Mandos, the Vala of doom, to permit the two to return to the world as "the dead that live again," though now with mortal lifespans (41).

It is therefore as a sanctified revenant that Beren carries out his last act of heroism, leading a host of elven archers to ambush the dwarf Naugladur, who has murdered Tinúviel's father and looted the Silmaril:

10 Cf. Christopher Tolkien's comments, *LT II* 257, 265.

> Suddenly is all that place filled with the sound of elfin horns, and one [?brays] with a clearer blast above the rest, and it is the horn of Beren, the huntsman of the woods. Then is the air thick with the slender arrows of the Eldar that err not neither doth the wind bear them aside, and lo, from every tree and boulder do the brown Elves and the green spring suddenly and loose unceasingly from full quivers. Then was there a panic and a noise in the host of Naugladur [...] but many were stricken with those pitiless darts and fell [...] and thus got the Eldar few hurts and the Dwarf-folk fell dead unceasingly. (*LT II* 237)

Beren's revenant status makes the c. 1919 episode an analogue, in a way, to the miraculous intervention of St George and the archers at Mons. But this could be a coincidence, a case of Tolkien, Machen and some of the promulgators of the Mons legend tapping into some of the same time-honoured narrative elements. More significant are the differences. I do not mean the trappings of bows and arrows and forests, drawn from the Tolkien's youthful fascination with stories of "Red Indians" (*OFS* 55), so much as the strategic scenario: an ambush of a caravan that is quite remote from a war-setting.

Revenant and angel

An angel and a revenant play the climactic role in battle, however, in Tolkien's next attempt to recount the full legendarium. This 1926 "Sketch of the Mythology" (written to explain his mythology to an old schoolmaster) ends with two divine military showdowns: the War of Wrath that overthrows Morgoth in his stronghold at Angband; and then, foretold in prophecy, the Last Battle of the world, when Morgoth will return.[11] Then, he will ultimately be defeated by two figures: Fionwë, a lesser Vala; and Túrin Turambar, a mortal dragonslayer who has returned from death. It will bring the renewal of the world in fairer form, like the Norse Ragnarök; with youth restored to all who live, and life to all who have died.

A personal note continues to undercut the full orchestral force Tolkien might have marshalled. In dealing Morgoth his death-blow, Túrin is said to avenge both himself and his sister, whose lives Morgoth had blighted; but the "Sketch"

---

11 For clarity and convenience, I adopt the name "the War of Wrath" from 1937 "Quenta Silmarillion" for the defeat of Morgoth at Angband, and "the Last Battle" for the end-of-the-world conflict. The "Sketch" calls both "the Last Battle" (*SM* 39, 40-41).

says nothing of justice for the other multitudes who suffered under Morgoth's evil. With Túrin, it was always personal, and the motive is true to Tolkien's sources for him: grim lone Germanic heroes and the troubled, troublesome Kullervo of the Finnish *Kalevala*. The earlier segment of the "Sketch" retelling Eärendel's story also retains the mariner's purely personal motivations, together with the broad shape of his voyage (west and into the sky), his dissociation from the war with Morgoth, and the downbeat narrative trajectory (*SM* 37-38). All this happens before the War of Wrath.

In an afterthought right at the end of the "Sketch", however, Tolkien inserted a new stage into Eärendel's story which radically reconfigures him. After the War of Wrath, the Valar give the mariner one of the three stolen jewels recovered from Morgoth and then launch his ship into the sky a second time. "There he sails with the Silmaril upon his brow and Elwing at his side, the brightest of all stars [...]" (*SM* 40-41).[12]

Eärendel re-sanctified

Shining now like a star because of a light at his brow, Eärendel seems to guide us back to Tolkien's youthful favourites, the Dioscuri, generally depicted with stars above their heads in classical iconography; or the star as a sign of apotheosis, seen from the death of Julius Caesar onwards.[13]

A saviour needs a public motive, and Eärendel finally developed one in the next version of the mythology, the "Qenta Noldorinwa", written c. 1930-31. Eärendel's voyage west had always been a personal odyssey but now Eärendel has an additional motive that is altruistic and self-abnegating: to bring "ere he died a message to the Gods and Elves of the West, that should move their hearts to pity on the world and the sorrows of Mankind" (*SM* 149). At last, some 17 years after Tolkien first breathed life into Eärendel, the star-mariner

12 Christopher Tolkien's commentary (71-72) on how the Silmaril reaches Eärendel does not make plain that this seems an afterthought. But the "Sketch" narrates the second, hallowed sky-launch of Eärendel with his Silmaril *after* the recounting of the "last battle of all" and the ultimate destruction of the Silmarils (40-41).

13 I am extremely grateful to Sherrylyn Branchaw for a long and enriching discussion on these points, which I hope will bear fruit more fully elsewhere.

acquired the kind of purpose his father Tuor had developed in a few pages of the "The Fall of Gondolin".

Even so, in "Qenta Noldorinwa" Eärendel arrives "too late to bring messages to the Elves, for the Elves had gone" (*SM* 150). He remains a heroic failure; and the old downbeat narrative of his first voyage into the sky before the War of Wrath remains.

The star-mariner's significance, however, was soon to undergo a final metamorphosis. The end of "Qenta Noldorinwa" was rewritten, Eärendel's story substantially.

In the revised "Qenta Noldorinwa", the Silmaril that had been recovered by Beren and Lúthien is brought to Eärendel by their granddaughter, Elwing. Thus "the puissance of that holy jewel" helps bring the mariner to the "immortal shores alone of living Men" (153). When he carries it into the city of Kôr he is addressed by Fionwë: "Hail Eärendel, star most radiant, messenger most fair!" (154). The words closely echo the Anglo-Saxon *Crist*:

Éala éarendel, engla beorhtast
ofer middangeard monnum sended

"Hail Éarendel, brightest of angels, over Middle-earth sent unto men."[14] Fionwë's words continue in the same style, but the substance is all Tolkien's. Eärendel is no longer just the evening star, but he is morning star too: "Star of the sunset hail! Hail herald of the morn!" It is a neat piece of chiasmus: twin sentences meeting in twin salutation. But Fionwë's word *messenger* is doubly significant because English *angel* derives from Greek *ἄγγελος* (phonetically *ángelos*) "a messenger". Forbidden by the Valar to return to his kin in mortal lands (154), Eärendel will be a messenger in the same way as the *engla beorhtast* in *Crist*.

In the ensuing narrative, the raising of his ship into the firmament by "power divine" as a hallowed vessel takes place before the War of Wrath, not after it; so that "the folk of earth [...] looked up from despair" to see the Silmaril's "holy flame" (154, 164).[15] Here, then, Eärendel's star is a divine sign of the same

14 Note that Tolkien did not yet refer to the mortal lands of his legendarium as "Middle-earth".
15 *SM* 154, 164. This rewritten "Qenta Noldorinwa" dispenses with the idea that Eärendel had already sailed into the sky for his own personal purposes.

species as the cross seen by Constantine at Milvian; and it guides the armies from Valinor to overthrow Morgoth at Angband (154-55). It justifies Fionwë's words that Eärendel is "the looked-for that comest unawares, the longed-for that comest beyond hope!" Tolkien later coined a term for the kind of sudden, poignant narrative uplift provided by Eärendel's new story: *eucatastrophe*, "the good catastrophe, the sudden joyous 'turn'" restoring hope of deliverance from "sorrow and failure" (*OFS* 75).

Eärendel is also now transfigured into a divine saviour, so that Fionwë's description of him as "thou slayer of the dark" takes on both metaphorical and literal significance. As battle rages around Angband, the star-mariner comes "shining with white flame" and slays Ancalagon, greatest of flying dragons (*SM* 160).

In the rewritten ending of the "Qenta Noldorinwa", Tolkien also at last defined the end-of-the-world role he seems to have envisaged for the Silmaril-wearing star-mariner in his afterthought at the end of the 1926 "Sketch". In the Last Battle at the end of days, the Vala Fionwë is no longer mentioned; but the pairing of angel and revenant is retained. Now it is the angelic Eärendel who, by driving Morgoth down from the skies, participates with Túrin in the enemy's final defeat. The heroism of the revenant Túrin in dealing Morgoth's death, meanwhile, acquires universal purpose, for "so shall the children of Húrin *and all Men* be avenged" (165; my italics).

Disenchantment and re-enchantment

In "Qenta Noldorinwa", it is said that Elves who are slain may eventually live again in Valinor; but the fate of mortal Men after death provides nothing equivalent to this, nor to the Christian assurance of eternal life. Their spirits are said to pass to a kind of limbo, but "Mandos under Ilúvatar knew alone whither they went after the time in his wide halls beyond the western sea" (*SM* 100). The situation for mortals in the legendarium at this stage, then, might be summed up in words recounted by Bede in his *Ecclesiastical History of England*: "like to the swift flight of a sparrow through the house [...] in at one door and immediately out at another [...] from winter into winter again. So this life of man appears for a little while, but of what is to follow or what went before we know nothing at all" (117). In such darkness, all deeds might be in vain. "Qenta Noldorinwa" was effectively the debut for the full story of the Battle of Unnumbered Tears, as Christopher Tolkien notes (*SM* 179): a military botch in which hope crumbles in irony. Through the work as a whole, the mounting toll of destruction, loss and despair is almost relentless.

To a surprising degree, this makes common ground between Tolkien's legendarium around 1930 and a new wave of writers with a disenchanted view of the Great War. A decade's near-silence about the Great War had been followed by a flood of works in which horrors were recounted unsparingly, inherited values of heroism were severely thrown into question, and bitter irony ramped at large, seeming to render the whole war a fruitless shambles.[16] But the new version of the Great War, a world apart from 1914 and Machen's "The Bowmen", certainly had no room on its battlefields for saints, revenant archers or angels. As signs that the earthly war conformed with the eternal one between good and evil, such interventions were the literary guarantors of the very values that the disenchanted war writers would deny.

Tolkien's views demonstrably did not equate with those of the new, disenchanted war writers. In 1944 he wrote that the "utter stupid waste of war [...] is so staggering to those who have to endure it. And always was (despite the poets), and always will be (despite the propagandists) – not of course that it has not is and will be necessary to face it in an evil world" (*Letters* 75). There is no reason to think his views were any different in c. 1931, when "the poets" (the new war writers) were in the ascendant; nor in 1914-18, when the propagandists had been. Tolkien evidently felt that both the disenchanted writers and the wartime propagandists were wrong, but that there was a middle way, a balance.

With the transformation in Eärendel's story, "Qenta Noldorinwa" finally acquires the epic redemptive uplift without which it would be almost unbearable. It is the

16 R.C. Sheriff's play *Parade's End* ran for 594 consecutive performances from December 1928; Erich Maria Remarque's *All Quiet on the Western Front*, published in English in 1929, sold 300,000 copies in six months (Poplawski 511). Also influential were Robert Graves' *Goodbye to All That*, and Richard Aldington's *Death of a Hero*, both 1929; Frederic Manning's novel *The Middle Parts of Fortune* and Siegfried Sassoon's *Memoirs of an Infantry Officer*, both 1930; movies of *All Quiet* and *Journey's End* that same year; and a new edition of Wilfred Owen's poetry in 1931. I have discussed the general relationship between Tolkien's work and this literature of disenchantment and irony at length in the "Postscript" to *Tolkien and the Great War*, but I did not set out there to trace Tolkien's post-war development in any detail.

moment when the phenomenon I have observed elsewhere becomes a keystone of Tolkien's writing: through *eucatastrophe* he "makes despair or 'disenchantment' the prelude to a redemptive restoration of meaning" (Garth, *Tolkien and the Great War* 305). But this is not simply an artistic flourish. The changes to the end of "Qenta Noldorinwa" have deeper ramifications.

In the initial version, the Valar send an army against Morgoth simply because a Vala, Ulmo, demands it (*SM* 149); the divine intervention is *deus ex machina*. Eärendel reaches the immortal shores after the army has set forth; his good deeds are in vain and so, it might be felt, are those of all who ever fought Morgoth. In the revised version, the Valar intervene because Eärendel has crossed a perilous, spell-barred ocean and persuaded them to do so; his good deeds bear fruit, and so, therefore, do those of the many whose actions have gone before – not least Beren and Lúthien in recovering the Silmaril he carries. Eärendel's appearance with that Silmaril as a star in the sky is a sign visible to all that everything has not been in vain. It is a divine guarantor of meaning and a sign that a divinity shapes our ends.

The joyous turn

It is also a symbol of life beyond death. The transformation of Eärendel's story can probably be related to the last work on the "Lay of Leithian" in mid-September 1931 when Tolkien described the recovery by Lúthien and Beren of a "holy Silmaril", one of the three "gems of fate", from Morgoth's crown. Whether this scene was composed before or after the end of "Qenta Noldorinwa" was rewritten seems beyond proof, but they were closely contemporary.[17] The Lay profoundly deepened the sense of moment and sanctity surrounding this Silmaril. It is a poor fit for the unrevised "Qenta Noldorinwa" version of the jewel's ultimate fate, to be cast into the sea by Elwing in despair; but an excellent match for the revised version, in which the Silmaril becomes Eärendel's

17 *LB* 296, 307. That the rewritten "Q II" ending of "Qenta Noldorinwa" (§§16-19) was made around the time the "Lay of Leithian" was abandoned is evident from the name Tolkien used for the region of the wars with Morgoth. It was still called *Broseliand* in "Qenta Noldorinwa" §12 (*SM* 125 n3); and in an outline for a segment of "Leithian" written in September 1930 ("Synopsis V"; see *LB* 312). But it was written as *Beleriand* in "Qenta Noldorinwa" §13 onwards (*SM* 131 n10), and in the "Leithian" scene in Morgoth's throne room written in mid-September 1931 (*LB* 304, notes to lines 3957 and 4085).

star. This places Eärendel's transformation close to the time of the now-famous conversation of 19 September 1931 in which Tolkien persuaded C.S. Lewis to accept the incarnation of Christ as truth.

Initiation into Tolkien's legendarium and close friendship had happened at a stroke when Lewis read and approved the "Lay of Leithian" in 1929. Also a Great War veteran, Lewis had gone to war an atheist and yet in its immediate wake had contrived to lose his only faith – in the romance and myth that had fed his spirit and imagination since childhood. "No more Avalon, no more Hesperides. I had [...] 'seen through' them. And I was never going to be taken in again" (Lewis, *Surprised by Joy* 204). By the mid-1920s Lewis had opened his heart again to the ancient idea of the undying west, and to all of the myth, romance and ineffable "Joy" they represented for him. From late 1929 Tolkien's imagination seems to have been feeding Lewis's appetite. Tolkien recalled that he "read all or a considerable part of my 'mythology'" and "was for long my only audience" (*Letters* 361-62).[18] "Qenta Noldorinwa" was doubtless written very much with Lewis in mind.[19] It may be no coincidence that from autumn 1931, Tolkien's primary audience had a Christian hunger to assuage.

The notions of mythic death and return to life were central to Tolkien's case in the conversation that 19 September, as Lewis recorded it: "the idea of the dying and reviving god (Balder, Adonis, Bacchus) [...] moved me provided I met it anywhere *except* in the Gospels. [...] Now the story of Christ is simply a true myth: a myth working on us in the same way as the others, but with this tremendous difference that *it really happened*" (Lewis, *Collected Letters* I.977, italics in original). Tolkien helped Lewis look at the pagan myths in a new way: they were "the first, faint whisper of the wind from beyond the world," as Lewis characterised the Christian gospel (Lewis, *Collected Letters* II.12-13).

The ideas Tolkien shared with Lewis that night would have enriched the return of Beren and Lúthien as "the dead that live" in the "Lay of Leithian" – if the long poem had ever reached that point. But in the "Qenta Noldorinwa" the restoration

18 *Cf. Letters* 378, "we provided one another with stories to hear or read that we really liked." On claims by both men that Lewis did not influence Tolkien, see Glyer, *passim*.

19 He had written its predecessor, the "Sketch of the Mythology", explicitly "to explain background" of his long alliterative "Lay of the Children of Húrin" to another reader, his former schoolteacher R.W. Reynolds (*SM* 11).

of Eärendel to angelhood and his divine interventions in battle represent both a powerful resanctification of his mythology and a demonstration of his key argument to Lewis. The addition of the star-mariner's defeat of Ancalagon the dragon is otherwise rather incongruous: the slaying of the Spider of Night had always been Eärendel's defining moment in combat, whereas the legendarium's prime act of dragon-slaying belonged to Túrin in his defeat of Glorund. But in view of Tolkien's arguments about myth providing glimpses of the "true myth", Eärendel's defeat of Ancalagon at the War of Wrath can be read as a glimpse of the biblical end-of-the-world victory over Satan, "the dragon, that old serpent" of Revelations 20.2. Thus, in reworking his legendarium around the end of 1931, Tolkien focused particularly on earthly equivalents of "the dying and reviving god," seemingly to illustrate what he told Lewis that September: that pagan myth could be a glimpse of the "true myth" of Christianity.

Eärendel and the Forgotten

Eärendel's significance grew apace with the sudden enlargement of the legendarium, around the end of 1936, to encompass a further era, a new land, and a deeper concern with the mortal condition of humankind.[20] "The Fall of Númenor" tells how "kings of the seed of Eärendel" rule this isle given to "Men of the three faithful houses" who had aided the Elves against Morgoth.[21] As far as patron saints can exist in Tolkien's legendarium, the star-mariner is Númenor's (and like England's St George, he is a dragon-slayer).

The starkness of Eärendel's own situation becomes more apparent, too, in Tolkien's 1936-37 writings. For the first time, Tolkien reveals in "The Fall of Númenor" that it is an error to think Elves live forever and Men do not. The Elves' fate is "an end within the world," but Men have no end and their fate "is not within the world" (*LR* 18). The 1937 "Quenta Silmarillion" (written to replace "Qenta Noldorinwa") reveals that the half-elven Eärendel and Elwing are allowed "to choose freely under which kindred they shall be judged" (327). Eärendel chooses to be judged an Elf only because Elwing has done so. Thus

20 For dating of "The Fall of Númenor" and "The Lost Road", see Garth, "When Tolkien Reinvented Atlantis".

21 *LR* 26, 24. These quotations are from the second version, FN II, closely associated with 1937's "Lost Road" and no doubt written at the same time.

his fate remains bound within the world even while he is permanently separated from everything in it, shining above like an everlasting beacon but apparently cut off from true eternal life.

Marking a shift from an Elf-centred to a human-centred legendarium, the Númenor narrative is the first of Tolkien's writings to be primarily concerned with the mortal condition. Envy of elven immortality is exploited by Morgoth's former lieutenant, Sauron, to engineer the Númenóreans' destruction. In the unfinished 1937 Númenor story "The Lost Road", the legend of Eärendel himself is twisted into a noose for them: Sauron's propaganda asserts that the mariner's example shows the Númenóreans can become immortal by stepping ashore in Valinor.

As Christopher Tolkien comments, when his father reached back to the time of Númenor/Atlantis, "he found there an image of what he most condemned and feared in his own" (*LR* 77). Since writing the most powerful version of his mythology in 1931 or so, he had seen European civilisation fall prey to demagogues who twisted history and myth to execrable ends.

In the event, according to "The Fall of Númenor", those Númenóreans who do set foot in Valinor suffer an ironic inversion of Eärendel's fate: they are "buried under fallen hills, where legend saith that they lie imprisoned in the Forgotten Caves until the day of Doom and the Last Battle" (*LR* 16). They are sequestered from their kin until the end of the world, but buried under earth, not uplifted in the sky; hidden in darkness, not illuminating it.

The story also inverts European traditions of sleeping warriors who will return to aid their nations in time of war; traditions typically embodied in British tradition in King Arthur, *rex quondam, rexque futurus*, "the once and future king."[22] Tolkien wrote much later that under the immutable laws governing mortals in his legendarium "the return of Arthur would be quite impossible, a vain imagining" (*Letters* 199). Whether indeed the Númenóreans in the Caves of the Forgotten have achieved immortality in some version of living death or have become ghosts, we are not told. It is all "legend". Like the Angels of

22 "The Caves of the Forgotten" is the phrase in FN II, *LR* 27.

Mons, they are revenants who may exist or may amount to nothing more than "a vain imagining".

In the two decades since the Mons legend first took off, it had remained a cultural point of reference. The Spanish Civil War had brought at least one new rumoured instance of a saintly intervention: the appearance of St Teresa of Ávila, who lived in the 16th century, to block Republican troops advancing on her town with atrocity in mind in 1936.[23] In 1939, the Mons angels were being cited in medical literature about "war neuroses" ("Neuroses in War-time" 126). When the Second World War provided a new crop of supernatural claims, the precedent of the Angels of Mons was always wheeled out, as evidence of the claims' truth or falsehood alike.

This prominent element of myth distorted and legend unverifiable does not mean, however, that Tolkien's overarching mythological narrative was to be rejected out of hand. That would explode the legendarium completely, signalling a surrender by Tolkien to disenchantment. Rather, the distortions and blurred edges help to provide the legendarium with its patina of reality. They are not a hindrance to "secondary belief" but an aid to it.

Tolkien's description of eucatastrophe as *evangelium*, "good news", situates fairy-story in the context of the eternal war in which final victory is vouchsafed, whatever failures or sufferings may lie ahead in the story or in day-to-day reality. In his drafts from 1943 Tolkien called the glimpse of Joy a "breaking through to the source-reality [...] usually caused by a Triumph of Right, of eternal Justice, of Good (or its representatives) over evil (and its representatives)" (*OFS* 246). In a 1944 letter he illustrated his concept of eucatastrophe with what he considered a real miracle – the sudden return to health of a dying boy – showing that "the apparent Anankê [compulsion] of this world" is not immutable; and "that this is indeed how things really do work in the Great World for which our nature is made" (*Letters* 100-01).

By robbing multitudes of their freedom, loved ones and lives, war is a condition of "compulsion" *par excellence*. It is surely no coincidence that Tolkien introduced eucatastrophe and *evangelium* into "On Fairy-stories" in 1943, in the

23 Cardozo 64-65.

midst of war. His drafts and revisions to the lecture in 1943 deal profoundly with the need for consolation, recovery and a sense of everlasting justice. It was also in 1943 that he recorded how, for him as young man, a "real taste for fairy-stories was [...] quickened to full life by war" (*OFS* 56). Those same needs, which fuelled the growth of legends such as the Angels of Mons, and fuelled his youthful invention of a mythology, continued to animate Tolkien's creativity in *The Lord of the Rings*.

Bibliography

BEDE. *Ecclesiastical History of England*, trans. A.M. Sellar. London: George Bell & Sons, 1907.

BLEILER, Richard J. *The Strange Case of "The Angels of Mons": Arthur Machen's World War I Story, the Insistent Believers, and His Refutations.* Jefferson, NC: McFarland, 2015.

BURNS, Maggie. "Commentary: 'The Battle of the Eastern Field.'" *Mallorn* 46 (2008): 15-22.

CARDOZO, Harold G. *The March of a Nation: My Year of Spain's Civil War.* New York City, NY: Robert M. McBride, 1937.

CHESTERTON, G.K. *The Crimes of England*. London: Cecil Palmer & Hayward, 1915. US edition (New York City, NY: John Lane, 1916) online at https://archive.org/stream/crimesofengland00ches.

CLARKE, David. *The Angel of Mons: Phantom Soldiers and Ghostly Guardians.* Chichester: Wiley, 2004.

FUSSELL, Paul. *The Great War and Modern Memory.* Oxford University Press, 1975.

GARTH, John. "'The Road from Adaptation to Invention': How Tolkien Came to the Brink of Middle-earth in 1914." *Tolkien Studies* 11 (2014): 1-44.

Tolkien and the Great War: The Threshold of Middle-earth. London: HarperCollins, 2003.

Tolkien at Exeter College: How an Oxford Undergraduate Created Middle-earth. Oxford: Exeter College, 2014.

"When Tolkien reinvented Atlantis and Lewis went to Mars." John Garth blog, https://johngarth.wordpress.com/2017/03/31/when-tolkien-reinvented-atlantis-and-lewis-went-to-mars/. 31 March 2017.

Glyer, Diana. *The Company They Keep: C.S. Lewis and J.R.R. Tolkien as Writers in Community.* Kent, OH: Kent State University Press, 2007.

Lewis, C.S. *Collected Letters, vol. 1: Family Letters 1905-1931.* London: HarperCollins, 2004.

Collected Letters, vol. 2: Books, Broadcasts and War, 1931-1949. London: HarperCollins, 2004.

Surprised by Joy. New York City, NY: Harcourt, 1956.

Macaulay. *Lays of Ancient Rome.* London: Thomas Nelson, 1908. Online at https://archive.org/stream/laysofancientrom00macauoft.

Machen, Arthur. *The Bowmen and Other Legends of the War: The Angels of Mons.* London: Simpkin, Marshall, Hamilton, Kent and Co., 1915. https://archive.org/stream/angelsofmonsbowm00machuoft.

"Neuroses in War-Time: Course of Lectures at the Tavistock Clinic." *British Medical Journal*, 21 January 1939: 126-128.

Poplawski, Paul. "The Twentieth Century, 1901-1939." *English Literature in Context.* Ed. Paul Poplawski. Cambridge: Cambridge University Press, 2017, 470-532.

Scull, Christina and Wayne G. Hammond. *The J.R.R. Tolkien Companion and Guide.* Rev. & exp. ed. Boston, MA: Houghton Mifflin, 2017. v.3: Chronology.

Symons, Barend. "Heldensage." *Grundriss der germanischen Philologie*, vol. 2, part 1. Ed. Hermann Paul (1-64). Strassburg: Trübner, 1893.

Tolkien, J.R.R. "BBC Interview." Interview by Denys Gueroult. 26 November 1964. http://www.bbc.co.uk/programmes. 3 February 2019.

The Book of Lost Tales, Part Two (The History of Middle-earth, vol. 2). Ed. Christopher Tolkien. Boston, MA: Houghton Mifflin, 1984.

The Lays of Beleriand (The History of Middle-earth, vol. 3). Ed. Christopher Tolkien. Boston, MA: Houghton Mifflin, 1985.

The Letters of J.R.R. Tolkien. Eds. Humphrey Carpenter with Christopher Tolkien. Boston, MA: Houghton Mifflin, 2000.

The Lost Road and Other Writings: Language and Legend before The Lord of the Rings (The History of Middle-earth, vol. 5.). Ed. Christopher Tolkien. Boston, MA: Houghton Mifflin, 1987.

*The Shaping of Middle-earth: The Quenta, the Ambarkanta, and the Annals, Together with the Earliest 'Silmarillion' and the First Map (*The History of Middle-earth vol. 4). Ed. Christopher Tolkien. Boston, MA: Houghton Mifflin, 1986.

The Story of Kullervo. Ed. Verlyn Flieger. Boston, MA: Houghton Mifflin, 2015.

Tolkien On Fairy-stories. Eds. Verlyn Flieger and Douglas A. Anderson. London: HarperCollins, 2008.

Łukasz Neubauer

"Worried by Silence": Some Possible Resonances of Combat-related Stress in *The Lord of the Rings*

In his memorable war poem "Exposure" (published posthumously in 1920), Wilfred Owen sketches a thoroughly disheartening picture of a group of soldiers in a trench, waiting apprehensively for whatever should happen next. They are nervous and confused, wearied but awake, "worried by [the] silence" (l. 4) which seems to pierce their ears and hearts like the bullets that may sometimes be heard whistling above their heads. Although they are reported to be in some distance from the main theatre of war – "the flickering gunnery rumbles, / Far off, like a dull rumour of some other war" (ll. 8-9) – the soldiers are, nevertheless, under an incessant stress of impending combat, the most alarming thing for them being the fact that, despite the evident omnipresence of death, "nothing [as yet] happens" (ll. 5, 15, 20, 40).[1]

Indeed, this prolonged inaction of the people who, before long, will have to face the surging troops of the enemy, is almost as detrimental to their mental wellbeing as is to their mortal frames a direct physical exposure to their adversaries' weapons. Of course, the term "worried", which might also imply a certain, not necessarily very serious disturbance of mind, does not fully reflect the actual range of emotions that would accompany the combatants in their wartime ordeal, from the slight apprehension to well-nigh debilitating dread. It does, however, succeed in replicating, even in the somewhat condensed poetic form, one of the most frightening experiences of trench life during the First World War – the growing tension caused by prolonged silence. Not a peaceful, soothing silence which one could seek within the medieval walls of a Carthusian monastery or between the dusty shelves of an old university library. The silence that Owen refers to in his poem could descend upon the angst-ridden soldiers without prior notice, like a fog or cloud of smoke, not unlike,

1 Written in early 1918, "Exposure" is highly characteristic of Wilfred Owen's poetic style, focusing upon a number of war-related themes, such as the growing exhaustion of the combatants, destruction of the natural world and alleged silence of God (Shaheen 56).

perhaps, the lethal clouds of chlorine that the German troops deployed in the second battle of Ypres (Audoin-Rouzeau 181), or the Zeppelin airships that dropped bombs in the south-western parts of Britain (Gillespie 20). Moreover, the silence – momentary, intermittent or continuous – could take the form of a provisional ceasefire (declared by the conflicting sides for a number of reasons, such as the need to retrieve the bodies of the fallen ones from no man's land) or a creepy prelude to the ensuing round of combat. Last but not least, it could provide a sonorous background for the other sounds of warfare – the ear-splitting thunder of a bursting shell, the barely audible echo of a distant artillery cannonade or nerve-racking groans of the soldiers hastily operated in the relative safety of a field hospital.

All these horrifying experiences were not in the least unknown to the whole generation of young British authors – poets, novelists, short-story writers and playwrights – whom fate singled out for military service on the other side of the English Channel. Accordingly, various, sometimes very graphic allusions to the menacing dread of wartime silence may be detected in the works of Edward Thomas ("Lights Out"),[2] Robert Nichols ("The Day's March"),[3] or Margaret Sackville ("A Memory"),[4] to name only a few, not necessarily the most recognisable representatives of the Great War lyricists. Recurrent images of virtually noiseless trenches and the deadly stillness of no man's land could also be found in plenty in the reports, letters and diaries authored by the more and more disillusioned volunteers in "the war to end all wars," professional journalists such as Charles Edward Montague[5] or (wartime) nurses like the novelist Sarah Broom Macnaughtan.[6] Last of all, certain, not always instantly discernible resonances of the ghastly silence that would all too often accompany the soldiers of the First World War may be discerned in the works of those writers who are not always automatically associated with the horrors of trench combat in France and

2 "The tall forest towers; / Its cloudy foliage lowers / Ahead, shelf above shelf; / Its silence I hear and obey / That I may lose my way / And myself" (ll. 25-30).

3 "The battery grides and jingles, / Mile succeeds to mile; / Suddenly battering the silence / The guns burst awhile" (ll. 38-41).

4 "There was no sound at all, no crying in the village, / Nothing you would count as sound, that is, after the shells; [...] Silence which might be felt, no pity in the silence, / Horrible, soft like blood, down all the blood-stained ways" (ll. 1-2, 5-6).

5 "Then our guns, for an interval, fell almost silent – first lift of the barrage – a chance for hungry ears to assess the weight of the enemy's answering gunfire" (212).

6 "One was struck by their [i.e. the wounded soldiers'] silence. No one spoke or even, except on rare occasions, moaned much" (56).

Belgium – the future Inklings C.S. Lewis[7] and, in particular, J.R.R. Tolkien, to whose masterpiece, *The Lord of the Rings*, we shall soon turn.

The Battles of the Western Fields

That certain episodes, passages and images in the works of Tolkien should reflect his wartime experiences is a well-documented fact which does not require further justification.[8] Interestingly, though, it appears that despite his acknowledgement that the landscapes of *The Lord of the Rings* – in particular, the Dead Marshes and the approaches to the Morannon – may "owe something to Northern France after the Battle of the Somme" (*Letters* 303),[9] the writer rather consistently claimed that neither of the two global wars "had any influence upon either the plot [of the story of the Ring] or the manner of its unfolding" (303). Nevertheless, as may be seen particularly in *The Hobbit* (where, prior to the Battle of Five Armies, Thorin and his companions are trapped inside the Lonely Mountain in an, as yet, bloodless siege, much as the soldiers in the trenches in the First World War, waiting, in apprehension, for the enemy's next move) or in "The Homecoming of Beorhtnoth Beorhthelm's Son" (where the nocturnal quest of Torhthelm and Tídwald to recover the body of their fallen leader from the corpse-strewn battlefield was almost certainly inspired by the analogous experiences that their twentieth-century brothers-in-arms would have

7 Despite the fact that there is only one explicit reference to the global conflicts of the twentieth century in the entire series of books set in the magical world of Narnia, namely that of the civilian evacuations from London in 1939-1940 (*The Lion, the Witch and the Wardrobe* 11), the passage that seems most evocative of the trench warfare during the First World War is the terrifying cloud of Darkness, much as the gas inferno at Ypres, which Caspian and his crew come across in the twelfth chapter of *The Voyage of the Dawn Treader* (184-196). Not surprisingly, given the properties of the chlorine gas, the virtually invisible and noiseless enemy that could be accounted for the death of many a soldier of the Great War, the cloud into which the Narnians initially resolve to sail seems to generate "the total silence which surrounded the ship" (192), the silence in "which [everything] sounded louder than usual" (189).

8 The indebtedness of Tolkien's fiction to the trench warfare he was exposed to in 1916 has been examined by a number of scholars, including, amongst others, John Garth, Janet Brennan Croft, Margaret Hiley and Joseph Loconte.

9 He appears to dismiss the thought in the following sentence, though, claiming that the said locations probably "owe more to William Morris and his Huns and Romans, as in *The House of the Wolfings* or *The Roots of the Mountains*" (303). Naturally, one does not have to exclude the other, however, as may be seen in the so-called "First Map" of Middle-earth – the one that for many years served as Tolkien's reference map (Hammond and Scull 95), where, between the Dead Marshes and Dagorlad, is the area inscribed in plain capitals: NO MAN'S LAND (96) – his words may not always be depended upon.

during the Somme offensive),[10] the reflections are to be found there in plenty and one does not need to be an expert on early-twentieth-century warfare to see that they are by no means incidental.

Somewhat contrary to what Tolkien claims in the above-quoted letter, some of the most striking, if not necessarily easily detectable, recollections of the Great War may be found in *The Lord of the Rings*. Indeed, certain passages – with some minor alterations with regard to the toponymy and the characters' names – might well fit into the eyewitness accounts of the battles of Ypres or of the Somme. Consider, for instance, the following extract from *The Fellowship of the Ring*, in which the four hobbits, now in the company of Strider-Aragorn, set up a camp atop Amon Sûl: "For a breathless time they sat there, silent and alert, with their backs turned to the wood-fire, each gazing into the shadows that encircled them. Nothing happened. There was no sound or movement in the night. Frodo stirred, feeling that he must break the silence: he longed to shout out aloud" (*LotR* I.11.194-195). Or the passage from *The Two Towers*, in which Gandalf, Aragorn, Gimli and Legolas as well as King Théoden, Éomer and the men of Rohan decide to take a night's rest before they take the last stretch of the road that is to take them to Isengard:

> They camped beside the bed of the Isen river; it was still silent and empty. Some of them slept a little. But late in the night the watchmen cried out, and all awoke. The moon was gone. Stars were shining above; but over the ground there crept a darkness blacker than the night. On both sides of the river it rolled towards them, going northward.
>
> 'Stay where you are!' said Gandalf. 'Draw no weapons! Wait! and it will pass you by!' (*LotR* III.8.552)

or, in the same volume, when, having eaten some of the provisions they received earlier that day from Faramir, Frodo and Sam (as well as, for the time being absent, Gollum) prepare for the night: "Darkness came early to the silent woods, and before the fall of night they halted, weary, for they had walked seven leagues or more from Henneth Annûn" (IV.7.696).

---

10 See, for instance, my chapter in *Recalling War: Representations of the Two World Wars in British Literature and Culture*, in which I examine the post-combat reality of early medieval warfare in "The Homecoming of Beorhtnoth" by reading it in the context of the enormous death toll amongst the young British soldiers in the First World War (35-50).

What is interesting, there is one word that appears in all of them, and the word is "silent". It is, of course, quite conventional to envision the Great War in the way in which it came to be depicted in, say, Richard Aldington's novel *Death of a Hero*, as "a timeless confusion, a chaos of noise, fatigue, anxiety, and horror" (293). Indeed, on the first day of the Somme offensive, Martin Gilbert relates,

> So intense and so loud was the barrage that it was heard on Hampstead Heath in north London, almost two hundred miles away. It was an astonishing sound, as guns of all calibres fired simultaneously. In some parts of the line British soldiers sat on their parapets cheering at each explosion, but their enthusiastic shouts were lost in the thunder of the guns. The sound was so intense that if a man screamed at the top of his voice into another man's ear, he could not be heard. (50)

Nevertheless, it does not deny the fact that, more often than not, it seems, the battlefields of the Western Front were infused by the silence, a silence that, to use the words of Tolkien, as Aragorn and his two companions set out in pursuit of the orcs that have captured Marry and Pippin, "did not seem to be the quiet of peace" (*LotR* III.2.427). It would be incorrect, though, to claim that this menacing silence was at all times consistent in its character, duration and magnitude. Hence, examined below, will be four of the most common (and frightening) instances in which silence and fear are often found to play the main parts. These will include the moments in which stillness is an anticipated, though not warranted, prelude to some military confrontation ("The Land of Shadow"), situations when certain, often barely audible, evidence of the enemy presence might strike almost just as much fear in the hearts of the soldiers as the ensuing hostilities ("Riddles in the Dark") and, last but not least, the nerve-racking whiles when every sound appears to be magnified manifold either on account of the all-encompassing silence ("The Gathering of the Clouds") or the intensity of the sound itself ("The Clouds Burst").

The Land of Shadow

In his war memoir *The War the Infantry Knew*, the then medical officer James Churchill Dunn relates a series of false alarms and cancelled orders to move that would regularly threaten his fellow soldiers serving in the Royal Welch

Fusiliers. No wonder that, following a few such instances, the combatants felt utterly exhausted with the "dreary wait that has got on [their] nerves" (66). Indeed, this prolonged pressure of watchful expectancy, not infrequently, one could presume, in near silence or at least with not much happening within the trenches and out in no man's land, must have been a truly hair-raising experience for the thousands of young men, "Tommies" and "Huns" alike. "It is a weary game and extremely trying on one's nerves," explains Second Lieutenant H.E. Cooper from the Royal Warwickshire Regiment in a letter to his parents, "for hearing and sight are strained to the utmost." "There we lie and wait and listen. [...] For an hour we lie in absolute silence" (qtd. in Brown 108). "The [...] silence was uncanny," remarks Robert Cedric Sherriff, officer in the 9th battalion of the East Surrey Regiment and the future author of the play *Journey's End*. "A sort of stagnant emptiness surrounded us" (qtd. in Gore-Langton 53).

We have already seen that analogous experiences are not unknown to the Ring-bearer and his companions. The incident on top of Amon Sûl, related in the eleventh chapter of book I ("A Knife in the Dark"), is obviously but one in a series of similar occurrences where the lead roles are played by silence and fear and the stage is either the barren landscape of Mordor and its adjoining territories or some other part of Middle-earth where the servants of the Enemy would doubtlessly feel at home. These could have either direct military connotations – as in the passage where, with increasing apprehension (and decreasing hope), the defenders of the mountain fortress of Hornburg watch "the hosts of Isengard [advance] in silence" (*LotR* III.7.532) – or only invoke an indefinite sense of wartime drama, as is certainly the case with the description of Saruman's citadel of Isengard, even after it has been practically destroyed by the terrifying force of Entish fury: "It was a sad country, silent now but for the stony noise of quick waters. Smokes and steams drifted in sullen clouds and lurked in the hollows. The riders did not speak. Many doubted in their hearts, wondering to what dismal end their journey led" (*LotR* III.8.553).

Yet of all the passages in Tolkien's book in which the ever-thickening atmosphere of menacing silence clearly plays no small part, perhaps the most evocative one is to be found in the opening paragraphs of book VI, where Sam gets his first thorough glimpse of the Dark Land: "All was ominously quiet. The light was no more than that of dusk at a dark day's end. The vast vapours that arose in Mordor and went streaming westward passed low overhead, a great welter of cloud and smoke now lit again beneath with a sullen glow of red" (*LotR* VI.1.898).

Here, of course, Tolkien does not use the word "silence" (or any of its numerous possible derivatives, compounds etc.). Instead, the area within Sam's sight is described as being "quiet", or, more specifically, "ominously quiet". While the adjectives "silent" and "quiet" are regularly treated as synonymous, there are, in fact, certain semantic nuances between them, the former denoting the absence of any sounds, the latter usually meaning that some, hardly audible ones could still be heard. This way or another, though, it cannot be denied that what emerges in front of Sam is certainly not, for the time being, a beehive of activity, drowned in the cacophony of orcish cries and barked orders of their commanders, neighing of horses and trumpeting of mûmakil, hisses of the Nazgûl and screams of their fell beasts. Much as in the Dead Marshes, the "shadowy silent world, cut off from all view of the lands about" (*LotR* IV.2.626), or the Eastemnet, to the west of Isengard, "where the land was empty, and there was silence that did not seem to be the quiet of peace" (III.2.427), the plateau of Gorgoroth as seen from Cirith Ungol gives the impression of a land where the seemingly peaceful, if naturally dark and gloomy, look evidently portends some dreadful things to come. It is the proverbial calm before the storm and the worst, or, at any rate, most unnerving thing about it for the two hobbits is not the question whether the mighty hordes of Mordor will be unleashed or not, but when,[11] a dreadful feeling that many a soldier of the First World War would have been perfectly acquainted with. As in the afore-quoted poem by Wilfred Owen, they were "worried" not only by the uncanny silence which surrounded them ("Exposure" l. 4), but also, perhaps just as intensely, the sheer fact that (as yet) "nothing happens" (ll. 5ff.).[12]

11 The inevitable offensive has already been launched, with the army of Mordor laying siege to Minas Tirith. It should be noted, however, that, as Gandalf rightly observes, "the next [assault] will be greater" (*LotR* V.9.878), the first offensive being but a vanguard of what Sauron has amassed in his realm. Not surprisingly, then, during the battle of the Morannon, where he seems to have thrown the bulk of his forces, the seemingly infinite hosts of the Dark Lord are figuratively referred to as the "swirling waters", "sea of enemies" (V.10.891), or "gathering sea" (VI.4.948).

12 H.E. Cooper observes, for instance, that the fact that "no shots [were] being fired from the [opposite] trenches" (Brown 108) could well mean that, at that time, the enemy had their patrol out, a prospect that could hardly be referred to as promising.

What is more, having ventured into the land of the enemy, Frodo and Sam are under a continuous threat of being spotted by the watchful eyes of the not always visible (and audible) servants of the Dark Lord. In other words, trudging through the bleak landscape of Mordor, hiding behind rocks, in hollows or under a bridge, the hobbits are quite distinctly reminiscent of those combatants of the Great War who, having "gone over the top," proceed in silence at a snail's pace in a desperate attempt to get as close as possible to the opposite trenches. Their efforts to remain unseen were repeatedly doomed to fail and it was usually a matter of time before their hopes were brutally dashed by the vigilant snipers, machine gunners or other troops in the enemy dugouts. For them, the silence would always seem "ominous", more often than not meaning that the opponents were either not yet aware of the approaching troops or that they already knew of the oncoming assault, but their commanders chose not to react before the crawling soldiers should make easier targets. The two hobbits might have adopted a less confrontational attitude towards the forces of Sauron, of course. Clearly different is also the way in which they are treated by the orcs they come across on the third day following their escape from the Tower of Cirith Ungol (they are mistakenly taken for a pair of deserters). Nonetheless, the evident peril in which they find themselves in Mordor and the absolute necessity to remain undetected are crucial for our understanding of how they feel when, against all the odds, Frodo and Sam slog through the "ominously quiet" (*LotR* VI.1.898) realm of the Dark Lord, much as the anxious soldiers in Robert Nichols' "The Day's March" who, have to "keep [their] senses [continuously] straightened" (l. 20) before the guns ultimately "burst out" (l. 41), "suddenly battering the silence" (l. 40).

Riddles in the Dark

The numerous eyewitness accounts of trench warfare are obviously quite consistent in many details, not in the least because some of them happen to relate the very same incidents. One of the most frequently mentioned concerns of the British combatants was the fact that, on account of the proximity (the distance between the opposing dugouts could, in some cases, be astonishingly small, with less than thirty metres of no man's land in between; see Baker), clearly distinguishable voices of the enemy could sometimes be heard from the opposite trenches. H.E. Cooper, whose wartime correspondence has already been quoted from, relates that, as the soldiers from his regiment, the Royal Warwickshires, lay in utter silence, waiting for the order to advance, they could "hear the faint hum of conversation" (Brown 108) coming from the German trenches. Likewise, in his poignant narrative relating the events that led to the famous "Christmas truce",[13] Alfred Anderson, from the 5th Battalion of the Royal Regiment of Scotland, explains that for about two months – his first two months in the trenches – practically the only sounds that he would hear, apart from "the hissing, cracking and whining of bullets in flight [and] machine gun fire," were the "distant German voices" (qtd. in Cramb).

None of it would have been possible, of course, if it had not been for the various moments of silence. Sometimes brief, lasting for no more than a few seconds (which may, nevertheless, have seemed to last for eternity), sometimes more prolonged (particularly, though by no means exclusively, at night), these intervals could, on rare occasions, provide the soldiers with some much-needed respite. Quite often, however, they would find it far less comfortable than that. As has already been argued, such moments were more likely to give rise to their growing uneasiness, "extremely trying," H.E. Cooper testifies, "to one's apprehension" (qtd. in Brown 108). In this silence, the voices heard from the enemy trenches would doubtlessly sound disturbing. All the more disturbing, in fact, for those of the "Tommies" (the majority) who had little, if any, knowledge of the German tongue. For them, the harsh, consonant clusters that characterise the language of Goethe could have made an impression similar to the one that the participants of the Council of Elrond have upon hearing Gandalf, as he recalls the words inscribed on the One Ring, his voice being "menacing, powerful, harsh as stone" (*LotR* II.2.254). Besides, on the more practical side of it, it should be kept in mind that the British combatants simply could not understand what the enemy soldiers were actually doing, whether they were praying, cursing the foul weather, or discussing the oncoming assault.

---

13 The Christmas truce was a series of spontaneous cessations of hostilities along the Western Front around the time of Christmas 1914. A good and comprehensive examination of this remarkable moment of human solidarity might be found in Stanley Weintraub's book *Silent Night: The Remarkable Christmas Truce of 1914*.

The unremitting feeling of a continuous presence of the enemy, which various members of the Fellowship seem to experience as they draw nearer and nearer to the land of the Dark Lord, is in many instances comparable. From the very first day of their entrance into Mordor, Frodo and Sam know all too well that, although "there was [...] no sign of orcs, [and no] answer to the cry of the Nazgûl, [...] the silence [that followed the cry] would not last long" (*LotR* VI.2.916). Much as the First World War soldiers, waiting endlessly on tenterhooks in the trenches of the Somme, Ypres or Passchendaele, the hobbits understand that, notwithstanding the moment of silence and the fact that, to once again use the words of Wilfred Owen, "nothing happens," the chances that their bold foray into the territory of the enemy will pass without further consequences are very slim indeed. The servants of Sauron are practically everywhere (even if, for the moment, they cannot be seen) and the hunt for the intruders might begin "at any moment" (VI.2.916).

Indeed, within just two days or so, the harsh voices of orcs and "the tramp of [their] iron-shod feet" (VI.2.916) are to be heard as many as three times: first by the bridge near Cirith Ungol (916-917), then upon the eastern ridge in the Ephel Dúath (924-926) and, finally, as Frodo and Sam are heading east towards Isenmouthe, where they are taken for deserters and, in consequence, forced to join the company that are on their way to the valley of Ûdun (930-931). In each of these three incidents, the sound always comes before the sight (in the first case, the orcs are, in fact, never even seen by the hobbits), invariably amplifying rather than diminishing the horror of being discovered. One should also bear it in mind that, during the last ten days or so of their near-suicidal quest, the Ring-bearers are on the brink of almost complete exhaustion. They are cold, hungry and thirsty, overcome by the weight of their burden. Moreover, Frodo is far from being well as a result of the wound recently inflicted upon him by Shelob and the harsh treatment he subsequently suffers in the tower of Cirith Ungol.[14] Seen from this perspective, it is rather hard not to juxtapose them with the fatigued combatants in Wilfred Owen's other poem, possibly his best known and oft-discussed work, "*Dulce et Decorum Est*". "Bent double, like old

14 Not to mention the other wounds – the one dealt by the Witch-king of Angmar on top of Amon Sûl (*LotR* 195-196) and another, albeit a light one, he suffers during the skirmish in the Chamber of Mazarbul (325).

beggars under sacks" (l. 1), trudging towards their still remote destination, they have every reason in the world to be "worried by silence" and everything that should break it, particularly when the sounds that they hear are the agitated shouts of recently mobilised orcs, suddenly breaking "the stillness of the night" (*LotR* VI.2.930).

The Gathering of the Clouds

In the surrounding silence (often exacerbated by the lack of good, if any, visibility) every sound that might be heard is usually perceptibly amplified so that the resonance seems greater than under the usual circumstances, when it could be obscured or even completely neutralised by the accompaniment of various background noises. Also this phenomenon seems to have been quite well known to the soldiers of the First World War. In the afore-quoted letter to his parents, H.E. Cooper relates, for instance, that, as they were waiting quietly in their trenches, all the "tiny noises" they were able to hear every now and then would become "magnified a hundredfold," so that "a rat nibbling at the growing corn or a rabbit scuttling along [could give them] all the jumps until [they] learn[ed] to differentiate the different sounds" (qtd. in Brown 108). In fact it often seems that practically anywhere one's attention was turned, in the short-lived periods of silence between the usual pounding of the guns and shouts of men or during the more prolonged intervals (e.g. on account of a ceasefire or other ad hoc agreement to prevent unnecessary bloodshed), the air on the western front was, to use the words from Isaac Rosenberg's poem "Dead Man's Dump", always "loud with death" (l. 39), filled with all sorts of war-related sounds (combined or in isolation) that kept on reverberating over the devastated landscapes of France and Belgium.[15]

This nerve-racking sensation is obviously not unknown to the members of the Fellowship and their allies, the intensity naturally increasing whenever they find themselves in the areas where their progress could be tracked by the enemy. One such instance might be found in the third chapter of book II ("The

15 That these menacing sounds did not always have to be of strictly speaking military character may be seen in the fourth episode of the television series *The Passing Bells* where, "worried by silence," the teenage recruit Derek begins to confuse drops of rainwater with the rumble of guns.

Ring Goes South"), when Frodo and his companions reach what is left of the once-thriving elvish realm of Eregion. "Silent and restless," Aragorn leaves the others for a moment, "looking out southwards and westwards, with his head posed as if he was listening" (*LotR* II.3.284). Questioned by the mirthful Merry, he voices his growing uneasiness concerning the unnaturally silent area he has known for several years. "There is," he says, "no sound for miles about us, and [the] voices seem to make the ground echo" (284), a curious feeling the Ranger neither likes, nor understands, "a sense of watchfulness" (284) he claims he has never had there before.

This intriguing restlessness appears to be almost infectious, with other members of the fellowship also becoming aware of the fact that something is indeed going on, even if they are not yet capable of endowing it with any tangible form. When the times comes for Sam to take the watch, he soon finds out that he can also feel it: "The breathing of the sleepers could be plainly heard. The swish of the pony's tail and the occasional movements of his feet became loud noises. Sam could hear his own joints creaking, if he stirred. Dead silence was around him" (II.3.284).

What under other circumstances could perhaps be a source of comfort, a prerequisite for one's undisturbed sleep, here appears to be the very cause why Sam Gamgee's peace of mind cannot be attained. The reason for this is obviously to be found in the subliminal feeling that the company is being followed (they are indeed trailed by Gollum), yet it would not probably be so acute if it were not for the general circumstances: the impending military conflict with Sauron and the importance of the Ring-bearer's near-suicidal mission which necessitates a bold incursion into the Dark Lord's realm.

The enormous psychological strain which the said mission imposes upon the members of the Fellowship – not merely Frodo and Sam, who are the most likely of the nine to have to sneak into the land of Mordor, but also, in particular, Aragorn and, to a somewhat lesser degree, Boromir, whose loyalties are, at that point, not so easily defined – naturally results in their increased attentiveness (and reactivity) to the external stimuli. The reaction itself is, of course, chiefly involuntary. Moreover, as has already been observed, its primary cause is to be found elsewhere, i.e. not so much in the external stimuli themselves. In the case of the soldiers of the Great War, it should be attributed to their first-hand experience of the global conflict estimated to have claimed the lives of some ten million people (with roughly twice as many wounded).[16] Being under a constant threat of bombardment or direct assault, the combatants' nerves must have been almost incessantly on edge, every now and then provoking them to desertion, self-inflicted injuries[17] or even suicide attempts. It is little wonder then that, stuck in the cold, muddy, lice- and rat-infested trenches, the young men should, every now and then, be so terrified by even the most mundane of sounds, "a rat nibbling at the growing corn or a rabbit scuttling along" (Brown 180).

Taking the first night watch in the ruins of Eregion, Sam is obviously in a better situation than many a soldier in the trenches of the First World War. The company has had no immediate – or even eye-contact with the servants of Sauron since they left Rivendell. They do not have to see their fellows drop like flies in the battlefield, where the enemy bullets cut into the ranks of their battalion, or suffer in bed as a result of the diseases spread by the omnipresent lice. It would be wrong, however, to suppose that this makes Sam feel any better. Much as the thousands of "Tommies" (with whom he is often compared),[18] the son of Gaffer Gamgee is an inexperienced youth who, until recently, has never really been away from home, having spent all his hitherto life in the village of Hobbiton. Why should he be not "worried by [the creepy] silence" that surrounds the campsite and all those ostensibly innocuous sounds which every now and then break it (breathing of the sleepers, swish of the pony's tail, movements of feet, creaking of joints), particularly as that very same feeling, although, it seems, with less intensity, is not in the least unfamiliar to some of the more experienced members of the Fellowship, characters like Aragorn and Gandalf?

16 The estimates obviously vary here, mainly due to the fact that some countries, such as Russia, kept insufficient statistical records. According to the 1920 study of E.L. Bogart, more than ten million people (10,004,771) are known to have died in the conflict and almost three more (2,991,800) were presumed dead (Cruttwell 630).

17 The case of desertion seems rather obvious, but conscious attempts at inflicting damage to one's own body may call for further explanation. Perhaps a good illustration of it could be found in the eighth episode of the television series *Downton Abbey* (2011), where Thomas Barrow, one of the Abbey's footmen, now in the Army Medical Corps, gets himself shot in the hand, so that he could be sent back to England as permanently unsuitable.

18 In his *Biography*, Humphrey Carpenter quotes Tolkien as saying, "My 'Sam Gamgee' is indeed a reflexion of the English soldier, of the privates and batmen I knew in the 1914 war, and recognized as so far superior to myself" (214).

The Clouds Burst

Barring the usual clamours of warfare, if there has ever been anything more detrimental to the emotional state of the entrenched combatants of the Great War than the ordinary, if somewhat intermittent, sounds of life, "magnified a hundredfold" by the encompassing silence, it could only be the markedly less frequent though far more intense cries of distress, disbelief or pain that may have sometimes been heard in or around their own trenches. Perhaps nowhere is it better illustrated than in the account of Ernst Toller, a twenty-odd-year-old volunteer in the ranks of the First Royal Bavarian Foot Artillery. In his autobiographical book *I Was a German* (1933), he relates a most shocking incident involving a man entangled in a barbed wire fence in no man's land:

> One night we heard a cry, the cry of one in excruciating pain; then all was quiet again. Someone in his death agony, we thought. But an hour later the cry came again. It never ceased the whole night. Nor the following night. Naked and inarticulate, the cry persisted. We could not tell whether it came from the throat of German or Frenchman. It existed in its own right, an agonized indictment of heaven and earth. We thrust our fingers into our ears to stop its moan; but it was no good; the cry cut like a drill into our heads, dragging minutes into hours, hours into years. We withered and grew old between those cries. (77)

It is once again intriguing, though not in the least surprising, that the most distressing moments for the German soldiers, moments in the course of which they are reported (with little or no overemphasis) to have "withered and grew old", were the long seconds, perhaps minutes, between rather than during these agonising moans. Here again, the explanation of the combatants' amplified distress – so enormous that they would even commence to "pray [...] for his death" – is perfectly simple: the moments of silence could last for a while, of course, but every time the unfortunate man ceased to moan, there was absolutely no way of telling whether the next piercing cry should be heard in a matter of seconds, minutes or hours. Or, in fact, whether it should ever be heard again. "If he went on much longer", Toller concludes, "we should go mad". It was only on the third day that "Death closed his mouth" (77).

Likewise, in Middle-earth, the silence could be "broken suddenly" (*LotR* V.10.888). Suddenly, but not unexpectedly, as may be illustrated by the long seven days it takes the Host of the West to finally come to the Black Gate of

Mordor. Approaching the Morannon, they are well aware of the presence of the Ringwraiths (886) and other "things half-seen that walked and prowled all about them" (887). Not until a formal challenge is issued, though, "the Enemy [makes any] sign" (887), when there finally comes "a long rolling of great drums like thunder in the mountains [and] a braying of horns" (888). This breaking of the silence is reported to shake "the very stones" and stun "men's ears" (888), yet it might be assumed (with a rather high degree of probability) that, regardless of the actual volume of the noise, just as debilitating to them is the abruptness of the clamour, preceded, as has been observed, by the long days of dispiriting silence. No doubt, breading fear in the ranks of his enemies is one of Sauron's most powerful weapons, a weapon he clearly delights himself in, be it at the siege of Minas Tirith or the battle of the Morannon.[19]

Just as the brief moment(s) of silence between the notes could enable the sound to be more effectively exploited by the musician, producing the effects of, on the one hand, nostalgia and, on the other, some sort of uneasiness or anxiety, the ingeniously used intervals of near-perfect stillness (not infrequently extending over minutes or hours) might, particularly in the time of war, quite naturally intensify the growing apprehension in the ranks of the enemy. Even more threatening, in fact, in some measure analogous to the bloodcurdling incident so graphically outlined by Ernst Toller, are those situations in which the sound-induced terror is additionally enhanced by the recurrence of the menacing sound, not infrequently at varied intervals. Apart from the above-mentioned examples of pre-combat silence preceding the Dark Lord's assault on Minas Tirith and his seamlessly designed and, up to a certain point, well executed ambush at the Morannon, the most striking instances of the sounds that suddenly pierce one's heart with an incapacitating dread are evidently the cries uttered, under varying circumstances, by the Nazgûl. From the eastern parts of the Shire, where they are heard for the first time:

> They stopped short suddenly. Frodo sprang to his feet. A long-drawn wail came down the wind, like the cry of some evil and lonely creature. It rose and fell, and ended on a high piercing note. Even as they sat and stood, as if suddenly frozen, it was answered by another cry, fainter and further off, but no

19 Fear also seems to be Sauron's primary weapon in, particularly, the first book of *The Fellowship of the Ring*, when even the slightest mention of the Black Riders (or the land that they come from) instils terror in the hearts of the hobbits.

> less chilling to the blood. There was then a silence, broken only by the sound of the wind in the leaves. (*LotR* I.4.90)

to the barren landscape of Mordor and its whereabouts, where the menacing presence of the Ringwraiths is an ever-menacing threat:

> The earth groaned; and out of the city there came a cry. Mingled with harsh high voices as of birds of prey, and the shrill neighing of horses wild with rage and fear, there came a rending screech, shivering rising swiftly to a piercing pitch beyond the range of hearing. The hobbits wheeled round towards it, and cast themselves down, holding their hands upon their ears.
>
> As the terrible cry ended, falling back through a long sickening wail to silence, Frodo slowly raised his head. Across the narrow valley, now almost on a level with his eyes, the walls of the evil city stood, and its cavernous gate, shaped like an open mouth with gleaming teeth, was gaping wide. And out of the gate an army came. (*LotR* IV.8.706)

Despite some obvious discrepancies – in the first case the shrill cries of the Black Riders appear to be heard in isolation, in the second they may be singled out from a background of quite conventional war-related noises – it should not be hard to imagine that in each of these two cases, both Frodo and his companions[20] are perhaps just as much (if not more) frightened by the silence that pre- and postcedes the calls of the Nazgûl as the horrible cries themselves. One reason for this is, no doubt, the fact that the hobbits can never tell – with any reasonable degree of certainty – how long the cry is going to pierce their ears and hearts and, no less importantly, whether it will be followed by another one (two? three?) or not. That is to say, the silence that ensues gives them no assurance whatsoever that the worst is now over (if only for the time being). Hence, figuratively or not, one may easily visualise the hobbits "wither and grow old between the cries," to use the words of Ernst Toller, or, this time quoting Wilfred Owen, "worried by the silence [...] curious, nervous" ("Exposure" l. 4).

20 In the first passage, Frodo is accompanied by Sam and Pippin (Merry is yet to join them at Farmer Maggot's). In the second, his companions are Sam and Gollum.

Conclusions

It would be a bold overstatement to claim that, as he was writing *The Lord of the Rings*, deliberately or not, Tolkien made an attempt to shake off the often inevitable trauma of the First and, perhaps in some measure, the Second World Wars.[21] What is more, it does not seem quite plausible that, much as with the almost subliminal Catholic substratum of his most famous novel, the numerous, if not always clearly identifiable, reverberations of the two global conflicts should actually find their way into the book by dint of some premeditated scheme, "unconsciously so at first, but consciously in the revision."[22] Indeed, it is far more likely that the echoes of his own experiences were not always fully acknowledged by the author (hence his somewhat puzzling reluctance to admit that either of the two wars had any sizable influence upon his masterpiece) and that their presence in *The Lord of the Rings* in effect rests upon the fact that, regardless of the actual timeframe, certain elements of warfare are simply universal. Consequently, it is not so much Tolkien's first-hand experience of the Great War that in any way affected the plot of his novel (which he himself avows in the aforementioned letter) as the sheer artistic necessity to portray the events of the War of the Ring in as realistic a way as possible, a necessity that may have not only induced him to echo the daily horrors of trench warfare, but also seems to have resulted in a subconscious replication of the writer's personal feelings about war, particularly that the bulk of the book was written when Hitler and Stalin were trying to establish a new world order in Europe and beyond.

---

21 All of Tolkien's sons – John (b. 1917), Michael (b. 1920) and Christopher (b. 1924) – were already in their twenties when the war came to an end. From November 1939 until May 1940 John studied for the priesthood at the English College, a Catholic seminary in Rome. Even though Italy did not formally enter the conflict until 10 June 1940, there had already been numerous German troops in its capital (Scull and Hammond 249). In 1941 Michael became an officer cadet at the Royal Military College, Sandhurst (264). He would later be transferred to the Royal Air Force and see action as a rear-gunner in bomber aircraft in France and Germany (268). Tolkien's youngest son, Christopher, entered the Royal Air Force in July 1943 (278) and was sent to South Africa later that year. Given that, it is not hard to imagine his mounting paternal anxieties which, coupled with the more general concerns about the situation in the world (often voiced in Tolkien's letters), must have often troubled the heart of the author of *The Lord of the Rings*.

22 Cf. Tolkien's oft-quoted letter to Father Robert Murray SJ, in which he famously claims that "*The Lord of the Rings* is of course a fundamentally religious and Catholic work; unconsciously so at first, but consciously in the revision" (*Letters* 172).

The above examination is, of course, but a tip of the iceberg in the multithread study of the not always easily acknowledged (also by the writer himself) indebtedness of Tolkien's fiction to his wartime memories. Even as far as the various sound effects (or lack of them) of combat and combat-related issues are concerned, the present chapter does not by any means exhaust its central premise, namely that, even if not directly inspired by his experience of trench warfare, Tolkien's ability to capture the grim reality of military confrontations in his subcreated world is intriguingly consistent with the often highly disturbing images of the Great War preserved in the numerous poems, reports, letters and diaries that came to be written during and in the immediate aftermath of this global conflict. It is, nevertheless, hoped that, notwithstanding its inevitably sketchy form, it could spark further interest in the intricate web of sounds – not only in the strictly martial or otherwise war-related context – that *The Lord of the Rings* certainly is. After all, as Pythagoras is held to have once said of the cosmic order (a view that Tolkien seems to, at least partly, subscribe to in "The Ainulindalë"), all the sounds appear to underwrite the universal harmony of the world – the *musica universalis*, or the "music of the spheres" – a harmony in which every sound has its own function and character and, in this way, provides a meaningful contribution to the whole (Hahn 156-157).

Bibliography

ALDINGTON, Richard. *Death of a Hero.* London: Penguin Books, 2013.

AUDOIN-ROUZEAU, Stéphane. "Combat." *A Companion to World War I.* Ed. John Horne. Chichester: Blackwell Publishing Ltd, 2012, 173-187.

BAKER, Chris. "Life in the trenches of the First World War." *The Long, Long Trail.* 2019. https://www.longlongtrail.co.uk/soldiers/a-soldiers-life-1914-1918/life-in-the-trenches-of-the-first-world-war/. 23 Jan 2019.

BROWN, Malcolm. *The Imperial War Museum Book of the Western Front.* London: Pan Macmillan, 2001.

CARPENTER, Humphrey. *J.R.R. Tolkien: A Biography.* London: HarperCollins, 2002.

CRAMB, Auslan. "Last Soldier Serving in 1914 Christmas Truce Dies, Aged 109." 22 Nov 2005. https://www.telegraph.co.uk/news/uknews/1503618/Last-soldier-serving-in-1914-Christmas-truce-dies-aged-109.html.

CROFT, Janet Brennan. "War." *A Companion to J.R.R. Tolkien*. Ed. Stuart D. Lee. Chichester: Wiley Blackwell, 2014, 461-472.

War and the Works of J.R.R. Tolkien. Westport, CT and London: Praeger Publishers, 2004.

CRUTTWELL, Charles Robert Mowbray Fraser. *A History of the Great War 1914-1918*. Chicago, IL: Academy Chicago Publishers, 2007.

Downton Abbey. Complete Collector's Set. Universal Pictures UK. 2016. DVD.

DUNN, James Churchill. *The War the Infantry Knew*. London: Abacus, 2004.

GARTH, John. *Tolkien and the Great War: The Threshold of Middle-earth*. London: HarperCollins, 2003.

GILBERT, Martin. *Somme: The Heroism and Horror of War*. London: John Murray, 2006.

GILLESPIE, Alexander. *History of the Laws of War*. Vol. 2: "The Customs and Laws of War with Regards to Civilians in Times of Conflict." London: Bloomsbury Publishing, 2011.

GORE-LANGTON, Robert. *Journey's End: The Classic War Play Explored*. London: Oberon Books, 2013.

HAHN, Robert. *The Metaphysics of the Pythagorean Theorem. Thales, Pythagoras, Engineering, Diagrams, and the Construction of the Cosmos out of Right Triangles*. Albany: State University of New York Press, 2017.

HAMMOND, Wayne G. and Christina SCULL. *The Art of The Lord of the Rings by J.R.R. Tolkien*. London: HarperCollins, 2015.

HILEY, Margaret. *The Loss and the Silence. Aspects of Modernism in the Works of C.S. Lewis, J.R.R. Tolkien and Charles Williams*. Zurich and Jena: Walking Tree Publishers, 2011.

LEWIS, Clive Staples. *The Lion, the Witch and the Wardrobe*. London: HarperCollins, 2014.

The Voyage of the Dawn Treader. London: HarperCollins, 2014.

LOCONTE, Joseph. *A Hobbit, a Wardrobe, and a Great War*. Nashville, TN: Nelson Books, 2015.

MACNAUGHTAN, Sarah Broom. *A Woman's Diary of the War*. New York City, NY: Dutton, 1916.

MONTAGUE, Charles Edward. *Disenchantment*. New York City, NY: Brentano's Publisher's, 1922.

NEUBAUER, Łukasz. "'It's a wicked business to gather them ungrown': Tragic Echoes of the Great War in J.R.R. Tolkien's 'Homecoming of Beorhtnoth Beorhthelm's Son.'" *Recalling War: Representations of the Two World Wars in British Literature and Culture*. Ed. Wojciech Klepuszewski. Koszalin: Wydawnictwo Politechniki Koszalińskiej, 2014, 35-50.

NICHOLS, Robert. "The Day's March." *The Penguin Book of First World War Poetry*. Ed. George Walter. London: Penguin Books, 2006, 116-117.

OWEN, Wilfred. "Dulce et Decorum Est." *The Penguin Book of First World War Poetry*. Ed. George Walter. London: Penguin Books, 2006, 141-142.

"Exposure." *The Penguin Book of First World War Poetry*. Ed. George Walter. London: Penguin Books, 2006, 55-57.

The Passing Bells. Directed by Brendan Maher. BBC, 2014. DVD.

ROSENBERG, Isaac. "Dead Man's Dump." *The Penguin Book of First World War Poetry*. Ed. George Walter. London: Penguin Books, 2006, 146-148.

SACKVILLE, Margaret. "A Memory." *The Penguin Book of First World War Poetry*. Ed. George Walter. London: Penguin Books, 2006, 145.

SCULL, Christina, and Wayne G. HAMMOND. *The J.R.R. Tolkien Companion and Guide. Chronology*. London: HarperCollins, 2017.

SHAHEEN, Rubina. "A Post-Structuralist Analysis of Some of Wilfred Owen's War Poems". *Explorations* 21 (2010): 55-66.

THOMAS, Edward. "Lights Out." *The Penguin Book of First World War Poetry*. Ed. George Walter. London: Penguin Books, 2006, 103-104.

TOLKIEN, J.R.R. *The Hobbit*. London: HarperCollins, 2007.

"The Homecoming of Beorhtnoth Beorhthelm's Son". *Essays and Studies by Members of the English Association. New Series*. 6 (1953): 1-18.

The Letters of J.R.R. Tolkien. Eds. Humphrey Carpenter and Christopher Tolkien. London: George Allen & Unwin, 1981.

The Lord of the Rings. 50th Anniversary edition. Boston, MA: Houghton Mifflin, 2004.

The Silmarillion. Ed. Christopher Tolkien. London: HarperCollins, 2006.

TOLLER, Ernst. *I Was a German: An Autobiography*. London: John Lane the Bodley Head, 1934.

WEINTRAUB, Stanley. *Silent Night: The Remarkable Christmas Truce of 1914*. London: Simon and Schuster, 2014.

Victoria Holtz Wodzak

Tolkien Underground: The "Troglodyte War"[1] in *The Hobbit* and *The Lord of the Rings*

Smaug is uneasy. He wakes from his dream-troubled nap to find "a breath of strange air in his cave. [...] He stir[s] and stretche[s] forth his neck to sniff. Then he misse[s] the cup! Thieves! Fire! Murder! Such a thing had not happened since first he came to the Mountain!" (*Hobbit* 12:217). Far above, at the end of the little passageway that has annoyed Smaug over the years, the dwarves are alarmed as "a vast rumbling woke in the mountain underneath" (12:217). Cowering against the side of the mountain near the partially opened door they "heard the awful rumour of his flight, and they crouched against the walls of the grassy terrace cringing under boulders, hoping somehow to escape the frightful eyes of the hunting dragon" (12:218). They had just taken shelter in the tunnel

> when Smaug came hurtling from the North, licking the mountain-sides with flame, beating his great wings with a noise like a roaring wind. His hot breath shrivelled the grass before the door, and drove in through the crack they had left and scorched them as they lay hid. Flickering fires leaped up and black rock-shadows danced. Then darkness fell as he passed again. (*Hobbit* 12:219)

Smaug veers off to pursue their ponies, and for the moment, they are in luck: the dragon has not yet discovered the little bay in the rock or the door in the side of the mountain. But, while the dragon worked off his anger, the dwarves and Bilbo "lay and shivered though it was warm and stuffy, until dawn came pale through the crack of the door. Every now and again through the night they could hear the roar of the flying dragon grow and then pass and fade, as he hunted round and round the mountain-sides" (12:219).[2]

This is Smaug's first attack. His second is more focused, strategic, and intense. Fearing, or sensing, the worst, Bilbo insists that his companions close the door,

1 See Fussell ch. 2 for the term *troglodyte* war and a discussion of its significance.
2 It's worth noting that common German war-time practice was to shell trenches and bunkers while gradually recalibrating the aim to ensure maximum effectiveness. See Barton, Doyle and Vandewalle (207), for example.

sealing them inside the mountain. He is right. Hoping to catch his visitors unawares, Smaug "had left his lair in silent stealth, quietly soared into the air, and then floated heavy and slow in the dark like a monstrous crow, down the wind towards the west of the Mountain, in the hopes of catching unawares something or somebody there,[3] and of spying the outlet to the passage which the thief had used" (12:232).

Smaug knew, as Bilbo suspected, where the tunnel entered the mountain. Not finding the door, his frustration explodes. From inside the tunnel Bilbo and his companions experience his rage:

> [A] blow smote the side of the Mountain like the crash of battering-rams made of forest oaks and swung by giants. The rock boomed, the walls cracked and stones fell from the roof on their heads. [...] They fled further down the tunnel glad to be still alive, while behind them outside they heard the roar and rumble of Smaug's fury. He was breaking rocks to pieces, smashing wall and cliff with the lashings of his huge tail, till their little lofty camping ground, the scorched grass, the thrush's stone, the snail-covered walls, the narrow ledge, and all disappeared in a jumble of smithereens, and an avalanche of splintered stones fell over the cliff into the valley below. (*Hobbit* 12:232)

Without the secret tunnel, without the ability to disappear underground, their existence on the mountain is untenable.

This secret tunnel is not the work of amateurs. Thorin's map says the passage is "five feet high" and that "three may walk abreast" (1:26).[4] When the waning light of Durin's Day reveals both door and keyhole, the travelers peer through the newly-opened door: "It seemed as if darkness flowed out like a vapour from the hole in the mountain-side, and deep darkness in which nothing could be seen lay before their eyes, a yawning mouth leading in and down" (11:181). Bilbo realizes that "[t]his was no goblin entrance, or rough wood-elves' cave. It was a passage made by dwarves, at the height of their wealth and skill: straight

3 There may be resonances of wartime observation balloons used by both sides to gain altitude over no man's land. The balloons were used to gain intelligence about troop movements and to provide targeting information to artillery units on the ground.

4 Robinson and Cave note that, by 1916, the standard height for an explosives tunnel was 1.8 meters (5.9 feet), a height great enough for a man to swing a pick efficiently. Given the shorter stature of a dwarf, perhaps 1.5 meters (5 feet) would be sufficient. Tunnels were often built wide enough to allow men and burdens to pass each other going in opposite directions, with sufficient space in between to allow for either a rail track for removing spoil or for faster moving "runners" to pass through – hence the significance of "three may walk abreast." Also see Barrie.

as a ruler, smooth-floored and smooth-sided, going with a gentle never-varying slope direct – to some distant end in the blackness below" (12:183).

Here is another hole: "In a hole in the ground there lived a hobbit. Not a nasty, dirty, wet hole, filled with the ends of worms and an oozy smell, nor yet a dry, bare, sandy hole with nothing in it to sit down on or to eat; it was a hobbit-hole, and that means comfort" (1:11).[5] With these words, Tolkien introduces hobbits and their preferred living arrangements,[6] and he attends to the physical sensation of underground spaces – are they "nasty, dirty, and wet," "dry, spare, and sandy" or "smooth-floored, smooth-sided"? Tolkien focuses on the sensual qualities of hobbit holes just as he notes the "deep darkness" when the forgotten door in Erebor is opened. In both cases, he draws generally unremarked attention to his familiarity with underground spaces.

Writing to Christopher Tolkien in June of 1944, on the relationship between lived experience, memory, and writing, Tolkien observes

> As for what to try and write: I don't know. I tried a diary with portraits [...] of persons and events seen; but I found it was not my line. So I took to 'escapism': or really transforming experience into another form and symbol with Morgoth and Orcs and the Eldalie (representing beauty and grace of life and artefact) and so on; and it has stood me in good stead in many hard years since and I still draw on the conceptions then hammered out. But, of course, there was no time except on leave or in hospital . . . . . (*Letters* 85)

Escapism is sometimes criticized as an inward-looking and immature response to trauma. As Garth points out (*Great War* 107), that is not what Tolkien has in mind when he uses the word. In *On Fairy-stories,* Tolkien notes that, rather

5 Note the similarity to Lewis's cheery description of an underground dugout at the front near Arras. One suspects he was putting a brave face on things for the benefit of his worried father and brother: "You will be anxious to hear my first impressions of trench life. This is a very quiet part of the line and the dug outs are very much more comfortable than one imagines at home. They are very deep, you go down to them by a shaft of about 20 steps; they have wire bunks where a man can sleep quite snugly, and brasiers for warmth and cooking. Indeed the chief discomfort is that they tend to get *too* hot, while of course the bad air makes one rather headachy. I had quite a pleasant time, and was only once in a situation of unusual danger, owing to a shell falling near the latrines while I was using them." (*Letters* I.351-352)

6 Arguably, Bag End, with its capacious and comfortable living spaces, depicts hobbits' hole-building at the peak of their wealth and skill. It's little wonder that the Sackville-Bagginses covet it. Additionally, Barton, Doyle, and Vandewalle include a description of systems of dug-outs that sound very much like Bagshot Row: "Dugouts. These were the great feature. [...] [T]here were a row of dug-outs behind a bank. These were entered by a flight of steps leading into a sort of area in front of the actual dug-out. They were very roomy with plenty of room to stand up. Some were made with covered iron sheets, but most were made with timber and sandbags and had at least 12 feet of material on the roof" (210).

than "the Flight of the Deserter," he is more interested in "the Escape of the Prisoner" (69). In negotiating his escape, Tolkien has, as has been recognized by multiple scholars, reimagined many aspects of his Somme experience.[7] He himself notes that, while he does not think either of the wars of his lifetime influenced plot, the landscape in The Dead Marshes and the approaches to the Morannon "owe something to Northern France after the Battle of the Somme"[8] (*Letters* 303). One aspect of the relationship between lived experience, memory, and story-making that has not been carefully considered is his imagining of underground space and how, like his depictions of the approaches to Mordor, it may owe something to his wartime experience.

One distinct opportunity for Tolkien to have observed underground space came in the summer of 1916, at the beginning of his time on France's battlefields. John Garth's meticulous timeline of Tolkien's life on the Somme, based on Tolkien's diaries and on official regimental histories, initially stations Tolkien about three miles behind the front lines in the small, much-battered village of Bouzincourt. It is not far from Albert, and even though it was in no way safe from shelling, it was being used as a kind of staging area. Tolkien arrived there on 3 July 1916, lugging his signals officer equipment. When his brigade moved on to support trenches near La Boisselle on 5 July, Tolkien remained in Bouzincourt to help run communications for all of his division. He was in and out of the village over the next two months. Bouzincourt was the place he and his fellow Fusiliers returned to following time in the trenches, and Garth's research indicates that Tolkien spent additional time in the village with fellow TCBS-ite G.B. Smith 6-8 July 1916 and again on 22 August, and that he spent a further six days rest there in September, when he shared a tent with a friend from training camp, Leslie Risdon Huxtable.

Tolkien's familiarity with Bouzincourt and the area around it is important. Located beneath the village church is an old system of caves, hand-hewn into the chalk, which had been used for centuries as shelter in time of trouble. In 1916, these caves housed British soldiers, many of them enjoying their final moments before

7 See, for example, Garth, Croft, Livingston, Martsch.
8 One might also consider the Midgewater Marshes and the old fortifications on the overlooking hills as another landscape shaped by his wartime experience. In both cases, they have passed through Tolkien's imagination and emerged as artifacts of ancient conflicts whose memory still shapes both landscape and event.

emerging to the lethal gunfire of the battle front. Jeff Gusky, a photographer and independent researcher, estimates that about three hundred British soldiers left their names carved into the chalk during their time there. While there is no evidence that Tolkien was ever billeted in these caves, it seems unlikely that he would not have heard about these caves since they were the closest thing to safe shelter available. Gusky is convinced that these caves were an important part of the imaginative backdrop of what would become Middle-earth. He says

> This place is a netherworld. When you consider Tolkien's *Lord of the Rings* and Middle Earth, this is an alternative universe where people are living underground because the surface of the Earth has become inhospitable for human life.
>
> And so I believe that this is the place where *Lord of the Rings* was born into Tolkien's imagination. It's hard to imagine that he was not down there. Forty feet underground, it was the safest place in the village. (qtd. in "WW1 Photographer")

These underground spaces, generally known as *souterraines*, are ubiquitous in this area of France. Today, the most widely known are probably the Underground City of Naours, and Carrière Wellington, underneath Arras. According to Robinson and Cave, it would be unusual for any village in this area not to have a souterraine, generally accessed from church property, and many of them dating back to medieval, if not to Roman, times (22). These souterraines provided the stone for many of the pre-war buildings in the area and were often developed with a secondary purpose of providing a secure hiding place. Generally, they were a series of galleries supported by thick columns; sometimes they were equipped with water supplies, shop spaces, and sleeping spaces; others were less well developed, sometimes just a tunnel with an entrance point and an opening that allowed rock to be hauled to the surface. Military engineers on both sides of the conflict sought out these spaces for their defensive potential and in many cases equipped them with generators, electric lights, gas curtains, and in the larger ones, directional signage.[9] Even if Tolkien was never billeted in these souterraines, it

9 One significant aspect of any of these underground spaces is the problem of ventilation. For the tunnelers, this was often a problem with carbon monoxide which lingered in low-lying passages and could quickly overcome the unwary miner. For occupied spaces, such as the *souterraine*, or the bunkers Lewis describes in his letter home, the problem became "bad air." Put bluntly, they came to stink of large numbers of unwashed humans crammed into small spaces. Tolkien hints at the realities of such places when he alludes to the stench of Shelob's Lair that, combined with the oppressive darkness, robs Frodo and Sam of all senses but smell, and seems to leave them that only for their torment. One also thinks of Tolkien's apparent awareness of the relief of leaving underground spaces: "Thus at last, they came beyond hope under the sky and felt the wind on their faces" (*LotR* II.5.331) and of Frodo's "fey mood" (*LotR* IV.9.724) as he and Sam emerge from Cirith Ungol.

seems very unlikely that he would not have heard about their existence from soldiers who did, and given the bedraggled and forlorn state of Bouzincourt, it seems equally unlikely that he would have missed the opportunity to shelter and/or explore there.

A second opportunity for Tolkien to assimilate life underground into his fiction comes from the extensive tunneling the British undertook, beginning in 1914. By the time Tolkien arrived in France in the summer of 1916, the work was well underway, and while precautions were taken to make the activity as invisible as possible to the enemy, it was not unknown to British soldiers. In fact, soldiers were often put to work hauling out and concealing the spoil of the tunnelers' activities. In the area of the Somme where Tolkien was deployed, the underlying geology is primarily chalk,[10] and beginning in 1915, British miners were recruited, given rank as military engineers, and set to work digging deep, difficult-to-detect tunnels towards enemy lines, with the objective of laying explosives to counter similar German tunneling efforts. It was, by all reports, both back-breaking and nerve-wracking work. The slightest sound could reveal the location of the tunnelers and could provoke a defensive explosion.[11] The goal was to get as close to the enemy as possible undetected, and the best way to do that was to dig deep and dig fast. It was impossible to completely muffle the clink of metal tools on chalk if the tunnel was too close to the surface, so tunnels were delved deep, and entrances were often concealed within more conventional surface trenches and dugouts.

In addition to the risks of detection and explosion, another risk was meeting the enemy underground. On occasion, German and English tunnels connected.

10 Flanders' soil, further north, is primarily clay, so the engineering challenges of the two areas are very different. The chalk in the Picardy and Artois regions meant that mining and constructing underground spaces was rarely silent, but it lent itself well to reasonably stable structures. A persistent problem is that chalk is water-permeable, meaning that the resulting tunnels were often damp or flooded. See Barton, Doyle, and Vandewalle 74-78 for further information. For more information on underground efforts in general, and photographs see "WW1 Photographer" and Walford.

11 The urgent need to detect enemy mining activities lead to a rapid improvement in listening technology. Early in the war, often the best equipment miners had was a container of water on the ground to amplify sound. A man would lie on the ground with his ear in the water, listening. Soon, more sophisticated geophones were added along with a carefully organized system for trained listeners. See Barton, Doyle and Vandewalle 99-108 for further information.

Sometimes, this was an opportunity to blow up the enemy's tunnel, but sometimes, if there were miners present on both sides, it produced a lethal fight in dark, low, and narrow tunnels. Even when it did not produce a confrontation, the awareness of the possibility of a meeting, or of being detected and blown up (*lifted* was the term miners used) remained forefront in the imagination. In one instance, German troops took brief control of British front line trenches at Mount Sorrel when tunnelers were underground nearby and unaware of the German presence. When the miners emerged, they were spotted and pursued underground. Barton, Doyle, and Vandewalle summarize the ensuing fight: "[f]ighting with grenades, pistols, rifles, and hand to hand with knives, bayonets and even razor sharp spades in the tiny galleries, the encounter was horrific. [...] [S]ixty out of eighty of [the tunnelers] were killed or wounded. The struggle lasted almost twenty-four hours" (141).

While it is true, as Garth points out, that Tolkien makes no direct mention of these caves, or of the tunnels,[12] Gusky argues that it is not surprising. He says "soldiers on both sides of the conflict almost never wrote about the places underground where they found sanctuary" (qtd. in "WW1 Photographer"). Instead, Tolkien, respecting the classified nature of the information, concealed what he knew in plain sight, just as he did the blasted landscape of the Somme battlefield.[13]

The historical fact of the underground war as Tolkien experienced it manifests itself in his fiction. For example, Erebor: the tunnel is smooth and well-carved out of the stone. It is the work of skillful miners. It provides concealment and shelter, but it is also dangerous. In his fury at not being able to find his unwanted visitors, Smaug attacks the side of the mountain with fire and with lashes of his tail. It is "like the crash of battering-rams made of forest oaks and swung by giants." As Bilbo and the dwarves cower within, "the rock booms, the walls crack and stones

12 Garth remains skeptical: "'On the Somme, [Tolkien] certainly spent time in deep trench dugouts, and he would have been aware of the subterranean world of the army tunnelers – all of which would, I believe, have given his descriptions of Moria and other Middle-earth underworlds some of their vitality,' Garth [...] wrote in an email. 'But the caves at Bouzincourt? There's no evidence that Tolkien's battalion stayed in anything other than huts, bivouacs or conventional billets while there in the summer of 1916'" (qtd. in Leopold).

13 It's worth noting that, on 1 July 1916, as Tolkien waited in reserve trenches, the British set off nineteen separate mines, including the giant Glory Hole, as they launched the disastrous opening day of the Battle of the Somme.

fall from the roof on their heads." Given the historical background, this sounds very much like echoes of enemy shelling witnessed from underground shelter.[14]

Sound is not Bilbo's friend. Reprising the difficulties of Somme mining crews while making his way down the tunnel towards Smaug, Bilbo is "warned by the echoes to take more than hobbit's care to make no sound" (*Hobbit* 12:214). Further, his interior monologue places him in sympathy with the volunteer digger in the dangerous environment of the tunnels: "Now you are in for it at last, Bilbo Baggins [...]. You went and put your foot right in it that night of the party,[15] and now you have got to pull it out and pay for it! Dear me, what a fool I was and am!" (12:214). He is right. After Smaug misses his great golden cup, and he detects a foreign smell on the air, he glares at the small opening Bilbo had used: "of late, he had half fancied he had caught the dim echoes of a knocking sound" (12:217) coming from the opening. Why, he wonders, had he never blocked the opening?[16] The tunnelers, as well as the above-ground soldiers near their dig sites, could be exposed by the tiniest of noises of metal on chalk. Both sides feared being undermined and surprised by their enemy, and both sides developed and deployed sensitive underground listening devices designed to detect the faint tapping noises that meant danger. If they were detected, the tunnel would be packed with explosives and detonated, meaning certain death for enemy tunnelers and potential death if those above ground were too close to the point of detonation.

14 Garth offers another suggestion of linkages between Erebor and Tolkien's experience on the Somme: "A world away from subtle, magnificent Smaug of *The Hobbit*, Tolkien's first dragons are surreal hybrids of beast and machine. They lumber against the elf-city of Gondolin, spouting fire and clanking, with orctroops hidden inside. This was in the first Middle-earth story, begun by 2nd Lieut JRR Tolkien in hospital straight after the Battle of the Somme, where Britain's own secret weapon, the tank, had just been rolled out." (Garth, "Battle")

15 Impulsive enlistment seems to lurk behind Bilbo's observation here. Wilfred Owen's poem "Disabled" attributes his young man's underage enlistment, in part, to a decision to please "the giddy jilts" who told him, during a party celebrating a victorious football match, that he'd "look a god in kilts."

16 As well, the goblins, in their pursuit of Bilbo and the dwarves, initially make the mistake of pursuing them without care for sound or light. Having turned a corner and finding themselves confronted by "Beater and Biter," for their second attempt to recapture Bilbo and the dwarves, the goblins "put out their torches and they slipped on soft shoes, and they chose out their very quickest runners with the sharpest ears and eyes. These ran forward, as swift as weasels in the dark, and with hardly any more noise than bats" (*Hobbit* 4:67). Wrapping their shoes in cloth or covering the floor with rugs commandeered from civilian homes were common practices among miners hoping to deaden sound and conceal their presence.

Finally, there is the subjective, emotional quality of underground space. Other than hobbit holes, which were explicitly designed to overcome the negative qualities of being underground, Tolkien's underground spaces in *The Hobbit* emphasize the oppressive darkness, the need for stealth, and the lingering sense of danger above ground. When the door in the side of Erebor opens "[i]t seemed as if darkness flowed out like a vapour from the hole in the mountain-side, and deep darkness in which nothing could be seen lay before their eyes, a yawning mouth leading in and down" (*Hobbit* 11:210). Below, and later in the sky above them, there is a dragon, and there is always the possibility that, when the door is closed, they will be trapped.

This pattern of similarities to the Somme underground war is not limited to Erebor, nor indeed to *The Hobbit*. Helm's Gate is breached by tunneling orcs, who lay explosive charges in the culvert where the Deeping Stream passes out of the Deep, and the people of Rohan take shelter in the caves of Aglarond, natural formations perhaps, but also reminiscent of the chalk caves of Bouzincourt. More significantly, Moria echoes the pattern. The Nine Walkers must disappear from the surface. Gandalf says "I see now little hope, if we do not soon vanish from sight for a while, and cover our trail. Therefore I advise that we should go neither over the mountains, nor round them, but under them" (*LotR* II.4.296). Caradhras has defeated their attempts to cross the mountains; birds, *crebain*, have been scouring the land from the air, and the Wargs have come west of the mountains. "The hunt is up!" (*LotR* II.4.297), Gandalf says. The skies above them are unfriendly, and the land journey is untenable. The solution lies underground.[17]

When the doors to Moria finally swing open, they reveal a darkness that "was deeper than the night" (*LotR* II.4.308). Other than the oppressive darkness and danger, probably the most significant parallel here results from Pippin's curious attraction to the guards' broken well at the end of their first march. He peers over the edge of the well, and "a chill air seemed to strike his face, rising from invisible depths." He drops in a stone and waits many heart beats before there comes a "*plunk*, very distant, but magnified and repeated in the

17 One thinks also of Legolas' advice to hobbits unwilling to shelter up in the trees on the border of Lothlórien: "Then dig a hole in the ground [...] if that is more after the fashion of your kind. But you must dig swift and deep, if you wish to hide from Orcs" (*LotR* II.6.342).

hollow shaft." Alarmed, Gandalf scolds the "Fool of a Took!" and reminds him that they are "not a hobbit walking-party." He commands Pippin to "be quiet!" (*LotR* II.4.313).

The alarm over what would usually be an innocent sound and the magnification of its echoes matters here. If this were a British tunneling group, every entry into cave or tunnel would have been met by "chill air," and any sound risked betraying their presence to German tunnelers. Pippin's result is not dissimilar. His innocent "*plunk*" is met, several minutes later, by a series of faint knocks from the depths: "*tom-tap, tap-tom*" and minutes later, by "*tap-tom, tom-tap, tap-tap, tom.*" Gimli notes "That was the sound of a hammer, or I have never heard one" (*LotR* II.4.313).[18] Assuming that Gandalf is right that the hammer-taps are a signal, Pippin's "*plunk*" is likely what causes both the nearly-disastrous orc attack in the Chamber of Mazarbul and Gandalf's fatal confrontation with the Balrog.[19]

Of course, it is likely that Tolkien, scholar that he was, had multiple sources for his underground spaces. It is impossible to be encyclopedic here; one can only point to some suggestive sources where underground space is a significant part of the story. Clearly, one place to look would be in classical accounts of a hero's journey to the underworld, specifically, Odysseus, Aeneas,[20] or Orpheus. The Middle English romance "Sir Orfeo" is, in some ways, more interesting in this context. Tolkien, in collaboration with medievalist Kenneth Sisam, edited a Middle English version of the poem in the 1920s, and seems to have returned to the text in the 1940s to develop a modern English version (Hostetter). While 1944 is too late for the translation to provide direct evidence of influence, the earlier date, combined with the later one, suggests ongoing engagement with

18 About sound, Robinson and Cave quote miners from Vimy Ridge in the spring of 1916: "It was eerie work down there, far under the ground, watching the white-faced miners picking away at the chalky soil, which was filled into sandbags as it fell and carried away, especially when it was known that the German engineers were engaged in similar work only a few yards through the chalk! The working parties were fascinated by the listening apparatus used by the miners, through which the faint thud of the German picks could be plainly heard, and by which means their progress could be judged to a foot." (142)

19 Barton, Doyle, and Vandewalle (134-41) describe underground combat and pursuit in terms that sound very much like both the flight from the orcs in Moria (*LotR* II.5.325-332) and from the goblins under the Misty Mountains (*Hobbit* 9.76-78).

20 For an interesting comparative analysis of Aeneas in the Underworld and Frodo in Moria, see Obertino, who sees both explorations through a Jungian interpretive lens; however, like the other works mentioned, *The Aeneid* does little with either rounded character development or sensory detail.

the poem. In all of these stories, the protagonist enters the underworld on a quest. The focus is on the quest itself, on the characters met in the underworld, and the relative degree of success of their errand.

Alternatively, one could look to George MacDonald's *The Princess and the Goblin* (published 1872) or *The Princess and Curdie* (published 1883), both of which feature significant use of underground mines as both setting and plot device. In these novels, the underground space functions as a dark place of menace and mystery. Contrasting the following description of the entrance to MacDonald's mine with Tolkien's description of entering Moria provides an instructive example:

> [Miners Curdie and his father] entered the hill by a natural opening under a huge rock, where a little stream rushed out. They followed its course for a few yards, when the passage took a turn, and sloped steeply into the heart of the hill. With many angles and windings and branchings off, and sometimes with steps where it came upon a natural gulf, it led them deep into the hill before they arrived at the place where they were at present digging out the precious ore. This was of various kinds, for the mountain was very rich with the better sorts of metals. With flint and steel, and tinder box, they lighted their lamps, then fixed them on their heads, and were soon hard at work with their pickaxes and shovels and hammers. (47)

As is common in these types of stories, both character and setting remain flat; they do not seem to be the focus of the story. This stands in sharp contrast to Tolkien's handling of the "underworld" in his work.

Finally, given the long-standing and insightful attention Tolkien invested in the poem, one should consider underground space in *Beowulf*. Beowulf only goes underground once, when he confronts Grendel's mother in her cave at the bottom of the mere. The cave is air-filled, and he learns that the sword he brought with him has no power there. The poet provides some detail about Beowulf's fight with Grendel's mother, and about his passage through the water to enter and leave her cave, but few details about the cave itself.

In all of these examples, Tolkien's treatment of underground space differs in the extent to which he deploys sensory detail to evoke experience. Partly, that is bound up in the concerns of the twentieth century novelist, but partly, I would argue, it is also connected to the availability of sensory experience.[21] For example, Tolkien's own account of a journey to the underworld, Aragorn's passage through the Paths of the Dead to call oath-breakers to keep their word and break Isildur's curse, re-centers the narrative focus seen in the older narratives. The party arrives while

> light was still grey [...] for the sun had not yet climbed over the black ridges of the Haunted Mountain before them. [...] There under the gloom of black trees that not even Legolas could long endure they found a hollow place opening at the mountain's root, and right in their path stood a single mighty stone like a finger of doom. [...] And so they came at last deep into the glen; and there stood a sheer wall of rock, and in the wall the Dark Door gaped before them like the mouth of night. Signs and figures were carved above its wide arch too dim to read, and fear flowed from it like a grey vapour. (*LotR* V.II.786)[22]

After they pass through the Door of the Dead, the narrative focuses on Gimli: once he crosses the threshold, his feet are "like lead;" the "dread was so heavy on him that he could hardly walk;" he marvels at Aragorn's calm, noting that he evinces no fear of the "whispering darkness." Gimli "was ever hindmost, pursued by a groping horror that seemed just about to seize him; and a rumour came after him like the shadow-sound of many feet. He stumbled on until he was crawling like a beast on the ground and felt that he could endure no more; he must either find an ending and escape or run back in madness to meet the following fear" (*LotR* V.2.786-88). In Gimli's visceral terror, Tolkien gives us an organic response to underground space that is missing from many of the older accounts of the underworld and affords a glimpse of what his war-time experience of underground space can add to these likely additional sources.

---

21 Similarly, Croft observes that "Tolkien was surely aware of the mythological significance of underground adventures when he wrote about the goblin battle in the passages under the Misty Mountains and the terrifying uncertainty of entering Smaug's caverns in *The Hobbit*, or the disorienting tunnels of the mines of Moria, the ghosts crowding the Paths of the Dead, and the stench of Shelob's Lair in *The Lord of the Rings*. But the importance of this motif for Tolkien, and the vocabulary of images available to him for describing it, may well have been augmented by his underground experiences in the Great War." (52)

22 In this passage, Tolkien distantly echoes Beowulf and his companions arriving at the mere to confront Grendel's mother: "And now those men of noble race, steep stony slopes they overpassed, narrow tracks and one-man paths, down unfamiliar trails, past headlong crags, and many a house of demons of the deep. One [...] went on before to spy the land, until on a sudden he came upon the mountain-trees leaning o'er the hoar rock, a joyless forest. Bloodstained and troubled water loomed beneath." (Tolkien's *Beowulf* translation, lines 1174-1180)

In his 1936 *Beowulf: The Monsters and the Critics*, Tolkien explains that one of the great strengths of the poem is that "Grendel inhabits the visible world and eats the flesh and blood of men; he enters their houses by the doors. The dragon wields a physical fire, and covets gold not souls; he is slain with iron in his belly. Beowulf's *byrne* was made by Weland, and the iron shield he bore against the serpent by his own smiths" (23-4). Earlier in the same essay, he makes a similar point about Beowulf himself, pointing out that "[s]omething more significant than a standard hero, a man faced with a foe more evil than any human enemy of house or realm, is before us, and yet incarnate in time, walking in heroic history, and treading the named lands of the North" (17).[23] Three years later, in his 1939 essay *On Fairy-stories*, Tolkien returns to a similar idea: "Probably every writer making a secondary world, a fantasy, every sub-creator, wishes in some measure to be a real maker, or hopes that he is drawing on reality: hopes that the peculiar quality of this secondary world [is] derived from Reality, or is flowing into it" (77). While this is, at best, an observation leading into a main point in his argument, it does offer a glimpse of Tolkien's view of the relationship between the visible world and the fantastic, and between lived experience and the kind of story that melds that experience with story. This is a relationship that Tolkien takes seriously: "For the story-maker who allows himself to be 'free with' Nature can be her lover not her slave. It was in fairy-stories that I first divined the potency of the words, and the wonder of the things, such as stone, and wood, and iron; tree and grass; house and fire; bread and wine" (*OFS* 69). In melding the imagined and the experienced, in allowing himself the fantasist's freedom, Tolkien differentiates himself from many of his likely source writers. It is not my intent to suggest that these potential, and even likely, sources are irrelevant. Rather, I would suggest that here, as in so many other instances, Tolkien draws on multiple strands of knowledge and experience, and the tunnels and caves of the Somme should be considered among them.

23 Faramir, too, is "a man" who walks "in heroic history": "A new character has come on the scene (I am sure I did not invent him, I did not even want him, though I like him, but there he came walking into the woods of Ithilien): Faramir, the brother of Boromir" (*Letters* 79).

Bibliography

BARRIE, Alexander. *War Underground.* London: Tom Donovan, 1961.

BARTON, Peter, Peter DOYLE, and Johan VANDEWALLE. *Beneath Flanders Fields: The Tunnellers' War 1914-18.* Staplehurst: Spellmount, 2004.

CROFT, Janet Brennan. *War and the Works of JRR Tolkien.* Westport, CT: Praeger, 2004.

FUSSELL, Paul. *The Great War and Modern Memory.* Oxford: University Press, 2013.

GARTH, John. "The Battle of the Somme: The Animal Horror That Inspired J.R.R. Tolkien."*The Telegraph.* 4 Oct 2013. www.telegraph.co.uk/history/world-war-one/inside-first-world-war/part-two/10356085/jrr-tolkien-war.html. 20 Sept 2018.

Tolkien and the Great War: Threshold of Middle-earth. New York City, NY: Houghton Mifflin Harcourt, 2003.

GUSKY, Jeff. "Commonwealth Underground." 2011-19. *Dr. Jeff Gusky: Doctor, Artist, Explorer.* https://jeffgusky.com/portfolio/commonwealth-underground. 19 Mar 2017.

HOSTETTER, Carl. "Sir Orfeo: A Modern English Version by JRR Tolkien." *Tolkien Studies* 1 (2004): 85-123.

LEOPOLD, Todd. "WWI Site Offers Hints of JRR Tolkien." CNN.com. 23 July 2015. www.cnn.com/2015/07/22/world/tolkien-somme-bouzincourt-caves-wwi-feat/index.html. 20 Sept 2018.

LEWIS, C.S. *Collected Letters Vol. 1: Family Letters 1905-1931.* Ed. Walter Hooper. Vol. 1. London: Harper Collins, 2000.

LIVINGSTON, Michael. "The Shell-Shocked Hobbit: The First World War and Tolkien's Trauma of the Ring." Ed. Janet Brennan Croft. *Baptism of Fire: The Birth of the Modern British Fantastic in World War I.* Altadena, CA: Mythopoeic Press, 2015, 9-22.

MACDONALD, George. *The Princess and the Goblin.* Garden City, NY: Doubleday, Doran & Co., 1928.

MARTSCH, Nancy. "Thiepval Ridge and Minas Tirith." *Mythlore* 33:125 (2015), 153-56.

OBERTINO, James. "Moria and Hades: Underworld Journeys in Tolkien and Virgil." *Comparative Literature Studies* 30.2 (1993): 153-169.

OWEN, Wilfred. "Disabled." 1917. *Poetry Foundation*. www.poetryfoundation.org/poems/57285/disabled. 25 Sept 2018.

PRIESTLY, R.E. *The Signal Service in the European War 1914-1918*. Chatham: W&J MacKay, 1921. https://archive.org/stream/signalserviceine00prie#page/n7.

ROBINSON, Phillip, and Nigel CAVE. *The Underground War: Vimy Ridge to Arras*. Barnsley: Pen and Sword Books, 2011.

TOLKIEN, Christopher. "The Evolution of the Great Tales." Tolkien, J.R.R. *The Children of Húrin*. Boston, MA: Houghton Mifflin, 2007, 269-291.

TOLKIEN, J.R.R. Beowulf: *a Translation and Commentary*. Ed. Christopher Tolkien. Boston, MA: Houghton Mifflin Harcourt, 2014.

Beowulf: *The Monsters and the Critics*. London: Oxford UP, 1936.

The Hobbit. Boston, MA: Houghton Mifflin, 1994.

The Letters of JRR Tolkien. Boston, MA: Houghton Mifflin, 1981.

The Lord of the Rings. 50th Anniversary edition. Boston, MA: Houghton Mifflin, 2004.

On Fairy-stories: Expanded Edition with Commentary and Notes. Ed. Verlyn Flieger and Douglas Anderson. London: HarperCollins, 2008.

WALFORD, Charles. "Inside the Real Birdsong Tunnels: Never-Before-Seen Images of the Mines Dug by British 'Clay-Kickers' Under German Lines in First World War." 27 Jan 2012. www.dailymail.co.uk/news/article-2092768/Never-seen-images-Birdsong-tunnels-dug-British-pit-workers-undermine-German-lines-First-World-War.html.

"WW1 Photographer Jeff Gusky Reveals his New Pictures of the Hidden Somme." *Centenary News: First World War 1914-18*. 21 Aug 2015. www.centenarynews.com/article/ww1-photographer-jeff-gusky-reveals-his-new-pictures-of-the-hidden-somme-. 7 Jan 2019.

Molly Volanth Hall

Narrating the Missed Encounter with the Loss of a World: *The Lord of the Rings'* Testimony to Modern Ecology

Fantastic literary responses to World War I (WWI) are often seen merely as a Victorian holdover. The fantastic, however, exceeds its nineteenth century origins, offering a unique and important response that both complements and completes studies of modernity, especially two of modernity's more central issues – warfare and ecology. Literary WWI scholarship and the scholarship of modernity more generally have largely ignored fantastic testimony. This is in part due to the dominance of modernist and realist fiction. The divergence between realist, modernist, and fantastic literatures impacted by WWI becomes most clear in the fantastical use of the pastoral – through the lens of ecological subtexts inscribed into the war landscapes of a body of mid-century novels and poetry born out of WWI. It is the realist foreclosure – or fantastic opening up – of a formative interconnectivity between the internal and external, subject and object, and hence, subjectivity and ecology, that distinguishes these genres' disparate responses to WWI. Such a post-WWI cognitive shift is significant, I argue in this essay, because it conceptually divorces humanity from ecology – a separation that reverberated outward throughout Western culture, beyond the soldiers in the trenches, and forward in time to tinge the whole of modernity itself.

Fantasy writers address this separation of the subject and its environ differently than the writers of non-fantastical literature, the modernists and war memoirists of the period. J.R.R. Tolkien's *The Lord of the Rings* (*LotR*) trilogy serves as an excellent case study of this dynamic. In its fantastical form, the work functions as testimony to this phenomenon, negotiating the relationship between war and ecology in response to WWI in ways less accessible to Tolkien's fellow English modernist and war writers. This essay will discuss how the fantastical characteristics of *LotR's* reaction to WWI provide a more vivid encounter for the reader of the uncanny displacement at the center of the experience of that war. *LotR's* traumatic legibility comes from the fantastic tendency to displace the felt subjective gap between self and world into a fictional realm by creating a "secondary world".[1] This sets it apart from the impulse of modernist aesthetics, trench poetry, and war memoirs which stage such narratives in the "primary", or real world (*OFS* 132). Unlike fantasy texts, by setting this gap in "reality" modernist and realist works valorize and reinforce this sense of alienation by hailing the ultimate foreclosure of the subject's interiority. Reading a fantastical response as testimony underscores its ability to open up the possibility of productive historical witness for the reader. For this form of witness to be productive, it must be more memorial in function than elegiac. As a memorialization of the warzone of WWI and its larger impact on modern culture, *LotR* opens a space for both a grieving of a loss of world and a re-narrativization of the ecological relationship of self and culture to the surrounding world.

Though the typically elegiac style of ecological readings of *LotR* often reinforces the distance between subject and environment, Tolkien's tale subverts such simple divisions in its treatment of the relationship between loss and home-place throughout this narrative response to war. Modernist and realist texts emphasize the way in which the battle of the Somme was won slowly and at great cost due to the implementation and normalization of the new strategic combination of attrition and total war. In contradistinction, *LotR's* fantastic counterpart – the battle of Helm's Deep – lasts only two days and is ended not by pressing forward with morbid stubbornness, but through alliance with the landscape itself. When all hope is lost, Rohan rides out "driving forth the enemy," and as they reached the Dike, "they gazed down upon the Deeping-coomb. The land had changed. Where before the green dale had lain, its grassy slopes lapping the ever-mounting hills, there now a forest loomed. [...] [T]rees [...] rank on rank [...] their twisted roots were buried in the long green grass" (*LotR* III.7.540-1). This forest did not spring up overnight, but *travelled* there, to aid Rohan in

1 In his essay "On Fairy-stories", Tolkien theorizes the relation between the "primary" and "secondary" worlds of reality and of the author's creation respectively (132). Middle-earth is the secondary world of Tolkien's creation – for *The Lord of the Rings* and beyond. According to Tolkien, the goal of fantasy is to create in the secondary or fantastical literary world the same "belief that a thing exists or can happen" just as it would "in the real (primary) world" (132). This "literary belief" occurs "when the story-maker's art is good enough to produce it. That state of mind has been called 'willing suspension of disbelief'. But this does not seem to me a good description of what happens. What really happens is that the story-maker proves a successful 'sub-creator'. He makes a Secondary World which your mind can enter. Inside it, what he relates is 'true': it accords with the laws of that world. You therefore believe it, while you are, as it were, inside." (132)

defeating their common enemy, Saruman, who had destroyed their home near Isengard. This strategy succeeds. Trapped between the cavalry of Rohan and the translocated forest of Fangorn, the armies of Saruman panic and flee into death on the swords of the Rohirrim or into the forest itself where they will be killed by the trees (III.7.542). Unique to Tolkien's literary response to the war is the alliance of free peoples of Middle-earth with non-human elements of the local ecosystem, rejecting dehumanizing war tactics when faced with an uncanny enemy that threatens the annihilation of the world as all know it. In contrast to representations of the actual artillery and trenches, which depict nature as dark and deformed in its abandonment of humanity, Tolkien binds their fates together.

This does not erase the ecological sense of loss at the core of the narrative, however. Though the loss is not of place itself in the form of a divorce of self *from* place, Tolkien does depict a foundational place-related loss: the loss of a self as constituted by place-attachment. What is remembered in *LotR* is a dismemberment that severs both limb from body and self from home-place. As the bearer of the One Ring which must be destroyed to stop Sauron's enslavement and destruction of all the lands and peoples of Middle-earth, Frodo finally arrives at Mount Doom to destroy the ring and complete the purpose of his quest. His journey to the site of his quest's completion also culminates, however, in the realignment of his attachments – displacing them from the desire to save Middle-earth and the Shire to the possession of the Ring. When Sam finds his way into the mountain he sees Frodo on the edge of the crack from which lava spits and boils below and the following ensues:

> 'I have come,' [Frodo] said. 'But I do not choose now to do what I came to do. I will not do this deed. The Ring is mine!' And suddenly, as he set it on his finger, he vanished from Sam's sight. […] [T]hen [Sam] saw a strange and terrible thing. Gollum on the edge of the abyss was fighting like a mad thing with an unseen foe. (VI.3.945-6)

At the crucial moment, when Frodo is finally able to destroy the Ring, the hobbit cannot. Following a series of emphatic "I" statements, one can read in the exclamation, "The Ring *is* mine!," that Frodo's selfhood has been consumed by the Ring. One can read this possessive statement as a marker of his transformation. This "is", as the verb to be was intended to, facilitates a symbolic equation. Frodo does not simply claim ownership of the object, he expresses the deep entanglement of his subjectivity in it. Tolkien scholar Verlyn Flieger reads this concatenation, also, in the power of the Ring over the bearer's body. She writes, "in the case of Frodo [...] Tolkien is using invisibility as the outward and visible (or invisible) sign of an inward process, a progressive fading and loss of self" ("The Body in Question" 285). Donning the Ring, no longer does Frodo merely wear the Ring. He *is* the Ring. It has become a part of him, putting the self for whom the most important thing was his home-place – the Shire – under erasure. And with this conversion, his body also quite literally disappears.

Because the *LotR's* loss is an interior one, rather than a separation of self from external world, Tolkien's response highlights key post-war generic differences in reported subjective access to exteriority. Modernist poet W.H. Auden suggests that both modernist *and* fantasy writers attempt to bridge the "gulf between the subjectively real [...] and the objectively real" (44) in response to what fantasy and modernist scholar Margaret Hiley has described as "the loss of values and roots" as a result of the trauma of WWI (31). This breakage of cultural and temporal frames of reference, to borrow a phrase from trauma theorist Shoshana Felman, resulted in the "breakdown" of the "synthesis of objective reality and subjective reality" (Hiley 22).[2] The modernist reaction was to write under the assumption that "only the subjectively real could be fully known," while fantasy writers chose to conjure up a "fantastic secondary world [where] the gap between subjective and objective reality no longer exists" (Hiley 22). In fantastic narratives such as *LotR* this gap is displaced from the modernist subject-object split (of individual *from* direct access to the external world) to a gap that instead emerges *between* the primary world of reality and the secondary world of the story. The objective reality of the twentieth-century is marked by an acceleration of both war and ecological destruction. In response, the modernist tendency is to enforce a subjective distancing from such materialities by focusing on the all-important "I" of subjective reality. This tendency is reversed in fantasy literature with the creation of whole worlds lacking this

2 The breaking of frames of reference refers, quite plainly, to the lack of prior memories or knowledge to account for the newness of a traumatic experience, such as WWI. Because the mind integrates new information and experiences by associating them with existing images and ideas in the mind, something so new and strange as to lack any bridge at all back to expectations based on the past, would break the frame of reference of the average mind, resulting in a traumatic pathology in order to cope and maintain a semblance of subjective cohesion.

distance. This is the case in *LotR* where the stability of the individual self is bound irrevocably to the fate of the ecological interdependence (or fellowship) of Middle-earth. The reality-bound impulse of modernist aesthetics, war memoirists, and trench poets led to the creation of a multiplicity of individuated subjects liberated from the external world which brought them nothing but death and sorrow. Whereas, the fantastic impulse of speculative writers such as Tolkien and C.S. Lewis was to salvage the intra-connection between subject and world by manifesting its connection in the creation of a whole new world – a world always seeming to be invested simultaneously with both the mythic past and real potential future of modern Europe. Though by the story's end the gap is refigured as that between worlds rather than that between subject and world, even in the fantastical realm created by Tolkien this subjective displacement remains as the constitutive trauma around which the secondary world is maintained. In displacing the gap *itself* to a different world, however, I argue Tolkien succeeds in extending the possibility that one's relationship to reality can be remade, while also testifying to the seemingly insurmountable horror of historical traumas such as WWI.

The *Lord of the Ring's* function as testimony to a subjective trauma is encapsulated in the final moment of crisis at Mount Doom, when Gollum makes his final move to regain the Ring from Frodo who has taken it there to destroy it and avert the fall of Middle-earth to Sauron's annihilating power. Tolkien writes,

> To and fro he swayed, now so near the brink that almost he tumbled in, now dragging back, falling to the ground, rising, and falling again. […] Frodo gave a cry, and there he was, fallen upon his knees at the chasm's edge. But Gollum, dancing like a mad thing, held aloft the ring, a finger still thrust within its circle. […] [E]ven as his eyes were lifted up to gloat on his prize, he stepped too far, toppled, wavered for a moment on the brink, and then with a shriek he fell. (VI.3.946)

Here one finds a repeated sequence of falls. Four falls are described in reference to the bodies of Frodo and Gollum, two together, and one each alone. The ultimate fall is the crux of the scene because it is the fall that destroys the One Ring, not, as the fellowship intended, completed by Frodo, who in the end failed at his task, but by the unlikely Gollum himself. Hence, the fall of destruction is not intentional but *accidental*.

The significance of the traumatic fall is, as explained by trauma theorist Cathy Caruth, to be located in "the recurring image of the accident [...] as the illustration of the unexpected or the accidental [...] becom[ing] the exemplary scene of trauma *par excellence* [...] because it tells of what it is, in traumatic events, that is *not* precisely grasped" (6). It is within Gollum's absorption with his "Precious" that this accident is allowed to occur, and it is also his last word as he dies not thinking of his own survival but of what he has become, no longer a person but the beholder of the precious Ring. It is through this moment, the transpiring of both a bodily dismemberment (Frodo's finger) and a fall (Gollum's body), which I insist one must read the whole of *The Lord of the Rings'* response to the trauma of WWI. Caruth explains that, "the unexpected reality – the locus of referentiality – of the traumatic story [...] associates reference with an impact [...] the impact of the fall [...] the story of the falling body [...] the story of the impact of reference [in which] the story of trauma is inescapably bound to a referential return" (6-7). This impact or impact of reference literally means the force of knowledge – raw sensory data coming into the brain – which lacks the attendant processing, integrating, and conscious understanding of what is happening to one and why it matters. Gollum's fall, repeated literally and metaphorically in Frodo's fall to his knees, therefore, illustrates the moment of the impact of reference for Frodo, who is unable at the time to grasp its meaning because of its accidental nature. This is the moment of his trauma.

Though the core moment of Frodo's trauma is set in the anti-pastoral locale of Mordor, this moment must be read together with Frodo's return to that traditionally pastoral place – the Shire. As Paul Fussell has noted, this burgeoning division between self and external world appears most vividly in war literature's pastoral representations of nature (86-7, 255). Frodo's reason for embarking on the *LotR*'s quest is to save his beloved pastoral Shire. Many war writers evoked the pastoral ironically to describe both the geographic and cognitive dissonance between home front and front lines, but it was also evocative of a deeper loss, not felt as the first soldiers left in 1914, but constructed slowly in the collective war experience, resulting in a sense that all of time now seemed divided by the trenches of the Western Front.

Uses of pastoral nature in *LotR* have been much discussed in Tolkienian scholarship, always focused on themes of natural mysticism and anti-industrialization.

Matthew Dickerson and Jonathan Evans outline Tolkien's environmental ethic as a "deep and complex ecological vision" (xvi). In Middle-earth, they argue, people, "although they are a *part* of nature [...] also somehow *transcend* nature [...]. [F]rom the beginning, nature's purpose is intimately bound to their coming into the world" (51-52). This quasi-mystical stance overlaps ironically with Verlyn Flieger's interpretation of *LotR*'s response to an increasingly industrial world, noting the text deals often with the "problem [...] of how to answer growing human needs without sacrificing to them some portion of the natural environment," arguing Tolkien concludes this problem "is unsolvable [...]. [I]t is inevitable that we alter nature, and in that alteration it is also inevitable that some of the things we would wish to preserve will be irretrievably lost" ("Taking the Part of Trees" 274). Tolkien's pastoral vision in *LotR*, adds Christopher Brawley, embodies the belief that, "the industrialization of our world divorces us from an experience of the sacramental vision [of nature], and hence there is more of a need to experience it within literary forms [...]. [T]he Shire is a peaceful place, [its] pastoralism [...] is the first image of home [...], the Shire represents a closeness to nature" (304). While doubtless Tolkien was concerned about the impacts of industrialization on a natural world he held in highest esteem, this assigns the Shire alone the status of an archetypal pastoral homeland from which post-war industrialism has divorced humanity. Brawley's reading of the Shire mirrors WWI writers' common distortion of what "home" used to be before the war, taking on an almost sacred, Edenic air, and reinforcing modern humanity's inaccessible divorce from it. While Tolkien's Shire evokes this theme, I argue he complicates it as well.

Tolkien's evocation of the pastoral mode must be understood, therefore, in light of the events of one of the closing chapters, the "Scouring of the Shire", wherein for all but Frodo a recovery of a "closeness to nature" is allowed to follow the war. Many ecocritical readings of *LotR* and WWI literature seem to treat nature as something inaccessible to modern subjects – reading Shire or England as elegiac representations of the home front. Tolkien's conclusion, however, suggests no such foreclosure is inevitable. Ecocritical scholars Tim Matts and Aidan Tynan explain that "[i]t is necessary to reconceptualise, beyond this negative mode, the violence invoked whenever we speak of environmental damage. [We must] re-conside[r] what is meant by 'nature'" (154). The dominant conception of nature is, according to ecocritical philosopher Timothy Morton, "that there is a 'thing' called nature that is 'out there' beyond us" (*Ecology* 183). Matts and Tynan add that this conception "ignore[s] the very ecological relations that already characterize the specifically human" (154). Morton and Matts and Tynan suggest, therefore, that there is no "objective" reality which can rightfully be said to be "beyond" subjective reality.

Because of this, the "violence" of "environmental damage" – like that which characterizes the human-environmental relationship within the industrial culture born out of WWI – must be "reconceptualized" to acknowledge this not-beyond-ness. The environmental damage of *LotR* comes in the form of the destruction at Isengard, Mordor, and the Shire by Sauron and Saruman. Tolkien strives to achieve the "reconceptualization" Morton suggests in his narration of such ecological "violence" together with the narrative of the subjective trauma of war – mainly that of Frodo and the other Ring-bearers. The key to understanding Tolkien's "reconceptualization" as distinct from the dominant twentieth-century modernist and realist modes lies in the reader's ability to see how Tolkien goes beyond the pastoral in his uniquely ecological treatment of the much-discussed presence of loss throughout the text.

The wounded body of Frodo is key to an ecological understanding of trauma in *LotR* beyond the elegiac pastoral mode. The scarred body acts as the physical repository for the memories of accrued accidents – echoing the scarred landscape of the material war zone. In addition to losing his finger, the Ring, and his sense of self, each physical wound Frodo accrues in service to the War of the Ring comes to him also when he has used the Ring to become invisible. Despite all the horror witnessed and loss foreboded after Mount Doom, by the close of the penultimate chapter ("The Scouring of the Shire"), things seem to have been righted and Middle-earth has entered into a stage of renewal and rebirth, and in many ways a recovery – hence its title – "Scouring" which means to clean or purge. Yet, settled back into the Shire, even after righting many of the damages done by Saruman in the four Hobbit's absence, Frodo is not at peace. No *presence* of physical scarring remains upon him – by which I mean that though his finger is now missing, this constitutes an absence rather than the visually additive presence of a scar *upon* the skin. Accumulated by Frodo and cauterized by the fall of the Ring, these wounds which manifest as *absence*, remain unhealed. In signifying this trauma through absence rather than presence *LotR* echoes further the absent impact of reference at the core of Frodo's trauma. The lost finger mirrors the inarticulability of his subjective loss – both incurred in the same moment. Instead of a symbol of healing, Tolkien signifies an embodied dismemberment where the loss of finger registers also the loss of a version of the self who could still feel at home in the Shire. Tolkien depicts Frodo on the anniversary of a "war" wound from his journey: Frodo is "found [...] lying in his bed; he was clutching a white gem that hung from a chain about his neck and he seemed half in a dream. 'It is gone forever,' he said, 'and now all is dark and empty'" (VI.9.1024). Traumatized by the loss of the Ring, he often slips in an out of reality, declaring the deep and irreversible alteration wrought upon him by its destruction. Flieger writes that the loss of the Ring is Frodo's "final, awful test that he will fail [...]. [H]e will have lost his innocence [...] his ordinary physical and psychological self, and his home" ("The Body in Question" 289-90). She remarks here that the loss of the Ring does not bring to an end his suffering at its hands, but rather compounds all of his physical wounds gained under its spell of invisibility into a loss not merely of the body, but of the subjectivity it encloses.

Moments dominated by both loss and landscape within the text emphasize the continued dependence of subjective coherence upon the relative attachment to home-place. This attachment is shown to be disrupted or otherwise mitigated by the War of the Ring, echoing the dynamics of the historically real Great War which inspired it. Modernist and realist texts often seek to give the reader an individual experience of this conversion, asking poetic prose for help in conveying affective access to a felt loss which eludes vernacular communication. Tolkien's fantastic prose instead takes loss as always already implicit to the reader's experience. Though the temporal function of this fiction as a mythic past or future of the reader's timeline needs to be accrued throughout the reader's experience of the text, by virtue of its fantastic genre the world on display is experienced as inaccessible from the start. Though the reader moves slowly from inaccessibility to loss, the presence of an inevitable loss is almost omnipotent from the outset of the narrative.

One may recall an early moment of the presence of this loss in the fellowship's passage through Lothlórien. When Galadriel speaks with Frodo just before his departure, she expresses her sadness regardless of the outcome of the war and Frodo is perplexed. She explains,

> Do you not see wherefore your coming to us is as the footstep of Doom? For if you fail, then we are laid bare to the Enemy. Yet if you succeed, then our power is diminished, and Lothlórien will fade, and the tides of Time will sweep it away. We must depart into the West, or dwindle to a rustic folk of dell and cave, slowly to forget and to be forgotten. [...] The love of the Elves for their land and their work is deeper than the deeps of the Sea [...]. (II.7.365)

Here, Galadriel describes the relationship amongst the Elves, their land, and the One Ring. In destroying the One Ring the power of the others will be "diminished". The Elven rings, and not some inherent magic, lend supranatural power to the lands of the Elves on Middle-earth, which seem to exist in a place outside time and therefore the mortality of natural life cycles. The diminishment of the Elven rings is linked, then, to the fading of the Elven lands, and the presence of the Elves themselves on Middle-earth. Win the war to protect one's home and sacrifice the connection between self and home.

The stage on which the foreboded departure plays out in *LotR* is again constructed in the pastoral mode: the temporal and geographic journey from the pastoral Shire to the environmental dystopia of Mordor. Typical WWI literature uses ironic or inverted pastoral imagery to depict their responses to warscapes of death and dismemberment.[3] By drawing upon the pastoral tradition for expression of the "unnatural" terrors of the trauma of war, realist and modernist war writers, I argue, exacerbated the divide between nature and culture already implicit in the pastoral mode – a pitfall fantasy allows Tolkien to avoid. Ecocritic Dana Phillips explains that the pastoral mode performs a "reductive process" on the "hyperspaces" which constitute an environment, by constructing them primarily as "landscapes [which] are more easily apprehended than the environments in which they are situated in space" metonymically (19). He adds that when ecology functions merely as landscape and not as hyperspace, one loses the ecological sense of a space as "an ecological niche [that is] a multidimensional hypervolume" of which "not all of its dimensions are spatial" (20). I argue that one such non-spatial dimension of this hypervolume is subjective. Just as ecology

3 Discussed at length in both Kate McLaughlin's *Authoring War* and Paul Fussell's *The Great War and Modern Memory*, where war memoirists and trench poets used a dark natural pattern of imagery to underscore the difference from the life-affirming landscapes of home.

includes the human ecology of physical populations, so too does it count the cultural and psychological valences of humanity and other species. The pastoral, then, exacerbates the nature-culture divide. This allows such texts to contribute to the solidification and maintenance of a pathology of subjective displacement from ecology. Instead, *LotR* strives to make this dynamic transparent.

Tolkien's narrative attempts to place the loss and departure central to its characters' relationships to Middle-earth in a form of Phillips' ecological hyperspace. In doing so, he avoids the tendency to employ a traditional pastoral or its ironic inversion in order to project an anticipated departure from ecology, elegizing it fatalistically. This points to a personal rather than a complete or biological environmental loss. Hence, *LotR* testifies to the traumatic impact on the subject's relationship to landscape during and after war, but it does not foreclose the possibility of substantive interactions for all of modernity. Galadriel testifies to the magnitude of what is at stake in the loss of the ring-power. She underscores that her subjects will not simply leave the land, but that their very memory of an ecological connection to this specific place is threatened if they ignore that loss has occurred, continuing to inhabit the land without the knowledge of its being a "multidimensional hypervolume". This lost epistemology was made possible by their possession of the ring-power, which enabled certain ways of knowing and inhabiting their home-land. The Elves could stay, says Galadriel, but they would become a "rustic folk" who both "forget" and are "forgotten", and whom dwell, not in the forest any longer, but in "dell and cave". Regardless of the outcome of the War of the Ring, then, the Elves will experience a traumatic displacement from their memory and identity – displaced from their forest either into death, the West, or valleys and mountains. This is the nature of the trauma implicit in the forgetting of what it was they are displaced from.

Placing this strange multidimensional relation to place at the core of its narration of the war, *LotR* makes explicit what has always been known to be implicit in the requirements of writing the war experience. Literary war scholars have long discussed the uniquely fictional demands of communicating war-time reality. Lawrence L. Langer explains that in writing war atrocity "irrealism" must dominate because the situation being depicted is neither reality nor unreality, but a combination characterized by discontinuity and dislocation (33-47). Michael Rothberg situates irrealism within trauma, calling it "traumatic realism", which, rather than being mimetic, "evokes the real as a 'felt lack,'" calling attention to the site of the loss which constitutes the trauma and therefore the narrative of lack (99-104). When used to bear witness to trauma, I argue that functions much like this "traumatic realism". This is especially true in *LotR* which points to a loss always already implicit in its existence as a *secondary* world rather than one's own *primary* reality. Moreover, in these tentative generic definitions notions of place are key. Irrealism represents reality as "dis*located*" and traumatic realist writing "points" through its conspicuous absences, to the originary *site* of trauma. Fantasy, then, is ideal for the expression of a traumatic dis*place*ment, the term I use to qualify the aforementioned divorce of subject from ecology because of WWI. Depicting reality as dis*located*, as a world in which external reality has fallen away from the subject, fantasy points to the *site* of trauma as the moment of subjective dislocation from objective, environmental reality through the war experience.

Subjects in the war-zone still desire to express their complex entanglement in ecology despite the difficulties caused by their conceptual estrangement from it. This is because such texts are necessarily embedded in the place or landscape of war. "The challenge for war writing," Kate McLoughlin explicates, "is to convey this charged space, to communicate the complex situation – part psycho-physiological, part geographical – that is conflict" (84). The textual *mise en scène* of war, then, is inextricably tied to the material environment in which the writer-survivor experiences the trauma of war. Indeed, Fussell draws the reader's attention to the fact that, "to be in the trenches was to experience an unreal, unforgettable enclosure and constraint, as well as a sense of being unoriented and lost. One saw two things only: the walls of an unlocalized, undifferentiated earth and the sky above" (54). In this statement the "unreal"-ity, "unforgettable enclosure", and experience of disorientation and "lost"-ness which writers of WWI struggle to express is linked to an "unlocalized, undifferentiated earth".

In coming to experience the environment as undifferentiated sameness and the loss of a sense of place, these writers express a collapsing of complex ecological surroundings into an objectified "other" disconnected from the experience of the self. Starkly distanced from their cultural inheritance as rife with detailed pastoral descriptions of the English countryside, the British soldier's experience of place as ecological often becomes as inaccessible in the trauma of WWI as his experience of the Western Front is from his memories of home. For example, Max Plowman noted the change between Victorian and modern conceptions of nature among soldiers, writing in his memoirs:

> [In the nineteenth century] the upper and more glorious half of Nature's pageant [the sky] goes unseen by the majority of people [...]. [T]he trenches have altered that. *Shutting off the landscape*, they compel us to observe the sky; and when it is a canopy of blue [...] and when the earth below is a shell-stricken waste, one looks up with delight, recalling perhaps the days when, as a small boy, one lay on the garden lawn at home counting the clouds as they passed. (italics mine, 72)

Plowman's comments on the "Shutting off" of "the landscape" indicate a deeper division than that between allied and enemy territory. Trench warfare where the "earth below is a shell-stricken waste" often caused a foreclosure of connection between subject and place. It replaces this link with a repositioning of the subject upwards and backwards in space and time, away from the ecological reality of one's groundedness in *this* particular material and ecological place, and towards a rewriting of memories of home.

The traumatic and testimonial aspects of *LotR* literalize the strangeness of encounters between post-war interiority and the external world of ecology which Plowman expresses above as a surreal alienation from place itself. Like modernist and war literature, *LotR* estranges the reader from nature or post-war landscapes as ecological as it references the dark nature of the waste lands of the western front. But in contrast to these dominant forms, the fantastic world of *LotR* represents a more intimate estrangement, not from the recognizability of the war zone as earthly space, but from home-place altogether. In Shoshana Felman's pivotal work on literature and traumatic testimony she asserts that in order to bear witness to another's testimony the narrative must "make the [reader] feel [and] progressively discover, how the testimony cannot be subsumed by its familiar notion, how the texts that testify do not simply *report facts* but, in different ways, encounter – and make us encounter – *strangeness*" (7). While it seems obvious that presenting the historical reality of WWI to modern readers through the lens of a fantasy tale about Elves, Hobbits, and talking trees (Ents) might be convincing enough evidence of making the reader "feel", "discover", and "encounter" a "*strangeness*", it is less the strangeness of the obvious deviations from empirical reality which testify to the trauma. Rather, in *LotR*, it is an experience of strangeness in the sense of an *estrangement* at the core of the story, a becoming-stranger in your own home, which the Ring-bearers experience when they must leave at the end of the tale. The reader is progressively awakened from what comes to seem like a dream of Middle-earth – a place that, through the reader's trust in its relegation to the realm of fantasy, comes to feel almost more real than the real world of the reader – a world from which many a modern subject feels alienated. The reader is awakened from Frodo and the Fellowship's quest and defeat of evil to an encounter with their own history, and potentially awakening to their estrangement from an ecological experience of place as well. Likewise, Frodo experiences the fall of the One Ring into the fires of Mount Doom. The Ring's destruction then becomes the core of the quest. As Frodo's traumatic fall, it becomes the inscrutable impact – the realization which Frodo cannot fully understand – of his imminent and inevitable departure from his home-place.

The inscrutability of Frodo's loss in Mount Doom, when read together with the Doom of Lothlórien, can be seen as the product of a gradual accrual of loss, undetected in the same sense that the creation of the grand canyon would be no great surprise to one who managed to live through the millennia that it took erosion to create it – unless of course one were to fall in, not knowing the great chasm had appeared. A similar gradual erosion is evoked in Galadriel's speech to Frodo, an oceanic conceit within the passage which indicates the Elves may have a different awareness of their inevitable displacement than Frodo does of his. Rife with both metaphors of the sea and of forgetting, the two ideas become conflated by the end of her speech. Tolkien writes, "tides of Time will sweep it away," and "the love of the Elves for their land and their work is deeper than the deeps of the Sea" amidst his description of that which will "fade", be "diminished", and "dwindle" "slowly to forget and to be forgotten." This forgetting resembles the erosion of earth by water, in which, rather than a sudden moment of unprocessed shock (such as shell-bombing), the mind awakens to a loss which has built up so gradually that it went unnoticed until it was brought to mind by a comparison with that which once was. *The Lord of the Rings* presents this as one way to conceive of the loss of the ecological emplacement of modern subjectivity.

For readers, the imaginary visitation in Lothlórien, like Frodo's, is an introduction to magical realms only in the moment of their disintegration, similar to David Lowe's description of the summer of 1914 on the eve of war, wherein the world "seemed most beautiful just before it disappeared" (155). Modern Europe seemed to many to awaken from the dream of imperial expansion just in time to witness the fall of the British empire and the engulfing of a whole generation of citizens and soldiers in the cracks left behind by its quaking and crumbling. Unable to cope with their own role in the destruction, this generation sacrificed nature as the effigetic victim of war, and created a modern identity built on that very loss of pastoral landscapes and lifestyles. Beyond the trench poets, the modernist focus on urban landscapes over rural locales is exemplary of the always already death of nature at the core of the modernist imaginary. *LotR*, and other fantasy reactions to the war, focus instead on the persistence of natural spaces. Hence, in *LotR* what dies is the subject who is displaced, not the place of dislodgement.

Paul Fussell identifies this death and displacement as a common "rhetoric of Conversion" in the literature of WWI (123). This conversion is evoked by war memoirist Henry Williamson, who writes of the trenches that soldiers who "passed through the estranging remoteness of battle" found themselves "not broken, but reborn" (x). What is meant by this reborn but not broken selfhood is that their trauma is not simply an experience of the personal (broken) self, but an externally refashioned or reborn self. The reborn self, I argue, is a subjectivity that is disconnected from ecology or shut off from the landscape in the paradigm of the trench memoirists. The trauma of the post-world-war-one-subjectivity is not just the lack of preparation and incommunicability of the horrors of this particular war, as scholars such as Paul Fussell and Modris Eksteins have dutifully outlined, but also the "rebirth" out of ecology into a pathological rather than fictional fantasy of an ontologically individuated subjectivity.

Although many Tolkien scholars have explored *LotR* as a literary response to WWI, few have discussed his work in relationship to this "rhetoric of Conversion" without recourse to readings of anti-industrialization didacticism – a line of argument which places heavy emphasis on a lamented disconnect between the modern subject and the dead or dying natural world. Those who address *LotR*'s relationship to WWI acknowledge the influence of

Tolkien's war experiences on his writing, as mentioned above, but are most careful to resist allegorical oversimplifications of his work. Janet Brennan Croft notes that Tolkien denied that *LotR* was directly about the Great War (15). Because "Tolkien famously despised allegory," it is not so much that it is unrelated to the war, but that "none of his works are *allegories* of World War I or any other war" (13, emphasis added). Croft points out, however, that *LotR* shares many of the common themes of WWI literature pointed out by Paul Fussell. Indeed, Mark Heberle argues that rather than being *about* the war, the "narrative" of *LotR* is "haunted by the Great War" (142), adding that more than just *LotR*, the whole mythology of which it is a part "has many of the earmarks of post-traumatic narratives, including fragmentation, reversal of chronology, repetition, and lack of closure" (138). The difference between those writers commenting directly on the reality of the war, and Tolkien's fantastical approach, Croft explains, is that "Tolkien [...] avoided the ironic response of his contemporaries and instead mythologized his experiences" (10). In doing so, he "transformed" the "common themes" of "post-World War I literature" (10) by using the genre of the fairy-story, or fantastic, to get at a "more heroic interpretation of war" (28) and "illustrate Tolkien's ideal of courage" – of "going on in spite of being without hope" (28). Furthermore, his choice of sub-creating a secondary world over the ironic depictions donned by modernist and realist responses to the war grew out of a desire to create a "mythology for England" (27-8). This English mythos was itself a direct response to WWI. He began creating Middle-earth and its language while convalescing from his war wounds (17). Though Croft describes this world-building as "an escape," "a way to wrest meaning from an incomprehensible experience by transforming it into something more familiar" (28), where he created the "Shire", which "like England" was "no longer a safe haven from the troubles of the world" (20), I argue here that what Croft identified as his valorization of "going on in spite of being without hope" is tied also to the traumatic and memorial functions of *The Lord of the Rings* – whose textual function sought to remake "something" which "has gone crack" as he wrote to a friend from the trenches in August of 1916 (Tolkien, *Letters* 10). More than rupturing his own fellowship of four friends rent by WWI, this breakage signifies also that the world itself seemed to have "gone crack". But cracks may be repaired; and they can let in the light as well as the cold.

In her discussion of the scenes in the Dead Marshes – where Frodo, Sam, and Gollum approach Mordor in the latter segment of the narrative – Rebecca Long calls this textual site Tolkien's way of remembering the war, evoking a sense of reparation that does not, however, forget the wound it binds. She writes, "Tolkien and his contemporaries were raised on 'Victorian pseudo-medieval romance' and brought these dreams of war into the trenches, while the language of euphemism obscured the actualities of the war" (131). The use of the elements of the Victorian romance ironically alongside dark pastoralisms is a frequent occurrence in war poetry and memoir (Fussell 146-7). Tolkien, however, seems to have rejected this strategy wholesale, seeing no value in using a broken mirror to reflect the present through the past. Rebekah Long explains that, distancing himself from the reality-obscuring effects of such outdated tropes, Tolkien "searches for a new language of violence" (131). Tolkien's language, adds John Garth, creates a "Middle-earth [which] looks so engagingly familiar to us and speaks to us so eloquently because it was born with the modern world and marked by the same terrible birth pangs" (309).

In searching for a language of violence capable of representing the wounds of both subjects and nature, Tolkien shares some of the broken imagery of the modernists but diverges in distinct ways as well. In his fantastic remerging of the forces of people and nature throughout the secondary world he has created in response to WWI "we can view *The Lord of the Rings* not as an allegory of the Great War [...] but as a recollection of it [...] which investigates the creative work of memory in reply to the trauma of war. Fantasy, conceived in Tolkien's novel as a dialogic process of invention and remembrance, allows for a return to the war that is not documentary or allegorical in approach but *memorial*" (Long 126). It is what readers are called upon to re-member, to reconstruct or recover, that distinguishes Tolkien from his modernist and realist brethren.

Though the narrative as a whole is memorial, not all re-membering is made possible within *LotR*. As a result of Frodo's unhealed wounds, the survivor's return does not lead to a recovery of the self in a broken world, so much as it does to the departure of a broken self from a world in recovery. After the War of the Ring is over, the reader soon learns that Frodo and the others will have to leave Middle-earth, departing in the final chapter of the book. This represents the official end of the Third Age when the last of the Ring-bearers leave from the Grey Havens over the sea and into the West. When the reader believes the worst is over and desires only a happy ending, one is met with a belated loss – with a leaving. Concerning the presence of a leave-taking within narratives of trauma, Caruth writes that the narration of the "trauma of leaving [inscribes] words that do not simply refer, but [...] convey the impact of a history precisely as what *cannot be grasped* about leaving" (21). The leaving, then, is the narrative performance of the fall, the traumatic moment of the inscrutable impact of reference. It tells us that this impact or meaning (of the war) is missed in the encounter with leaving, remaining incomprehensible. It is this referential awareness which Tolkien seeks to re-place, awakening us to the link between the war and displacement. Sam, distraught at Frodo's departure at the close of the book, asks, "and I can't come"; to which Frodo replies,

> No, Sam. Not yet anyway [...]. You cannot be always torn in two. You will have to be one and whole, for many years. [...] I have been too deeply hurt, Sam. I tried to save the Shire, and it has been saved, but not for me. It must often be so, Sam, when things are in danger: some one has to give them up, lose them, so that others may keep them. [...] [K]eep alive the memory of the age that is gone, so that people will remember the Great Danger and love their beloved land all the more. (VI.9.1029)

And then all of the Ring-bearers – Gandalf, the High Elves, Frodo, and Bilbo – board the ship and sail into the West. Note that it is not all who experience loss and change due to the war who leave Middle-earth. There are no Ents present, nor Dwarves, other Hobbits, or Aragorn. These folk – though they were also deeply involved in the conflict – do not pass away.

Using as her prime example founding psychoanalyst Sigmund Freud's *Moses and Monotheism* – a text on leaving which is itself a mix of history and fantasy, Caruth demonstrates that "a falling [...] is transmitted precisely in the unconscious act of leaving. It is this *unconsciousness of leaving* that bears the impact of history" (22), but, she continues, "Leaving home [...] is also a kind of freedom, the freedom to [...] bring [one's] voice to another place [...]. [The] freedom to leave is, paradoxically, not to live but to die: to bring forth [one's] voice to others in dying. [The] voice emerges, that is, as a departure [...] that addresses us" (23). The Ring-bearers, therefore, do not leave their home to live but to die, the symbolic death of their life on Middle-earth being the consequence of remaining while the One Ring perishes. In Tolkien's authoring of a story of leaving, the voice of the displaced "emerges" "as a departure" and "addresses us." It is this address which makes *LotR* distinctly testimonial. And moreover, it is only through this departure, this narration of loss and tale of traumatic displacement, that Tolkien may give his testimony to the traumatic birth of the dominant modern subjectivity out of WWI in a way that obligates his readers. This address compels the reader to bear witness in turn *to* LotR's testimony of what one is displaced from – ecology – and how this came to be historically realized.

In deciding not to give up the Ring, but rather to give himself to it, Frodo makes it evident that he is not prepared to be without the Ring. According to Freud's theories on traumatic war neuroses, this lack of preparation for a shock is exactly what makes it traumatic for the mind; its occurrence is inconceivable.[4] The fall which traumatizes Frodo on Mount Doom is due, as Flieger asserts, to "Frodo's failure [and his] sacrifice" which depict Middle-earth as a place where "the Fall [...] is a gradual process [and] is continual [...]. We might say that Tolkien's world is falling rather than fallen [...] leaving at the center a space for the audience to see itself, and thus to participate in the story" ("Missing Person" 230-231). This compelling reading of Frodo's fall and narrative of trauma, although Flieger does not name it as such, introduces an interesting notion of a "gradual", "continual" fall. In this sense the trauma of the ring, as symbolic of ecologically displaced subjectivity, is not simply a result of the moment of the Ring's destruction, just as the split between subjective reality and objective reality cannot have grown solely from the moment of WWI's happening or commencement. The impact of the reference of history, the unknowable meaning at the core of the traumatic experience of the war, is, therefore, in part so traumatic and unknowable *because* of its gradual and continual nature. It lacks the climactic impact of a great battle, just as the real war did.[5] Furthermore, Tolkien's "leaving at the center a space for the audience to see itself" can be read as the space between battle epic and quest narrative in which he houses his testimonial address to the reader, as a modern subject.

---

4 See Freud (10-11, 30-34).

5 Apropos of the environmental themes of *LotR*, this dynamic is similar to the incomprehensible nature of hyperobjects such as global warming, which are "massively distributed in time and space relative to humans" so as to seem uncannily undetectable until their sudden accrual is felt with the shock or impact of a Hurricane Katrina-like accident, as discussed by Timothy Morton, *Hyperobjects* (1).

As noted above, Sam, and the reader along with him, is asked not only to embody the whole self – both a culturally viable and ecologically embedded subjectivity – remaining fully present, mind *and* body, in the Shire, but also to keep alive the memory of the trauma of the War of the Ring. Frodo asks him to do this by telling him to be a keeper of memory, a teller or recorder of history. In other words, as the key witness to the whole of this central narrative, and most importantly to the missed moment of the traumatic event itself – the fall of the ring and its subsequent loss, Sam is asked by those wounded beyond reparation to testify or bear witness to this historical trauma as Tolkien has. By testifying to the "Great Danger" of the trauma of the ring, Sam may re-engender a love of their "beloved land", which can be read as a step towards an ecological re-placement of the subject, a collapsing of the perceived divide between subject and object – subject and ecological world.

It is not then, based on my reading of *LotR,* the loss of objective reality itself, a loss of "nature" as material thing, which is the core trauma of WWI as several ecocritical treatments of the text have suggested. Such a trauma would be purely material and, as Freud notes, it is a mental not mechanical agent which causes war neuroses of the new, severe, and widespread type – the type which Caruth and others have theorized in their treatments of historical trauma. What, then, is being lost from Middle-earth which reflects WWI's greatest trauma? It is not simply the trees, mountains, rivers, or any "purely objective" aspect of nature evoked by the text, and not just the Ring-bearers. The loss, in the completion of the story, is characters themselves – entities, people, subjects: Elves, Ents, Frodo, Gandalf, even Shadowfax. They must go or pass or dwindle. They suffer the separation from this place – their homeland – and the "magic" of the "sacramental" relationship to nature, as Brawley would say, is lost to the Fourth (or should I say Modern) Age.

The trauma of WWI is not enacted, therefore, *upon* ecology, but *within* us, people, and our perceived separation from it. As Tom Bombadil and Treebeard, the Ent, have implied, they, and "nature", in the end, are indifferent to the fate of humanity. When Frodo encounters Bombadil en route to Rivendell, Tom describes himself as: "old. Eldest [...]. Tom was here before the rivers and trees; Tom remembers the first raindrop and the first acorn" (I.7.131). The implication is also that Tom will persist after the last. Later, as the Hobbits are further along in the journey towards the front-lines of the War of the Ring, Treebeard explains to Merry and Pippin "perhaps [the Entwives and Ents, long separated] shall find somewhere a land where we can live together and both be content. But it is foreboded that that will only be when we have both lost all that we now have. And it may well be that that time is drawing near at last. For if Sauron of old destroyed the gardens, the Enemy today seems likely to wither all the woods" (III.4.476-7). As with Bombadil, Tolkien suggests that the Ents' story does not *end* with the destruction of a version of nature legible to "men" but this enlivened and timeless nature which they represent persists, though the woods and fields of Hobbits and humans may not.

In the reader's own real, primary world, this is also true. Ecology will persist regardless of people's actions, it just may not persist in a fashion conducive to the sustainability of the human species. *LotR* is, after all, a work of literature and we are literary scholars and not scientists. Although there are very "real" material consequences both of WWI and this subjective disjuncture, what I address here is *our loss* not the loss of a world. Throughout *LotR*, as many people from scholars to fans have noted, one experiences wondrous magical things, places, and creatures. One may desire strongly to actualize and dwell in that fantastic realm; one may desire for all this to be "true". But the tragic beauty of *The Lord of the Rings* is that at every step on Frodo and the Fellowship's journey they (and we) experience the magic of a world where one's absence from it is always already implicit. This absence is felt both in its nature as fantasy and through the pervasive sense of loss throughout the story: future, past, or actualized in the plot. What one gets in reading *LotR* is a reenactment – a performance – of the missed encounter with the fall from, or leaving of, ecology or attachment to home-place within one's own psyche – a placement humanity was quite possibly never fully conscious of holding in the first place. World War I did not create this displacement. Yet, it can be said to have awoken western subjects to it belatedly – awoken them to a traumatic impact of reference for which one has no frame of reference, and to a reality whose framework Tolkien tries diligently to recreate for the reader in this epic fantastic tale. The Men of Middle-earth are created, empowered as modern people in the world constituted by this leave-taking. Fourth-Agers are forged in the very historical act of losing all that once defined their home-place of Middle-earth: the place where Elves and Men and talking trees may mingle. At the end of history. After the war to end all wars.

Bibliography

AUDEN, W.H. "At the End of the Quest, Victory." *The Tolkien Scrapbook*. Ed. Alida Becker. Philadelphia, PA: Running Press, 1978, 44-48.

BRAWLEY, Chris. "The Fading of the World: Tolkien's Ecology and Loss in *The Lord of the Rings*." *Journal of the Fantastic in the Arts* 18.3 (2007): 292-307.

CARUTH, Cathy. *Unclaimed Experience: Trauma, Narrative, and History*. Baltimore, MA: John's Hopkins University Press, 1996.

CROFT, Janet Brennan. *War and the Works of J.R.R. Tolkien*. Westport, CT: Praeger, 2004.

DICKERSON, Matthew, and Jonathan EVANS. *Ents, Elves, and Eriador: The Environmental Vision of J.R.R. Tolkien*. Lexington, KY: The University Press of Kentucky, 2006.

EKSTEINS, Modris. *Rites of Spring: The Great War and the Birth of the Modern Age*. Boston, MA: Houghton Mifflin, 1989.

FELMAN, Shoshana, and Dori LAUB. *Testimony: Crises of Witnessing in Literature, Psychoanalysis, and History*. New York City, NY: Routledge, 1992.

FLIEGER, Verlyn. "The Body in Question: The Unhealed Wounds of Frodo Baggins." *Green Suns and Faërie: Essays on J.R.R. Tolkien*. Kent, OH: Kent State University Press, 2012, 283-291.

"Missing Person." *Green Suns and Faërie: Essays on J.R.R. Tolkien*. Kent, OH: Kent State University Press, 2012, 223-231.

"Taking the Part of Trees: Eco-conflict in Middle-earth." *Green Suns and Faërie: Essays on J.R.R. Tolkien*. Kent, OH: Kent State University Press, 2012, 262-274.

FREUD, Sigmund. *Beyond the Pleasure Principle*. Trans. and Ed. James Strachey New York City, NY: W.W. Norton, 1961.

FUSSELL, Paul. *The Great War and Modern Memory*. Oxford: Oxford University Press, 1975.

GARTH, John. *Tolkien and the Great War: The Threshold of Middle-earth*. Boston, MA: Houghton Mifflin, 2003.

HEBERLE, Mark. "The Shadow of War: Tolkien, Trauma, Childhood, and Fantasy." *Under Fire: Childhood in the Shadow of War*. Eds. Andrea Immel and Elizabeth Goodenough. Detroit, MI: Wayne State University Press, 2008, 129-142.

HILEY, Margaret. *The Loss and the Silence: Aspects of Modernism in the Works of C.S. Lewis, J.R.R. Tolkien, & Charles Williams*. Zurich and Jena: Walking Tree Publishers, 2011.

LANGER, Lawrence L. *The Holocaust and the Literary Imagination*. New Haven, CT: Yale University Press, 1975.

LONG, Rebekah. "Fantastic Medievalism and the Great War in J.R.R. Tolkien's *The Lord of the Rings*." *Tolkien's Modern Middle Ages*. Eds. Jane Chance and Alfred K. Siewers. New York City, NY: Palgrave Macmillan, 2005.

LOWE, David. "Bourbon Country." *Prose* VI (1973): 137-156.

MATTS, Tim and Aidan TYNAN. "Geotrauma and the Eco-clinic: Nature, Violence, and Ideology." *Symplokē* 20 (2012): 153-172.

MCLOUGHLIN, Kate. *Authoring War: The Literary Representation of War from Iliad to Iraq*. Cambridge: Cambridge University Press, 2011.

MORTON, Timothy. *Ecology Without Nature: Rethinking Environmental Aesthetics*. Cambridge, MA: Harvard University Press, 2007.

Hyperobjects: Philosophy and Ecology after the End of the World. Minneapolis, MN: University of Minnesota Press, 2013.

PHILLIPS, Dana. *The Truth of Ecology: Nature, Culture, and Literature in America*. Oxford: Oxford University Press, 2003.

PLOWMAN, Max. *A Subaltern on the Somme in 1916 by Mark VII*. New York City, NY: E.P. Dutton & Company, 1928.

ROTHBERG, Michael. *Traumatic Realism: The Demands of Holocaust Representation*. Minneapolis, MN: University of Minnesota Press, 2000.

TOLKIEN, J.R.R. *The Letters of J.R.R. Tolkien*. Ed. Humphrey Carpenter, with the assistance of Christopher Tolkien. London: George Allen & Unwin; Boston, MA: Houghton Mifflin, 1981.

The Lord of the Rings. 50th Anniversary edition. Boston, MA: Houghton Mifflin, 2004.

"On Fairy-stories." *The Monsters and the Critics and Other Essays*. Ed. Christopher Tolkien. Boston, MA: Houghton Mifflin, 1984, 109-161

WILLIAMSON, Henry. "Forward." *The Wipers Times*. Ed. Patrick Beaver. London: Papermac, 1973.

Anna Smol

Bodies in War: Medieval and Modern Tensions in "The Homecoming"

At the end of June 1916, the newly-married Tolkien, a young man of twenty-four, received his orders to join the men of the 11th Lancashire Fusiliers behind the Somme front line where, waiting to go into action, his battalion dug graves in the cemetery while witnessing hundreds of wounded and mutilated men coming back from the trenches (Garth 158). On 14 July, Tolkien's battalion was moved in preparation for an assault. Their eventual view of no man's land revealed bodies that had lain there for up to two weeks (Garth 163). As Tolkien moved forward into position, the wounded were being evacuated. John Garth describes what the experience must have been like:

> Going was slow, and single-file. Part way along they passed through an open area containing a broken-down ambulance wagon. This was land newly taken from the Germans, and at high cost. So it was on the approach to Ovillers that Tolkien first encountered the lost of the Somme: heralded by their stench, darkly hunched or prone, or hanging on the wire until a stab of brightness revealed them, the bloated and putrescent dead. (Garth 164)

Decades later, Tolkien writes *HBBS*, a verse-drama that comments on the tenth-century Old English poem, "The Battle of Maldon", a situation that at first glance may seem both historically and personally far removed from his service on the front lines. However, I propose that *HBBS* be considered in the light of Tolkien's war experiences. That he can be considered a Great War writer is generally accepted. For example, Tom Shippey includes Tolkien in a group of twentieth-century writers who had experienced the horrors of war directly and who chose to write about unspeakable evils, among other modern concerns, through fantasy (*Author* viii-ix). John Garth provides a detailed biographical account of Tolkien and his friends' experiences in the First World War and the effect it had on his early literary work. Brian Rosebury comments on the effects of wartime bereavement on works such as *The Lord of the Rings*, even though it was published some forty years after the war's end (139), and Janet Brennan Croft, in her 2004 book *War and The Works of J.R.R. Tolkien,* surveys earlier critics who comment on the influence of war in his fiction (22-27). In her discussion of war themes in Tolkien's work, she notes that "rare is the work in which there is no mention of war" (Croft 21). As Margaret Hiley reminds us, "war forms a major topic of the literature of the twentieth century" (33), and I believe that *HBBS* is no exception. Like Tolkien's better-known works of fiction, *HBBS* addresses issues of war and heroism that are relevant to a modern writer who is transforming his past experiences into fiction, and, as is not uncommon with Tolkien, doing so through the lens of medieval literature.

In *HBBS*, Tolkien creates a verse-drama set on the battlefield after an English defeat at Maldon in 991 CE where two men must retrieve the body of their lord Beorhtnoth. Although "The Battle of Maldon", which commemorates Beorhtnoth and his followers in their losing battle against Viking invaders, is missing its beginning and conclusion, it is safe to say that it did not include such a scene where men collect the dead in the aftermath of the fighting. Of course, realistically, someone has to dispose of corpses after a battle in any historical period. In Old English poetry, lone heroes like Beowulf are lamented, praised, and placed on a funeral pyre, but Anglo-Saxon poets were generally not interested in horrific, frightening scenes of mass slaughter after the action or in ordinary people just getting on with the nasty, practical matters of burial in obedience to commands from invisible superiors.

Perhaps the closest version of an Old English poem focusing on the war dead is "The Battle of Brunanburh". In that poem, we are told that "The field flowed / with the blood of warriors" (Liuzza 259, lines 12-13) from sunrise to sunset. The speaker's general view tells us how "many a man / lay spattered by spears, men of the North / shot over their shields, and Scotsmen as well, / weary, dazed with war" (Liuzza 259, 17-20). The poet counts the important dead: five young kings and seven earls among many others, and when he gets more personal, he adds that the lord Constantinus had to leave his son "on the killing field, ground down by wounds" (Liuzza 260, 43). Perhaps the closest we get to feeling the grimness of those left behind in battle comes in the poem's formulaic Beasts of Battle theme, a conventional element of Old English poetry that enumerates the raven, eagle, and wolf as the animals that gather to feed on corpses – but their actions are left to the imagination. The aim of this poet is to take a general view of the battle and its place in English history while praising the victors.

Tolkien, too, could have taken a general approach to the aftermath of the battle. He could have written his response to "The Battle of Maldon" with different characters in a different setting. One can imagine a scene between the abbot and his monks, for example, discussing the results of the battle and praising or criticizing Beorhtnoth. Or Tolkien could have set the scene in King Æthelræd's hall, with his band of advisors and a court poet commenting on the battle – a similar scene occurs in "The Notion Club Papers", where King Edweard sits in a hall with his warriors after one of many skirmishes with invaders and calls for songs (SD 269-73). Instead, Tolkien imagines a scene in the night after the Maldon defeat, on the battlefield, where a farmer and a minstrel's son experience threats of violence lurking in the dark, where masses of the dead must be identified, and where they must haul away a corpse in a wagon over dangerous footing. In other words, in *HBBS* Tolkien imagines a common Great War scene.

According to Scull and Hammond, Tolkien might have conceived of the play as early as 1931 to 1933 (547). Tolkien's manuscripts (Oxford, Bodleian Library, MS. Tolkien 5) consist of ten drafts, including one fragment, labelled A to J by Thomas Honegger. These drafts contain no indication of dates, but it is highly likely that a good number of them were revised through the Second World War, when Tolkien's memories of his previous experiences must have intensified with his concern for his sons' safety during their war service. Tolkien's biographer, Humphrey Carpenter, believes that *HBBS* was in existence by 1945 (218), although the final typescript, version K, which still contains minor revisions, was only sent off for publication to the journal *Essays and Studies* in 1953. In the final typescript, Tolkien appends a short essay titled "Ofermod" which states at the outset that his drama, "was composed primarily as verse, to be condemned or approved as such" (143). While Tolkien illustrates many of his ideas about Old English alliterative verse in his play, which is written in various alliterative styles, it is his critique in this essay of the actions of Beorhtnoth in the Old English poem that has preoccupied scholars for decades. The verse drama itself certainly demonstrates the flexibility of alliterative meter in modern English, but in doing so it also puts the subject matter of traditional alliterative poetry, specifically the subject of war and heroism in "The Battle of Maldon", in dialogue with a modern perspective.

The two characters who enact this dialogue, a young minstrel's son named Totta, short for Torhthelm, and an older farmer Tída, short for Tídwald, represent different interests, experiences, and perspectives on the battle. Tom Shippey emphatically sides with the more experienced and war-weary Tída, reading him as "Tolkien's verse-mouthpiece" and mocking the idealistic poetry-loving Totta as "a fool and braggart" ("Boar and Badger" 233), and further enumerating his flaws as being cowardly, boastful, and murderous, and flawed in prophesy ("Tolkien and 'The Homecoming'" 326-27). Shippey equates Tída with a realistic and Christian perspective on heroism that he believes is shared by Tolkien. Totta, in Shippey's view, represents the side of the dialogue that Tolkien rejects: heathen heroism and Old English poetry. I would suggest that the distinctions between the two characters are not as clear cut as Shippey argues. As I hope to show, both characters appear to be Christians, both are familiar with and, to varying degrees, approve of traditional poetry. Admittedly, their dialogue creates a tension between disenchantment and heroic ideals, but this is the same kind of negotiation that many Great War soldiers typically had to undertake during and after the war. For example, in a letter to his son Christopher in 1944, Tolkien writes of the "animal horror" of trench life that he had experienced in the war (*Letters* 72), but only a few years earlier, in his *Beowulf* essay published in 1937, he states that "[e]ven to-day (despite the critics) you may find men not ignorant of tragic legend and history, who have heard of heroes and indeed seen them [...]" (*MC* 16). Tolkien hated war but acknowledged the existence of heroism; in HBBS he dramatizes that tension without rejecting either side entirely.

Tolkien's *HBBS* is not the only work in which he imagines the aftermath of a battle, likely influenced by what he had seen in the war. Perhaps the eeriest and most intense representation of war experience occurs in Tolkien's depiction of the Dead Marshes in *The Lord of the Rings*. Tolkien admits that the Great War could have been one of several influences on that scene: "The Dead Marshes and the approaches to the Morannon owe something to Northern France after the Battle of the Somme" (*Letters* 303). The primary emotion evoked in Frodo and Sam's first close-up view of the Marshes is uncanny horror. The presence of long-dead faces in the waters, faces that should not have been present there on the ancient battlefield, violates the normal boundaries between life and death. Frodo, Sam, and Gollum have difficulty trudging single-file in the mud and avoiding the pools of the Marshes, and, as Sam says to Gollum: "The stink nearly knocks me down with my nose held. You stink, and master stinks; the whole place stinks" (*LotR* IV.2.629). The uneasy ghostliness of the Marshes, with its corpse-candles and Frodo's dream-like state, gives way eventually to a blasted landscape. Leaving behind "the arid moors of the Noman-lands" they come to the land before Sauron's gate: "The gasping pools were choked with ash and crawling muds, sickly white and grey, as if the mountains had vomited the filth of their entrails upon the lands about" (IV.2.631) where fear of surveillance and sudden attack in the dark further marks the scene as typical of WWI narratives. As I have suggested elsewhere, Tolkien's description is in line with other Great War writers who depict what Sandra Gilbert calls the "antipastoral deathscape" characteristic of First World War writers such as Wilfred Owen, who in his letters describes no man's land: "It is pock-marked like a body of foulest disease and its odour is the breath of cancer" (qtd. in Smol 47). This is the most intense psychological evocation of the realities of war that Tolkien produced, fittingly representing two small characters who are willingly advancing to a likely death in war. However, other scenes in *The Lord of the Rings* and *The Hobbit* also present the battlefield after the main action.

As the Battle of Pelennor Fields winds down, Éowyn – of noble birth and so a person of some consequence – is borne away on a stretcher, whose bearers at first believe she is dead. Merry is overlooked and wanders confused and wounded towards safety:

> He gave little heed to the wreck and slaughter that lay about all. Fire and smoke and stench was in the air; for many engines had been burned or cast into the fire-pits, and many of the slain also, while here and there lay many carcases of the great Southron monsters, half-burned, or broken by stone-cast, or shot through the eyes by the valiant archers of Morthond (*LotR* V.8.858).

Fortunately, Pippin is sent out to the battlefield to search for Merry, only to find him at the city gates. Later, we are told that Pippin himself was rescued by Gimli from under a heap of dead bodies after the fighting at the Black Gate. A similar lucky find occurs in *The Hobbit*, when Bilbo, struck unconscious early in the battle action, comes to and, realizing he is still wearing the ring, takes it off, only to be discovered by a man who had been sent out one last time by Gandalf to look for the hobbit among the dead. These battlefield scenes include mangled or unnatural corpses and a destroyed landscape; only in *The Hobbit* is the tone lighter, though the search for bodies is common to all and the inability at first to distinguish living from dead is part of the action in most of these passages. In none of these scenes do heroic warriors march triumphantly home. We see instead limping, horrified, or just very lucky people making their ways or being carried to safety. This is not the heroic world of *Beowulf*, where warriors ride triumphantly back to the hall from Grendel's mere; Tolkien's scenes are more evocative of Wilfred Owen's "Dulce et Decorum est" which describes WWI soldiers trudging back from the front lines: "Bent double, like old beggars under sacks, / Knock-kneed, coughing like hags" (Owen 141.1-2).

As the Battle of Five Armies gets underway in *The Hobbit*, Bilbo expresses the characteristic disillusionment of the Great War soldier, albeit with hobbit-like understatement: "I have heard songs of many battles, and I have always understood that defeat may be glorious. It seems very uncomfortable, not to say distressing. I wish I was well out of it." (*Hobbit* XVII:260).[1] Songs of glorious defeat as opposed to the distressing realities of war are what the two characters in *HBBS* also discuss as they do their job of searching for the body of the English leader Beorhtnoth among the dead to bring it back to the abbot for burial. Unlike Frodo and Sam or Bilbo or Merry and Pippin, the two characters in the verse drama are not soldiers; neither one has seen action on the day of the battle, although the older one, Tída, has served in the levies before and the younger man, Totta, is eager to do so. While they may not feel the urgency and despair of those caught in the midst of fighting, they do find themselves in the dark after the battle walking among the dead, trying to make sense of the war as they witness its aftermath, and even facing mortal danger at one point.

The action begins in the dark, with the younger Totta frightened by the sound of someone approaching whom he can't see. Although it turns out only to be his companion Tída, Totta is further startled in the next few moments by an owl hooting and flying by. He explains how being alone among the dead on the battlefield has affected him, first because "They lie so queer" (125) and

1 Mary R. Bowman posits that Tolkien might have been thinking of "The Battle of Maldon" as one of these songs of battle in this passage (93-94).

then "the wind sighing / was like words whispered by waking ghosts / that in my ears muttered" (125). He defends himself against Tída's mocking by pointing out that others would find the presence of the dead bodies unnerving too: "more men than I find the mirk gruesome / among the dead unshrouded" (126). Totta compares the dead bodies lying in the dark to a "heathen hell" (126). When Tída overturns the body of one of the enemy fighters, Totta can't bear to look at the corpse: "I can't abide his eyes, bleak and evil / as Grendel's in the moon" (129). His ghostly imaginings and superstitious belief in bad omens were common reactions among Great War soldiers, as reported by Paul Fussell, who points out that "inexpressible terror long and inexplicably endured" resulted in "a plethora of very un-modern superstitions, talismans, wonders, miracles, relics, legend and rumours" (115). Tída and Totta are not active combatants, but Totta's reactions are very much in line with Great War soldiers who were haunted by the ghostly or nightmarish visions of the dead. For example, Frederic Manning in his poem "The Face" describes the face of a young boy whom he saw die and which "cometh again / As a wraith of sleep" (Manning 129.11-12), and Charles Hamilton Sorely writes: "When you see millions of the mouthless dead / Across your dreams in pale battalions go / Say not soft things [...]" (Sorley 158.1-3).

When Totta spots some creeping shapes in the dark, he interprets them as ghostly or supernatural "Troll-shapes" or "hell-walkers" (133). As they come nearer, Tída confronts them and in the scuffle Totta kills one of them. The incident proves that mortal danger could come suddenly and unexpectedly, even when one thinks the battle is over. Totta is further alarmed by the thought that the enemy Danes might return to attack them. In other words, Totta reacts like many a Great War soldier, frightened by the dead around him, expecting sudden death from unseen foes. One can again turn to some of the best-known Great War poems for analogous situations: Isaac Rosenberg writes of the joy of hearing the songs of larks while marching back to camp, but then adds that the soldiers know "What sinister threat lurks there" (Rosenberg 65.3) and that "Death could drop from the dark / As easily as song – " (Rosenberg, "Returning" 65.10-11). And indeed, it does in Wilfred Owen's "*Dulce et decorum est*" which describes a sudden attack and the ensuing panic: "Gas! GAS! Quick, boys!" (Owen 141.9).

Of course, the nature of an attack would be different on an Anglo-Saxon battlefield, and Tída rejects Totta's imaginings and superstitions: an owl is just an owl, in his view; all the ghosts are underground, and the Vikings have no reason to turn back for another attack. He disapproves of killing one of the corpse-robbers as unnecessary violence, though he claims he would be glad to see some of the Vikings slain. His experience – or one might argue his literal-mindedness – enables him to assess the situation in a more realistic, level-headed way than the inexperienced, imaginative Totta. And while there would always be innocent young men and experienced older warriors in any historical period, one might be reminded in the Great War context of the idealistic young men who volunteered at first, eager to prove themselves, as is Totta, as opposed to the seasoned career soldiers who they had to serve beside or preside over, in the case of untried officers. One is not more medieval or modern in outlook than the other. What is decidedly modern, however, is the subject and setting of this verse-drama, its focus on the aftermath of a defeat in battle, on the uncanny feelings it evokes, and on the conversations that arise among those low in status contemplating the deeds of more famous people of high status.

Both Tída and Totta discuss what they see on the battlefield and relate the gossip circulating in town. Totta wonders how the Vikings came across a causeway over the river without evidence of a great fight. He is alluding to the decision by Beorhtnoth in "The Battle of Maldon" to allow the invading army to cross the causeway without resistance so that the two forces could face off on ample ground. Tída explains that "our lord was at fault, / or so in Maldon this morning men were saying" (137); the fault is attributed to Beorhtnoth's desire "to give minstrels matter for mighty songs" (137); in other words, a desire for personal heroic fame. This criticism of a leader's disastrous maneuver and the loss of young lives is commented on by both Tída and Totta, when they regret, for example, the death of Ælfwine, "barely bearded" (128). And the young Totta is especially critical of the "bearded men" who fled from the battle, "while the red heathen / beat down their boys" (128). The general tenor of their comments suggests that those in charge or those who should have led acted in misguided or cowardly fashions, leaving the young men to die unnecessarily. As Tída observes, "It's a wicked business / to gather them ungrown" (127). Tolkien's argument in the "Ofermod" essay is that the "Maldon" poet thought so too, although it is significant that the Old English poem does not emphasize in all cases the youth of the men who fell bravely alongside Beorhtnoth as a result of his decisions. This is Tolkien's own emphasis, a particularly modern one, in keeping with the writers and observers who were appalled by the record numbers of young men, the "lost generation", killed in the Great War.

And that is what marks this play most strongly as a reflection of the experience of the Great War: the setting filled with dead bodies. Of course, if presented as a radio play or a drama for two voices, the bodies have to be imagined by the listener. But the characters' dialogue insistently brings corpses to the fore, and even more tellingly, body parts. As Paul Kocher remarks, "By putting the reader right among the corpses on the battlefield after nightfall it drives home with utter immediacy the horror of a carnage that need never have taken place" (185). The horror of WWI included record numbers of men killed and wounded in new ways due to new weapons. Joanna Bourke points out how new technologies proved "more effective instruments of dismemberment than ever before," with amputations becoming a common sight (34). According to Allyson Booth, "Soldiers inhabited a world of corpses" (21); for this reason, Samuel Hynes suggests that the battlefields could be termed "landscape-with-corpse" (192). Soldier-poets emphasized the grim reality of dead and dismembered men who were a common sight in the trenches. Isaac Rosenberg, in "Dead Man's Dump", expresses the inescapable horror: "A man's brains splattered on / A stretcher-bearer's face" (Rosenberg 147.48-49) while Ivor Gurney's poem "To his Love" tries not to articulate the reality of the corpse until the truth bursts out in the last stanza:

> Cover him, cover him soon!
>   And with thick-set
> Masses of memoried flowers –
>   Hide that red wet
>   Thing I must somehow forget.
>   (Gurney 97.16-20)

Tolkien shares this focus on physical and psychological disability and death. Margaret Sinex examines iterations of the Túrin story and concludes that "Tolkien should be counted among those WWI veterans – memoirists, novelists and especially the poets – who highlight the grievous fragility of the human body and psyche caught up in the battlefield slaughter of the Great

War" (39); and I take a similar approach to Frodo, comparing Tolkien's representation of his increasingly damaged body and mind to other WWI writers ("Frodo's Body").

In *HBBS*, it is Tída who emphasizes the materiality of the dead bodies that the two characters are searching among. Tída comments on the corpses and dismembered bodies – albeit killed by sword rather than Great War technological weaponry – with a straightforward attitude, as if very little of the scene disgusts or frightens him. He seems inured to such devastation and just wants to get on with the job he has been given. It is Tída who always calls on Totta to help him, thereby bringing to the fore the idea that they are among dead, heavy bodies that must be turned about and identified: "Help me to heave' em! It's heavy labour / to lug them alone: long ones and short ones, / the thick and the thin" (126). The dialogue leads one to imagine that Tída is sorting through piles of the dead: "Look here, my lad, where they lie thickest! / Here! lend a hand! This head we know!" (127). The weight of the corpses is again emphasized when Tída uncovers one of the Vikings: "Help me with this one! / There, heave him over – the hound's carcase, / hulking heathen!" (129). It is no different when Tída is carrying his lord Beorhtnoth (or what's left of him) to a wagon for transport to the abbey. Again, he's giving orders to Totta: "Lift your end there! Lift up, I say" (136) and commenting on how, even though his lord's head has been cut off, his body is not light, causing Tída to sweat while working to move him. Even the younger Totta asks for a break because he is out of breath (132). In the final heaving of the body into the wagon, Tída specifies the body parts they should grab hold of: "Hold the shanks now, while I heave the shoulders" (138). The effect is to reduce the great lord Beorhtnoth to disparate body parts, dead and heavy. As Totta realizes, "Dead men drag earthward" (132).

However, that is not the only perspective on the dead that we are presented with in this play. Totta may comment on the downward pull of dead men, but he has a remedy for that, and it comes through poetry. From the earliest manuscript versions of the play, it is suggested that Totta is a poet, the son of a minstrel, and his poetry is revised and expanded as the drama develops into its final form. One could say that Totta's poetry, steeped in traditional style and subject matter, moves in a different direction from the dead. While corpses are weighty and drag earthward, poetry looks upwards from the grim ground and reintegrates the fallen.

Nowhere is this more evident than in the moments when the two men finally come across Beorhtnoth's body. The first sight of him is through a body part – his long, thick legs, identified by Totta: "Look! Here's a limb! A long yard, and thick / as three men's thighs" (129). Tída confirms that this is Beorhtnoth, "or what Heaven's left us:/ the longest legs in the land, I guess" (130). Their silent contemplation of what is left of the lord's body on the ground gives way to Totta's chanting verses. The first thing he does in his poem of praise is to raise up Beorhtnoth, in a literal sense, above all others: "His head was higher than the helm of kings / with heathen crowns" (130). In the midst of the dark and the "mirk" in which neither man can barely see anything, Totta represents Beorhtnoth metaphorically in clear, shining, golden lights: "his soul clearer than swords of heroes/ polished and proven; than plated gold/ his worth was greater" (130); he is further compared to "golden lords of long ago" (130). The poem praises the lord's heart and soul, his judgement and generosity – metaphorical and personal qualities that keep attention away from the mangled reality that lies before the poet.

Nevertheless, Totta is faced with a grim vision of Beorhtnoth's body when he realizes that not only is his body badly mangled but also that his head has been cut off. Previously, Totta was wondering where his lord lay that night, imagining his head on a "hard pillow" and his limbs "in long slumber" (127). The shocking reality leads Totta to another poetic song, introduced by his lines declaring, "Dear still shall be this dead body, / though men have marred it" (131), and from there, he begins to chant again. This time, in a lament closely modelled on the ending of *Beowulf*, Totta imagines a burial mound for his lord, filled with weapons and treasure. The lament is set in the present and future: "women are weeping; the wood is blazing" (131); "his grave shall be green" (132). The vision accords Beorhtnoth a funeral that exists in poetic tradition only. Of course, the two men have been assigned the task of bringing Beorhtnoth's body to the abbey, where it will be buried, and not cremated, Beowulf-like, on a funeral pyre piled high with his treasures.

Another moment of disillusionment leads to another poetic re-making by Totta when Tída explains that the reason Totta doesn't see a lot of dead Vikings by the causeway is that Beorhtnoth made a mistake in letting the enemy cross unimpeded. Totta's response is to lament Beorhtnoth's death by placing him in a broad historical context. He does not consider Beorhtnoth's specific and possibly disastrous battle strategy; instead, he elevates him poetically by seeing him as a descendant of a long line of Saxon conquerors of Britain. His set piece echoes the ending of the Old English poem "The Battle of Brunanburh", which commemorates an English victory in 937 CE. The last lines of that poem are as follows:

> There was never a greater slaughter
> on this island, nor ever yet so many
> people slain by the sword's edges
> before this, as books tell us,
> old wise men, since from the east
> the Angles and Saxons came up
> across the broad sea to seek Britain,
> proud war-smiths; they overcame the Welsh,
> and those men of glory gained a land.
> (Liuzza 260-61, 65-73)

Compare Totta's version:

> So the last is fallen of the line of earls,
> From Saxon lords long-descended
> Who sailed the seas, as songs tell us,
> From Angel in the East, with eager swords
> Upon war's anvil the Welsh smiting.
> Realms here they won and royal kingdoms,
> And in olden days this isle conquered. (137)

It is noteworthy that Totta echoes a poem celebrating a victory at Brunanburh for his present vision of a defeat at Maldon. His added conclusion, though, that Britain is once again in need, might suggest that he is hoping for a similar turn of events as in the past where victorious warriors would conquer their enemies. Totta looks for a recurrence in the future of what he knows of the past.

Totta's frequent recourse to poetic tradition allows him to escape the bounds of time. He can understand the present in the light of the past, and possibly even foresee a future. His poetry reintegrates and elevates the dead, transforming the grim reality he sees before him. His greatest poetic vision occurs near the end of the drama, when he is no longer chanting as in a couple of previous instances, but speaking as if he is in a dream-like state. As he travels in the wagon, he can see lights flickering in the distance. He starts by saying he's hearing the mass being chanted for Beorhtnoth in Ely, then moves into a vision of time passing and the world generally deteriorating: "The world withers and the wind rises; / the candles are quenched. Cold falls the night" (140). The stage direction calls for the lights to disappear as he speaks, and the next phase of his dream-like vision is more immediate and intense. He calls for a light, and seems to see one: "Lo! Fire now wakens, / hearth is burning, house is lighted, / men there gather" (141). His words evoke a ghostly atmosphere in which he can see men mysteriously appear out of the dark: "Out of the mists they come / through darkling doors whereat doom waiteth" (141). Is he seeing a vision of the future or the past? What he hears these visionary men singing is what Tolkien considered a proverbial saying from the Old English poetic tradition, "the finest expression of the northern heroic spirit, Norse or English; the clearest statement of the doctrine of uttermost endurance in the service of indomitable will" (143). They are a version of the lines given to Byrhtwold in "The Battle of Maldon", although Tolkien adds two more lines here: "Heart shall be bolder, harder be purpose, / more proud the spirit as our power lessens! / Mind shall not falter nor mood waver, / though doom shall come and dark conquer" (141).[2] My view, that Totta is penetrating to the heart of heroic tradition in his dream vision, disagrees markedly with Shippey's in this instance. Shippey argues that Totta's mind is "addled" and that Tolkien intends the dream vision to be interpreted negatively because Totta is half asleep ("Tolkien and 'The Homecoming'" 329, 336). But I view this scene as placing Totta in an entirely different light. I think that he is partaking in a significant event that recurs in Tolkien's fiction: the dream-like state in which poetry or song or a story is heard, allowing the listener to experience other times and places. In whatever form the story takes, it seems to have an independent life, absorbing the listener / dreamer. We can see this happening in *The Lord of the Rings* as the hobbits listen to Bombadil's tale of Middle-earth's history. As Bombadil goes on in his talking, singing, and even dancing, his tale seems to take on a

2 Honegger compares the evolution and different versions of these lines in Tolkien's various drafts.

life of its own: "Suddenly Tom's talk left the woods and went leaping up the young stream [...]" (*LotR* I.7.130). By the end of the tale, the hobbits end up "enchanted [...] under the spell of his words" (I.7.131) while Tom appears to be nodding as if falling asleep. The same kind of enchanted dream-like spell falls over Frodo when listening to the songs in Rivendell:

> Almost it seemed that the words took shape, and visions of far lands and bright things that he had never yet imagined opened out before him; and the firelit hall became like a golden mist above seas of foam that sighed upon the margins of the world. Then the enchantment became more and more dreamlike, until he felt that an endless river of swelling gold and silver was flowing over him, too multitudinous for its pattern to be comprehended; it became part of the throbbing air about him, and it drenched and drowned him. Swiftly he sank under its shining weight into a deep realm of sleep. (*LotR* II.1.233)

In "The Notion Club Papers", to cite one more example, those listening to the tale of Lowdham and Jeremy's adventures also enter a dream-like state in which they seem to be transported to an Anglo-Saxon hall where they listen to the story of King Sheave. When Lowdham stops talking, "we jumped like men waked suddenly from a dream. It seemed as if one man had vanished and another had sprung up in his place [...]" (*SD* 276). All of these dream visions enable access to "far lands", ancient kingdoms, traditional stories. I contend that Totta momentarily experiences the same kind of vision. Because this is a play for voices, he narrates what he sees, but the vision seems to come to him independently and to transport him – significantly, half-asleep – to another time and place.

It is easy to forget that Totta is experiencing this vision while lying on the headless corpse of Beorhtnoth. Moments before, Tída suggested that Totta can rest in the wagon with Beorhtnoth's "body for bolster" (139). While Totta finds the suggestion brutal, Tída reverses roles and mockingly takes on the role of poet, demonstrating that he, too, can compose alliterative verse if he wants to, remaking his "plain language" into a scenario that is more acceptable to Totta: "If a poet sang you: 'I bowed my head on his breast beloved, / and weary of weeping woeful slept I; / thus joined we journeyed, gentle master / and faithful servant [...],' / you'd not call it cruel" (139-40). The poetic version, even when composed by Tída, reinvigorates Beorhtnoth by imagining him and Totta in a human relationship as a master and servant, journeying together, and not by treating him like a lifeless thing, a mangled body that is being hauled in a cart, covered by a dirty blanket (138).

Which version speaks the truth? Yes, Beorhtnoth is a dismembered corpse; he is also the great lord who was a beloved master, with both Tída and Totta expressing their loyalty to and love of him, someone who inspired others with unyielding courage. Tída is the more literal-minded, plain-speaking, experienced character, and Totta is the innocent who is seeing the aftermath of real war for the first time, though inspired by poetic tradition to re-vision what he sees. Shippey points out that Totta is usually wrong, but one could argue that his optimism and his uncertainties simply come from inexperience. The divide between the two that Shippey sees is not as sharp as he might believe. For example, after Totta chants his first set-piece, "His head was higher than the helm of kings." Tída commends the verses: "Brave words, my lad! / The woven staves have yet worth in them / for woeful hearts" (130). After Totta's re-vision of Beowulf's funeral, Tída remarks, "Good words enough, gleeman Totta! / You laboured long as you lay, I guess, / in the watches of the night, while the wise slumbered" (132). And even though Tída often asks Totta to shut up and stop versifying, he can still appreciate – even compose – traditional metres himself, as he proves when he versifies a different image of Beorhtnoth's corpse lying in the cart for Tída's delicate feelings. It is difficult to imagine that Tolkien, who took such care with composing and revising over many years this alliterative drama, and whose habits, according to his biographer Humphry Carpenter, might lead us to believe that he too "laboured long [...] in the watches of the night" (132) over his verses, would think that Totta was "simply a stooge" (Shippey, "Tolkien and 'The Homecoming'" 329).

Shippey further views Tída as Tolkien's "mouthpiece" because he is the one who expresses Christian beliefs and tells Totta that his dream vision sounded "heathenish" – and "I don't hold with that" (141). Totta is not entirely or explicitly a heathen though. He is frightened by what looks like a "heathen hell" to him at the beginning, but he calls on "Heaven" to blast the cowards who ran from battle. Totta further expresses his love of Beorhtnoth, swearing: "By the Cross" (129). Totta proclaims that Beorhtnoth has "Gone to God glory seeking" (130) while exclaiming against the "wolfish heathens" (131), and after he kills one of the corpse-robbers, he says "Christ forgive me" (135). In other words, both of the men appear to be Christians. Furthermore, Tída's vision of Christianity is not exactly inspiring. Immediately after rejecting Totta's "heathenish" vision, which "sounded fey and fell-hearted" (141) to Tída, he makes a rather "fell-hearted" remark of his own, commenting that "When morning comes, it'll be much like others: / more labour and loss till the land's ruined; / ever work and war till the world passes" (141). This is not far from Totta's "doom" and "dark" conquering all. One could say that Tída expresses an appropriate theme on the transience of worldly things, but it lacks the consolation of Christian hope.

In other words, neither character can be singled out as an exact representative of what we know of Tolkien's expressed views and beliefs. Or to put it another way, both characters represent a tension between different experiences and views. To align only one or the other with Tolkien is unnecessary. It might be more productive to recognize that Tída and Totta engage in a dialectic that Margaret Hiley identifies as particularly modernist, in which traditional heroism is invoked but also criticized. Hiley points out, for example, that in Tolkien's (and other Inklings') fantasy, traditional heroes such as Aragorn exist side-by-side with unlikely heroes such as the comic hobbits, and that traditional heroism is found wanting when Frodo ultimately fails in his quest (85). While the *HBBS* is not set in Tolkien's fantasy Secondary World but in the early medieval period, the same split is evident. Tída pulls strongly in the direction of a disillusioned view of war that undermines traditional heroism. Totta takes us in another direction, using language and poetic tradition to make sense of the reality he sees, to find hope and meaning in the heroic past for the present and the future.

Totta's remaking of what he sees on the battlefield, supplemented by what he learns from Tída while also drawing on poetic tradition, results in the poem "The Battle of Maldon", according to Tolkien's fiction. The sequence of events can be confusing, as *HBBS* takes place after the battle represented in the Old English poem. One could say that *HBBS* represents a sequel to the *events* of the battle, but for this reason, many critics think of *HBBS* as a sequel to "The Battle of Maldon", the poem itself. However, while the events in *HBBS* occur after the battle, the drama actually presents a *prequel* to the Old English poem. In Tolkien's fiction, the Old English poem does not yet exist. Totta's dream vision, which includes the famous verses of "The Battle of Maldon" ("Heart shall be keener" etc.), is one moment that will inspire the Old English poem.

The young gleeman will return home and compose the poem that we know as "The Battle of Maldon". In fact, in one marginal note in his draft manuscripts, Tolkien says as much: "It is here supposed that Totta afterwards becomes the author of the poem the fragment of which survives. It is based (on this theory) partly on survivors' reports, partly on imagination & epic tradition" (Oxford, Bodleian Library, MS. Tolkien 5, fol. 65v).

If we accept Tolkien's fiction[3] and read from *HBBS* back to "The Battle of Maldon" (instead of the other way around, which is more usual when dealing with adaptations), we will see that Totta as the "Maldon" poet does the same things as in *HBBS*: having seen the dead bodies, he reintegrates and animates the dead, investing them with heroic glory. He also, in Tolkien's imagination, incorporates what he's learned from Tída. Marie Nelson discusses how Tída can "read" a battlefield. He understands where Beorhtnoth is likely to have fallen and identifies various warriors of his household retinue – as Nelson points out, in the same order as they appear in "The Battle of Maldon" (74-75). If we're reading *HBBS* as an adaptation of an earlier source, as is the more usual practice, this provides an interesting fact about Tolkien's adherence to the Old English poem in composing his verse drama. However, if we transfer this insight to Tolkien's fictional representation of Totta as the "Maldon" poet, we can see that Tída's identification of the dead is reproduced in the same order in Totta's "Maldon" poem: Wulfmær (including the momentary confusion over which Wulfmær this is), Ælfnoth, Ælfwine, Offa. Totta does add other warriors as well in "The Battle of Maldon", including Dunnere, a "ceorl", or "churl" in modern English, a man of lower status. We might be reminded of Totta exclaiming how he had loved Beorhtnoth as well as any lord and that "a poor freeman may prove in the end / more tough when tested than titled earls" (129). Following Tolkien's conceit of Totta as the "Maldon" poet, we could say that Totta included just such a poor man in his array of heroic warriors. The proverbial heroic lines

3 Honegger cites a similar statement by Tolkien a couple of pages earlier in the manuscript (Honegger 197, n. 17), but he discounts the idea of Totta being the author of "The Battle of Maldon" because he agrees with Shippey's assessment of the character as foolish and therefore incapable of composing such a poem. Honegger further points out that the entire page where the comment occurs has a line drawn through it, suggesting Tolkien's rejection of the idea of Totta as the "Maldon" poet. The comment that I cite above is also on a page that has been crossed out, but the content on both pages mostly reappears in later revisions as the introduction to the final text. In other words, the crossing out does not indicate rejection; it just illustrates the process of revision. My reasons for taking Tolkien's comments on Totta at face value are further explained in the discussion above.

that he heard in his dream vision he gives to an old warrior, Byrhtwold, who appropriately expresses the age-old saying that emerges from a long tradition. As for Beorhtnoth, Totta invests him with heroic glory in keeping with his love of his lord, but (in Tolkien's opinion of "Maldon" at least), he also incorporates some criticism of Beorhtnoth's strategy in letting the enemy cross the causeway, which he attributes to Beorhtnoth's "ofermod" or "overmastering pride" (143) as Tolkien translates it. Again, one might recall that in *HBBS*, it is Tída who explains that people in town were already criticizing Beorhtnoth for this tactic. Tída's opinion instructs Totta's poetic representation of his lord. Tída, who is continually asking Totta to be quiet, does not have any interest in expressing his thoughts. Totta, however, finds the language to articulate what happened on the battlefield, incorporating his poetic ideals of traditional heroism as well as the practical and realistic view of the war-weary Tída. In a way, he speaks for both of them in "The Battle of Maldon".

Although Tolkien's views of the Old English poem are not shared by all critics, his interpretation has been influential in discussions of what is and is not acceptable heroism in "Maldon", which he defines in the concluding "Ofermod" essay. Both *HBBS* and the Old English "Battle of Maldon", in Tolkien's view, present heroism that is tempered by an awareness that warriors can make disastrous tactical errors, and that the personal pride of a leader is not as admirable as the love and loyalty of his subordinates. I do not see a rejection of Old English poetry in this – certainly not a rejection of "The Battle of Maldon". Both texts, *HBBS* and "Maldon", help Tolkien to redefine what heroism can and should look like, a project that he carries out in other works of fiction as well, such as *LotR*, where, for example, in comparing Faramir and Boromir, S. Brett Carter concludes, "the role of the warrior that defined heroes since the poetry of Homer is cast aside in favour of a heroic model that prefers peace and only fights when his way of life is threatened and there is no alternative" (34).

Although Tolkien shares experiences and literary elements with other war writers, he did not develop the overwhelming cynicism of some of the Great War writers. In other words, Tolkien's views are not represented by Tída's alone. Neither are his views only those of the naive Totta. It is the dialogue between the two, the push and the pull, that enables him to continually negotiate between the two, to identify what is flawed and sorrowful about the waste of war and what is worthwhile and lasting in traditions of heroism.

Acknowledgments

The author would like to acknowledge the support of a Mount Saint Vincent University Research Grant and to thank the Tolkien Estate for permission to quote from Tolkien's manuscript.

Bibliography

BOOTH, Allyson. *Postcards from the Trenches: Negotiating the Space Between Modernism and the First World War.* Oxford: Oxford University Press, 1996.

BOURKE, Joanna. *Dismembering the Male: Men's Bodies, Britain and the Great War.* Chicago, IL: University of Chicago Press, 1996.

BOWMAN, Mary R. "Refining the Gold: Tolkien, *The Battle of Maldon*, and the Northern Theory of Courage." *Tolkien Studies* 7 (2010): 91-115.

CARPENTER, Humphrey. *J.R.R. Tolkien: A Biography.* Boston, MA and New York City, NY: Houghton Mifflin, 2000.

CARTER, S. Brett. "Faramir and the Heroic Ideal of the Twentieth Century; or, How Aragorn Died at the Somme." *Baptism of Fire: The Birth of the Modern British Fantastic in World War I.* Ed. Janet Brennan Croft, Altadena, CA: Mythopoeic Press, 2015, 23-37.

CROFT, Janet Brennan. *War and the Works of J.R.R. Tolkien.* Contributions to the Study of Science Fiction and Fantasy 106. Westport, CT and London: Praeger, 2004.

FUSSELL, Paul. *The Great War and Modern Memory.* Oxford: Oxford University Press, 2000.

GARTH, John. *Tolkien and the Great War: The Threshold of Middle-earth.* London: HarperCollins, 2003.

GILBERT, Sandra. "'Rat's Alley': The Great War, Modernism, and the (Anti) Pastoral Elegy." *New Literary History* 30.1 (1999): 179-201.

GURNEY, Ivor. "To His Love." *The Penguin Book of First World War Poetry.* Ed. George Walter. London: Penguin, 2006, 97.

HILEY, Margaret. *The Loss and the Silence: Aspects of Modernism in the Works of C.S. Lewis, J.R.R. Tolkien and Charles Williams*. Cormarë Series 22. Zurich and Jena: Walking Tree Publishers, 2011.

HONEGGER, Thomas. "*The Homecoming of Beorhtnoth*: Philology and the Literary Muse." *Tolkien Studies* 4 (2007): 189-99.

HYNES, Samuel. *A War Imagined: The First World War and English Culture*. New York City, NY: Atheneum, 1991.

KOCHER, Paul H. *Master of Middle-earth: The Fiction of J.R.R. Tolkien*. New York City, NY: Ballantine Books, 1972.

LIUZZA, R.M. (ed. and trans.). "The Battle at Brunanburh." *Old English Poetry: An Anthology*. Broadview Anthology of British Literature edition. Peterborough, Ontario: Broadview Press, 2014, 256-61.

MANNING, Frederic. "The Face." *The Penguin Book of First World War Poetry*. Ed. George Walter. London: Penguin, 2006, 129.

NELSON, Marie. "'The Homecoming of Beorhtnoth Beorhthelm's Son': J.R.R. Tolkien's Sequel to 'The Battle of Maldon'." *Mythlore* 26 (2008): 65-87,

OWEN, Wilfrid. "Dulce et Decorum est." *The Penguin Book of First World War Poetry*. Ed. George Walter. London: Penguin, 2006, 141-42.

ROSEBURY, Brian. *Tolkien: A Cultural Phenomenon*. New York City, NY: Palgrave Macmillan, 2003.

ROSENBERG, Isaac. "Dead Man's Dump." *The Penguin Book of First World War Poetry*. Ed. George Walter. London: Penguin, 2006, 146-48.

"Returning, We Hear The Larks." *The Penguin Book of First World War Poetry*. Ed. George Walter. London: Penguin, 2006, 65.

SCULL, Christina and Wayne G. HAMMOND. *The J.R.R. Tolkien Companion and Guide*. Revised and Expanded Edition. London: HarperCollins, 2017.

SHIPPEY, Tom. "Boar and Badger: An Old English Heroic Antithesis?" *Leeds Studies in English* 16 (1985): 220-39.

J.R.R. Tolkien: Author of the Century. London: HarperCollins, 2001.

"Tolkien and 'The Homecoming of Beorhtnoth'." *Roots and Branches: Selected Papers on Tolkien by Tom Shippey*. Cormarë Series 11. Zurich and Jena: Walking Tree Publishers, 2007, 323-339.

SINEX, Margaret. "Wounded by War: Men's Bodies in the Prose Tradition of *The Children of Húrin*." *Baptism of Fire: The Birth of the Modern British Fantastic in World War I*. Ed. Janet Brennan Croft. Altadena, CA: Mythopoeic Press, 2015, 38-59.

SMOL, Anna. "Frodo's Body: Liminality and the Experience of War." *The Body in Tolkien's Legendarium: Essays on Middle-earth Corporeality*. Ed. Christopher Vaccaro. Jefferson, NC: McFarland, 2013, 39-62.

SORLEY, Charles Hamilton. "When you see millions of the mouthless dead." *The Penguin Book of First World War Poetry*. Ed. George Walter. London: Penguin, 200, 158.

TOLKIEN, J.R.R. "*Beowulf*: The Monsters and the Critics." *The Monsters and the Critics and Other Essays*. Ed. Christopher Tolkien. London: HarperCollins, 1997, 5-48.

The Hobbit or There and Back Again. Boston, MA: Houghton Mifflin, 2007.

The Homecoming of Beorhtnoth Beorhthelm's Son. Oxford, Bodleian Library, MS. Tolkien 5.

"The Homecoming of Beorhtnoth Beorhthelm's Son." *Tree and Leaf, including Mythopoeia*. London: HarperCollins, 2001.

The Letters of J.R.R. Tolkien. Edited by Humphrey Carpenter, with the assistance of Christopher Tolkien. London: George Allen and Unwin, 1981; London: HarperCollins, 1995.

The Lord of the Rings. 50th Anniversary edition. London: HarperCollins; Boston, MA: Houghton Mifflin, 2004.

"The Notion Club Papers." *Sauron Defeated*. (The History of Middle-earth 9). Ed. Christopher Tolkien. London: HarperCollins; Boston, MA: Houghton Mifflin, 1992, 145-327.

Section IV:

Alterity: Race, Class, Gender, and Sexuality in War

Lynn Schlesinger

Angels of Care and Houses of Healing in World War I: Their Possible Influence on Tolkien's *The Lord of the Rings*

In J.R.R. Tolkien's *The Lord of the Rings* healing is an overarching theme. Characters and communities suffer physical, psychic and spiritual wounds. Some wounds may be cured (Éowyn, Faramir, Merry), many are fatal (Théoden, Saruman), while others may be ameliorated but never completely healed (Frodo's shoulder; Arwen's grief after Aragorn's death). Some experiences are transformative: Gandalf goes from grey wizard to white, and Éowyn chooses to "battle" as a healer rather than a warrior. Some hurts occur all at once, while others develop over time, festering (Gollum). Healers employ technical skills, but some also have a healing touch that cannot be easily explained or taught (Elrond, Aragorn). Tolkien associates both males (Aragorn, Elrond) and females (Éowyn, Ioreth) with healing, and at the end of *The Lord of the Rings* the land needs healing, as well as those who survived the war.

Tolkien expressed displeasure with those who sought to compare *LotR* to WWI and/or WWII directly, or described the work as an allegory. Yet Tolkien also acknowledged some connections between his biographical experiences and his fiction (*Letters* 303; see also Carpenter; Garth, Preface).[1] John Garth's detailed timeline, description of Tolkien's early years with the TCBS, the Somme trenches, and Tolkien's illness, help us understand the context within which Tolkien wrote some of his early works, and the possible influence of WWI on his later works as well.[2]

In his book Garth exposes myths about being a soldier in WWI, and uses primary sources to give readers a sense of what it was like to be a soldier at the Battle of the Somme, to survive when so many others died, to be separated from family, to be given a "blighty" and sent back home, to convalesce, to

---

1 Tolkien's reflections on war are particularly apparent in his letters to his sons during WWII. (e.g., *Letters* 45, 66).

2 Regarding possible biographical relevance, the following authors examine links between Tolkien's faith, belief in grace and afterlife, and his writings: Brenner; Mitchell; Sandner.

renew relationships, and to mourn. In this paper I suggest that we expand our study of Tolkien and WWI to include the role of women as "healers" in WWI, particularly those working on the Western Front, on hospital ships, and in British hospitals and convalescent facilities. Many women saw themselves as fighters *and* as care workers. Are there connections between Tolkien's characterization of women such as Éowyn and Ioreth, and the actions of those wartime women, who directed and worked in hospitals, drove ambulances, ran canteens, etc.?[3]

World War I Women Care Workers on Two Fronts

Wartime Options for Nurses and Other Caregivers

Hallett notes that in 1914 "the Allied military nursing services were a curious amalgam of highly trained elite professionals, semi-trained volunteers, and confident but largely untrained lady-nurses" (*Veiled Warriors* 18). Queen Alexandra's Imperial Military Nursing Service (QAIMNS) and Queen Alexandra's Royal Naval Nursing Service (QARNNS) were the primary military nursing organizations in Britain when WWI began. In 1914 the QAIMNS had less than 300 members, and approximately 800 Reservists, who had agreed to serve within 24 hours' notice. The QARNNS had fewer than 100 active staff, and some reservists. These nurses spent years training, and viewed themselves as professionals (Hallett, *Veiled Warriors*).

After the Boer War, the government established the Territorial Force Nursing Service (TFNS) to address the need for qualified medical staff in times of war. Civilian nurses who had at least 3 years of training could join the TFNS. The Act establishing the TFNS also called for plans that would establish 23 hospitals throughout Britain. Schools, universities, and other public buildings

3 An essay by Amy Amendt-Raduege, published when this chapter was already substantially complete, also makes the case for the influence of women who served in World War I: "[Tolkien] had modern examples [of women as heroes], too: the women who participated in WWI. [...] I have so far found nothing in Tolkien's published writings about the influence these remarkable women had on his writings; perhaps he himself did not know. All we can say for certain is that he very likely saw for himself the sacrifices and valor of women serving at the front, and that those events happen to coincide with the first germs of the great legendarium. And they were all heroes" (80-81).

were chosen to be converted *if needed* to hospitals. When WWI began, between 2000-3000 nurses had volunteered to be part of the TFNS. During the war additional Territorial hospitals were established in France, Belgium, and other war fronts (Hallett, *Veiled Warriors*; Light).

The First Aid Nursing Yeomanry (FANY) was another organization of trained health care workers. Captain Edward Baker, a veteran of the Boer War, wanted to train women in First Aid, but also prepare them to get close enough to the wounded to make a difference: "the original members of FANY were trained in cavalry work, signaling and camping out" as well as first aid (Trueman, "First Aid Nursing Yeomanry"). Late in 1915 the British Red Cross formally agreed to have FANY provide ambulance convoys for the British Army. In 1916 the organization also began to provide drivers for the Belgian Army. In addition to first aid and driving, members established canteens, organized plays and other diversions (Lee, "'I Wish My Mother'"; Trueman, "First Aid").

As the war progressed "[t]housands of young women from middle-class homes with little experience of domestic work, not much relevant education and total ignorance of male bodies, volunteered and found themselves pitched into military hospitals" (Williams). Associated with the British Red Cross and the Order of St. John, these VADs (Voluntary Aid Detachments) necessarily came from more well-off families; they had to supply their own uniforms and cover other expenses. The VAD regulations specified employment criteria (e.g., aged 23-42 if working abroad) and job requirements. For example:

> They will be required to work under fully trained Nurses, and will be under the direct control of the Officer in charge and the Matron of the Hospital in which employed. Their duties will be similar to those carried out by probationers in Civil Hospitals. These include sweeping, dusting polishing of brasses, cleaning of ward tables and patients' lockers, cleaning of ward sinks and ward utensils, washing of patients' crockery and sorting of linen. These, and any nursing duties which they are considered qualified to perform, will be allotted to them by the Matron of the Hospital. (A.C.I. 1244 of 1916) ("Regulations Governing the Employment of Nursing V.A.D. Members in Military Hospitals")

Some trained nurses, who were struggling for professional recognition, resented those who joined the VADs (Voluntary Aid Detachments). Some VADs, coming from a higher social status, criticized the professional nurses, and felt that they were treated "little better than [...] domestic servants" (Williams).

In 1917, the Women's Army Auxiliary Corps (WAAC) "became the first example of a Western nation employing women within the armed services" (Kempshall, "Women's Army Auxiliary Corps"; see also Crosthwait; Trueman).[4] While this policy represented a "first", WAACs were limited to activities considered suitable for women: "clerks, domestic services, mechanical maintenance, cookery and tending war graves" (Kempshall, "Women's Army"). They were not allowed to use military titles. Those in charge were called Administrators or Controllers, and were typically from the middle/upper classes. Forewomen (the equivalent of NCOs) and workers were more likely to be working class (Trueman, "Women's Army Auxiliary Corps"). Although the WAAC formed after Tolkien's service in France, I would think he would have been aware of the debates regarding women entering the military.

At the beginning of the war the British army only recognized trained nurses who were in the QAIMNS and QARNNS.[5] Some nurses on their own volunteered to serve with the French and Belgian armies. Two of the most famous women, Elsie Knocker and Mairi Chisholm, established a first aid station in Pervyse, Belgium. Not wanting to deal with the bureaucratic delays they would face if they sought government funding, Elsie and Mairi engaged in fundraising, traveling back to England. They became known as "the Angels of Pervyse" ("Barnfield Theatre"; Hosie). One soldier wrote in his diary:

> Christmas this year appeared as a British angel. She emerged in my observation post, dressed in a leather coat, with twinkling eyes and her hands filled with presents. There were small, useful gifts and also a piece of plum cake.
>
> The presents were bowed with a Belgian tricoloured ribbon. Thank you for the presents, thank you for this surprise, and thank you for the smile. Christmas Day 1914 – diary entry by artillery observer Captain Robert De Wilde. (Hosie)

Some women physicians, not accepted in the military, established hospitals both in France and Great Britain, hospitals administered and staffed by women (Murray).

---

4 The Women's Land Army was founded in the same year "to maintain Britain's agricultural interests" (Trueman, "Women's Army Auxiliary Corps").

5 Other women's organizations included: Women's Hospital Corps, Women's Auxiliary Force, and The Women's Legion (*Women and the British Army in the First World War – The Long, Long Trail*).

Social Activism and Conflicting Expectations at Home and Abroad

Whether paid or unpaid, women participated in WWI through a variety of organizations, with the majority engaged in some form of caregiving. Hallett mentions two gender-related social causes that influenced many women in the early 20th century to challenge prescribed social roles. Women active in the suffrage movement sought to achieve voting rights through political organizing and outright demonstrations (*Veiled Warriors* 11-12). Suffragette protests conflicted with middle- and upper-class expectations for women as homemakers and mothers.[6] At the same time, nurses were increasingly concerned about promoting nursing as a profession and limiting inclusion to those who could meet certain criteria. People involved in healthcare in Britain were divided on the subject of registration for nurses. Some felt that a registry of trained nurses would raise the standard of nursing and promote professionalization. Others, especially hospital administrators, opposed the establishment of a closed registry. Administrators did not want to lose control, and some nurses questioned whether a registry would effectively raise standards (Hallett, *Veiled Warriors* 16-18).

With the advent of war, women from differing backgrounds and political perspectives put aside debates, in order to participate in the war effort. Women had many reasons for wanting to be more involved, whether at home or abroad. For some, involvement reflected personal concerns for loved ones in service, and a desire to support their efforts. Some women also saw clearly that their involvement could help make a stronger case for women's rights and full participation in social life. Regarding nurses on hospital ships, Hallett writes: "behind the lines of nurses' narratives there is a sense that, in doing such extraordinary work, these women believed they were both carving out an identity for themselves as female professionals on a world stage, and discovering their own strength and power as individuals" ("Argonauts" 198).

At the same time, social expectations for women reflected conflicting ideas of what women could and should do. During WWI women on all sides of the conflicts were recruited to do a variety of "men's" work, yet still "keep the home fires burning":

6 Of course some women have always had to work, often in addition to the work of homemaking/mothering, whether they wanted to or not.

> There's a silver lining
> Through the dark clouds shining,
> Turn the dark cloud inside out
> Till the boys come home.
> (Novello and Ford)

The lyrics acknowledged how much the "boys" were missed, and emphasized the importance for those at home to maintain some consistency and continuity; to not give in. Those lads/boys dreamed of returning to a home that they hoped would be as they remembered. Initially many people believed the war would end quickly, and that life would be little changed ("Voices of the First World War: Over by Christmas"). Popular images on posters at home, and the caring and dedication shown to battle-weary soldiers on the front, contributed to an almost mythic vision of women as "The girl behind the man behind the gun" (Smith, A.).[7] Shirley Williams wrote for the BBC news on "World War One: The Many Battles Faced by WW1's Nurses":

> [T]he myth of the gentle young nurse, often a voluntary and untrained VAD (Voluntary Aid Detachment), in her starched and spotless white uniform, was universally admired. It echoed centuries of stories from King Arthur and the Round Table to Shakespeare's Henry V, where rough but brave warriors encountered graceful young women who cared for them. (Williams)[8]

Hallett, in her detailed history of allied nurses during WWI, describes three myths that arose: "the myth of the courageous, mistreated VAD; the myth of the romantic nurse, who falls in love with her patient; and the myth of the nurse-heroine, who risks everything, not only to save individual patients' lives, but also to win the war" (*Veiled Warriors* 2). After the war, authors continued to utilize such images in fiction, poetry, biographical and autobiographical accounts (Bell; McGowan; Geiger). However, life for British women and men, at home and abroad, was grittier and more complex. Writings about heroic acts as if performed by Heroes (capital H) created a distance between readers and the everyday people who indeed often performed heroically, at great

7 Women in Germany as well as Allied countries had a patriotic duty to contribute to maintaining their homeland (Marchesi).

8 Shirley Williams's mother was Vera Brittain (1893-1970), known as a nurse, poet, novelist, and pacifist. Much of Brittain's poetry is raw, angry, refusing to romanticize war (McClellan). Like Tolkien, during WWI Brittain lost some of the most important people in her young life (brother, fiancé, friends). She did not retreat from life in her anger, but through her writing and activism pursued pacifism and conveyed what Tolkien referred to as the "animal horror" of war (*Letters* 72).

physical and psychic cost. Just as Garth utilized primary data to describe the experiences of Tolkien's peers in WWI, oral and written histories of women in WWI may provide a more accurate, less mythic, sense of the kinds of women Tolkien might have encountered, in France and at home. For example, Grace McDougall wrote: "War was no romantic, heroic epic, only this dreary reality of gaping wounds and quivering flesh" (132). Whatever work they did, in leaving home for France and other war fronts women faced some of the same physical and emotional challenges as men.

Leaving the "Lonely Isle"

> O lonely, sparkling isle, farewell!
> (Tolkien, "The Lonely Isle", reprinted in Garth 145)

> The ship began to move, and I shall never forget the awful feeling I had as I saw my beloved country slipping away from view. It was the first time I'd been away from England.
> (Kathleen Charlotte Bottomley; Reel 2)

Trained or untrained, paid or volunteer, members of an organization or on their own, women who traveled to the war fronts placed themselves in danger as soon as they left Britain, before they even neared a battlefield or land-based military hospital. Military hospital ships, and transport ships, might be attacked (Christie; "WWI Hospital Ships"). Annie Johnston was a young Canadian nurse who volunteered in 1915, and served in Malta, France, and England before returning to Canada in 1919. Annie's sister Maud noted in her diary:

> Annie's ship departed for England on May 1, 1915. They sailed through the Irish Sea only a few hours before the *Lusitania*, traveling over the same dangerous water with lights out and life preservers on. They did not know that the *Lusitania* had been torpedoed until they reached Liverpool (Giffin 42; see also "23 West Street, Newport").

Kit and Eve Dodsworth, two sisters from York, England, survived the sinking of the military transport ship Aragon on 30 December 1917 as they approached Alexandria, Egypt. In her diary Kit described a torpedo attack, the harrowing lifeboat lowering over the edge of the ship, local boats arriving to help, and men jumping from the sinking ship: "It was an extraordinary and awful sight" ("Marygate York: Wartime Adventures of Two Sisters"; see also "Sinking of the

S.S. Aragon"). Although all the nurses on board survived, 610 soldiers died. The following day another military ship, the Osmanieh, struck a mine, killing 197 people, 8 of whom were nurses ("CWGC Remembers").

Edith Elizabeth Appleton (1877-1958) was a member of Queen Alexandra's Imperial Military Nursing Service. In one of her first letters home she described her journey to her mother:

> We left [Dover] in the dark. A dark ship racing full speed through the night. No light was allowed to show from any of the cabins, no lights at all on deck, only one much-shaded one from the mizzen mast. [...] I felt a little eerie; especially as we had been saying perhaps the crossing was unsafe [...]. I knew we had arrived when I woke – first I heard a dog bark, then a little later heard Church bells ringing, and should have been quite pleased to attend the service to say, "Thank you for a safe crossing." (Letter, 11 October 1914)

Edith's 1914 journey was long, from Southampton to Dover, then Ostende, Dunkirk, finally landing at Boulogne. Edith ends her letter by saying "I hope I am not greedy, but after four days of boulli, roast mutton and lamb begin to sound very delicious, but we should be thankful for all the care taken of us [...]. It has been a great eye-opener of the seriousness of navigation just now."[9] Edith served until 1919 and kept a diary during almost the entire time.

In her book *A VAD in France*, Olive Dent describes leaving England, and her first impressions of France.

> *Tuesday* Our party of a hundred V.A.D.s – members of St. John's Ambulance Association, St. John's Ambulance Brigade and the British Red Cross Society – left Charing Cross Station this morning. It may be the station of Infinite Sorrows, of heart-breaking farewells, but our going, at any rate, was quite unheroic. [...] We had a very good and very quick crossing with not even a floating bottle to deceive ourselves that an enemy submarine was near. [...] Arrived at Boulogne [...] we nurses went to an hotel where we were allocated to various hospitals – all in Northern France, – and to which we were to proceed on the morrow. It was here we saw a new aspect of hotel life. I shared a room with a girl I had never before seen. It was seven feet by nine, with a sloping

9 Thank you to Dick Robinson, Edie's grand-nephew, for initial online access to Edie Appleton's diaries. Edith's diaries are available as *A Nurse at the Front: The Great War Diaries of Sister Edith Appleton*. Edited by Ruth Cowen. Simon & Schuster, 2012. After the book was published a relative found three letters from Edith, including the one quoted above, and shared them with Mr. Robinson. All three letters may be found at http://anurseatthefront.org.uk/introduction-to-the-diaries/early-letters/, and additional information about Edith may be found at "Edith Elizabeth Appleton O.B.E. R.R.C.", http://anurseatthefront.org.uk.

> roof having two rafters and a skylight, and with lime-washed walls. Ce n'est pas magnifique mais c'est la guerre. (19-21)

On Wednesday Olive's group visited a cemetery that now included an area for members of the British military. During the night Olive and other V.A.D.s arrived at their assigned hospital.

> We were taken to the night duty room, and in about three minutes time were wondering why on earth we were so consummately foolish as to volunteer for nursing service. It was 2.30 in the morning, the door of the duty room was swollen and would not close, an icy draught played along the floor, the kettle refused to boil for some time […] (29).

Kathleen Charlotte Bottomley, a trained telephonist, joined the WAAC in 1917, against her mother's wishes ("My mother was a real martinet, women in the army was unthinkable."). She wasn't sure what tasks she would be assigned, but that didn't matter: "I'd go as anything … I wanted to go to France." When Kathleen applied, she lied about her age ("I was only 19," not 21). She described the physical performed by six "lady" physicians who "turned me inside out practically." During her training Kathleen learned about more than she expected. At first, she thought urinals were vases, and recalling the lectures on venereal diseases Kathleen said: "hadn't heard of it before … put us on our guard" (Reel 1). The first night in France, Kathleen and the other new WAACs slept on the floor, with blankets that hadn't been cleaned; some got body lice. Years later, at a get together with other WAACs a woman recognized Kathleen and reminded her: "We deloused together" (Reel 2). Kathleen soon learned that the rules they had to follow might reflect propriety more than common sense. In Abbeville, their second night in France, Kathleen and the other young women tried to fight the cold by sharing blankets but were told that was not allowed. Contact with men was often monitored strictly and women were expected to represent their country appropriately. The work that women did, however, often would not have been considered ladylike, or even typical "women's work", in another context.

Women at Work

In France, women's work varied depending on several factors, both formal (affiliated organization, training) and informal. Sometimes need superseded tradition or rules. At first Kathleen Bottomley was assigned to different jobs. She cleaned lavatories, cleaned out candle "fat" and put in new candles (no electricity), and "mark[ed] out" a tennis court "on my knees." She was excited at first to learn about the tennis court, but it turned out that the court was only for the officers (Reel 3). Kathleen knew some French, which helped when she had to run errands: delivering and picking up laundry and shoes to be repaired. For some time, Kathleen worked as a store-woman, sorting uniforms: "if ever I smell new material now it reminds me of that time …" (Reel 1). Kathleen then replaced a male telephonist: "Men weren't so keen on working with women" (Reel 3). She was given "unofficial" errands to do: caring for the commandant's horse, buying presents for soldiers to bring home to their wives. In the camp they had to boil water, and Kathleen remembered finding nonfood items in her meals more than once: a soldier's button, a key, a piece of tin; she equated Army biscuits with dog biscuits. The camp took in increasing numbers of POWs, which "under some convention agreement" meant less food for the British soldiers and staff (Reel 4).

Alice Christobel Remington saw volunteering as "my big chance of getting out and away" (Reel 1). She was from a well-off family. Alice was not interested in nursing, so in 1914 she took the initiative to go to a garage and asked for training. She learned to drive, and to work on tires and engines, doing "everything that the men did" (Reel 1). By 1915 she was a driver for Lady Angela Forbes. Lady Forbes established canteens in Le Touquet, Étaples, and Boulogne (which Alice described as a "beautiful spot if you had time to enjoy it"). Alice also picked up stores for the canteens. Later, she became a VAD ambulance driver. Alice would drive as carefully as possible, especially if the ambulance had soldiers with fractures or spinal injuries. However, even though those injuries meant driving more slowly, Alice considered other types of medical problems were more difficult: "Ones that had trench fever and the ones that had dysentery, they were the most depressed." She further said: "The ones that had dysentery, poor things … they were so ashamed of themselves, they couldn't help it … to feel they were in that state, and that we girls were doing things for them, wouldn't have minded the nurses, but we were not the same, we were sort of drivers, we were different from the nurses, they expected that in hospitals." Amy Bell notes that "the relationship between female nurse and male patient during the war was a powerful example of the breakdown of boundaries between the sexes" as female nurses saw and treated male bodies, men damaged physically and psychologically by war (419).[10] To minimize the tension, some women would try to frame their relationship to men in neutral or more typically gendered ways (Bell 420). In August 1916 Edith Appleton referred to the 69 patients for whom she was responsible as her "family" (*A Nurse at the Front* 177).

Nora Barker joined the WAAC as a gardener and served from 1917-1919. Men did the actual digging, but Nora and others filled in the graves, planted grass, left space for future plants, a cross. Nora said the "French people looked upon us with horror. 'Khaki girl, ne bon.' Dreadful." When asked whether she found the work depressing Nora replied: "No … just a job … cut grass, and look after the flowers, and save the seed … [Nurses] avoided us … [Men] just put up with us" (Reel 1).

Grace McDougall was the FANY Commandant. In her book, *A Nurse at the War*, Grace describes a moment of strange calm, during a rainstorm, with the sound of guns booming. In the midst of war she recognizes how her life has changed:

> Up here alone, far from civilization, very far from the homes where perhaps our people thought of us, but certainly did not imagine our surroundings – here we were, girls of the twentieth century in this atmosphere of storm and war living what surely few women ever dreamt in their wildest fancies until this war began. This was life! My ears tingled; I breathed in long, deep breaths. Had I spoken, a sort of wild war song would have come from my lips. The Highland blood in me bubbled and frothed; I wanted to run for miles – to race, to climb – action at all costs. (132)

Reality quickly challenged Grace's excitement and romanticizing:

> And then … well, along the road came weary, stumbling figures, and most of them carried stretchers or long strange bundles. There was no romance or triumph here, no wild war cry and exaltation – just these men, dirty and muddy

---

10 See also Acton's "'Dangerous Daughters': American Nurses and Gender Identity in World War One and Vietnam": "The woman who enters the 'forbidden zone' of the male arena of war reveals the 'forbidden zone' of the fragmented male body" (106).

> and footsore, bringing in their comrades, broken and maimed and moaning … or very quiet … (132; ellipsis in the original)

You returned to work and kept going. When supplies were scarce, you employed creativity. Olive Dent wrote: "On active service it is a case of improvising, improvising, improvising, and one article in its time plays many parts. Thus the other day a hut door was being propped open with a tin of bully beef – the beef being subsequently eaten at the night orderlies' supper" (36-37).

Women as well as men became patients, whether through injury or illness. In addition to the dangers associated with ship duty, nurses in hospitals might be wounded or killed by the same artillery that affected the soldiers they treated. Alice Thomasson was 21 when she died at Abbeville in 1918.

> During the night of May 29th-30th, the Germans launched a bombing raid on Abbeville and one of the bombs fell into a protection trench where Alice and her QMAAC [Queen Mary's Army Auxiliary Corps] colleagues were sheltering. Eight women, including Alice, were killed outright, whilst another died later of her wounds. Seven other women were wounded, but survived, thanks largely to the efforts of three women who attended to them – Dr Phoebe Chapple of the Royal Army Medical Corps, Ethel Cartledge, a forewoman clerk and assistant administrator Sophy Cross. (Dean)

Some contracted flu or other diseases (Bennett). Nora Barker got food poisoning, probably from poorly reheated food (Reel 2). Only recently have scholars started to explore the effects of stress experienced by the women who worked on or near the WW1 battlefields (Groch-Begley).

Kathleen Bottomley needed an emergency appendectomy. After surgery she convalesced first at Woodside Convalescent Home, in Le Touquet: "enjoying good food and excellent nursing." She was sent back to England on leave, to find herself in a "spot of bother." When she arrived at Victoria Stations, Kathleen met a soldier who "hinted that we were more or less prostitutes sent out to amuse the army, which naturally I took exception to, and stood up to him and told him off." As people gathered, military police arrived, and told Kathleen to take off the blue and white arm band she wore on her coat. Kathleen refused, "as it was part of my uniform, being a signaler." When she got back to Abbeville, in France, she was concerned that she might be in trouble. Her supervisor told her that it was good that she "had acted on behalf of our comrades in defending our good name, etc., and the MPs had no authority over me when in England on leave." In recalling the story, you can hear the delight in Kathleen's voice, proud of herself and of the support she received (Reel 5).

War Front – Battle of the Somme

Before and during the Battle of the Somme Edith Appleton was at General Hospital #1 in Etretat, on the French Coast (approximately 220 km from the British Red Cross Hospital #1 at Le Touquet at which Tolkien was hospitalized from 10 October to 7 November, prior to being sent back to England on a hospital ship.) The battle of the Somme began on 1 July 2016. In Etretat Edie anxiously awaited word of a hoped-for advance. Tolkien's battalion was not part of the initial battle (in which his friend Rob Gilson was killed). Tolkien also waited for news: "On Sunday 2 July 1916, Tolkien attended Mass in front of a portable altar in a field at Warloy. [...] The British were rumoured to have taken the entire German frontline system, but no official news had come" (Garth 157). Edie's diary vividly demonstrates how quickly optimism shifted to horror during the first week of July:

> **July 2.** The last eight days the guns have been firing the whole time. Fine big ones they need to be for us to hear them so distinctly ... There was a wonderful sunset last night, the sea like a millpond ...
>
> **July 3.** Our much longed for advance has begun after many days of heavy bombardment, and we launched an attack at 7.30 on Saturday morning. They went over in waves, the second one so many minutes after the first, and so on. Where one man came from the first wave was wiped out, so was the second, which gave the Germans time to adjust their machine-guns to receive the rest... We had a couple of train loads of wounded down – 1100, in all – 153 officers very dirty), and the London Scottish kilts were a sight to behold ...
>
> **July 4.** Wounded! hundreds upon hundreds on stretchers, being carried, walking – all covered from head to foot in well-caked mud. The rush and buzz of ambulances & motor-buses is the only thing I can remember of yesterday outside my wards. Inside it took us longer than the whole day to anything like cope with the work of changing, feeding, and dressing the wounds of our share of them. We had horribly bad wounds in numbers – some crawling with maggots, some stinking and tense with gangrene. One poor lad had both eyes shot through and there they were, all smashed and mixed up with the eye lashes. He was quite calm, and very tired. He said "Shall I need an operation? I can't see anything." Poor boy, he never will. Three men died in the train and two only just reached hospital before they went west too. Three were completely

> dumb. They say we are serving the division that has acted as a "draw" to save the other divisions. If any are left they deserve all honour.
>
> **July 6th.** I give up trying to describe it – It beats me. In ordinary times we get a telegram from Abbeville saying a train with so many on board has left and is coming to us. Then they stopped giving numbers – just said "full train". Now not even a telegram comes – but the full trains do … (*A Nurse at the Front* 160-62)

Carola Oman served as a British Red Cross VAD, and in her book *The Menin Road and Other Poems* she wrote about such trains:

> Is it an ancient chanty
> Won from some classic shore?
> The stretcher-bearers stand
> Two on either hand.
> They bend and lift and raise
> Where the doors open wide
> With yellow light ablaze.
> Into the dark outside
> Each stretcher passes.
> (From "Song of the Ambulance Train", reprinted in Connie)

Oman went on to have a successful writing career, yet she renewed her involvement with the Red Cross in 1939, and even served as a regional President in the 1950's ("Carola Oman Entry").[11]

In early July, Tolkien's battalion was waiting in Warloy, and then Bouzincourt, for orders. Warloy was an "operating center", and Tolkien observed the numbers of wounded soldiers being brought there. Tolkien's battalion helped dig graves during this time. Tolkien also met with his friend G.B. Smith in Bouzincourt, on 6 July. Smith had already seen battle, and shared his experiences with Tolkien (Garth 158-59). Edie Appleton and J.R.R. Tolkien both survived the "animal horror" of the Somme (Tolkien, *Letters* 72). By the end of October 1916 Tolkien was ill with trench fever,[12] and caregivers like Edie tended to him in France, and back home in England.

---

11 I have not been able to find an accounting of the number of women who served in both World Wars, but Carola Oman certainly was not alone (for an example, see Devlin).

12 See "Lice and Men: Trench Fever and Trench Life in the AIF".

To Home Again – "Houses of Healing"

Caring for and transporting the sick and wounded required organization: "The principle upon which the Medical Service is built up is that the troops must be kept fit for service, but when they become unfit they must be evacuated from the field of operations as rapidly as possible" ("Evacuation of the Sick and Wounded in the Great War").[13]

Wounded and ill soldiers who needed additional care before they returned to the war (if at all) might be transferred to a hospital ship and/or facilities outside the immediate war zones (including transport to England). The journey could be arduous. In her diary Edith Elizabeth Appleton noted:

> One motor V.A.D. told me things last night that, if true, are horrible. She said sometimes on the way to Le Havre the men on stretchers cried out with pain caused by jolting, and one man told her that he would rather stay in France for 20 years than do that journey again. Another started bleeding badly from the jolting – but what is to be done? (*A Nurse at the Front,* 166-67)

Tolkien returned to England aboard the military hospital ship Asturias. Less than one year later the ship was torpedoed. Among the dead were two women: Bridget Trenerry (a "Stewardess") and Jessie Josephine Phillips, a QAIMNS Nurse ("Hospital Ship HMHS 'Asturias' sunk"; "HMHS Asturias").

With the advent of WW1, the number of British military hospitals and convalescent homes increased, as did private facilities ("Auxiliary Hospitals"; "Hospitals and Convalescent Homes"; "Military Hospitals in the British Isles"; Talbot). Upon returning to England J.R.R. Tolkien recuperated in Birmingham, at the 1st Southern Hospital. For the rest of the war he was hospitalized several times and posted to several different communities (by 1918 Edith did not want to move again; when J.R.R. was discharged, the family moved to Oxford). Tolkien spent two of the longer stays at Brooklands Officers Hospital, in Hull (August-October 1917; June-October 1918). Garth describes how Brooklands

13 The protocol further stated: "As the removal of the sick and wounded starts from the firing line, we shall follow them down the lines of communication, and will start our studies at the firing line itself. Every soldier in the field carries a first field dressing, which is sewn in the small pocket on the inner side of the tunic at the left corner of the skirt of the coat" ("Evacuation of the Sick and Wounded in the Great War"; see also "The Evacuation Chain").

provided Tolkien with time and space to write, which had been very difficult when he was fighting in France:

> [During his second stay at] Brooklands, Tolkien managed to pursue his mythological work, further developing Qenya and Goldogrin. He brushed up on his Spanish and Italian and – just as the Western Allies effectively joined the White Russians' war against the Bolsheviks – he began to study Russian. But military duties of any sort were beyond Tolkien. Meals were followed by pain and stomach upsets. He lost two stone and regaining it proved to be a slow struggle. (Garth 247-48)

Brooklands was run by Margaret Strickland-Constable. Michael Flowers has written about Tolkien's stays at Brooklands, and other Yorkshire sites. He notes that although Strickland-Constable's diaries do not mention Tolkien, they do give some sense of how Brooklands was run, the standards of care, etc. (Flowers).[14]

Margaret Goodwin Warren worked at Brooklands during the time of Tolkien's stays. In a 90-minute interview Margaret does not mention Tolkien but does supply a sense of what working there was like, how she viewed the patients, and how she felt they viewed their care (Warren). Margaret was a VAD, and therefore from a relatively well-off family. She received some training to be a VAD and remembered that in the "practical lectures" she learned "you had to cope with the men's mentalities as well as their wounds" (Reel 1). Since her family lived nearby Margaret was able to bring home her laundry and considered herself "very lucky" to eat approximately 3 meals a week at home. She described the food at the hospital as "adequate for the men and very inadequate for the nurses" (Reel 2). Margaret was definitely aware of her class privilege, "people who could afford to be voluntary aid people" (Reel 3).

Margaret observed and learned, and gradually was allowed to do more: "if you got a good sister . . . the [fully trained sisters] could impart their learning to the VADs" (Reel 3). Doing more was not always desirable. Margaret didn't like being in the surgery. Once when a patient asked her to attend his operation, Margaret was left holding his leg; the physician said "unceremoniously … put it in the bucket, nurse" (Reel 5). Night shifts were busy, with dressing

14 See also: Mathison; "Doing Their Bit: Brooklands Women in the Great War"; and "Red Cross Field Day at Brooklands".

changes, and nightmares: "you nursed with your own personality. Nowadays you give them a pill and hope they'll get better ... [it was] real nursing" (Reel 5). Margaret described patients who had been gassed or had spinal injuries as the most difficult: "minds had gone peculiar." Patients were there for many different reasons and had varying attitudes towards the future: "many people were getting reorganized for their life to come, many of them were desperately ill, it was an all sorts of hospital" (Reel 5).

Those patients who were more mobile had more of an opportunity to socialize, and/or engage in activities beyond the wards. Margaret noted meals could be "great fun" with those patients who could go to main hall to eat (Reel 2). A map had been put up for the nurses, but the men found it, and posted flags on it to follow the war. "It was their life," Margaret said, but could also upset the men (Reel 6). Some men would try to sabotage their recovery, putting thermometers in warm water, using "every trick under the sun ... I don't wonder" (Reel 2).

Margaret said "whatever spare time you had, you had fun and made your own fun ... you remember the nice" (Reel 3). There were "masses of visitors," and patients liked to give parties (Reel 6).[15] Staff were not allowed to give the men presents, but often the men gave presents to the staff, and Margaret notes that the men "loved sewing for me" (Reel 6).[16] In this environment, Tolkien would have had time to write. And when Edith was living away, Tolkien would also have had opportunities for social contact, if he desired.

One of the qualities I have found most interesting while listening to some oral histories was the ways in which women and men in tense, often horrific circumstances, used humor during the war. I have focused research so far primarily on women workers. However, in looking for soldiers who might have been at one of the same facilities as Tolkien, I came across Norman Edwards, a British NCO, 1/6th Bn Gloucestershire Regiment ("Norman Edwards" 1991). On 1 July 1916 his group was supposed to be the third wave of soldiers to cross no man's land. An officer had told Edwards that "the most important order in

---

15 Hospitals sponsored various nonmedical activities to promote healing and distract patients from their physical and psychological injuries. For an example see "The show must go on: How wounded First World War soldiers were entertained to help their recovery".

16 Nurse Mabel Earp worked at a hospital, caring for returning soldiers. The notebooks she kept contain poems, art, and remembrances given to her by her patients, as well as her own artwork (Arkell).

the British army is 'follow me chaps'" (Reel 8). Like the troops before them, Edwards's group followed "over the top", or rather tried to follow, and were stopped by German machine gun fire. "There was no question of not going" (Reel 8). Edwards was wounded, and in his interview, he described the process by which he eventually got to a hospital in Birmingham.

As one of the "walking wounded" he had to make his own way to a Dressing Station (called "Crucifix Corner"). After "patching up" by one officer, he took a coach to see another officer, who gave Edwards his "blighty ticket": "worth thousands of quid to me at that time" (Reel 8). After a tetanus shot, Edwards went by coach to another hospital, then coach to a train that took him to a port, and then a steamer across the Channel to Southampton. From there he took a coach to someplace to another coach to an ambulance to somewhere, and finally to Dudley Road Hospital in Birmingham.

On Reel 8 of his Oral history Edwards gave the following account. He described the nurses as "very skillful and very pleasant." He was not so impressed with the physicians. After one week a nurse, Sister Carter, said "Corporal, I would like you to write something in my autograph book." Edwards said he would try, and a week later returned the book with the following:

> You can talk about the Spanish Inquisition,
> You can rave about the martyrs on the rack,
> When they pulled their arms and legs out of position,
> And took their eyeballs out and put them back,
> For his wickedness the Hun is rightly hated,
> And for dirty deeds we blame the mighty Turk,
> But they're nothing to the tortures perpetrated
> in Ward C7 when Sister gets to work.

Edwards told the interviewer: "I thought she was going to slap my face, which I deserved." But instead Sister Carter said: "Corporal, if I promise some extra strong iodine in your wound, do you think it would inspire you to write a second verse?" Edwards replied, "I don't know, I'll try." One week later he gave the following to Nurse Carter:

> First she prods me with a prober long and pointed,
> Then she squeezes me until I howl and squeal,
> I feel as though my limbs were all disjointed,
> And I tingle from my head unto my heel.

The hair upon my head is growing skywards,
A clammy sweat breaks out upon my brow
When she whispers to me sweetly "Corporal Edwards,
We're going to put the iodine in now."

After reciting the second verse during the interview Edwards immediately said: "Very very fine, skillful, and very nice nurses" (Reel 8). Edwards' reminiscence illustrates what Margaret Goodwin Warren called nursing "with your own personality." Edwards' appreciation for the care he received is apparent. Most of all, the banter between Norman Edwards and Sister Carter, and his witty poem, are reminiscent of Tolkien's own sense of humor, his use of ballads, and appreciation of satire.

Tolkien, Women, and World War I

Tolkien and "The Woman Question"

Regarding women characters, Tolkien has been criticized primarily for two broad reasons: quantity, meaning including too few women characters, and quality, portraying women, when he does, in limited, stereotypical roles. Some authors have maintained that Tolkien's women simply represented then-contemporary gender and class norms of the passive female (better to be seen than heard, and best at home). Tolkien's specific experiences in male-centered contexts, such as school, university, and the army has also been cited as an influence (Fredrick and McBride 32). However, according to Viars and Coker "[p]opular history and criticism dwell overmuch on Tolkien himself as being a man of his time" as if this would serve as either an adequate explanation for the number and characterization of women in his writing, or a reason to dismiss his work as at least "old fashioned", if not misogynist (35). Viars and Coker then argue that this argument does not accurately reflect Tolkien or his writing, citing Anwyn (36):

> [T]he text of *Lord of the Rings* does not for a moment bear out the idea that Tolkien had any kind of derogatory opinion about women. Three things are clear: that he was far from a misogynist, that the female characters in his masterpiece *collectively* represent everything that is great about being a woman, and less representation does not equal less importance. (Anwyn 115, emphasis in original; qtd. in Viars and Coker 36)

In his essay "The Missing Women: J.R.R. Tolkien's Lifelong Support for Women's Higher Education" John Rateliff provides evidence of Tolkien's positive regard for women students and scholars.[17] Neither Tolkien's relationships with women, nor how he handles femininity and gender in his writings, can be reduced to the explanation that he was a man, living and working in male-dominated settings (school, army, academia, or in a conventional marriage).

Éowyn, Warrior/Healer

Garth and others have demonstrated ways in which WWI may have influenced themes in Tolkien's writing, including comradeship (Garth), good/evil (Shippey), and enchantment/ disenchantment (Rosegrant). There is no reason to think that Tolkien's WWI experiences were only relevant for considering his male characters, and we know that he would have had direct contact with women such as those described in this paper. Much of the scholarship on Tolkien and gender has focused on Éowyn, as a – if not the – heroine of *The Lord of the Rings*. Reflecting the arguments just mentioned, Éowyn has been characterized as going to battle in a self-centered act of rebellion, "distraught" over Aragorn's rejection, being "healed by Faramir's love", and/or assuming a more gender appropriate domestic role as healer and wife; no more battlefield for her.

Although Fredrick & McBride acknowledge the importance of the few female characters in Tolkien, they maintain that Tolkien had a binary view of masculine and feminine based on patriarchal norms. Éowyn can only survive if she makes the right choice: "Tolkien's choices for a would-be woman warrior; submit to your allotted role as wife, or die" (35). They go on to state:

> From Tolkien's perspective, even if, like Éowyn, a woman is capable of fighting (perhaps even destined to fight), she should choose not to, except in the direst need. And then afterwards, she should cheerfully resume her domestic role, much as "Rosie the Riveter" was expected to return to managing the household in order to make room in the workforce for returning male veterans following World War II. (36)

---

17 Sue Parman eloquently conveys Tolkien's impact on her, both as a young student, and as an older, reflective professor. She sees the tension between Tolkien, the increasingly well-known author, and Tolkien the man dealing with the matters of everyday life.

Several recent scholars question whether past criticisms have themselves reflected a limited understanding of relationships between gender and power, and a portrayal of Tolkien that is too simplistic. Enright argues that in assuming Tolkien's understanding of gender roles could only reflect the status quo, Fredrick and McBride miss ways in which Éowyn could experience a transformation.[18] Rather than a "return" to a domestic role controlled by others, she chooses new roles – to be a healer, to love, to move on. Éowyn becomes more, not less, powerful and effective: "Her personal healing involves, not only being open to love, but a movement from a desire for power and domination (i.e. as a queen) to the desire to heal and to help things grow" (Enright 133). Similarly, Hatcher notes:

> Modern scholars have seen this [Éowyn's decision] as a choice to accept conventional female submissiveness. However, in choosing the path of protecting and preserving the earth, Éowyn acts in accordance with Tolkien's highest ideal: a fierce commitment to peace. Rather than submission, Éowyn embodies the full-blooded subjectivity that Tolkien posits as essential for peace. (43)

Possible links between Tolkien's experiences in WWI and women caregivers in France and England become more explicit in scholarship by Johnson, who sees in Éowyn's story a "model of recovery" (126). Fife writes: "Healing for Éowyn is more than physical or psychological; she learns that she must have a sense of place, and she chooses that place, to be a healer by the side of Faramir, not a Lady of Rohan or a great Queen" (154).

Through Éowyn, Tolkien highlights qualities that he admired. Rather than a reactionary portrayal, Éowyn can be viewed as a transgressive figure, acknowledging her femininity and her power. In evaluating Tolkien's view of women, Branco examines Éowyn's statement that what she is most afraid of is "to stay behind bars, until use and old age accept them, and all chance of doing great deeds is gone beyond recall or desire" (qtd. 73). Branco concludes: "this is an amazingly modern sentiment in a work by a male Catholic medievalist in his sixties, published just after the English translation (1953) of Simone de Beauvoir's *The Second Sex*, where the idea of the cage is strongly connected to that of the female body" (73).

---

18 See also Workman for a critique of Fredrick and McBride.

If Galadriel represents the chivalric Lady, and Rosie the class-based norm of woman as home-maker, then Éowyn may be seen as transitional. She is grounded, but not bound by tradition, able to make choices in part because of her privilege. Łaszkiewicz points out that "after her participation in battle Éowyn is not punished for her transgression, but praised and respected – not a likely outcome if Middle-earth's society were truly so patriarchal as some critics assume. In the end, Éowyn does not insist on remaining a warrior, but redirects her courage and determination to her new social roles."

Thanks to Christopher Tolkien's years of work on *The History of Middle-earth*, we have the extraordinary opportunity to trace an author's process. The Éowyn in *The Lord of the Rings* evolved, which is especially evident in volume 8, *The War of the Ring*. Tolkien made choices. Éowyn could have died, married Aragorn, not killed the Nazgûl, disappeared altogether from the story. Tolkien *could have* exploited the gendered romanticized images of women that were popular during and after the war. Some women, as well as men, writing about their experiences through poetry, fiction, and nonfictional accounts chose to employ such myths (Hallett, *Veiled Warriors*). In "I Wish My Mother Could See Me Now" Lee demonstrates ways in which women who joined the FANY were able to accomplish much by both challenging and using gender- and class-based expectations. In 1918 the FANY Gazette Supplement included the following poem "One of the Saints" (Lee, "I Wish My Mother" 138):

> I wish my mother could see me now with a grease gun under my car
> Filling my universal, 'ere I start for the sea afar
> On top of the sheet of frozen iron in a cold that would make you cry
> "Why do we do it?" you ask. "Why? We're the FANY."
>
> I used to be in Society once
> Danced, hunted, and flirted once
> Had white hands and complexion once
> Now I'm a FANY!
> ("One of the Saints" 1918, 3)

We should avoid adopting another "myth" however, that women's wartime experiences were generally or necessarily liberating and transformative. In the "Afterword" of *First World War Nursing: New Perspectives* Fell writes:

> [W]itnessing the war as a nurse was a complex and sometimes conflictual role for women. It required the simultaneous adoption of different, sometimes clashing, perspectives: nurses were observers of suffering, active participants in the war effort, professional carers, and stand-ins for a male patient's mother, sister, or lover. The nurses whose voices are quoted in this volume often express both a sense of pride in their ability to carry out these roles well and a sense of unease about the ways in which these multiple roles were not always compatible. (188)[19]

With Éowyn, Tolkien provides us with a character who is not perfect, who challenges social expectations, and experiences confusion and loss, and transformation. Consistent with Tolkien's emphasis on comradeship, Éowyn's actions as a woman make a difference, though not alone; she and Merry together attack the Nazgûl. Her commitment to making the world a better place through healing is also in keeping with Tolkien's concerns (Coutras; Dickerson and Evans; Hatcher).

At the beginning of this essay I presented healing as a central theme for Tolkien. Éowyn is just one character, and *The Lord of the Rings* just one of Tolkien's works. Other characters associated with healing could be studied. In *The Lord of the Rings* alone I could have examined both female healers (Ioreth, Galadriel, Goldberry) and male (the Master of the House of Healing, Aragorn, Elrond).

It is also not possible in this paper to examine the lives and contributions of women like Edith Tolkien, the friends and family of those who went to war, and returned (if they returned) often physically and/or psychologically injured. After all, it would seem unlikely that *only* formal women caregivers would have influenced either Tolkien's life or his writing. What did "the home front" contribute (see Holtz-Wodzak; Robert; Smith, M.)? It would also be simplistic to reduce Tolkien's view of Edith to a narrow conception of women's roles and potentials. From what we know, Edith was capable of, and did, make her views

19 Similarly, although many women went to work, and went to work in jobs previously designated as "men's work", we should not assume that the war completely changed social expectations or economic organization. Women were often viewed as simply filling in for a man, until the war was over ("What Did World War One Really Do for Women?").

known. Edith lived in over 20 different places between 1915-1918 (Garth 246). When Edith was still recovering from their son's John birth she refused to move again. Tolkien's willingness to relocate to Bournemouth after his retirement illustrated his respect for, and recognition of the sacrifices that Edith had made, so that he could pursue his academic career (Carpenter 247 et seq.).[20]

Unfortunately, we have little direct evidence from Tolkien about his experiences in France, his illness and recovery, and the impacts on both Edith and J.R.R. (Garth; Carpenter; Cater; Gilbert). We do not know how Edith occupied herself while separated from Tolkien, or how she viewed the nurses and other caregivers where Tolkien was hospitalized, nor what it was like for the couple when they were finally able to establish a home of their own. In 1972 Tolkien wrote a moving letter to his son Christopher. Bereaved after Edith's death, Tolkien acknowledges both his disinclination to focus on his biography, and his desire that someone understand the complex, multi-layered, human (and therefore imperfect) relationship he shared with Edith:

> [S]omeone close in heart to me should know something about things that records do not record: the dreadful sufferings of our childhoods, from which we rescued one another, but could not wholly heal the wounds that later often proved disabling; the sufferings that we endured after our love began – all of which (over and above our personal weaknesses) might help to make pardonable, or understandable, the lapses and darknesses which at times marred our lives – and to explain how these never touched our depths nor dimmed our memories of our youthful love. (*Letters* 421)

Unless there are unpublished letters, and/or a Tolkien family member shares her/his thoughts about the impact of WWI on J.R.R. and Edith Tolkien, we can only continue to extrapolate from other data. With the centenary of WWI more primary materials have been digitized, both by organizations and individuals. Through examination of online data, and through visits to specific archives and museums, it may be possible to find additional examples of caregivers like Margaret Goodwin Warren, or soldiers like Norman Edwards, who worked or were patients where Tolkien was treated. What I have tried to show in this paper is that the kind of women Tolkien likely would have met during WWI could have influenced a richer perspective of women than the "old fashioned" viewpoint often attributed to him.

20 Although Garth describes the move as Tolkien "hiding from fame" (283).

Finally, what became clearer to me while writing this paper was the extent to which Tolkien's contributions are linked to ways in which both the man and his writings resist "pigeonholing". I first read *The Hobbit* and *The Lord of the Rings* in my early teens. Decades later I reread Tolkien and have not stopped. As a scholar whose past research focused on gender, I was surprised that I was not more upset by the lack of female characters. After reading the following, I felt validated:

> As a woman reader and writer, I often find myself in the position of explaining that I love Tolkien *despite* ... Despite the absence of women, despite the late Victorian/Edwardian aspects of the ones that are there, despite the uneasy racialization of Orcs and Númenóreans, despite the hierarchical social structures – despite all of this, I continue to love *The Lord of the Rings* [...]. (McCormack 309)

That is not to say that we should ignore the issues McCormack mentioned, and fortunately scholars have pursued them (see, for example, other essays in the collection edited by Croft and Donovan). However, it is remarkable how Tolkien could be so much a "man of his time" and yet – not. As Chance says:

> Tolkien reveals an understanding of the limited gender roles demanded by different societies for women, modern and medieval, real and fantastic. He aptly anticipates and understands female difference as the result of a culture in which men play a dominant role biologically, socially, and philosophically, but in his fantasies – his "fairy-stories" – that difference offers another form of enforced abjection that his female heroes overcome. (208)

Currently, it has become depressingly clear the extent to which gender equality has not been achieved, either in social organization or social interaction. Tolkien, his writings, and the memoirs of women such as those described in this paper convey something that transcends their time. They remind us that ordinary people can do extraordinary things, grounded in and slogging through the imperfect inconsistency of everyday life. Decades after his death, and a century since WWI ended, Tolkien scholars are fortunate that we still have so much to discover and pursue.

Bibliography

ACTON, Carol. "'Dangerous Daughters': American Nurses and Gender Identity in World War One." *War, Literature & the Arts: An International Journal of the Humanities* 13 (2001): 87-113.

AMENDT-RADUEGE, Amy. "Revising Lobelia." *Tolkien and Alterity.* Eds. Christopher Vaccaro and Yvette Kisor. New York City, NY: Palgrave, 2017, 77-93.

APPLETON, Edith Elizabeth. Letter written 11 Oct 1914. http://anurseatthefront.org.uk/introduction-to-the-diaries/early-letters/.

A Nurse at the Front: The Great War Diaries of Sister Edith Appleton. Ed. Ruth Cowen. New York City, NY: Simon & Schuster, 2012.

ARKELL, Harriet. "Mabel's War: Diaries of World War One nurse reveal lives of horrifically injured soldiers as she treated them back home." *Daily Mail.* 26 Nov 2013. www.dailymail.co.uk/news/article-2513723/Mables-War-Diaries-World-War-One-nurse-reveal-lives-horrifically-injured-soldiers-treated-home.html.

"Auxiliary Hospitals." *British Red Cross.* https://vad.redcross.org.uk/en/Auxiliary-Hospitals.

BARKER, Nora. *Imperial War Museum Lives of the First World War Oral History.* Recorded by Lyn E. Smith, 1987. www.iwm.org.uk/collections/item/object/80009516.

BELL, Amy. "Women's Politics, Poetry, and the Feminist Historiography of the Great War." *Canadian Journal of History,* 42.3 (2007): 411-37.

"Barnfield Theatre, Devon: The Angels of Pervyse." Audio clip from *World War One At Home.* BBC. www.bbc.co.uk/programmes/p01s2hcp.

BENNETT, Olive Louise. "Olive Louise Bennett." *Imperial War Museum Lives of the First World War Oral History.* http://livesofthefirstworldwar.org/lifestory/7669190.

"Bolton, Manchester: Killed Whilst Treating the Wounded." Audio clip from *World War One At Home.* BBC. www.bbc.co.uk/programmes/p01x3gdv.

BOTTOMLEY, Kathleen Charlotte. "Kathleen Charlotte Bottomley." *Imperial War Museum Lives of the First World War Oral History.* Recorded by Margaret A. BROOKS, 1973. www.iwm.org.uk /collections/item/object/80000171.

BRANCO, Patrícia. "Exploring Justitia Through Éowyn and Niobe: On Gender, Race and the Legal." *Liverpool Law Review* 38.1 (2017): 63-82.

BRENNER, David C. "Grace & Truce." *Touchstone: A Journal of Mere Christianity* 26 (2013): 16-18.

Cater, Bill. "We Talked of Love, Death and Fairy Tales." *The Telegraph.* 4 Dec 2001. www.telegraph.co.uk/culture/4726863/We-talked-of-love-death-and-fairy-tales.html.

"Carola Oman Entry." *Orlando: Women's Writing in the British Isles from the Beginnings to the Present.* Eds. Susan Brown, Patricia Clements, and Isobel Grundy. Cambridge: Cambridge University Press Online, 2006. http://orlando.cambridge.org/.

Carpenter, Humphrey. *J.R.R. Tolkien: A Biography.* 1977. New York City, NY: Harper Collins, 2002.

Chance, Jane. "'Usually Slighted': Gudrún, Other Medieval Women, and *The Lord of the Rings*, Book 3 (1925-1943)." *Tolkien, Self and Other: "This Queer Creature."* New York City, NY: Palgrave Macmillan, 2016, 177-214.

Christie, Sarah. "Gender, Remembrance, and the Sinking of the Marquette." *Women's Studies Journal* 30 (2016): 30-46.

Crosthwait, E. "'The Girl Behind the Man Behind the Gun': The Women's Army Auxiliary Corps, 1914-18." *Our* Work, *Our Lives, Our Words. Women in Society.* Ed. L. Davidoff and B. Westover. London: Palgrave, 1986, 161-181.

"CWGC Remembers the Brave Nurses Lost During the World Wars on International Nurses Day." *Commonwealth War Graves Commission.* 11 May 2018. www.cwgc.org/learn/news-and-events/news/2018/05/11/14/03/cwgc-remembers-the-brave-nurses-lost-during-the-world-wars-on-international-nurses-day.

Connie, R. "Behind Their Lines: Song of the Ambulance Train." *Behind Their Lines.* 10 May 2017. http://behindtheirlines.blogspot.com/2017/05/song-of-ambulance-train.html.

Coutras, Lisa. *Tolkien's Theology of Beauty: Majesty, Splendor and Transcendence in Middle-earth.* London: Palgrave, 2016.

Croft, Janet Brennan and Leslie A. Donovan (eds.). *Perilous and Fair: Women in the Works and Life of J.R.R. Tolkien.* Altadena, CA: Mythopoeic Press, 2015.

Dean, Lois. "Alice Thomasson." *GM 1914, The First World War in Greater Manchester.* 10 Nov 2016. http://gm1914.wordpress.com/2016/11/10/alice-thomasson.

Dent, Olive. *A V.A.D. in France.* London: Grant Richards, 1917.

Devlin, Ron. "History Book: The area nurse who served in both world wars." *Reading Eagle.* Reading, PN, 17 May 2016.

DICKERSON, Matthew T. and Jonathan EVANS. *Ents, Elves, and Eriador: The Environmental Vision of J.R.R. Tolkien.* Lexington, KY: University of Kentucky Press, 2011.

"Doing Their Bit: Brooklands Women in the Great War." *Brooklands Museum.* www.brooklands museum.com/about/latest-news/doing-their-bit-brooklands-women-in-the-great-war.

"Edith Elizabeth Appleton O.B.E. R.R.C." 2017. http://anurseatthefront.org.uk.

EDWARDS, Norman. "Norman Edwards." *Imperial War Museum Lives of the First World War Oral History.* Recorded by Peter M. Hart, 1991. www.iwm.org.uk/collections/item/object/80014528.

ENRIGHT, Nancy. "Tolkien's Females and the Defining of Power." *Perilous and Fair: Women in the Works and Life of J.R.R. Tolkien.* Ed. Janet Brennan Croft and Leslie A. Donovan. Altadena, CA: Mythopoeic Press, 2015, 118-35.

"The Evacuation Chain for Wounded and Sick Soldiers." *The Long, Long Trail.* www.longlongtrail.co.uk/soldiers/a-soldiers-life-1914-1918/the-evacuation-chain-for-wounded-and-sick-soldiers.

"Evacuation Of The Sick And Wounded In The Great War." *Medical Front WWI.* www.vlib.us/medical/evacn/evacn.htm.

FELL, Alison S. *First World War Nursing, New Perspectives.* Eds. Alison S. Fell and Christine E. Hallett. New York City, NY: Routledge, 2013.

FIFE, Ernelle. "Wise Warriors in Tolkien, Lewis, and Rowling." *Mythlore* 25.1/2 (2006): 147-62.

FLOWERS, Michael. "A Hemlock Glade, The Houses of Healing, Two Towers, and a Beacon: Tolkien in East Yorkshire, Part 4: Brooklands Officers' Hospital and the Godwin Battery." July 2015. http://eybirdwatching.blogspot.com/2015/07/tolkiens-hemlock-glade-part-4.html.

FORD, Lena Guilbert (words) and Ivor NOVELLO (music). "Keep the Home-Fires Burning ('Till the Boys Come Home)." New York City, NY: Chappell & Co. Ltd. 1915. Available at *A Multimedia History of World War One.* www.first worldwar.com/audio/keepthehomefiresburning.htm.

FREDRICK, Candice and Sam MCBRIDE. "Battling the Woman Warrior: Females and Combat in Tolkien and Lewis." *Mythlore* 25.3/4 (2007): 29-42.

GARTH, John. *Tolkien and the Great War: The Threshold of Middle-Earth.* Boston, MA: Houghton Mifflin Harcourt, 2003.

GEIGER, Maria. "No Trench Required." *War, Literature & the Arts: An International Journal of the Humanities* 27 (2015): 1-13.

GIFFIN, Phillip. "Annie's War." *Manitoba History* 55.2 (2007): 40-50.

GROCH-BEGLEY, Hannah. "The Forgotten Female Shell-Shock Victims of World War I." *The Atlantic*. www.theatlantic.com/health/archive/2014/09/world-war-ones-forgotten-female-shell-shock-victims/378995.

HALLETT, Christine E. "Argonauts of the Eastern Mediterranean: Military Nurses on Hospital and Transport Ships, 1914-18." *Journal of War & Culture Studies* 10.3 (2017): 198-210.

Veiled Warriors, Allied Nurses of the First World War. Oxford: Oxford University Press, 2014.

HATCHER, Melissa McCrory. "Finding Woman's Role in *The Lord of the Rings*." *Mythlore* 25.3/4 (2007): 43-54.

"HMHS Asturias." *Maritime Archeology Trust*. http://forgottenwrecks.maritime archaeologytrust.org/asturias.

HOLTZ-WODZAK, Victoria. "Tolkien Sidelined: Constructing the Non-Combatant in *The Children of Húrin*." *Mythlore* 33.2 (2015): 93-109.

HOSIE, Rachel. "British 'Angels' Who Braved WW1 Trenches." *BBC News*. 5 Aug 2014. www.bbc.com/news/world-europe-28609597.

"Hospital Ship HMHS 'Asturias' sunk 20th-21st March 1917 off Start Point in the English Channel." *Inspirational Women of World War One*. http://inspiration alwomenofww1.blogspot.com/2017/03/hospital-ship-hmhs-asturias-sunk-20th.html.

"Hospitals and Convalescent Homes." *Historic England*. http://historicengland.org.uk/whats-new/first-world-war-home-front/what-we-already-know/land/hospitals-convalescent-homes.

JOHNSON, Brent D. "Éowyn's Grief." *Mythlore* 27.3/4 (2009): 117-27.

KEMPSHALL, Chris. "Women's Army Auxiliary Corps." *WW1 East Sussex*. 28 Mar 2017. www.eastsussexww1.org.uk/womens-army-auxiliary-corps.

ŁASZKIEWICZ, Weronika. "J.R.R. Tolkien's Portrayal of Femininity and Its Transformations." *Crossroads*. 10 Dec 2016. www.crossroads.uwb.edu.pl/tolkiens-femininity-transformations.

LEE, Janet. "'I Wish My Mother Could See Me Now': The First Aid Nursing Yeomanry (FANY) and Negotiation of Gender and Class Relations, 1907-1918." *NWSA Journal* 19.2 (2007): 138-158.

"A Nurse and a Soldier: Gender, Class and National Identity in the First World War Adventures of Grace McDougall and Flora Sandes." *Women's History Review* 15 (2006): 83-103.

"Lice and Men: Trench Fever and Trench Life in the AIF." *Medical Front WWI*. www.vlib.us/medical/liceand.htm.

LIGHT, Sue. "The Territorial Force Nursing Service 1908-1921." www.scarletfinders.co.uk/92.html.

MARCHESI, Patricia. "Boundaries, Borders, and Female Identity in German Women Writers of World War I." *Women & Language* 27 (2004): 51-57.

"Marygate, York: The Wartime Adventures of Two Sisters." Audio clip from *World War One At Home.* BBC. www.bbc.co.uk/programmes/p02b5nl1.

MATHISON, Phil. *Tolkien in East Yorkshire 1917-1918: An Illustrated Tour.* Brough: Deadgood Publications, 2012.

MCCLELLAN, Ann K. "'I Was My War; My War Was I': Vera Brittain, Autobiography and University Fiction during the Great War." *Paedagogica Historica* 52 (2016): 121-36.

MCCORMACK, Una. "Finding Ourselves in the (Un)Mapped Lands: Women's Reparative Readings of *The Lord of the Rings.*" *Perilous and Fair: Women in the Works and Life of J.R.R. Tolkien.* Eds. Janet Brennan Croft and Leslie A. Donovan. Altadena, CA: Mythopoeic Press, 2015, 309-326.

MCDOUGALL, Grace. *A Nurse at the War, Nursing Adventures in Belgium and France.* New York City, NY: Robert M. McBride & Co., 1917.

MCGOWAN, Marcia Phillips. "'A Nearer Approach to the Truth': Mary Borden's Journey Down a Blind Alley." *War, Literature & the Arts: An International Journal of the Humanities* 16 (2004): 198-210.

"Military hospitals in the British Isles 1914-1918." *The Long, Long Trail.* www.longlongtrail.co.uk/soldiers/a-soldiers-life-1914-1918/the-evacuation-chain-for-wounded-and-sick-soldiers/military-hospitals-in-the-british-isles-1914-1918.

MITCHELL, Phillip Irving. "'But Grace is Not Infinite': Tolkien's Explorations of Nature and Grace in His Catholic Context." *Mythlore* 31.3/4 (2013): 61-81.

MOFFETT, James. "Ioreth of Gondor." *A Tolkienist's Perspective.* 11 Nov 2017. https://atolkienistperspective.wordpress.com/2017/11/11/ioreth-of-gondor.

MURRAY, Flora. *Women as Army Surgeons, Being the History of the Women's Hospital Corps in Paris, Wimereux and Endell Street; September 1914-October 1919 (Classic Reprint).* London: Forgotten Books, 2017 (1920).

PARMAN, Sue. "A Song for J.R.R. Tolkien." *The Antioch Review* 73.1 (2015): 34-44.

RATELIFF, John. "The Missing Women: J.R.R. Tolkien's Lifelong Support for Women's Higher Education." *Perilous and Fair: Women in the Works and Life of J.R.R. Tolkien.* Eds. Janet Brennan Croft and Leslie A. Donovan. Altadena, CA: Mythopoeic Press, 2015, 41-69.

"Red Cross Field Day at Brooklands." *Surrey in the Great War.* www.surreyinthegreatwar.org.uk/story/red-cross-field-day-at-brooklands.

"Regulations Governing the Employment of Nursing V.A.D. Members in Military Hospitals." *The Medical Front WWI.* WWW Virtual Libraries. www.vlib.us/medical/vad/vadregs.htm.

Remington, Alice Christobel. *Imperial War Museum Lives of the First World War Oral History.* Recorded by Margaret A. Brooks, 1974. www.iwm.org.uk/collections/item/object/80000507.

Robert, Krisztina. "Constructions of 'Home,' 'Front,' and women's military employment in first-world-war Britain: A spatial interpretation." *History and Theory* 52 (2013): 319-43.

Sandner, David. "Between Eucatastrophe and Grace: J.R.R. Tolkien and Flannery O'Connor." *Soundings: An Interdisciplinary Journal* 89 (2006): 171-198.

Shippey, Tom. "Tolkien as a Post-War Writer." *Mythlore* 21.2 (1996): 84-93.

"The show must go on: How wounded First World War soldiers were entertained to help their recovery." *Manchester Evening News.* 26 Jun 2014. www.manchestereveningnews.co.uk/news/nostalgia/first-world-war-one-how-7329455.

"Sinking of the SS Aragon, 30th December 1917." *The Bedfordshire Regiment in the Great* War. http://bedfordregiment.org.uk/5thbn/ssaragon.html.

Smith, Angela. "The Girl behind the Man behind the Gun: Women as Carers in Recruitment Posters of the First World War." *Journal of War & Culture Studies* 1 (2008): 223-241.

Smith, Melissa. "At Home and Abroad: Éowyn's Two-fold Figuring as War Bride in *The Lord of the Rings.*" *Mythlore* 26.1/2 (2007): 161-72. Also in *Perilous and Fair: Women in the Works and Life of J.R.R. Tolkien.* Ed. Janet Brennan Croft and Leslie A. Donovan. Altadena, CA: Mythopoeic Press, 2015, 203-17.

Talbot, Charlotte. "World War One: Surrey's Country Homes Converted into Hospitals." *SurreyLive.* 27 Aug 2017. www.getsurrey.co.uk/news/nostalgia/country-homes-became-ww1-hospitals-7680032.

Tolkien, J.R.R., *The Letters of J.R.R. Tolkien.* Eds. Humphrey Carpenter and Christopher Tolkien. Boston, MA: Houghton Mifflin, 1981.

The Lord of the Rings. 50th Anniversary edition. Boston, MA: Houghton Mifflin, 2004. London: George Allen & Unwin, 1954.

Tolkien, J.R.R. and Christopher Tolkien. *The War of the Ring* (The History of Middle-earth 8). Boston, MA: Houghton Mifflin, 2000.

Trueman, C.N. "First Aid Nursing Yeomanry." *The History Learning Site.* 17 Mar 2015. www.historylearningsite.co.uk/the-role-of-british-women-in-the-twentieth-century/first-aid-nursing-yeomanry. 28 Nov 2018.

"The Women's Army Auxiliary Corps." *The History Learning Site.* 17 Mar 2015. www.historylearningsite.co.uk/the-role-of-british-women-in-the-twentieth-century/the-womens-army-auxiliary-corps. 28 Nov 2018.

"23 West Street, Newport: Annie's War." Audio clip from *World War One At Home.* BBC. http://www.bbc.co.uk/programmes/p02c5lfp.

Viars, Karen and Cait Coker. "Constructing Lothíriel: Rewriting and Rescuing the Women of Middle-earth From the Margins." *Mythlore* 33.2 (2015): 35-48.

"Voices of the First World War: Over by Christmas." Imperial War Museum. www.iwm.org.uk/history/voices-of-the-first-world-war-over-by-christmas.

Warren, Margaret Goodwin. "Voluntary Aid Detachment Margaret Goodwin Warren." *Imperial War Museum Lives of the First World War Oral History.* Recorded by Margaret A. Brooks, 1974. www.iwm.org.uk/collections/item/object/80000508.

"What Did World War One Really Do for Women?" *BBC Guides.* 2019. www.bbc.co.uk/guides/z9bf9j6.

Williams, Shirley. "World War One: The Many Battles Faced by WWI's Nurses." *BBC News.* 2 Apr 2014. www.bbc.com/news/magazine-26838077.

Workman, Sarah. "Female Valor Without Renown: Memory, Mourning and Loss at the Center of Middle-earth." *A Quest of Her Own: Essays on the Female Hero in Modern Fantasy.* Ed. Lori M. Campbell. Jefferson, NC: McFarland, 2014.

"WWI Hospital Ships Destroyed By Submarines Or Mines." *Medical Front WWI.* www.vlib.us/medical/hospships.htm.

Felicity Gilbert

Mighty Men of War: The Impact of Gender and War in the Work of J.R.R. Tolkien

Homoeroticism and masculinity in Middle-earth

Gender politics and culturally contrived gender norms have long been contentious subjects in historic as well as contemporary civilized society. When applying these norms to the concept of human warfare we see a substantially male-dominated area of human history; an area that is traditionally prohibited from any female presence altogether. Furthermore, indulgent, rose-tinted imagery and associations have often been fashioned and linked to male participation in war and combat alike; with gallantry and glory associated largely with triumphant victory in the name of land or sovereign. Death in battle often brings further glory to the soldier's/warrior's memory and remaining family. Music, art and other cultural artefacts adulating the male participation in war propagate this romanticising of warfare.

We bear witness to this phenomenon throughout our history, but also throughout folklore and mythical stories. We find its presence in varying cultures – examples include Nordic tales of conquer and glorified death in Valhalla, or Celtic folklore surrounding exalted warrior figures such as Cú Chulainn;[1] such tales lend support to the global ubiquity of this representation. Literature acts as a vehicle through which one may explore such social issues. Tolkien's trilogy, *The Lord of the Rings*, is no exception.

Written by J.R.R. Tolkien between 1937 and 1949, *The Lord of the Rings* reflects the inescapable subject of war. The main storyline itself revolves around a great and devastating war between two powerful, yet opposing forces. While many have since analysed his texts for hidden meanings and metaphors, Tolkien has

1 In Irish folklore, Cú Chulainn is an example of everlasting fame and glory taking precedence over a long-lived life (Ford 255-261).

firmly stated that his work is in no form a representation of his experiences in both World Wars. He firmly expresses a disdain for allegory, stating that:

> As for any inner meaning or 'message', it has in the intention of the author none. It is neither allegorical nor topical. [...] I cordially dislike allegory in all its manifestations, and always have done so since I grew old and wary enough to detect its presence. I much prefer history, true or feigned, with its varied applicability to the thought and experience of readers. I think that many confuse 'applicability' with 'allegory'; but the one resides in the freedom of the reader, and the other in the purposed domination of the author. (*LotR* Foreword.xxiii-xxiv)

He appears to have avoided direct reference to his experiences during the war altogether, apart from mentions in his lectures on occasion (Croft 16). However, later critics and academics alike agree that his work must have some connection to his experiences in some shape or form, whether it be conscious or not. This essay is no different in that respect. Many writers feel differently; drawing links between far too many aspects of his work and the vivid horrors of war, as well as the intense comradery and friendships, to simply dismiss it. It would be foolish to ignore the reality of the effects of the Great War on Tolkien's work; a vast and ubiquitous subject matter in the writings of so many of his contemporaries. Both readers and critics have associated Middle-earth's dark and dejected landscapes, such as the Dead Marshes, to the horrific trenches on the battlegrounds. Tolkien himself, in a letter to his peer, L.W. Forster, admits that "The Dead Marshes and the approaches to the Morannon owe something to Northern France after the Battle of the Somme" (*Letters* 303). Tolkien similarly stated that the "darkness of the present days has had some effect on it" (*Letters* 41).

One may argue that the concept of war is specifically constructed to be viewed in a particular light in androcentric society – as masculine, patriotic and with deep feelings of nationhood. It is a man's role to fight for his country – his motherland, his fellow male comrades, as well as *his* women. Characteristically, these women would patiently await his return and simultaneously mourn fallen soldiers. This zealous patriotism corresponds to the national symbolism of man as representative of his entire people and, more importantly, his cultural origins. It becomes his duty to uphold this representation with fervour. His loyalty and nationhood are proven as he takes up arms in the name of his country. In other words, this nationhood is contrived specifically by imperial forces or a similar governing force. Its purpose is to foster an undying loyalty to a nation so as to act as willing fodder for warfare; one that serves the imperial (largely colonial) cause.

Benedict Anderson discusses this notion in his work, *Imagined Communities*, published in 1991. He examined such "imagined communities" regarding core ideologically-driven definitions of a nation. These nations, according to Anderson, exist solely due to a common and mutual feeling of community among a population. However, "even the smallest nation will never know most of their fellow-members, meet them, or even hear of them, yet in the minds of each lives the image of their communion" (6). Such a communal belief based on likeness to one another in terms of shared cultural ideals forms a "deep, horizontal comradeship" (Anderson 7). This enables a personal and naturalised connection to one's "community" (Anderson 143). He similarly claims that these nationalistic undertones of any nation do not naturally emerge by themselves, but are used as a driving political force (McClintock 352 et seq.). Anderson also argues that a gendered vocabulary of kinship is incorporated into the purpose of fostering such nationhood. This propagandized vocabulary, with terms such as 'motherland' (one that must be protected) and 'our boys/men,' help perpetuate this exclusively androcentric sphere. In other words, this culturally propagated myth of masculine-driven nationhood is purposed specifically as a means of creating a selflessness and willingness to serve and sacrifice oneself for a nation, its people, and its governing institutions. He asserts that "ultimately it is this fraternity that makes it possible [...] for so many millions of people, not so much to kill [but], as willing to die for such limited imaginings" (Anderson 7). Originating in this mythologizing of nationhood, death is valorised and glorified in order to perpetuate undying loyalty to a leader or nation. The concept of death is therefore linked to stereotyped notions of masculinity and warmongering, and war is perceived as a solely masculine zone. There have indeed been women who fought in combat; most notably are the mythological female warriors, the Amazons. Similarly, female warriors have been found in cultures worldwide, such as female gladiators and generals in Greek and Roman times, as well as African, Asian, Middle-Eastern, Nordic, Celtic as well as Anglo-Saxon cultures (Fredrick and McBride). Yet, in spite of this, the unequivocal majority of those who participate in combat and war alike are male. Thus spawns the traditional perception of soldiers being exclusively male.

In Middle-earth, the people of Rohan, the Rohirrim, have an undying loyalty to their King, Théoden and their country. They fearlessly ride to war with elevated feelings of nationhood as they seek glory in the name of their king and people. Interestingly, the chief concern of the Rohirrim includes the association of king Théoden's eventual death in battle with everlasting fame and honour; his death is indeed glorified as he "died in splendour" (*LotR* VI.6.976). His niece, Éowyn, obsessively admires her kin as they ride to battle; the cultural norms and ideology of Rohan dictate that fighting merits admiration much more than diplomacy or intellect. Éomer, Éowyn's brother, is made king after the death of Théoden; this similarly perpetuates such cultural norms. He laments his uncle, while weeping "Mourn not overmuch! Mighty was the fallen, / meet was his ending. When his mound is raised, / women then shall weep. War now calls us!" (*LotR* V.6.843). The Rohirrim attach significance to death in battle as it justifies their unconscious need for nationhood and solidarity. Théoden's death is glorified as he died with "both honour and peace" (*LotR* VI.5.960). This respect for bravery and willingness to fight for one's nation is a reflection of our own societies.[2] Evidently, one sees the lengths to which a community, such as the Rohirrim, will go in order to maintain their national pride and love of king. Théoden becomes a symbol for his people, a symbol that validates warmongering and a desire to prove their loyalty in battle: "Out of doubt, out of dark, to the day's rising / he rode singing in the sun, sword unsheathing. / Hope he rekindled, and in hope ended; / over death, over dread, over doom lifted / out of loss, out of life, unto long glory" (*LotR* VI.6.976).

While Tolkien witnessed both World Wars in his lifetime, the main focus here will be on the First World War, the Great War. Early twentieth century Britain was in the early stages of moving on from the stranglehold of traditional Victorian ideology, however, it was still largely present in British culture during the Great War. Such norms include a rigid socio-cultural gender structure, particularly in terms of fixed economic boundaries or gendered vocations. Similarly, a naturalised love of Crown and country was instilled. Tolkien was indeed a man of British ideals – specifically in relation to his duty to his country. At the time, there was

2 Schopenhauer's claim seems fitting at this time: "Every miserable fool who has nothing at all of which he can be proud, adopts as a last resource pride in the nation to which he belongs; he is ready and happy to defend all its faults and follies tooth and nail, thus reimbursing himself for his own inferiority" (51).

an immense pressure on the men of Britain to join the British army and to go to war. Following a resonance from the renowned phrase "*Dulce et decorum est pro patria mori*" (It is sweet and honourable to die for one's fatherland), many men felt obliged to enlist and Tolkien was no exception. He himself reported that "in those days chaps joined up, or were scorned publicly" (*Letters* 53).[3] This pressure seemed to cause Tolkien a great deal of stress as he was faced with the decision of choosing between either completing his degree or carrying out his family's expectations that he should enlist (Carpenter 75). He was thankful to stumble upon a scheme that allowed him to train for the army whilst finishing his studies. Tolkien was therefore no exception to the men who fell prey to the national obligation of enlisting as a direct result of societal pressure.

We also see this clear devotion to one's country and culture in Tolkien's texts, specifically in *The Lord of the Rings*. From mighty king to little hobbit, the protagonists take on their duty in the name of peace and goodness, to face the evil that is Sauron. This unflinching bravery against the enemy is very much a cultural ideal of Tolkien's time; an ideal rooted firmly in cultural expectations of men who must adhere to gendered characteristics. Tolkien's text largely deals with the act of accepting one's fate and taking up arms in the name of destroying evil, with the exception of Frodo's largely interpreted pacifistic message. However, Tolkien also writes about later disillusionment in war and its destructive forces, admitting his reluctance to enter into this horrific environment in his youth. He addresses the emotional turmoil and bereavement associated with soldiers in the Great War as he notes that "by 1918 all but one of my close friends were dead" (*LotR* Foreword.xxix). This all too common disillusionment is also seen in the character of Samwise Gamgee as he feels he cannot go on when the reality of Frodo's apparent death from Shelob's venom sinks in (Smol 961): "And then black despair came down on him, and Sam bowed to the ground, and drew his grey hood over his head, and night came into his heart, and he knew no more. When at last the blackness passed, Sam looked up and shadows were about him; but for how many minutes or hours the world had gone dragging on he could not tell" (*LotR* IV.10.731).

3 Tolkien's words are fitting in the context of wartime Britain as it was seen as cowardice to refuse to fight. Many men deemed as cowards would be "publicly humiliated by a lady with a white feather" (Gullace 178), the white feather being a prominent symbol of cowardice.

Sam has travelled a great distance, enduring depleted supplies of food and water as well as extremely little sleep. Combined with Shelob's attack and Gollum's treachery to boot, Sam's disorientation and disillusionment is made all the greater by the apparent death of his beloved master. The horror of this scene resonates with the grim and disorientating circumstances of soldiers on the battlefields of World War I. Tolkien struggled with grief when the first of his friends to die in service, Rob Gilman, was claimed by the war. He articulated that he and his friends attempted to make some sense of the chaos of the war, in which he felt as if abruptly, "something has gone crack" (*Letters* 10). This makes Tolkien's characters, and their journey to an unfamiliar land in extreme and uncomfortable conditions, all the more idealised due to their staunchness and bravery in the face of war with a foreign enemy.

Similarly, *The Lord of the Rings*, as noted by a plethora of critics, contains many of the same rigid gender roles; not just in relation to men, but also women. While there is a notable absence of a female presence in the novels as a whole, there is but a small cadre of women who are granted entry into the androcentric sphere of the battlegrounds. The women of Middle-earth, adhering to their social positions, are situated safely far away from any fighting that occurs. Arwen, while heroicized and constructed with much more depth in Peter Jackson's film adaptation, is kept out of sight in the original text and Galadriel remains similarly "peripheral to the action and we learn little of her history and relationships" (Rawls 99). This too is a salient reflection of traditional patriarchal society of Tolkien's time, with the character of Éowyn being the main exception.

As a result of the lack of any feminine presence, men would form close bonds with one another. Previous writers have explored the subject of male friendship during the war; among them, ex-soldiers such as W.A. Quintin, in his unpublished memoirs.[4] Similarly, writers have examined "the widely held view that during the Great War, male friendship provided the stable anchoring point for a world in crisis" (Cole 140). Many of those who fought in World War I have recounted the close friendships that were established during their service in the war (most notably the friendship developed between British war poets

4 Unpublished memoirs, W.A. Quintin, 75/32/1, Imperial War Museum.

Sassoon and Owen). Tolkien is also among them, forming close bonds with his wartime friends. This male bonding was therefore heavily bolstered by the living conditions and irreversible horrors witnessed during the war.[5] Being exposed to this exclusively male space for prolonged periods undoubtedly had a dramatic effect on soldiers – mainly in terms of male intimacy and bonding. This topic has been applied repeatedly to the relationship between the two Hobbits, Frodo and Sam as well as the apparent homoerotic undertones perceived. This essay explores this similar theme, while avoiding the conclusory labelling of concrete terms such as homosexual or heterosexual.

Like a carefully balanced formula that occurs through random chance, the chaotic and unpredictable trauma of war fostered such intense homosocial relations; both emotional as well as tactile relationships which appeared to act as a primary source of comfort for soldiers. Das aptly described these conditions and their effect on early twentieth century gender norms:

> In the trenches of World War I, the norms of tactile contact between men changed profoundly. Mutilation and mortality, loneliness and boredom, the strain of constant bombardment, the breakdown of language, and the sense of alienation from home led to a new level of intimacy and intensity under which the carefully constructed mores of civilian society broke down. (Das 52)

In this very sense, such intimate relationships between men exclusively could never have occurred in early twentieth century society without ridicule or even imprisonment. The war as such allowed for a brief relief from social norms when death could come at any moment. As such, homosocial intimacy, based on mutual understanding and experiences, could potentially alleviate some inner turmoil triggered by the horrific experiences of war. With an absence of any female presence, men would take up the traditionally feminine role of nurturing and comfort-giving; they would substitute female gender roles for something other – a makeshift substitute for love (which was traditionally only to be experienced from wives or significant others in Victorian society) or temporary feeling of comfort.

---

5 C.S. Lewis, in his writings on Tolkien's work, lent support to the connections between Middle Earth and Tolkien's experience of the war; he wrote: "[Tolkien's] war has the very quality of the war my generation knew. It is all here: the endless, unintelligible movement, the sinister quiet of the front when 'everything is now ready,' the flying civilians, the lively, vivid friendships, the background of something like despair and the merry foreground, and such heaven-sent windfalls as a cache of choice tobacco 'salvaged' from a ruin'" (Lewis 39-40)

Numerous sources cite historian Joanna Bourke's research on this subject. According to Bourke, the soldiers would nurse their friends and comrades back to health when they fell ill, including feeding and washing them as well as keeping them warm. Soldiers would hold each other as they danced and shared blankets as "their bodies 'spooned' together in sleep" (Das 52). By adopting these feminine characteristics, the men could have some sort of emotional balance and a psychological fulfilment based on a need for comfort. These moments of tenderness possibly helped soldiers to adopt a solidarity and thus form a passionate bond. A man must have owed his comrades more than his life in situations where they would care and provide a physical closeness for him in an environment as hostile and uncaring as the trenches. The physical intimacy and comfort it brought appears to have had an ameliorative effect on the mental health of the soldiers, providing a sense of refuge. However, what is more interesting is the shame it would bring once a man came home from war and back into his society. Male intimacy was taboo and so could not be spoken of.

A key factor in the alienating feelings of homosocial intimacy is the perpetuating stigma of breaking prescribed gender constructs. While homosocial bonding, in the form of comradery, was accepted (and helped to perpetuate the stereotype of men as naturally born warriors), it was the inversion of gender roles that was not acceptable. Judith Butler argues for the abolition of heavily loaded terms 'male' and 'female' in relation to gender and derided the indistinguishability of gender from sex in society. Butler argued that these rigid structures are hurtful and amount to great social pressures and stigmas in terms of identity. She maintained that "the presumption of a binary gender system implicitly retains the belief in a mimetic relation of gender to sex whereby gender mirrors sex or is otherwise restricted by it" (Butler 10). In other words, Butler's apt observation involving the redundancy of traditionally prescribed gender lends support to the subversion and temporary abandonment of these norms by the closeness and tactile intimacy experienced during wartime. The notion that men cannot be intimate with other men – for it would be 'unmanly' and would cross boundaries and therefore taboo – is but a contrived social structure constructed within patriarchal society. McLarty argues that Tolkien's text, and more specifically Peter Jackson's film adaptation, "disengages maleness from patriarchy and in doing so not only offers a spectrum of masculinities but holds the 'Law of the Father' responsible for a potential apocalypse" (181). McLarty argues that characters in Middle-earth often display different 'degrees' of masculinity, in varying ways. However, the key point is that it is only the traditionally structured masculinity in the patriarchal sense that creates problems. Sauron, Saruman and Denethor embody this problematic patriarchal masculinity as they threaten to dominate the natural world to make room for their singular patriarchal vision. It is this that places them in the category of evil.

Many previous readings have all too readily assigned sexual identities to the relationship between Sam and Frodo; they are either heterosexual, but unequivocally intimate, or else, they harbour inhibited homoerotic feelings for one another. Yet, to categorise them as one or the other is to presume that their sexual identity is in line with the traditional gender roles as detailed above. We have explored the redundancy of these traditional gender roles – being culturally/socially constructed facets of western society; the characters can indeed openly display both feminine and masculine characteristics. As such, the claim that they are plainly homosexual or heterosexual loses some credibility. Just as one may not identify with being wholly one gender, an individual may not necessarily fit into just one box denoting their sexual alignment. Likewise, the phenomenon of male intimacy during the war does not necessarily indicate repressed homoerotic thoughts and feelings. The concept of gender and sexuality is much more fluid and complex – different circumstances may impact such aspects of oneself. To rearticulate Smol's point (955), the topic of homosexuality and homoeroticism is a grey area at best. Yet it is undeniably clear that it was linked to issues of gender and their normative practices within early twentieth British society.

Typically, Tolkien's text is believed to ascribe to characters traditional gender roles in direct accordance with their sex. Melanie Rawls, in her essay "The Feminine Principle in Tolkien", argues for a different approach to interpreting gender roles in Middle-earth. Rawls argues that Tolkien separates gender from sex, and that the characters are comprised of both feminine as well as masculine characteristics. These characteristics augment each other and fall within the categories of positive and negative respectively and are therefore tied to the concepts of good and evil. It is a balance of the two that characterises a moral, solid character. For example, Aragorn is the most suitable ruler of Gondor as he possesses both feminine and masculine traits. He is a strong active character, who carries out law and order (all belonging to the masculine category of power). Additionally, he also skilled in healing, wise counsel, and expresses intuition, love, and mercy (all feminine traits of 'understanding'). His character is comprised of an equal balance of both masculine and feminine traits in comparison to Sauron, who displays only exaggerated negative masculine characteristics such as rashness and aggression; "Sauron is what happens when the masculine predilection toward outer-directed activity is taken to the extreme" (102). His only goal is in remaking Middle-earth in his own image and as such does not exemplify just rule or foresight. This inevitably sets up his downfall. Rawls also draws on Elrond as an example of femininity in a masculine character. Elrond is a wise counsellor (which Rawls categorises under feminine insight), and he also expresses love for his kin and is an inactive character (similarly feminine traits). Here Elrond challenges the Victorian notion that men must go, without showing any feelings, and fight in battle. This then lends support to the notion that gender, and its attributes, are indeed flexible. Likewise, Samwise displays the typically non-masculine traits of caring for and expressing love for his master: "I love him. He's like that, and sometimes it shines through, somehow. But I love him, whether or no" (*LotR* IV.4.652).

More and more individuals nowadays understand the concept of gender as an outdated social construction and therefore ideally irrelevant in modern society; gender is now more commonly seen as a spectrum or fluidity by a steadily growing, forward-thinking, community. However, traditional thought still plays a heavy hand in comprehension. As such, the social and cultural norm was (and still is to some degree) to assume that an individual must adhere to their rigidly prescribed gender roles in accordance with their sex. Following this rule, previous critics have assumed that the nature of the hobbits' relationship is simply homoerotic. Yet more recent readings from Das, Smol, and Goldberg and Gabbard, have noted the complexities and numerous factors that surround their relationship; such complexities may sway the individual examining the text to understand that Sam and Frodo cannot be simply labelled as 'gay' or 'straight'. The hobbits display an "unselfconsciously physical relationship because the culture of the Shire permits this kind of closeness" (Croft 54). In such times of hardship where one would feel alienated from the world they know, it is easy to understand the closeness of the two hobbits in non-erotic circumstances.

It is important to note that the text, based on its cultural context and social position (as well as the staunch traditional and pious views) of the author, could not be claimed to have been written with homoerotic or subversive undertones in mind. Nor would it have been likely to have figured into the creative process of the author based on his views of marital relations and the position of women. Partridge, in her 1983 paper, drew on Tolkien's background for the study in which she discusses the influence of his segregated personal, as well as, professional life. Tolkien grew up in a segregated educational system for boys and girls, who would then take up careers in areas that would largely also be separated by gender. Tolkien's peers therefore would have consisted solely of other men, including his fellow academics and friends. Partridge notes that this is probably the reason for Tolkien's strong belief in fraternity and therefore his investment in male bonding in his texts. She also believes it to be the reason for a lack of investment in any real depth or development for female characters within the text.[6]

Before delving into previous analyses, let us begin by looking how the two hobbits react to one another within the text (as well as the film adaptation). The hobbits are undoubtedly loyal to one another. Sam acts as a faithful servant to Frodo, referring to him as his master. This automatically grants Frodo power over Sam. It also replicates that of the batman-officer relationship as seen throughout the Great War. However, it seems as though moments of tactile intimacy between the Hobbits – such as Sam's touch of Frodo's hand or a caress of his master's face – does indeed "cross class, gender, and sexual boundaries" (Vaccaro 286). This, combined with Barthe's famous assertion of the *death of the author* (Lodge and Wood 146) – regardless of the author's intended message, a text's meaning will ultimately come down to the interpretations of readers – paves the way for various readings to be applied freely. Sam does indeed appear to display a readiness for tactile intimacy and affection for his Master. Throughout the text,

6 It is important to note that several authors have disagreed with this opinion, such as Rateliff (41), who compiled a list of women whom Tolkien admired. Similarly, it is indisputable that he sympathised with women's plight for equal education. Yet, it may also be true that he did have traditional views on gender roles as seen in his letter to his son, Michael (*Letters* 48-54).

he engages in acts such as reaching for and grasping his master's hand as well as holding Frodo while they both sleep. In the chapter "The Stairs of Cirith Ungol", Gollum furtively observes the two hobbits as they lie asleep together. He notes Sam and how "[i]n his lap lay Frodo's head, drowned deep in sleep; upon his white forehead lay one of Sam's brown hands, and the other lay softly upon his master's breast. Peace was in both their faces" (*LotR* IV.8.714). There is clearly a deep connection between the hobbits which manifests itself physically in such a way that it is noteworthy to other characters, even a character as warped and malicious as Gollum. As noted by author and sexologist Magnus Hirschfield: "the comradeship which developed between the soldiers who shared all the trials and dangers of war [...] penetrated beyond the outer limits of the homoerotic and was thus, to speak the language of psychoanalysis, characterized by libidinous components" (116-117).

Goldberg and Gabbard argue that an "undercurrent of sexual ambivalence" runs throughout the text in regards to the relationship between the hobbits (268). They argue that, specifically in Jackson's portrayal, the vast amount of imagery portraying an unconscious sexual anxiety is representative of the Hobbit's relationship. Deep caves, fiery pits, cavernous mines, and thick spears and swords are all representative of a hesitation to question their sexuality, as well as a fear of the female body. While this is by no means conclusive evidence for homoeroticism present, there are many interpretations that support the flexibility of their sexuality. Similarly, Craig's essay "Queer Lodgings" claims that the boundaries between male friendship and homoeroticism became somewhat fluid during World War I.

We have discussed the homoerotic undertones of the text, and can comprehend that these do not dictate homosexual feelings between the two friends. Regardless, they display 'unmanly', and therefore feminine, traits such as caring and nurturing qualities. However, bearing in mind that we have deconstructed the need for constructed gender roles or boundaries surrounding them, can we claim homoerotic undertones for the relationship? No overt sexuality is ever confirmed. As such, given the restrictions of masculine friendships, the hobbits have a heterodoxy in their relationship. Sam shifts between a masculine protector role (defending his master from enemies) and the feminine nurturer (selflessly caring for his master). Frodo, too, displays traits traditionally understood as feminine as he does not partake in combat where the other male characters thrive in such an environment. This leads one to, at the very least, recognise gender identity as being somewhat fluid, specifically in turbulent times of turmoil or in environments that exist outside and subvert traditional societal norms. A man may possess both female as well as traditionally male traits, while the same may be true of a woman. We will explore this taboo of the feminine experience in/outside of the androcentric zone of war further.

Gender constructs in Middle Earth

The subject of women and gender have long been areas of fascination for academics and Tolkien enthusiasts alike; specifically, in regards to Tolkien's representations of women, or lack of. There is also quite some debate over their overly romanticised hyperfemininity. Tolkien has received much criticism for his depiction of women in *The Lord of the Rings*. But there are also those who have defended Tolkien in this respect, such as Rawls, who upholds that

> The societies of Arda are patriarchal, but Tolkien appears to desire this arrangement to be attributed to the masculine talent for public affairs, rather than to general masculine superiority coupled with feminine weakness and incompetence, or the inappropriateness of females in public roles, the rationales given for male dominance in our public arenas. (112-113)

This statement is in alignment with Tolkien's perception of gender norms as experienced within early twentieth century society. As we have noted, Tolkien was exposed to the societal and cultural demonstration of segregated social spheres and gender-based ideologies. Rawls attempts to defend Tolkien against accusations of misogyny and chauvinism, and she does indeed do so to some extent. However, she also admits that Tolkien, as a man of his time, still appoints men and women to two separate spheres. While Tolkien believes in the autonomy of women, in that she may still obtain individuality even when married, the gendered public and private spheres are still relatively in place. Critics such as Doris Myers draw from the typical gendered cultural practises of Tolkien's time, specifically in relation to his androcentric-orientated academic and social communities. She expresses a disappointment in the likes of Tolkien and his fellow contemporary author and close friend, C.S. Lewis. This disappointment emerges from the authors' emphasis on world-building as well as a vast number of opportunities not taken by both writers to explore social issues or norms when sub-creating a fictional world; "a world which operates on a set of assumptions different from the world as we know it" (13). The women of Middle-earth are very limited in terms of their character depth and available opportunities, as Tolkien's writing does not break free from traditional gender ideologies of his time. For Myers, Tolkien provides women with "nothing but the same old bouquet of medieval" attitudes and values (15).

Even the shield maiden, Éowyn, who enters combat alongside her kin, must adhere to strict traditional roles located in the domestic sphere. The only way in which she can break free from her allotted role is to disobey her uncle's direct order for her to stay behind. She then disguises herself as her male alias Dernhelm and secretly enters the battlefields unbeknownst to others of her actual sex. Éowyn is quite aware that the cause of her melancholy is largely due to her entrapment in her social position as a woman. When asked what she fears, Éowyn replies "[a] cage" as well as "[t]o stay behind bars, until use and old age accept them, and all chance of doing great deeds is gone beyond recall or desire" (*LotR* V.2.784). In order to gain any actual autonomy, she must challenge her position and disregard it; a position typically followed by other female characters within the text. However, Éowyn eventually aligns herself with the societal demands of women and conforms to her gender role as a healer. Even the Lady of Lothlórien, Galadriel, follows the usual tropes of female passivity in the face of combat and war; famed for her beauty and enchanting features. While readers are aware of her power, specifically her magic and clairvoyance, Galadriel does not actively take part in the War of the Ring.

Furthermore, the role of Arwen complies with that of the traditional passively demure beauty belonging to nobility in medieval literature. Arwen is barely assigned any direct dialogue and is infrequently referred to throughout the text. Her sole function seems to be to act as a desired object that is handed over from her father to Aragorn once he is crowned king of Gondor: "Elrond surrendered the sceptre, and laid the hand of his daughter in the hand of the king" (*LotR* VI.5.972). It is obvious that Arwen does love Aragorn and is willing to marry him. Their love is a reflection of the happy marriage between Tolkien himself and his wife Edith, whom he adored. However, Tolkien's depiction of this archaic rite that takes place subscribes to traditional patriarchal thought – that is the exchange of women as a commodity. Renowned theorist Luce Irigaray may be drawn on to support this statement. In her book *This Sex Which is Not One*, she proceeds to detail the conditions upon which patriarchal economy is based; the commodity or transaction of women. Irigaray claims that the "production of women, signs, and commodities is always referred back to men" and that these transactions only ever take place between men (171). She states that when a man 'purchases' a woman, he only ever deals with the father or brother, never the mother. Irigaray argues that societal laws are constructed around the valorisation of, and cater to, the needs and desires of men, and this is where patriarchy thrives. While Irigaray is overly aggressive in her denunciation of men (and I say this as an admirer of her work), her essay "Women on the Market" lends itself to the exploration of patriarchal undertones within Tolkien's work. He leaves little room for the development of female characters based on their own desires: "[O]ur societies thus [require] that women lend themselves to alienation in consumption, and to exchanges in which they do not participate, and that men be exempt from being used and circulated like commodities" (Irigaray 172). Indeed, Tolkien's women in *LotR* appear to possess largely muted characteristics and traits. The only characteristic that appears to be amplified for the female characters is their beauty and elegance.

Beauty appears to have a key role in regards to the portrayal of women in *The Lord of the Rings*. While there are no women present on the battlefield in traditional society and literature, women often appear as a central component of war. That is, their role exists outside of combat, yet they still influence war itself. According to medieval codes of chivalry, men must fight in order to defend the honour of a lady, as well as for her beauty. This is present in Gimli's fervent desire to defend the name and image of the Lady Galadriel (Fredrick and McBride 29). In their 2007 study, Fredrick and McBride continue to argue for the role of feminine beauty as an aspect, and sometimes a catalyst, of war. They make the point that while men fight over women, it is interesting to note that they specifically fight "over exceedingly beautiful women" (29). One might recall Helen of Troy and her pivotal role in the Trojan wars, which was essentially men fighting over the most beautiful woman in the world (bearing in mind other key social and political factors which influenced the war). While women can directly influence the beginnings of combat between men, they must not enter this sphere for fear it would display them as less than perfect.

In order for Éowyn to enter the field of battle, she must first disguise her beauty. She cannot be both warrior and woman at the same time and as such, in order to enter the androcentric zone of war, she must become a man. Finally, Fredrick and McBride boldly note that war is not a pretty sight, and highlight the traditional view that to see a woman in combat would sully the idealised and projected image of a woman as delicate, impeccable and pure; men would prefer not to see that. For them, this is the reason that women are deliberately not portrayed as being on the battlefield.

We have noted the consequential catalytic role of women in the portrayal of war in literature. We have also explored the function of women in Middle-earth. Let us now draw from the work of the feminist theorist and existentialist philosopher, Simone de Beauvoir. Her work is focused primarily on the position of women as second-class citizens in traditional patriarchal society and falls into the category of second-wave feminism:

> History has shown that men have always held all the concrete powers; from patriarchy's earliest times they have deemed it useful to keep woman in a state of dependence; their codes were set up against her; she was thus concretely established as the Other. This condition served males' economic interests; but it also suited their ontological and moral ambitions. (193)

It is these rigid gender roles assigned to men and women that construct women as subservient, and therefore, as *Other*. Beauvoir argues that women "have passively accepted the meanings men have imposed on them" (Weil 156). For Beauvoir, women must learn to survive in a male-orientated society, where they are positioned as subordinate. Man, according to Beauvoir, is the centre of the universe and women have "been made into man's other and so robbed of their own ability to define themselves" (Weil 155).

Beauvoir also argues the paradoxical nature of women; she must exist as two separate entities at once. In the domestic sphere, she has some control over her life and she dedicates herself and her energies to her duties within this sphere diligently to lessen the discord inside her – to give her a sense of self and purpose. However, once she steps outside into the public sphere, an exclusively male area, she is lost. She has no place here and is reliant on men. Women are therefore trapped, willingly due to a state of ignorance, in their own personal world that is separate to that of patriarchal society: "The sphere she belongs to is closed everywhere, limited, dominated by the male universe: as high as she climbs, as far as she dares go, there will always be a ceiling over her head, walls that block her path" (Beauvoir 359).

This can be applied to Tolkien's text, where traditional gender norms are very much at play. We have already outlined the passivity and generally demure 'lady-like' nature of the women of Middle-earth. This passivity of women arguably falls under Beauvoir's concept of patriarchy; "seeing clearly is not her business: she was taught to accept masculine authority [...]. She leaves it to the superior caste" (272). However, this paradox that Beauvoir speaks of is simultaneously present within the text. One primary example is that of Goldberry. Many previous critics[7] have discussed the portrayal of Goldberry as a domestic goddess, an enchanting beauty as well as her origins in folklore. However, we shall focus on the domesticity of women in wartime, such as the character of Éowyn.

We have already discussed the role of Éowyn in the subversion of gender roles in Middle-earth. However, it is her inner conflict that is of importance in light of Beauvoir's theory. Éowyn suffers from a deep despair and melancholy. This is brought about from her feelings of disconnect to her kin – she desires to fight for her people just as her brother and uncle do. Many even comment on her strength and ability, as well as her fearlessness. Yet cultural norms dictate that she must stay far away from any actual combat, simply because she is a woman. She must also come to terms with the fact that she can never be suited to Aragorn. The paradox exists in Éowyn in that she must choose between fulfilling her own desires and obeying her king, and thus remaining behind. This conflict is furthered as she breaks her promise to her king and kin, and disconnects herself from her loved ones when she chooses to go to war in secret. Smith interestingly discusses Éowyn in relation to her position as a 'war bride', giving some insight in to her position, as well as the depth of her character as a woman. It was a trend during Tolkien's time to hastily marry, whether it be to a foreign allied soldier, or a childhood sweetheart, as it seemed as if doom was near and men were disappearing to fight in the war. Éowyn falls into both categories according to Smith, but most interestingly as a foreign war bride to Faramir, where she is placed in a culture and

7 E.g. Basso, Taylor.

society that is alien to her (167). Here, Éowyn attempts to overcome her feelings of powerlessness through determination to 'do her bit' in the war. It is interesting that she still retains her individuality even after she decides to wed Faramir, in contrast to Arwen. Here we see Tolkien's redeeming view that no "wedding ring converts a woman from a highly desirable individual (or love object) to a household fixture" (Rawls 113).

The portrayal of women as sublime mythical beings must be explored in relation to the turmoil of wartime. As we have already discussed in depth, the lack of women in the war arguably fostered the phenomenon of men adopting traditional feminine traits as well as taboo male bonding. Tolkien's experience of war as an exclusively male zone, teamed with the lack of women that would have existed in Tolkien's scholarly and social circles, arguably led to the typical romanticising of women in Tolkien's works. Women's feminine characteristics are over-emphasized, such as their beauty and grace. They radiate like goddesses; men witness them as if they are some rare creature that they have never had the pleasure to behold beforehand. Of the few passages in *The Lord of the Rings* in which the lady Arwen is mentioned, she is rarely an active participant in the story and remains modestly reticent. Upon first seeing her, Frodo describes her enchanting qualities, even comparing her to a mythic beautiful maiden in Middle-earth lore: "So it was that Frodo saw her whom few mortals had yet seen; Arwen, daughter of Elrond, in whom it was said that the likeness of Lúthien had come on earth again; and she was called Undómiel, for she was the Evenstar of her people" (*LotR* II.1.227). Arwen is a descendent of Lúthien, known as the most beautiful woman to have ever graced the men and Elves of Middle-earth and the 'morning star' of her people. Already we envision Arwen as an enchanting beauty with angelic qualities. When Frodo encounters her once again he notes her magnificence: "And Frodo when he saw her come glimmering in the evening, with stars on her brow and a sweet fragrance about her, was moved with great wonder" (*LotR* VI.5.972).

Similarly, Galadriel is described as fair and angelic. Gimli becomes enamoured with her beauty and grace and describes her as both "the fairest of ladies" (*LotR* III.6.524) and "above all the jewels that lie beneath the earth!" (*LotR* II.7.356). Gimli is not the only man to comment on her loveliness; Sam too attempts to describe her divine qualities, yet feels as though his words are inadequate:

> But I wish I could make a song about her. Beautiful she is, sir! Lovely! Sometimes like a great tree in flower, sometimes like a white daffadowndilly, small and slender like. Hard as di'monds, soft as moonlight. Warm as sunlight, cold as frost in the stars. Proud and far-off as a snow-mountain, and as merry as any lass I ever saw with daisies in her hair in springtime. (*LotR* IV.5.680)

Even the less exalted, more down to earth, Rose Cotton is romanticised for Sam when he exaggerates her feminine qualities as he fantasises about her. This is reminiscent of soldiers in war as they carried valuable pictures of lovers with them while away at war and highlights the lack of women in these circumstances. Finally, the mortal woman Éowyn, while we see her depicted as strong and wilful, is also famed for her physical beauty. Both Aragorn and Faramir comment on her beauty, with Faramir falling in love with her. He proclaims "Éowyn of Rohan, I say to you that you are beautiful. In the valleys of our hills there are flowers fair and bright, and maidens fairer still; but neither flower nor lady have I seen till now in Gondor so lovely, and so sorrowful" (*LotR* VI.5.960).

It would appear as if women are regarded for the beauty above all in Middle-earth; this is reminiscent of medieval literature and poetry. It also highlights the clear divide in the positions available for women and men in such stories. Another means of perpetuating stereotypes of women (romanticised with hyper-feminine traits due to a lack of physical presence) is their link to nature. Male-dominated academic practices, such as science, are "often mediated in images that are tendentiously gendered"; nature is similarly "gendered as female" (Kennedy 234). Sharrock furthers this notion with the example of ancient Greek poetry. Here nature has the power to be an active force which influences the story: "Nature will be seen to be completely free and independent of arrogant masters, doing her will herself, of her own accord, without the gods" (261, Sharrock's translation from Lucretius). As discussed, the beauty of the women is often romanticised with metaphors of nature. Arwen is compared to the stars, Éowyn to flowers, and Galadriel to all of that and more. Similarly, Faramir recounts his memory of his mother in which he describes her as lovely and fair.

It is important to bear in mind that *The Lord of the Rings* does not represent a large number of female characters, but there are indeed much stronger female characters in his other works, such as the tale of Beren and Lúthien (also referred to as *The Lay of Leithian).* I have described Lúthien earlier, and shall continue to recount her relevance to the portrayal of femininity in Tolkien's *The Lord of the Rings.* The recently published *Beren and Lúthien* (2017) provides a direct contrast and comparison to the women of *The Lord of the Rings.* What is interesting about this story is the contrasting elements of Lúthien which both perpetuate and challenge traditional patriarchal ideals of femininity (specifically in terms of traditional storytelling). Lúthien is coveted by all men due to her divine beauty and demure manner. She is joyful and enchants those who witness her dancing. She is similarly confined to her traditional gendered roles and, like Éowyn, she also challenges these roles by disobeying the main patriarch in her life.

Lúthien is an object of desire for men, and many try to capture her and take her as their own. Descriptions of her beauty include "[S]he beguiled Thû to come forth, for the fame of the loveliness of Lúthien had gone through all the lands and the wonder of her song. Even Morgoth desired her, and had promised the greatest award to any who could capture her" (*B&L* 134). Similarly, in another excerpt, she is described:

> Heard ye not then
> of that pretty fay, of Lúthien?
> Her body is fair, very white and fair.
> Morgoth would possess her in his lair.
> (*B&L* 128)

Lúthien displays the traditional meek qualities of femininity; she does not fight and indeed her power is located in her charm. Characters such as Huan, the hound of Valinor, are moved by her distress and take it upon themselves to aid her. However, it is also Lúthien who comes to the rescue of Beren when he is made prisoner. This reversal of traditional roles in storytelling is interesting to say the least, especially when compared to the famous lines of Éowyn as she slays the dreaded Witch-king and exclaims "But no living man am I! You look upon a woman" (*LotR* V.6.841). Another interesting subversion of gender norms is present in *The Silmarillion*. Beren's mother, Emeldir, is briefly mentioned in regard to her strong characteristics for which she is given the nickname 'Manhearted'. She arms the people of her tribe against the evil forces of Morgoth and "these masculine activities are, apparently, the qualifications behind her nickname" (Fredrick and McBride 32). Any strength in character is therefore linked to masculinity rather than femininity. While these characters are an interesting comparison to the females of Tolkien's other text, it does unfortunately appear that Tolkien is eager to conform to traditional gender stereotypes in storytelling; specifically, in regard to the role of women in wartime.

What is also interesting about this text is the concept of the physical body and its relationship with power and gender. Agan's essay "Lúthien Tinúviel and Bodily Desire in the Lay of Leithian" discusses this notion in depth. Agan begins by describing how Lúthien challenges gender norms by being an active agent in the story. There is, at first glance, the potential for dismissal as a typical demure, chaste damsel as she is assigned hyper-feminine, ethereal attributes and desirability. However, "the text also allows space for Lúthien to move against the will of her father, her lover, the enemy Sauron, and of course, even Morgoth" (169). Aggressively dominant male characters such as Thingol, Celegorm, and Curufin are typified exponents of the law of the patriarch. Their upholding of patriarchal beliefs, particularly that of the husband-father control, present a problem for the development of Lúthien's character (Brücker 12). However, it is precisely through being entrapped by her father that she is able to craft her magical cloak from her hair; it is her bodily expression of power. It is through her entrapment within the domestic sphere that Lúthien chooses to become an active agent. Unlike Éowyn who must don the disguise of a man in order to leave her sphere, Lúthien remains feminine in nature as she begins her perilous journey in search of her beloved. It is precisely this device that she uses to gain power over her enemies, allowing her some form of control when the threat of sexual violence and control encroaches on her from those who desire her as a possession. While Lúthien does not enter into combat, and is protected by either Beren or Huan when threatened, she does subvert the gender norm in that she is able to move freely, be it through the challenging of her father and other captors.

Throughout Tolkien's works we witness the historical contingencies that still perpetuate the divisive ideals of gender heteronormativity. Regardless of

Tolkien's refutations regarding wartime allegories in his writing, it is clear that it had some impact concerning male bonding, or wartime gender stereotypes. Tolkien appears to categorise characters according to prescriptive societal roles and expectations of traditional patriarchal society. His depictions of gender and sexuality highlight the pervasive nature of ideologies in terms of the creation of fictional and inverted realities. Yet Tolkien's experiences of war helped to shape his work. If it were not for the traumatic experience of the Great War, Tolkien would not so astutely understand the relationship between two soldiers and friends. He also understood the loss and alienation involved, as manifested in his characters and the landscapes of Middle-earth. It could be argued that these issues are contributing factors to why the very phenomenon of war exists, or is justified, as its animalistic territorialism is symptomatically mirrored in the injustices that is implicit in creating definitions of what gender or sexuality should be. The forced repression of instinctual desires (often denied) leads to the overt and frustrated physical violence we witness, not just in wartime, but also throughout patriarchal, masculine, and phallocentric behaviours. While some characters do attempt to subvert the norms, the relationship between Frodo and Sam challenges the heteronormativity of war and the willing active participation in violence. It simultaneously challenges notions of rigid gender roles during wartime bonding and intimacy. Likewise, Éowyn challenges these norms, yet eventually submits to her prescribed role as a healer. In comparison, we witness characters such as Lúthien, who contrast with the passive women in *The Lord of the Rings*. In many varying aspects, the gender roles of Tolkien's time have an enormous impact on Tolkien's writing.

Bibliography

AGAN, Cami D. "Lúthien Tinúviel and Bodily Desire in the Lay of Leithian." *Perilous and Fair: Women in the Works and Life of J.R.R. Tolkien*. Eds. Janet Brennan Croft and Leslie A. Donovan. Altadena, CA: Mythopoetic Press, 2015, 168-187.

ANDERSON, Benedict. *Imagined Communities*. London: Verso, 1991.

BASSO, Ann McCauley. "Fair Lady Goldberry, Daughter of the River." *Mythlore* 27.1/2 (2008): 137-46.

BEAUVOIR, Simone de. *The Second Sex*. New York City, NY: Vintage Books, 2010.

BOURKE, Joanna. *Dismembering the Male: Men's Bodies, Britain and the Great War.* Chicago, IL: University of Chicago Press, 1996.

BRÜCKER, Patrick. "Tolkien on Love: Concepts of 'Love' in the *Silmarillion* and *The Lord of the Rings*." *Tolkien and Modernity 2.* Eds. Thomas Honegger and Frank Weinreich. Zurich and Berne: Walking Tree Publishers, 2006, 1-52.

BUTLER, Judith. *Gender Trouble: Feminism and the Subversion of Identity.* New York City, NY: Routledge, 1999.

COLE, Sarah. *Modernism, Male Friendship, and the First World War.* Cambridge: Cambridge University Press, 2003.

CRAIG, David M. "'Queer Lodgings': Gender and Sexuality in *The Lord of the Rings*." *Mallorn: The Journal of the Tolkien Society* 38 (2001): 11-18.

CROFT, Janet Brennan. *War and the Works of J.R.R. Tolkien.* Westport, CT: Praeger Publishers, 2004.

DAS, Santanu. "'Kiss Me, Hardy': Intimacy, Gender, and Gesture in World War I Trench Literature." *Modernism/Modernity* 9(1) (2002): 51-74.

FORD, Patrick K. "The Idea of Everlasting Fame in the Táin." *Ulidia: Proceedings of the First International Conference on the Ulster Cycle of Tales.* Eds. James P. Mallory and Gerard Stockman. Belfast: December Publications, 1994, 255-61.

FREDRICK, Candice and Sam MCBRIDE. "Battling the Woman Warrior: Females and Combat in Tolkien and Lewis." *Mythlore* 25.3/4 (2007): 29-42.

GOLDBERG, Ruth and Krin GABBARD. "'What Does the Eye Demand': Sexuality, Forbidden Vision and Embodiment in *The Lord of the Rings*." *From Hobbits to Hollywood: Essays on Peter Jackson's Lord of the Rings.* Eds. Ernest Mathijs and Steven Jay Schneider. New York City, NY: Rodopi, 2006, 265-282.

GULLACE, Nicoletta F. "White Feathers and Wounded Men: Female Patriotism and the Memory of the Great War." *Journal of British Studies* 36 (1997): 178-206.

HIRSCHFELD, Magnus. *The Sexual History of the World War.* New York City, NY: Cadillac, 1946.

IRIGARAY, Luce. *This Sex Which is Not One.* Trans. Catherine Porter. New York City, NY: Cornell University Press, 1985.

KENNEDY, Duncan. "Atoms, Individuals, and Myths." *Laughing with Medusa.* Eds. Vanda Zajko and Miriam Leonard. Oxford: University of Oxford, 2006, 233-253.

LEWIS, C.S. "The Dethronement of Power." *A Reader's Companion to* The Hobbit *and* The Lord of the Rings. New York City, NY: Quality Paperback Book Club, 2005, 37-42.

Lodge, David and Nigel Wood. *Modern Criticism and Theory: A Reader.* 2nd ed. Harlow: Pearson: 2000.

McClintock, Anne. *Imperial Leather: Race, Gender and Sexuality in the Colonial Contest.* New York City, NY: Routledge, 1995.

McLarty, Lianne. "Masculinity, Whiteness and Social Class in *The Lord of the Rings.*" *From Hobbits to Hollywood: Essays on Peter Jackson's Lord of the Rings.* Eds. Ernest Mathijs and Steven Jay Schneider. New York City, NY: Rodopi (2006): 173-188.

Myers, Doris T. "'Brave New World': The Status of Women According to Tolkien, Lewis, and Williams." *Cimarron Review* October 1971: 13-19.

Partridge, Brenda. "No Sex Please – We're Hobbits: The Construction of Female Sexuality in *The Lord of the Rings.*" *J.R.R. Tolkien: This Far Land.* Ed. Robert Giddings. New Jersey: Vision – Barnes & Noble, 1983, 179-197.

Rateliff, John D. "The Missing Woman: J.R.R. Tolkien's Lifelong Support for Women's Higher Education." *Perilous and Fair: Women in the Works and Life of J.R.R. Tolkien.* Eds. Janet Brennan Croft and Leslie A. Donovan. Altadena, CA: Mythopoeic Press, 2015, 41-69.

Rawls, Melanie. "The Feminine Principle in Tolkien." *Perilous and Fair: Women in the Works and Life of J.R.R. Tolkien.* Eds. Janet Brennan Croft and Leslie A. Donovan, Altadena, CA: Mythopoeic Press, 2015, 99-117.

Schopenhauer, Arthur. *The Wisdom of Life.* Trans. Thomas Bailey Saunders. University Park, PN: Pennsylvania State University Press, 2005.

Seton-Watson, Hugh. *Nations and States: An Enquiry into the Origins of Nations and the Politics of Nationalism.* Boulder, CO: Westview Press, 1977.

Sharrock, Alison. "The Philosopher and the Mother Cow: Towards a Gendered Reading of Lucretius, *De Rerum Natura.*" *Laughing with Medusa.* Eds. Vanda Zajko and Miriam Leonard. Oxford: Oxford University Press, 2006, 253-275.

Smol, Anna. "'Oh... oh... Frodo!': Readings of Male Intimacy in *The Lord of the Rings.*" *MFS Modern Fiction Studies* 50.4 (2004): 949-979.

Taylor, Taryne Jade. "Investigating the Role and Origin of Goldberry in Tolkien's Mythology." *Mythlore* 27.1/2 (2008): 147-56.

Tolkien, J.R.R. *Beren and Lúthien.* Ed. Christopher Tolkien. London: Harper Collins Publishers, 2017.

The Letters of J.R.R. Tolkien: A Selection. Eds. Humphrey Carpenter and Christopher Tolkien. 1st ed. Boston, MA: Houghton Mifflin, 2000.

The Lord of the Rings. 50th Anniversary edition. Boston, MA: Houghton Mifflin, 2004.

The Silmarillion. London: Harper Collins Publishers, 2013.

VACCARO, Christopher. "Homosexuality." *J.R.R. Tolkien Encyclopedia: Scholarship and Critical Assessment*. Ed. Michael D.C. Drout. New York City, NY: Routledge, 2007, 285-286.

WEIL, Kari. "French Feminism's Écriture Féminine." *The Cambridge Companion to Feminist Literary Theory*. Ed. Ellen Rooney. Cambridge: Cambridge University Press, 2006.

Alicia Fox-Lenz

Contemporary Reflections of War: Soldier-Servant Relationships in *The Lord of the Rings* and *Downton Abbey*

It's no new information for even the most casual Tolkien scholar that *The Lord of the Rings* is heavily rooted in Tolkien's experience during World War I. The most haunting depiction of his time there being Sam and Frodo's trek through the desolate slag heaps and withered ground of the Dagorlad and Gorgoroth on their way into Mordor – a similar landscape to what Tolkien would have seen in the trenches during the Battle of the Somme. The extremely close master and servant relationship shown between Frodo and Sam was also informed by Tolkien's experience in the war. Sam is based on an officer's soldier-servant, or batman, who were used in the British armed forces from the eighteenth through the early twentieth century. This arrangement of an officer having a private servant is somewhat alien to a modern American, being rooted in the prevailing rigid class structure of England at the time. The idea of a soldier-servant was not solely a British one – other European countries, such as Germany, also made use of this arrangement – however, the *batman* is uniquely British. He lives on in English literature, within the biographical poems and novels of the canonical World War I authors and poets, and also within a scant number of fictionalizations such as *The Lord of the Rings.* The relationship of Sam and Frodo, of the batman and his officer, and their "battle" gives the reader a glimpse into the contemporary view of war in the early to mid-twentieth century. This historical view can then be contrasted by stepping outside Tolkien entirely, into Masterpiece Theater's historical drama *Downton Abbey,* which shows fictionalized batman relationships in a real world setting and showcases a more modern, twenty-first century view of war.

The word *batman* comes from the Old French word *bât,* meaning "pack saddle". The job of a batman began as the soldier who tended the officer's luggage on a pack-horse but expanded in scope over time (Hooker 125). By the time of the World Wars, a batman was an officer's valet, who performed a variety of domestic chores such as cooking his food and cleaning his clothing, as well as taking care of his baggage (Garth 171; Hooker 125). In return for his service, a batman, who was also a private in the army, would be relieved of his sentry duties and receive additional compensation (Fellowes and Briggs 246).

The purpose of having these soldier-servants was two-fold. Firstly, it was a practical arrangement: by having a servant to tend to his basic needs, the officer would be free to focus solely on his many military activities (Garth 171). Secondly, this relationship recreated the social structure of the life left behind in England. Officers were gentlemen, pulled from the British nobility and educated middle class, and many were accustomed to having servants such as valets (Hooker 125). Far from being a simple luxury for the officer, recreating this familiar social structure was seen as a way to introduce structure to the chaos of trench warfare. The fear being that social equality in the ranks would lead to the dissolution of unthinking obedience to authority, something the British thought imperative to winning on the battlefield (Fellowes and Briggs 245). Thus, one has the privates, specifically the batmen, who were men of humble origins in servitude to the gentlemen officers (Seton Hutchison 222).

Men facing death together can forge bonds in a way that is hard for the civilians left back home to understand; in the case of officers and batmen, these bonds span social class. Officers often became especially close to their batmen, and the literature of World War I is littered with officers admiring the loyalty and devotion of the batmen who cared for them (Hooker 125). In his article "Frodo's Batman", Mark T. Hooker explores the writings of two World War I officers, William Noel Hodgson and Lieutenant Colonel Graham Seton Hutchison, focusing on their relationships with their batmen: Pearson and Peter McLintock, respectively. Through the passages quoted in this article, one can piece together a list of traits that World War I officers ascribe to their batmen.

According to Hodgson and Seton Hutchison, a batman is resourceful to the point of nearly being a conjuror, being able to produce wine, bread, and eggs for a starving officer in a deserted village (Hodgson 77). A batman is a force of nature within his servitude; he does not know his own limitations since they have never been reached (Hodgson 77). A batman is a light in dark places, lending his officer confidence and good cheer within the darkness (Seton Hutchison

215). A batman never left his officer's side, "an ever-present companion" fighting side-by-side and falling together in battle (Seton Hutchison 215, 219-20). Based on the number of times it is mentioned, the batman's relationship to the officer is one of his central traits. Seton Hutchison describes his batman, McLintock, as "the best, most intimate friend man ever had," mentioning McLintock's "little acts of vigilant kindness," and calling him "a faithful servant, a friend and counselor" (211, 221, 215).

Although not widely considered a World War I writer like Hodgson and Seton Hutchison, Tolkien also served in the British military during the conflict, along with most of his childhood friends, many of whom died over the course of the war. One of Tolkien's closest friends, a member of the Tea Club and Barrovian Society (TCBS), Rob Gilson, was one of the millions of men who lost their lives during the war. After Gilson's death, his batman, Bradnam, wrote a letter to Gilson's parents telling them how well-loved and respected their son has been. The closeness of Gilson and Bradnam is evident in the substantial amount of money Gilson bequeathed to his former batman, £50, which is nearly £2000 today. Sadly, Bradnam did not live to receive it, he was mortally wounded as he fought alongside Gilson and lost his life soon after penning the letter to Gilson's parents (Garth 170).

Tolkien was separated from his friends during the war and found it difficult to befriend his fellow officers. Tolkien came to befriend many of the batmen and developed a profound admiration for them, although officers were not permitted to make friends among the privates (Carpenter 89; Garth 171). This admiration was far from an anomaly; Hodgson claims that good batmen are one of the "greatest marvels of modern civilization," and mentions that officers boasting of their batmen was a common occurrence (77, 81).

The strong bonds forged in the strain of combat between officers and their batmen helped to contribute to a post-war cultural shift in Britain. A good batman became respected and admired amongst the higher-class officers, and through that admiration, he could glimpse the possibility of a world without rigid class barriers back home (Garth 171; Hooker 133). It was not only batmen who discovered a different life. Due to a shortage of officers, many privates were promoted up the ranks, getting a taste of life in a different social sphere.

After the war, these men were suddenly stripped of their status and found it difficult to revert to their old lives. Because of these displaced former officers and the attachments between the gentlemen officers and their former batmen, as Britain began to recover from the war it became obvious there was no hope of returning to its pre-war state (Fellowes et al. 17). The period surrounding the world wars in Britain, roughly from 1890 to 1940 forms a bridge between the old world with its rigid class structure and primarily agrarian economy and the new, urban society with a flatter, more mobile, class structure (Fellowes and Briggs 9).

It can be difficult for a modern reader to really understand the importance of class in English society during this era, and therefore difficult to see how groundbreaking these close relationships between officers and batmen were. The depth of the close bond between soldiers is similarly outside the grasp of civilians living in relative peace. An officer was a gentleman, and as referenced earlier, he was born into greatness and greatness was expected of him. A batman was a commoner with no such social expectations of greatness; it was a fact of life that those of the lower classes would know their place (Hooker 131). This is in stark contrast to the present day where, for the most part, people of different classes are treated as more or less equal in terms of aptitude and there is more social mobility.

Along with this flattening of the social hierarchy, there is a marked shift in the British sense of masculinity. The soldiers, particularly the officers and batmen, frequently nursed chaste homoerotic crushes in the all-male environment of the trenches. These crushes are generally from the officer to the batman, as the officer sees his subordinate's vulnerability and seeks to protect it, but they might also flow the other way as a sense of hero worship (Croft 52). In the inter-war period, Britain saw a rejection of the aggressive, military values it held pre-war. The definition of traditional masculinity expanded to include more nurturing, feminine behaviors. At the same time, there was a conservative backlash to these social changes, resulting in a rigid separation of men and women in an effort to maintain social order (Craig 11).

Tolkien has said that Sam Gamgee is a reflection of the batmen he came to know over the course of World War I (Carpenter 81). Sam is an amalgamation of all beloved batmen, and similarly to how Hodgson describes other officers boasting of their batmen, Tolkien is boasting about them all in unison. Tolkien is a champion of batmen, stating that he found them as superior to himself (Carpenter 89; Garth 310). In "The Shell-Shocked Hobbit", an article exploring Frodo as a sufferer of Post-Traumatic Stress Disorder, Michael Livingston proposes that what Tolkien identifies as superiority in these soldiers is their ability to fully divorce themselves from the war and move on with their lives, which is not something Tolkien seems to have been able to fully do, as evidenced by the heavy influence of the war on the entirety of his creative output and his tendency to form primarily strong homosocial bonds (20). Frodo sees within Sam this ability to leave behind trauma, telling him: "[Y]ou will be healed. You were meant to be solid and whole, and you will be" (*LotR* VI.9.1026). Frodo lacks this ability, as evidenced by his inability to loosen the tight bond of friendship with Sam, moving the Gamgees into Bag End with him, as well as his inability to rejoin life in the Shire and subsequent sailing into the West.

Frodo and Sam have a relationship that is unequivocally "master" and "servant", which is made clear by Tolkien's liberal use of these words throughout *The Lord of the Rings*. In his *Letters*, Tolkien tells a reader that Sam does not see himself as admirable except for his loyalty to Frodo; Sam is not a hero nor does he see himself as being particularly brave (329). In a clear comparison to the batmen who served him during the war, Tolkien explicitly has Sam leaving the Shire "to do for Mr. Frodo" (*LotR* I.3.69), indicating that Sam would be acting as Frodo's valet, taking on the same responsibilities as a batman (Hooker 128).

On the journey from Bad End to Mordor and back again, Sam shows many of the traits Hodgson and Seton Hutchison point to when describing their excellent batmen. Sam is a constant companion who refuses to leave Frodo's side, even when Frodo explicitly tries to leave him behind at Amon Hen to save him the danger of the journey into Mordor. Sam's knowledge of his master allows him to catch Frodo before he leaves, and, although Frodo's decision to leave alone was made at the last moment, Sam has predicted his master's actions, and his pack lay nearby loaded with extra food ready to accompany Frodo (*LotR* II.10.406).

In laying aside this extra food Sam is resourceful, but his resourcefulness also ventures, in Frodo's mind, near to conjuration in the Tower of Cirith Ungol. Frodo has been captured by Orcs, and he fears they have stripped him of the Ring. When Sam appears in the tower, beyond hope, to save him and then produces the Ring that he had presumed lost, Frodo calls Sam a marvel (*LotR* VI.1.911). It does not matter to Frodo what steps Sam took to get the ring back to him – fighting Shelob, his existential crisis over taking the ring and leaving Frodo behind, and chasing the Orcs back to the tower – much like it did not matter to Hodgson how his batman managed to produce a meal from a destroyed town, it is enough just to know the near magic of which their companions were capable.

Sam falls squarely into a morale support role in the long trek through Mordor, providing Frodo with comfort and reminding him of the world outside and above the darkness on the steps of Mount Doom, tying their fate to the fate of the heroes in the great stories of the past (*LotR* IV.8.712-713). Much like his historical counterpart, Sam's most important role is as Frodo's closest friend and devoted companion. At the end of the novel, Sam has been elevated from being solely Frodo's gardener and servant to living within Bag End alongside Frodo, a testament to the closeness of their relationship as well as Frodo's inability to let go of his trauma. When Frodo leaves to sail into the West, Sam becomes the master of Bag End, one of the richest delvings in Hobbiton (*LotR* VI.9.1029). This reversal of Sam's fortunes in being thrust into greatness, also parallels the aforementioned democratization of the cultural hierarchy within post-war Britain. Sam had come from a family of gardeners and tradesmen, evidence of a previous lack of social mobility within Hobbit society. In "Balaam and His Ass", W.H. Auden states that although the master-servant relationship is an unequal and contractual one, when one party risks his life for the other, the nature of the contract is transcended; this is seen again and again in Frodo and Sam's journey to the depths of Mordor and successfully rewrites their relationship into one between social equals (108). Sam's ability to become upwardly mobile is firmly based in Frodo's affections for him, and their altered relationship, both forged in trauma.

Within *The Lord of the Rings*, Tolkien presents us with two models of war. One is a medieval pastiche of a heroic, just war, a depiction of war that had thoroughly fallen out of favor in the post-War period. The battles of Men – Helm's Deep, Pelennor Fields, the battle of the Morannon – and their simplistic pitting of good versus evil lead many critics to decry *The Lord of the Rings* as being juvenile. These critics overlooked the depiction of modern war found in Frodo and Sam's journey into Mordor. Tolkien weaves the horrors of modern war through the landscape of Mordor – the faces of fallen soldiers in the Dead Marshes; the pitted, desolate landscape of the Dagorlad – as well as through their slow, plodding progress toward their goal, unseen terrors screeching overhead. It is truly a depiction of war without any valor, which rings true to the experience of World War I as depicted by the war poets. It is an utter condemnation of the modern way of waging war, which destroys the landscape and demoralizes soldiers, sending them back broken and shell-shocked or not at all. Almost an entire generation of men were killed during World War I, likely driving the rejection of the aggressive, highly masculinized, military focus of pre-war Britain in the inter-war period.

In contrast, *Downton Abbey* has a very modern vision of war. Though set in the World War I period, there is none of the silent horror of Tolkien's depiction of his experiences during the war. *Downton Abbey* is considered a "costume drama", meaning that it shoots for historical authenticity, but not necessarily historical accuracy. Being written by writers who have had no experience living in the early twentieth century, the narrative becomes clouded with contemporary sensibilities. According to Julian Fellowes, writer and director of *Downton Abbey*, the main inspiration for writing the show was to explore the intersecting lives of the family and the help residing in a large estate, giving each group equal weight in the narrative and characterization. This move to treat the classes equally is vastly different to what would have been produced if this television show had been produced closer to the era it is portraying (2-3). This modernity-tinged treatment of life in a large estate masks the social turmoil surrounding World War I to some extent, manifesting itself in the increased social value of the women in the family, a servant marrying into nobility, and Lord Grantham being at a complete loss as to what his role is in the shifting society. Lords of estates were previously large employers in the old agrarian economy of England, but as the population shifted into cities due to an increased reliance on industry, large tracts of land were no longer needed (Fellowes et al. 24-5).

There are two batman relationships depicted in the show, the primary one being between Lord Grantham and Bates, which shows the emotional closeness of Sam and Frodo's relationship. Bates served as Grantham's batman during the Boer war, the war immediately preceding World War I in British history. Their relationship faithfully captures the historical relationship it is based upon: after a harrowing time at war the two forged a class-defying friendship that never would have formed outside of the pressure of battle. There is an incredible amount of empathy shown between the two, enough that when Bates was invalided out of the military due to an injury, Grantham offered him a high-status job at Downton as his valet (Fellowes et al. 124). A valet was a senior role, one of a very few which worked directly with the family and enjoyed their trust, along with the lady's maid and the butler and footmen. The valet was a very similar role to a batman, helping the gentleman dress and keeping his schedule, and other duties that align with a personal assistant-type role (Fellowes et al. 121).

Bates's relationship with Lord Grantham is treated as queerly intimate in the series. When Bates arrives at Downton, the butler, Carson, who seems to be unaware of the previous history between the Lord and the new valet, greets him with a speech about the daunting standards of the house. Carson goes on to counsel Bates about feeling intimidated by Lord Grantham and assuring him that Grantham will lead him through any awkwardness with grace. These words are hardly out of Carson's mouth when Grantham bursts into the servants' quarters – something quite unusual which shocks the other servants – to enthusiastically greet Bates, calling him his "old comrade-in-arms" and "my dear man" (*Downton Abbey* 1:1).

Grantham affords Bates a voice that is not often allowed to servants, not only due to Bates's place in the servant hierarchy, but also because of their war-forged friendship. He inquires into how Bates is "settling in" and if he likes life at Downton with real concern. Grantham also reminiscences with Bates about the good times they had together in spite of the war when they were both enlisted. Most notably, his care for Bates is shown through the storyline of two other servants attempting to have Bates fired over his disability – using a cane due to a war injury, a piece of shrapnel that had become embedded in his knee. Grantham is genuinely concerned about Bates, not as a Lord would be concerned about a servant, in terms of Bates not being able to perform the duties of his job, but as a friend not wanting his friend to be in pain. Bates continuously minimizes his injury, culminating in a stint in leg braces that cause constant pain in an effort to fix his lameness. Bates refuses to bow to his limitations, going so far as to suggest a wage garnishment to hire someone part time to do the duties he can't (*Downton Abbey* 1:1, 1:3).

The two servants who try to get Bates fired, eventually convince Lady Grantham that Bates needs to go. This sparks a massive argument between the Lord and Lady when she demands Bates be fired for being too injured to be able to properly perform his duties. After this argument, one of the servants trips Bates in front of a visiting Duke, and Grantham is forced into letting Bates go by his wife and Carson, the butler, who manages all of the servants. Visibly upset, Grantham offers to pay Bates's salary until he could find gainful employment, which Bates refuses and Grantham pushes at least a month's wages upon him. As Bates is sitting in the carriage to travel to the train station, Grantham pulls him out and tells him to go back inside, telling Carson "I just didn't think it was right." This is the culmination of the friendship that has blossomed between Grantham and Bates, that Grantham would defy everyone in his world to do right by his faithful servant (*Downton Abbey* 1:1).

It is in the second batman-officer relationship where *Downton Abbey*'s depiction of war comes into play. The second series begins in the midst of World War I and features Matthew Crawley and William Mason in the trenches. Crawley is the heir to Downton, and is an officer in the trenches of World War I with his soldier-servant, Mason, who was previously the second footman at Downton. This relationship is useful to compare to *The Lord of the Rings* not only because of its portrayal of the undying friendship forged between Crawley and Mason (in contrast to the way the emotional closeness and intimacy within male friendship that Tolkien depicted has been stripped within the Peter Jackson adaptations, for example) but as a foil to the depiction of war within *The Lord of the Rings*. Where Tolkien treats the war as one of isolation and desolation, much like others of his generation, *Downton Abbey* depicts the war as a time of chaos and excitement. The effect is jarring within the show, as the camera cuts between a costume drama and what is essentially an action movie. The focus is on the explosions and gunshots as opposed to the psychological effects of the war. This is a focus that is very in-line with the contemporary view of violence as something to titillate, where war is glorified and simplified: brave men dodging gunfire and killing enemies, coming home victorious. This is reminiscent of the simplistic wars of men within *The Lord of the Rings*, where battles are glorious, and more importantly, can be won. However, even then Tolkien never goes so far as to glorify war. Faramir, who is a great captain of men, says that it is lesser men who delight in war for the sake of war and war should instead be fought to protect a land's culture and people. *Downton*'s portrayal is slightly more nuanced than a simple feel-good narrative about victory against evil accompanied by exciting explosions. Neither Crawley nor Mason comes back completely psychologically unscathed from the war, but it is far from the devastation visited upon Frodo in *The Lord of the Rings*: both can still function in their assigned roles in their day-to-day lives.

It may seem curious that Tolkien, who lived through the war, would turn the narrative so far away from the reality of the combat of that era while the modern eye revels in the danger of battle. This could be due to our relative distance to war. In the early twentieth century, more lives were touched by war through the two World Wars, where millions of men died in combat. Now relatively few people enlist in the military and of those, even fewer die in combat. The modern way of waging war through drones and airstrikes is as remote to the trench warfare of World War I as Tolkien's portrayal of archaic war through Aragorn's battles is to his experience in the trenches. Perhaps the distance modern society has from the bloodier types of war has engendered a type of nostalgia where depicting the bloody horror of battle only serves to prove the heroism of the soldiers, and no longer invokes animal horror. No doubt, to an inter-war reader, graphic depictions of the violence visited to soldiers in trench warfare would have been seen as obscene, whereas Tolkien's depictions of battle have the distance of history to soften the blow.

The relationships between batmen and the officers they served were instrumental in the British military through the mid-twentieth century. These relationships served to reinforce the social structure the soldiers had left behind to defend, making the strong cross-class relationships that were forged surprising to the people back home, as hard to understand to them as a rigid class structure is for a modern American. These relationships live on in the biographical writings of the soldiers of World War I, as well as *The Lord of the Rings*. Tolkien's depiction of the batman relationship is based on his experiences as a soldier during the war and Sam is turned into a symbol of the collective batman and everything that makes them great. Within Sam's character arc, we see represented the loosening of the class structure of post-war Britain due to these strong relationships forged in battle. We are also introduced to British culture's softening of what it means to be traditionally masculine and its rejection of hawkishness in the inter-war period through Frodo and Sam's journey into Mordor. Contrasting this with the modern view of *Downton Abbey*'s glorification of the chaos and excitement of war, *The Lord of the Rings*'s more sober concentration on the desolation left in the aftermath of the battle shows a clear divide between the modern focus on war as an acceptable means to an end and the post-war era disillusionment in the purpose of war.

Bibliography

AUDEN, W.H. "Balaam and His Ass." *The Dyer's Hand and Other Essays*. London: Penguin Random House, 1962, 107-145.

CARPENTER, Humphrey. *J.R.R. Tolkien: A Biography*. London: George Allen & Unwin, 1977.

CRAIG, David M. "'Queer Lodgings': Gender and Sexuality in *The Lord of the Rings*." *Mallorn* 38 (2001): 11-18.

CROFT, Janet Brennan. *War and the Works of J.R.R. Tolkien*. Westport, CT: Praeger, 2004.

"Downton Abbey, Series I (Episode I)." Masterpiece Theatre. PBS. GPB, Atlanta, 26 Sep. 2010.

"Downton Abbey, Series I (Episode 3)." Masterpiece Theatre. PBS. GPB, Atlanta, 10 Oct. 2010.

"Downton Abbey, Series II (Episode I)." Masterpiece Theatre. PBS. GPB, Atlanta, 18 Sep. 2011.

FELLOWES, Jessica and Nick BRIGGS. *The World of Downton Abbey*. New York City, NY: St. Martin's, 2011.

FELLOWES, Jessica, Matthew STURGIS, Joss BARRATT, Nick BRIGGS, and Giles KEYTE. *The Chronicles of Downton Abbey: A New Era*. New York City, NY: St. Martin's, 2012.

GARTH, John. *Tolkien and the Great War: The Threshold of Middle-earth*. Boston, MA: Houghton Mifflin, 2003.

HODGSON, William Noel. *Verse and Prose in Peace and War*. London: Smith, Elder & Co., 1917.

HOOKER, Mark T. "Frodo's Batman." *Tolkien Studies* 1.1 (2004): 125-36.

LIVINGSTON, Michael. "The Shell-shocked Hobbit: The First World War and Tolkien's Trauma of the Ring." *Baptism of Fire: The Birth of the Modern British Fantastic in World War I*. Ed. Janet Brennan Croft. Altadenta, CA: Mythopoeic Press, 2015, 9-22.

SETON HUTCHINSON, Graham. *Biography of a Batman*. London: Eyre and Spottiswoode. 1929. (Reprinted from *English Review*, August 1929. 211-222, where it was originally published under the name Graham Seton.)

TOLKIEN, J.R.R. *The Letters of J.R.R. Tolkien: A Selection*. Eds. Humphrey Carpenter and Christopher Tolkien. Boston, MA: Houghton Mifflin, 2000.

The Lord of the Rings: 50th Anniversary edition. Boston, MA: Houghton Mifflin, 2004.

Giovanni Costabile

'No Englander May Hinder Me': Éowyn the Highland Pipe Major and Other Highlights of Tolkien's Awareness of Sexual, Class and Ethnic Divisions in Wartime

In recent years, gender studies have focused more broadly on the complex field of relations between femininity and war. Among other things being thoroughly analyzed, a serious subject of research is the convoluted interplay of political, social and gender dynamics in wartime. In the *Introduction* to the 2012 Routledge volume *Making Gender, Making War: Violence, Military and Peacekeeping Practices*, editors Annika Kronsell and Erika Svedberg pointed out the following very clearly: "What happens in war is that sexual divisions become even deeper through war-making and so do class and ethnic divisions" (Kronsell and Svedberg 6).

Any Tolkien reader might see Tolkien's works as reflecting actual war-experiences in this respect. I shall offer two random examples of ethnic divisions. Hobbits are generally seen as unfit for war. Gondorians doubt Rohan's will to aid them in defending Minas Tirith under siege. Concerning class divisions, I think it is sufficient to observe how, in the same city of Minas Tirith, Pippin is saluted and celebrated in the streets, rather than once more diminished and despised, as soon as the rumour spreads: he is a Prince of the Halflings. Furthermore, sexual and age divisions are also represented: Beregond shows the same Pippin "the road to the vales of Tumladen and Lossarnach, and the mountain-villages, and then on to Lebennin [...] [where] go the last of the wains that bear away to refuge the aged, the children, and the women that must go with them" (*LotR* V.1.764).[1]

More relevant to the present article, in the character of Éowyn, especially if a proposed source was proved to be factual, Tolkien might have envisioned the coming together of the instances of the rights of alterities. Ethnic, political

1 A passage first related to Tolkien's war experience in Croft 16-17.

and social minorities[2] have more to do with women's rights[3] than might be immediately evident, as revealed in the face of the extreme peril and hardship of war, in a way which I shall now endeavour to explain.

If we take into account the crucial passage in *The Return of the King* where Éowyn tries to convince Aragorn to take her with him on his ride to the Paths of the Dead, she does not stress gender in her speech, but altogether the contrary: she sounds like gender is the last thing she wants to be taken into account. Instead the only thing that counts is nobility, entailing lordship and battle-prowess, and especially Eorl nobility. In fact, she repeatedly stresses her belonging to the House of Eorl: "But am I not of the House of Eorl, a shieldmaiden and not a dry-nurse?" and "I am of the House of Eorl and not a serving-woman. I can ride and wield blade, and I do not fear either pain or death" (*LotR* V.2.784).

In other words, here she is not claiming that womanhood is fit (or unfit) for war and fighting, but advocating the separation of the whole sphere of nobility and warfare from gender issues. She turns the gender prejudice into a class prejudice, thereby inverting the outcome: as a woman, she would be unfit for war. As a noble of the House of Eorl, war is what best suits her. If one puts the two scales of values together, she implies, it does not mean that woman (supposedly negative) and noble of the House of Eorl (positive) nullify each other in their opposition. On the contrary, she is stating that the positivity of Rohirric nobility is unquestionably greater than the alleged negativity of womanhood, thereby making her fit for war.

Moreover, she is trying to subtly insinuate that refusing her a chance to prove her worth in battle is an offence against the House of Eorl itself, either if it is done by Aragorn or even by other descendants of Eorl. She might as well have argued that leaving her behind meant to question the nobility of Eorl's blood, in her opinion recognized in theory but *de facto* here ignored. While this is noteworthy in its own right, it must become especially interesting in the light

2 I am aware there was some controversy about Tolkien's alleged racism, but I argue that this is preposterous, since Middle-earth is clearly a place where the cooperation of the different races and peoples is key to their prosperity. See Young. For a comprehensive treatment of the bibliography concerning racial issues in Tolkien's works, see Reid.

3 Tolkien was indeed interested in supporting women's advancement in society, especially in education, as it was clearly shown by Rateliff.

of the fact that two necessary consequences may be drawn from her words. In the first place, that there must have been some tradition of female warriors in the House of Eorl, or she could not have invented the term 'shieldmaiden' herself and used it as an argument.[4] Secondly, and perhaps more importantly, she is implying that the very association of military prowess and valour with manhood is accidental, whereas their occurrence does not in her opinion depend on gender at all, in either direction.

The irony in the whole thing is that, when Théoden had decided to appoint the regency to her in his absence, that was supposed to be a honour tributed to her, intended to recognize her value, not to question, or even diminish it, as also Aragorn points out to her.

> [Théoden said:] 'But to some one I must now entrust my people that I leave behind, to rule them in my place. Which of you will stay?'
>
> No man spoke.
>
> 'Is there none whom you would name? In whom do my people trust?'
>
> 'In the House of Eorl,' answered Háma.
>
> 'But Éomer I cannot spare, nor would he stay,' said the king; 'and he is the last of that House.'
>
> 'I said not Éomer,' answered Háma. 'And he is not the last. There is Éowyn, daughter of Éomund, his sister. She is fearless and high-hearted. All love her. Let her be as lord to the Eorlingas, while we are gone.'
>
> 'It shall be so,' said Théoden. 'Let the heralds announce to the folk that the Lady Éowyn will lead them!' (LotR III.6.523)

I would like to stress how neither Háma nor Théoden see her as powerless in her womanhood, nor question her valour, prowess, courage or strength. On the contrary, Háma says she should be "*as lord* to the Eorlingas" (my emphasis), thereby attributing her with both power and (spiritual) manhood. Théoden, even if he uses the more usual female title, "Lady," says that she "will *lead* them" (my emphasis), in all effects appointing her their *leader*. This, if anyone doubts it, is not a word intended to refer to a mere puppet who acts out the will of the true masters, but an active figure who holds real responsibility for their people and can theoretically even declare war and conduct an army on the battlefield.

4 On Éowyn and the Norse shieldmaiden tradition see Donovan, Wallace.

It is then clear that gender issues in Éowyn's case are intertwined with class-related concerns, as I stated I would prove. Furthermore, it is hardly ever pointed out an important aspect in her later powerfully and very impressively claiming her womanhood against the Witch King. Éowyn once more does not only claim her womanhood, as she was very superficially portrayed in the film adaptation by Peter Jackson. Instead she underlines her lineage once more. The Witch King hisses: "Hinder me? Thou fool, no living man may hinder me." And she replies: "But no living man am I! You look upon a woman. Éowyn I am, Éomund's daughter. You stand between me and my lord and kin. Begone, if you be not deathless!" (*LotR* V.6.841).

"Éomund's daughter" and "You stand between me and *my lord and kin*" (emphasis mine). In other words, she is saying that the royal blood runs through her veins because of her family, which implies she is bound to protect that same blood, even in other kinsmen. That is so both according to the "Germanic", or "feudal", law of the Eorlingas ("my lord") and because of that bond of kinship itself ("my kin").

This is even beyond class preoccupations, rather surpassing even the medieval and especially Germanic concern for loyalty, to delve deep into the tribal ancestorship of mankind as a whole. Something which makes a worthy pair to the Middle English poem *Sir Gawain and the Green Knight*. In fact, this 14th century alliterative poem is equally concerned with loyalty, also seen as related to womanhood. Besides, both stories hint in the direction of a remote and nowadays obscure European past.

This is also perhaps underlined by Tolkien in the meeting of the host of the Rohirrim (among whom Éowyn is disguised as Dernhelm, carrying Merry along) with the Wild Men of Ghân-buri-ghân during the ride towards Gondor. This episode might well parallel Gawain's fight with the *wodwos*, or Wild Men, on the way to the Green Chapel. In both cases there are heroes on an errand (which will almost certainly end up in death) having to face the wild nature (of their own hearts?) in a humanized form. To borrow a phrase from Lou Reed, they are "taking a walk on the wild side." After all, the fact that Tolkien seems to draw heavily from the medieval tradition of the Wild Men has been often pointed out.[5]

Besides, one of the most "deep-rooted" tales of the Middle Ages, apart from *Sir Gawain* and *Beowulf*, is probably *Le Roman de Silence*. This work precisely treats, once more in the common Arthurian framework, the subject of a woman disguised as a knight achieving wondrous feats of valour.[6] As C.S. Lewis points out,[7] stories were once concerned with the unusual and the exceptional rather than with the modern "depicting life as it is everyday." And what could have been more striking in a traditional society of the remote past than a proud female warrior? Therefore I think the substratum behind tales such as *Silence* might well be very old.

What, if anything, might Éowyn have to do with the Wild Men? I shall explain my idea. The shieldmaiden's warlike re-appropriation of her own femininity is vehemently tied in her own words to the tribal bonds which enforce the defence of leadership and kin at all costs. This fact implies that the whole thing must evoke a very primal picture to us: a scene of a primitive[8] tribe of long ago, when the culturization of gender had not yet become so widespread as it is today, not even as it was in the Middle Ages. Now, let us say this tribe is exposed to a violent attack by wild animals or another tribe, and has to employ

---

5 Flieger; Fimi, "Wildman".

6 Taken into account as possibly related to Éowyn in Linton.

7 "[W]e cannot help noticing that until quite modern times nearly all stories [...] belonged to the family of the *Oedipus*, not to that of *Middlemarch*. Just as all except bores relate in conversation not what is normal but what is exceptional – you mention having seen a giraffe in Petty Cury, but don't mention having seen an undergraduate – so authors told of the exceptional. [...] We can learn the world-wide and immemorial attitude of man to stories from noticing how stories are introduced in conversation. Men begin 'The strangest sight I ever saw was – ', or 'I'll tell you something queerer even than that', or 'Here's something you'll hardly believe'. Such was the spirit of nearly all stories before the nineteenth century" (Lewis 62-63).

8 By picturing this primitive scene I am by no mean trying to imply that Tolkien was a primitivist. Primitivism could easily become anti-moral, as the following comments by scholar Modris Eksteins to Igor Stravinskij's 1913 ballet *The Rite of Spring*, which represented a maiden who danced herself to death, prove: "devoid of readily identifiable moral purpose. Primitive, pre-ethical, pre-individual man was portrayed in nature. Rebirth, life, and death were depicted without obvious ethical comment. [...] In this portrayal of the continuity of life, fundamental, brutal, and tragic, beyond individual fate, there was no suggestion of sentiment. There was only energy, exultation, and necessity. The victim was not mourned but honored. The chosen maiden joined in the rite automatically, without sign of comprehension or interpretation. She submitted to a fate that transcended her. The theme was basic and at the same time brutal. If there was any hope, it was in the energy and fertility of life, not in morality." (Eksteins 50)

all of its forces in the desperate attempt to resist the attack, repel the enemies and survive as a whole.

In this situation, especially if there are many of them, and some of them are childless, women might well be sent to fight. Those who are not might have to fight all the same. And the defence of women by warriors of the tribe must share the first place among the defenders' concerns with the defence of each warrior's kin, and the defence of the leader(s). In other words, if we employ the terminology of gender studies, close relatives (the precise definition of 'close' might vary substantially depending on specific cultures) and leaders are feminized by dire situations of peril such as those which are recurrent in warfare. Feminized in both senses, negative and positive: they are seen as weak, no matter what the actual reality of their powers might be, and they are seen as incomparably precious.

I should then sum up my argument as far as class and family issues are concerned: Éowyn is actually arguing that there are three feminines in society: the individual feminine (a given woman), the familial feminine (which includes the affections of all members of the family towards each other, and not only females) and the sociopolitical feminine (loyalty and duty to protect and save the leaders). And, she claims, the sociopolitical is the most important, to which the familial and the individual can be sacrificed, while the individual can also be sacrificed to the familial.

Loyalty, and sacrifice: this is what, I argue, creates the shieldmaiden, the invincible woman who defeats Death itself, at least if we believe the Witch King claiming he is Death. And this is also very hard to process for modern readers, who might like the abstract idea of the powerful woman, but live in a society where the idea of patriotic sacrifice seems something very distant, rather belonging to their grandfathers, or even great-grandfathers. But loyalty and sacrifice are no doubt ways to relate to alterity which valourize it, and in their valourizing it both gender and other forms of alterity are restored to their supreme dignity.

Enough with family and class. Instead there is still another kind of divisions based on alterity which have been mentioned earlier and which war terribly proves and stresses: I am referring to the ethnic divisions. As related to Éowyn's story, there are two ethnic groups which are seen as different and, at least potentially, inferior to Gondorians: the Rohirrim and the Hobbits. The Hobbits are seen as different and frowned upon also in Rohan, thus commenting on the fact that everyone is both (seen as) superior and inferior to someone else (in any respect), and inviting to the suspension of arrogance and to humility.

The role played by Merry in the killing of the Witch-king is also crucial, which means that ethnic variables (the Hobbits as a different race) and age variables (the Hobbits as childlike) also come into play in this very powerful scene. Returning to the primitive picture I envisioned, it is obvious that, once women are forced by circumstance to fight, children must also be ready to help the fighters. It is less obvious why a different race, or people, or tribe, seen as inferior, should enter this picture.

But then we have to take the history of our imagined tribe into account. Probably our tribe had previous fights with beasts as well as with other hostile tribes, and in the latter case someone was taken prisoner and made into a slave, or maybe even might have joined the enemy. Primitiveness is no prejudice against either recruitment or betrayal. Both, in fact, are very primal social phenomena. And in both cases the newcomer into the tribe has to earn the respect and the full acceptance of the tribe members, which implies there will be prejudice and resistance against him.

Indeed war (or the attack of beasts or other tribes which we imagined, in the case of the primitive tribe) is precisely one of the best situations in which to prove oneself and get the aforesaid acceptance and respect, and this is exactly what Merry does among the Rohirrim, as Pippin also does among the Gondorians. But in both cases it is the threat of death to the leader and to the kinsman which empowers the feminine, as in women, also in children and even in well-meaning foreigners. If saving the leader reveals the feminine as a virtue in a woman, it must also reveal the foreign element as a virtue in a foreigner. The heroic gesture does not cancel femininity nor one's being foreign, but it revaluates and transvaluates them, showing them as they are, or at least as they can be: good, very good.

The Rohirrim's case in Gondor seems considerably easier: since they appear like the saviours who come in the moment of utmost need to save the day, nobody would point out that they are also frowned upon in Gondor, but the truth is that, behind a longlasting alliance, there are also some hidden seeds of Gondorian pride and prejudice towards Rohan. This is no doubt what the saviours would have had to face as a welcome from the Steward, had Denethor not taken his own life. He was already so darkened in his mind that he might have talked to them as Saruman does to Théoden in Orthanc, calling them Northern Barbarians and other things. But then perhaps it is not a coincidence that Denethor's death and Éowyn's feat of extraordinary valour are roughly simultaneous. Éomer might cry: "Death!" after seeing his sister wounded in the field, but what she represents is Life in both its tremendous power and its fragile delicacy, which often go together.

And Tolkien certainly did not learn about this only in books, but personally experienced many different things, when he served in the British Army as a Signal Officer in the Great War. To begin with, I have two remarks. In the first place, I would like to point out how what I have said so far concerning the Lady of Rohan and Meriadoc Brandybuck is possibly rooted in Tolkien's First World War experience through two poems also cited in John Garth's fundamental work *Tolkien and the Great War*. Secondly, I wish to rehearse what I already stated in a previously published article, where I proposed among other ideas a suggestion of mine in particular which I had the pleasure to discuss personally with Verlyn Flieger, who agreed there was at least a good possibility I had a point.

John Garth compares two quotes from very famous poems, the first one from the Anglo-Saxon *The Battle of Maldon* (although Tolkien points out that these lines are not key to the poem as much as they have been usually taken to be):[9] "Hige sceal þe heardra, heorte þe cenre, / mod sceal þe mare þe ure maegen lytlað" (124). These same lines are later (than 1915) translated by Tolkien himself as: "Will shall be the sterner, heart the bolder, spirit the greater as our strength lessens" (Garth 71). I think it is clear how this applies very well to Éowyn, whose stern will, bold heart and great spirit are revealed precisely by

9 "They are the best-known lines of the poem, possibly of all Old English verse. Yet except in the excellence of the expression, they seem to me of less interest than the earlier lines [89-90]" (*HBBS* 143).

desperate situations when the strength of her people and allies was lessened. The same applies to Merry.

The second quote is from a poem which we are not sure Tolkien read, and we might even doubt that, if he had read it, he would have appreciated it. In fact, it was read by Garth as if it "implied that a soldier's worth to his nation was greater in death than life" (71). It is a poem by Rupert Brooke, titled *The Soldier*, the famous ending of which reads: "If I should die, think only this of me: / That there's some corner of a foreign field / That is for ever England" (qtd. in Garth 72).

It does not seem to me that this means a dead soldier is better than a live one. It would rather appear as a way of consoling relatives for one's own death, which was not a remote possibility after all on the front. In fact, Garth himself relates that "G.B. Smith admired Brooke's poetry and thought Tolkien should read it" (72), something which I do not find surprising, coming as it does from the man who himself wrote:

> O God, the God of battles,
> To us who intercede,
> Give only strength to follow
> Until there's no more need,
> And grant us at that ending
> Of the unkindly quest
> To come unto the quiet isles
> Beyond Death's starry West.
> ("Intercessional")

Neither does it seem to me a big stretch of the imagination to picture the shieldmaiden of the Rohirrim declaring: "If I should die, think only this of me: / That there's some corner of a foreign field / That is forever Rohan." Admittedly it would be harder for Merry to say anything like that as related to the Shire, and yet picturing home and the Shire when abroad is something Hobbits do all the time in the tale, and especially when things get particularly difficult. It is only the colonialist side of the statement which makes it so hard to connect it with the Shire, whose inhabitants are generally so glad to stay within their borders.

The unintended irony which results if we apply the words of G.B. Smith's poem to Éowyn's situation is also interesting.[10] By unintended irony I mean the irony that consists in the fact that *following* means two distinct actions. On one hand, it means to obey orders, and that is what she does not do by leaving Meduseld to take part in the ride of the Rohirrim. On the other hand, *following* also means to actually go after someone, and that is precisely what she does, since she leaves the Golden Hall after Théoden.

And, having mentioned G.B. Smith, I can proceed to propose my second point by recalling how Smith and Rob Gilson were on the front when John Ronald had barely begun attending the training (December 1914). Apart from noting how peculiar it is that lateness was permitted in times when any suitable youth was enrolled, I shall briefly recall one thing. In a previous article of mine I argued that the poem "Goblin Feet" might actually be read as a metaphor for Tolkien's desire to go to the front. A similar desire might be caused by the fact that, back then, in England whoever had not was openly frowned upon,[11] as much as by the awareness that all his friends had. Therefore he might well have felt as much left behind by the "padding feet" of his dear goblin- and leprechaun-friends (the other T.C.B.S. members) as the lyrical *I* in the poem was (Costabile 48). "O! the magic! o! the sorrow when it dies!" This might also explain why he later hated this poem so much, as he might have later connected it with their deaths (except with Christopher Wiseman's, though, which was many, many years ahead).

This is especially pertinent to my present treatment because, while Janet Brennan Croft connects Éowyn's anxiety at being left behind with Edith's (71),[12] I cannot recall anybody connecting the former's wish to actually fight with Tolkien's

---

10 Obviously, instead, Death's starry West, which to us readers of Tolkien sounds so much like Aman, if so taken, could much better be seen as a thought by Frodo, or Bilbo. And, even so, by calling it "Death's", it would either remind us of Tolkien's early concepts of Valinor as the Afterlife, discussed by Christopher Tolkien in *The Book of Lost Tales: Part I*, or inspire in us some memory of the speech on the Afterlife between Gandalf and Pippin in the scene in the siege of Minas Tirith from Peter Jackson's *The Return of the King*, a scene which is actually a transposition of words intended for a very different context in the books.

11 Garth recalls Tolkien's own later words: "In those days chaps joined up, or were scorned publicly. It was a nasty cleft to be in" (qtd. 41).

12 See also M. Smith, who cites Croft and further discusses the subject (207).

own wish to face the front for his country, in a war which "is for all the evil of our own side with large view good against evil" (*Letters* 10).[13]

It goes without saying that Tolkien was not a woman nor had any kind of impediment preventing his getting into action. Nevertheless, the psychological dilemma whether to go or not was complicated by more than just the public scorn toward people seen as cowards. Even more than the very human fear of death which every man in war faces. There was also the prospect of having to leave his wife behind, maybe never seeing her again. And furthermore there was the concurrent desire, perhaps even supported by his mentor Joseph Wright, to finish his degree before going.

So, when he was writing the scene of the Lady of Rohan's appointment to regent, the dialogue between her and Aragorn, and perhaps even her bold defiance in the face of the Witch King's terrifying presence of Death, Tolkien might well have drawn from his own personal feelings and experience in World War One. This could very well be true besides any reference to Edith, which is not my purpose to contradict, but only to add to the broader picture and perhaps show something more of its inherent complexity.

In fact someone might even, as Carpenter actually did, call into question the notion that Tolkien is representing women in war at all through his female characters. He cites a passage from C.S. Lewis' *The Four Loves* in this light: "What were the women doing meanwhile? How should I know? I am a man and never spied on the mysteries of the Bona Dea" (qtd. in Carpenter 153).

Now, apart from the fact that Lewis is clearly ironic in his statement here,[14] I would like to make it explicit that I do not intend to suggest that there might be something of Tolkien in Éowyn. On the contrary, I hope it is seen as I myself

13 This statement is in my opinion unjustly underestimated by Garth, when he lists all the reasons for Tolkien's expected predisposition to respond to Kitchener's call to arms straightaway. In fact Garth does not include a sense of morality, although he writes that Tolkien "felt a duty to crown and country." But it is not only to the King and to England that Tolkien was going eventually to respond, but also to his own conscience, and not only because he "was Catholic, whereas the German invaders [...] were Lutheran zealots who raped nuns and slaughtered priests. He was outraged by the German destruction of Louvain [and] its library of 230,000 books that included hundreds of unique medieval manuscripts" (41).

14 He did write an entire novel, *That Hideous Strength*, devoting half of the chapters to the point of view of an English middle-class wife of the 20th century's, while she is forced to come to terms with her own special call and the reality of a supernatural threat.

see it: a hypothesis which, were it to be proven, would further stress how much in Tolkien's works there is a balance between the masculine and the feminine which entails the presence of a masculine aspect inside women and a feminine side of men, as Melanie A. Rawls aptly put it.[15]

It was also a good way to introduce what should now seem a quite more modest proposal. On 22 July 2015 Michael Flowers posted an article of his on the Tolkien Society webpage, in which he made known the finding of a Tolkien head-and-shoulder portrait realized by Glasgow's official Great War artist Frederick Arthur Farrell. It was first published in the Australian Catholic newspaper *The Advocate* on 9 August 1934.

Portrait of Professor J.R.R. Tolkien by Frederick A. Farrell, published in *The Advocate*, Melburne on 9 August 1934 (published with the permission of the MDHC Catholic Archdiocese of Melbourne)

15 Rawls might have devised the concept by herself, but it is interesting to notice that, although she is undoubtedly the first to specifically apply it to Tolkien's literature, the theory was first formulated by Otto Weininger as a sexual philosophy of character in his controversial 1903 work titled *Sex and Character*.

As Michael Flowers reported, the text which accompanied the article was:

> Professor John Tolkien has been Rawlinson and Bosworth Professor of Anglo-Saxon in Oxford University since 1925. He served with the Lancashire Fusiliers from 1915-18. Born of a South African family in 1892, he was educated at the King Edward VI. School, Birmingham, and Exeter College, Oxford. He was Professor of English Language in Leeds University in 1924-5.

In the article there is also an extensive biography of Fred A. Farrell, too long to report here, as well as the report that esteemed Tolkien scholar Charles Noad thinks the portrait was taken from life but not earlier than 1932. Also further information about *The Advocate* is included:

> In 1934 *The Advocate* was a six-penny weekly newspaper specialising in supplying newsworthy items to Catholics in Melbourne, Australia. *The Advocate* still appears today, but is now a monthly magazine and a web page. The feature itself appeared in the regular column, "A Letter from London", but the only clue as to authorship was that it was supplied by "*The Advocate's* Special Correspondent." In 1930 and earlier the column was supplied by a named author, Denis Gwynn.

It is especially interesting that Charles Noad thinks the portrait was taken from life, because it means that Farrell and Tolkien probably met; although we cannot be completely certain in this respect, we cannot either exclude the possibility. A possibility which meant that Farrell could have mentioned to Tolkien another of his works, a World War I painting titled: *'"Surrender Englander!" / 8th Argyll incident'* or *'Surrender Englander!' – Neuville St. Vaast.* Tolkien obviously might also have otherwise known the painting, or the episode it pictures.

The painting, reproduced in black-and-white on the following page, is found in the artbook *Fred A. Farrell, Glasgow's War Artist* (51),[16] accompanied by this text:

> This poster-like propagandist piece is a reconstruction of a much recounted event that reportedly took place in April 1916. During darkness a German officer climbed the barbed wire, pointed his revolver into a British trench and shouted, 'Surrender Englander!' An NCO of the 8th Argyll & Sutherland Highlanders, who was stationed in the trench, had a hand grenade in his hand. Without pulling the pin, he threw it at the German, shouting, 'I am no Englander; I'm a Scotsman!' The force of the blow killed the German. Apparently it was

16 The black-and-white rendition of the picture can, of course, only hint at the effect of the painting on the viewer. For full effect, have a look at the full colour rendition in Meacock or as found on the internet.

later discovered from German prisoners that this incident prevented a further attack. (Meacock)

Painting 'Surrender Englander!' – Neuville St Vaast by Frederick A. Farrell

I think it is evident how, if the episode and/or the painting were known to Tolkien, it would be very hard to argue that the scene of Éowyn confronting the Witch King was completely independent from the "8th Argyll incident". This observation would apply even if the influence was only present in the leaf-mould of Tolkien's mind. In fact, "Thou fool, no living man may hinder me!" works very well as an epic analogue to the intimation "Surrender Englander!" And there is more: in fact, both of the exclamations are immediately subverted. In *The Lord of the Rings* we read Éowyn's powerful reply: "But no living man am I! You look upon a woman." In the previously cited version of the "8th Argyll incident" we find the Scotsman yelling to the German soldier: "I am no Englander! I am a Scotsman!" The result of the action, the killing of the enemy, is also the same.

Therefore, if this parallel was correct as an influence, we would have even further proof than what I already argued in the rest of the present writing. Proof, i.e. according to Tolkien gender issues are related to the instances of other groups who are too often unjustly prevaricated and oppressed in Western societies, today as a century ago. In the specific case, Tolkien would be advocating the rights of the so-called Celtic minorities in the British Empire,[17] which is not too surprising for a whole series of reasons. First of all, since Tolkien was a great lover of "things Celtic" himself.[18] He owned a Celtic library[19] and travelled to both Ireland and Scotland for conferences (*Letters* 219). Furthermore, one of his favourite languages was Welsh.

Further research into the "8th Argyll incident" produced interesting results, and at the very least I argue that what I found might be of interest in order to evaluate the other possibility, i.e. that Tolkien might have known the episode before meeting Farrell. In fact, the 8th Argyll was the most distinguished even among the implacable Territorial Battalions of the outstanding 51st Highland Division. The book *The Argyll and Sutherland Highlanders* makes it evident in their words:

---

17 Which might also be related to the often-proposed Celtic connection of Éowyn to Boudica, the female leader of the British Celtic Iceni tribe who rebelled against the Romans in 60-61 AD.

18 Fimi, "Tolkien's 'Celtic' Type of Legends".

19 The full contents of which are going to be published in Cilli.

> Volumes could be, and indeed have been, written on the achievements of the five Territorial battalions and six Service battalions which the Argylls put into the field between 1914 and 1918. Special mention should perhaps be made of the 8th Argyllshire Battalion, the most genuinely Highland of all, which distinguished itself even within the 51st Highland Division which the Germans listed as one of the most formidable fighting formations in the Allied Army. (McElwee 27)

This is also confirmed by van de Pas, when she writes: "That the 51st Highland Division – paradoxically mainly composed of Lowland Scots – was the most popular British Division of all at home should surprise no one by now" (15). She thereafter cites in support of this statement no less than four other historians.[20]

From Craig F. French, the author of the 2006 book *The 51st (Highland) Division during the First World War*, it is possible to learn more about the 8th Argyll, for example that their being "the most genuinely Highland of all," to cite McElwee, might also lead to feuds amongst divisions. In particular, the 6th Division was seen by the 8th as unfit to call themselves Highlanders, since the "distinction between the 1/8th Battalion and the others in the regiment was essentially to set apart the 1/8th as a purer body of fighting men in the proper martial traditions of the Highland clansmen" (French 2006). This might conceivably be compared to the elitism of the House of Eorl in Rohan, and Éowyn's astonished remarks that she has been left home while she is one of the Eorlingas.

There I also read that "Military piping was another signifier of Scottish culture and was very prominent in the 51st Division during the First World War. The sight of the piper and the sound of the pipes often affected officers and men in a highly emotional way, conjuring up an array of images that inspired them to 'do their duty'" (French 161).

Fascinated by the idea that the NCO might be a Piper, and already imagining fantastic parallels between the horns of Rohan and the Scottish pipes,[21] I

20 Spiers (4-17, 203-214); MacKenzie (226); Attridge (45-46), Devine (84).

21 Concerning parades and marches involving the pipe band, Major-General Harper "was decidedly the right man for this somewhat feudal gathering of the clans. Moreover, he knew how to stimulate this feeling. For state and other occasions he massed the pipers of his three infantry brigades – a retreat played by a hundred and more pipers was worth coming some distance to hear. Once heard and seen it was not easily forgotten" (cited French 162). Although the author mentions retreats instead of charges, I cannot help, when I read about a "somewhat feudal gathering of the clans," but to picture the Rohirrim blowing their horns upon their arrival to the Pelennor Fields.

consulted *The Pipes of War: A Record of the Achievements of Pipers of Scottish and Overseas Regiments during the War 1914-18*, written by Brevet-Colonel Bruce Seton and Pipe-Major John Grant. Therein I checked the documents concerning Scottish Pipers in the Argyll & Sutherland Highlanders. I found that in the 8th Argyll they had 29 pipers, plus a Lance Corporal, two Pipe Majors, a Captain, four Lieutenants, an Adjutant and a Quartermaster Lieutenant. In the Great War 9 of the pipers were wounded, including the Lance Corporal, 6 were invalided, including a Pipe Major, and one was awarded a Military Medal at the Somme in July 1916. The Pipe Major who was not invalided was also awarded a Divisional certificate for gallant conduct by the Division Commander in May 1916.

Since the medal was awarded to a private, while our NCO was obviously an officer, I was rather struck by the Divisional certificate tributed to the Pipe Major, and, upon further search within the book, I found the following record:

> Pipe Major J. Wilson, 8th Argyll and Sutherland Highlanders: On the 8th April, 1916, a German raiding party of considerable strength entered our trenches in the Labyrinth after the explosion of several mines which inflicted heavy casualties. Pipe Major Wilson at once organised a counter attack and drove out the enemy. He received a Divisional certificate of gallant conduct. (Seton and Grant 58)

I think all the evidence of the case points toward the identification of the NCO officer with Pipe Major J. Wilson, even though the actual reality of the events might have been romanticised in the telling, becoming what we read in the text attached to Farrell's painting and see in his painting itself.

Although complete certainty cannot be assured, I think that the fact that the 51st Highlanders was the most popular division back home also means quite a few things. It certainly entails that stories about them travelled a lot, especially those concerning heroic deeds, which lifted the morals of the troops and encouraged them to keep their position and their obedience to superiors. Tolkien might well have heard of the extraordinary undertaking of Pipe Major J. Wilson, either in a report which mentioned his name or not. The story might have reached him already in a popular "romantic" form, but even so it might have conceivably maintained a grain of truth (and who knows whether or not the Major actually did shout that he was a Scotsman).[22] Maybe Tolkien was inspired by this story when, many years later, he devised the story of Éowyn for his new book *The Lord of the Rings*.[23] Perhaps meanwhile he had also seen Fred A. Farrell's painting of the scene, when the painter had come to meet him to sketch his portrait. Or perhaps that was the very first occasion when Tolkien learnt about the story. We cannot claim for sure that he never knew anything of it, but personally I think it possible he did. Words have a tendency to escape one's tongue, things in common tend to be shared, and soldiers especially talk a lot, because they have to avoid, as long as they can, the thought of their own death. Posing for a portrait inevitably leads to a conversation with the artist, and the subjects of the ensuing exchange might be unpredictable, as well as very predictable.

Thus, in the end, we can return to the initial quote and confirm that in times of war divisions based on gender, class, and ethnic identity are stressed much more than the usual, so much so that war might be an occasion for solidarity amongst despised categories and lead to some form of overcoming of the (perceived) difference between sexes, and between social and ethnic groups.[24]

Enlisted soldiers came to the Western Front in the Great War carrying books of legends such as the *Iliad* and the *Mabinogion*.[25] Some of them, though, would also bring back legends from the Front, as J.R.R. Tolkien and arguably Pipe Major J. Wilson did. Tolkien would write *The Book of Lost Tales* and Wilson would probably bring home the pride of having become a legend himself. And,

22 We should not underestimate the probability that a prominent role in the extraordinary prowess showed by Wilson was actually played by the aforementioned Major-General Harper's "views on the importance of the inculcation of initiative" (French 54). Harper thought that soldiers should not depend completely on superiors but also be able to take decisions and bear the ensuing responsibility based on their own rights.

23 Incidentally, during another World War.

24 M. Smith defines the Lady of Rohan after her decision to accept Faramir's love as a realized "foreign war-bride [...] perhaps symbolizing the way in which the women of his time aided the reforging of society after the war, and the bravery with which they and their husbands faced a new post-war culture, determined to look forward and heal the ravages that war had wreaked upon their way of life" (216). I would like to propose to stress the foreign element in marriage much more, consistently with all of what I stated in the present writing. A foreign war-bride is a further invitation for her husband (and hopefully vice-versa as well) to reconsider things in a new light and offers Recovery through a detachment from trite possessivity, as Tolkien describes the effects of the Fairy-story in *OFS*. Surely marriage can be a Fairy-story, if so many Fairy-stories end up with Eucatastrophic marriages.

25 "Although the stereotypical picture of the Western Front does not include soldiers reading the *Mabinogion* with its Welsh Arthuriana, as G.B. Smith did, or William Morris's *The Earthly Paradise*, which Tolkien carried, in fact quest literature was profoundly popular" (Garth 296).

perhaps, who knows, the former might also, even unknowingly, have made immortal the legend of the latter and brought it into the realm of transcendental Myth. In the process the tale acquired a form which was transfigured by the writer's love for his own wife and by the power of his imagination, thereby turning the whole episode into the heroic adventure of Éowyn, the shield-maiden of Rohan. Or, why not, Éowyn, the 51st Highland Division 8th Argyll & Sutherland Battalion Pipe Major.

Bibliography

Attridge, Steve. *Nationalism, Imperialism, and Identity in Late Victorian Culture: Civil and Military Worlds.* Basingstoke and New York City, NY: Palgrave Macmillan, 2003.

Carpenter, Humphrey. *J.R.R. Tolkien: A Biography.* 2nd ed. London: Harper Collins, 2002.

Cilli, Oronzo. *Tolkien's Library: An Annotated Checklist.* Edinburgh: Luna Press Publishing, forthcoming 2019.

Costabile, Giovanni Carmine. "The Trumpets of Faërie and the Great War." *Inklings Jahrbuch für Literatur und Ästhetik* 34 (2017): 45-52.

Croft, Janet Brennan. *War and the Works of J.R.R. Tolkien.* Westport, CT, and London: Praeger, 2004.

Devine, Thomas Martin. *Clanship to Crofter's War: The Social Transformation of the Scottish Highlands.* Manchester: Manchester University Press, 1994.

Donovan, Leslie A. "The Valkyrie Reflex in J.R.R. Tolkien's *The Lord of the Rings*: Galadriel, Shelob, Éowyn and Arwen." *Perilous and Fair: Women in the Works and Life of J.R.R. Tolkien.* Eds. Janet Brennan Croft and Leslie A. Donovan. Altadena, CA: Mythopoeic Press, 2015, 221-257.

Eksteins, Modris. *Rites of Spring: The Great War and the Birth of the Modern Age.* New York City, NY: Houghton Mifflin, 1989.

Fimi, Dimitra. "Tolkien's 'Celtic' Type of Legends: Merging Traditions." *Tolkien Studies* 4 (2007): 51-71.

"Wildman of the Woods: Inscribing Tragedy on the Landscape of Middle-earth in *The Children of Húrin.*" *Tolkien: The Forest and the City.* Eds. Helen Conrad-O'Briain and Gerald Hynes. Dublin: Four Courts Press, 2013, 43-56.

FLIEGER, Verlyn. "Tolkien's Wild Men from Medieval to Modern." *Green Suns and Faerie: Essays on J. R. R. Tolkien*. Kent, OH: Kent State University Press, 2012, 115-126.

FLOWERS, Michael. "1934 Sketch of Tolkien Discovered." *Tolkien Society*. July 2015. https://www.tolkiensociety.org/blog/2015/07/1934-sketch-of-tolkien-discovered/. 11 Aug. 2018.

FRENCH, Craig F. *The 51st (Highland) Division during the First World War*. PhD Thesis. University of Glasgow, 2012.

GARTH, John. *Tolkien and the Great War: The Threshold of Middle-earth*. London: Harper Collins, 2003.

KRONSELL, Annika and Erika SVEDBERG (eds.). *Making Gender, Making War: Violence, Military and Peacekeeping Practices*. New York City, NY and London: Routledge, 2012.

"A Letter from London." *The Advocate*, 9 Aug. 1934. https://trove.nla.gov.au/newspaper/article/171898324?searchTerm=tolkien&searchLimits/. 11. Aug. 2018.

LEWIS, C.S. *An Experiment in Criticism*. Cambridge: Cambridge University Press, 1967.

LINTON, Phoebe A. "Speech and Silence in *The Lord of the Rings*: Medieval Romance and the Transitions of Éowyn." *Perilous and Fair: Women in the Works and Life of J.R.R. Tolkien*. Eds. Janet Brennan Croft and Leslie A. Donovan. Altadena, CA: Mythopoeic Press, 2015, 258-280.

MACKENZIE, John M. "Empire and National Identities the Case of Scotland." *Transactions of the Royal Historical Society* 8 (1998): 215-231.

MCELWEE, William Lloyd. *Argyll & Sutherland Highlanders*. Oxford: Osprey Publishing, 1972.

MEACOCK, Joanna et al. *Fred A. Farrell Glasgow's War Artist*. Glasgow: Philip Wilson Publishers, 2014.

RATELIFF, John D. "The Missing Women: J.R.R. Tolkien's Lifelong Support for Women's Higher Education." *Perilous and Fair: Women in the Works and Life of J.R.R. Tolkien*. Eds. Janet Brennan Croft and Leslie A. Donovan. Altadena, CA: Mythopoeic Press, 2015, 204-220.

REID, Robin Anne. "Race in Tolkien Studies: A Bibliographic Essay." *Tolkien and Alterity*. Eds. Christopher Vaccaro and Yvette Kisor. New York City, NY: Palgrave Macmillan, 2017, 33-74.

SETON, Bruce and John GRANT. *The Pipes of War: A Record of the Achievements of Pipers of Scottish and Overseas Regiments during the War 1914-18*. Glasgow: MacLehose, Jackson & Co., 1920.

SMITH, Geoffrey Bache. "Intercessional." *A Spring Harvest*. Ed. J.R.R. Tolkien. London: Erskine MacDonald, 1918.

SMITH, Melissa A. "At Home and Abroad: Éowyn's Two-fold Figuring as War Bride in *The Lord of the Rings*." *Perilous and Fair: Women in the Works and Life of J.R.R. Tolkien*. Eds. Janet Brennan Croft and Leslie A. Donovan. Altadena, CA: Mythopoeic Press, 2015, 204-220.

SPIERS, Edward M. *The Scottish Soldier and Empire, 1854-1902*. Edinburgh: Edinburgh University Press, 2006.

TOLKIEN, J.R.R. "Goblin Feet." *The Annotated Hobbit*. Ed. Douglas A. Anderson. 2nd ed. Boston, MA: Houghton Mifflin, 2002, 113.

"The Homecoming of Beorhtnoth Beorhthelm's Son." *Tree and Leaf, Mythopoeia, the Homecoming of Beorhtnoth Beorhthelm's Son*. New ed. London: HarperCollinsPublishers, 2001.

The Letters of J.R.R. Tolkien: A Selection. Eds. Humphrey Carpenter and Christopher Tolkien. 1st Houghton Mifflin pbk. ed. Boston, MA: Houghton Mifflin, 2000.

The Lord of the Rings. 50th Anniversary edition. Boston, MA: Houghton Mifflin, 2004.

VAN DE PAS, Brigitte. *World War One through Scottish Eyes. Scots and Identity in the British Army during the First World War*. MA Thesis. Leiden University, 2015.

WALLACE, Anna. "A Wild Shieldmaiden of the North: Éowyn of Rohan and Old Norse Literature." *Philament* 17 (2011). The University of Sydney. https://philamentjournal.wordpress.com/issue17/. 11 Aug. 2018.

WEININGER, Otto. *Sex and Character*. New York City, NY and Chicago, IL: A.L. Burt Company, 1906.

YOUNG, Helen. "Diversity and Difference: Cosmopolitanism and *The Lord of the Rings*." *Journal of the Fantastic in the Arts* 21.3 (2010).

Janet Brennan Croft is Liaison to the School of Communication and Information and Librarian for Disability Services and Copyright at Rutgers University Libraries. She is the author of *War in the Works of J.R.R. Tolkien* and editor of *Baptism of Fire: The Birth of the Modern British Fantastic in World War I*. She has also written on the Peter Jackson films, J.K. Rowling, Terry Pratchett, Lois McMaster Bujold, *Orphan Black*, and other topics, and is editor of the refereed scholarly journal *Mythlore*.

Annika Röttinger completed her Master of Arts in Military History at Leibniz University, Hannover, with a thesis that examines the Great War experiences of J.R.R. Tolkien and their impact on *The Lord of the Rings*. Her Bachelor thesis explores similarities between Tolkien's Rohirrim and the Anglo-Saxons. She has also given talks and published articles on these topics. An active member of the German Tolkien Society, Röttinger is the Commissioner for International Connections and is also responsible for many other duties.

Tom Shippey is a notable Tolkien scholar and professor of philology. Author of acclaimed books *The Road to Middle-earth*, *J.R.R. Tolkien: Author of the Century*, and *Roots and Branches: Selected Papers on Tolkien*, the latter published with Walking Tree Publishers. He has also appeared in numerous documentaries, including on *The Lord of the Rings* film trilogy DVDs. Tom Shippey taught at six universities in the UK and US, and for a time held Tolkien's old Chair at Leeds, as well as playing rugby (like Tolkien) for Old Edwardians. In addition to his work on Tolkien, he has also published books on Old English, medievalism, and now the literature of Old Norse (*Laughing Shall I Die*).

John M. Bourne was formerly Senior Lecturer in Modern History and Director of the Centre for First World War Studies at the University of Birmingham, and is currently Honorary Professor of First World War Studies at the University of Wolverhampton. He is a Fellow of the Royal Historical Society and Vice-

President of the Western Front Association. Bourne is best known as the author of *Britain in the Great War 1914-1918*, *Who's Who in World War One*, co-editor of *Douglas Haig: War Diaries and Letters*, and the author of many articles and studies on the topic.

Glenn Peterson received his BS & MS in Aerospace Engineering from San Diego State University. Following two years of work at Johnson Space Center for Unisys designing simulations for astronaut training, he entered the doctoral program at the University of Texas at Austin where he received his PhD in 1997. Since then he has worked in the Astrodynamics Department of The Aerospace Corporation on a variety of topics including the Leonid meteor showers, formation flying of satellites, and collision analysis. Peterson has authored many papers on these topics and has written a book on the threat posed to orbiting satellites by meteor showers. He is also currently a student in the Masters program at Signum University.

Tal Tovy is Senior Lecturer at the History Department at Bar Ilan University, Israel. He holds a PhD from Haifa University, Israel, and his field of research focuses on Western Military Art and Science, specifically US Military History and US Foreign Policy since 1945, as well as terror, guerilla and counterinsurgency studies.

John Rosegrant is a clinical psychologist and psychoanalyst whose private practice with adults, teens, and children is in New Orleans. Rosegrant has published widely in the psychoanalytic literature on topics including psychoanalytic technique, short-term psychotherapy, play therapy, dreams, fairy tales, Tolkien, Harry Potter, and the World of Warcraft computer games. In the Tolkien literature Rosegrant has published "Tolkien's Dialogue between Enchantment and Loss" and "From the Ineluctable Wave to the Realization of Imagined Wonder" (both in *Mythlore*), and "Bilbo Baggins, Harry Potter, and the Fate of Enchantment" in the book *Critical Insights: The Hobbit.*

Michael Flowers graduated in English Language and Literature at the University of Hull and obtained an MPhil on the Victorian supernatural stories of Ellen [Mrs Henry] Wood at the University of Sheffield. He works as a teacher of natural history in East Yorkshire, and has been researching Tolkien's time in the area since 2012. Flowers has given several talks at Tolkien Society events and has contributed recent articles to *Amon Hen* and the Tolkien Society Website and blog.

Wilhelm Kuehs holds a PhD in German Literature and Comparatistics from the University of Klagenfurt. He is part of the science staff of the institute for Cultural Analysis at the University of Klagenfurt. Kuehs has published on mythologies, semiotics, and difficult heritage as well as on Tolkien's semiotics and his *On Fairy-stories* in the yearbook of the German Tolkien Society, *Hither Shore.*

John Garth is internationally recognised for his groundbreaking work on the creative development of J.R.R. Tolkien in the context of his times. *Tolkien and the Great War*, his 2003 biographical study exploring the invention of Middle-earth against the backdrop of the First World War, won the Mythopoeic Award for Inklings Scholarship. Ongoing research has produced a further study, *Tolkien at Exeter College*, on the formative undergraduate years. While a fellow of the Black Mountain Institute, Garth began work on his current project, to be titled *Tolkien's Mirror*. Garth has contributed biographical chapters to the book accompanying the major 2018 Bodleian exhibition, *Tolkien: Maker of Middle-earth*, and to the *Blackwell Companion to J.R.R. Tolkien*.

Łukasz Neubauer received his PhD in English Philology from the University of Łódź. He is a researcher and lecturer at the University of Koszalin, Poland, where he teaches courses on Tolkien and Lewis, Old English literature, and the Arthurian romances. Apart from his publications dealing with various medieval as well as Christian influences and resonances in *The Lord of the Rings*, he has written papers on *The Battle of Maldon*, *Beowulf*, *Hêliand*, Icelandic sagas and the so-called "beasts of battle" trope in, particularly but not exclusively, Old Germanic poetry.

Victoria Holtz Wodzak earned her doctorate from the University of Missouri-Columbia in medieval literature. She teaches literature and writing classes at Viterbo University in La Crosse, Wisconsin. She dates her love of Tolkien from her earliest days as a reader when she was given her first set of his books at the age of seven. One of the very first things she learned from Tolkien's books was that the best thing to do when you reach the end of a good book is to start over from the beginning.

Molly Volanth Hall is a doctoral candidate and instructor of literature at University of Rhode Island. Her dissertation focuses on the constitutive entanglements of the British national subject in landscape representation within modernist responses to World War I. Her work is forthcoming in the journal *Interdisciplinary Studies in Literature and the Environment* and she is also co-editing a collection of essays, *Affective Ecologies of the Modernist Body,* with University Press of Florida.

Anna Smol is a Professor of English at Mount Saint Vincent University in Nova Scotia, Canada, where she teaches courses on Tolkien, medievalism, and Old English literature. Her research on Tolkien as a war writer (focusing on *The Lord of the Rings*) has been published in *Modern Fiction Studies*, *Tolkien 2005: The Ring Goes Ever On*, and in collections edited by Chris Vaccaro (*The Body in Tolkien's Legendarium*) and Leslie Donovan (*Approaches to Teaching Tolkien's* The Lord of the Rings). Smol has also published on gender and sexuality in Tolkien's work in Michael Drout's *J.R.R. Tolkien Encyclopedia* and on Tolkien as an artist in *Tolkien Studies* and *Mythlore.*

Lynn Schlesinger received her PhD in Sociology and taught at State University of New York at Plattsburgh for 21 years. Her past research includes a qualitative study of women who live with chronic pain, and archival research on the history of residential schools for the deaf in the United States. She is currently pursuing a Master's degree in English Literature from Signum University.

Felicity Gilbert is currently a PhD candidate in the Dept. of English Literature in Mary Immaculate College, University of Limerick. Enamoured with the genres of fantasy and science fiction, as well as feminist and psychoanalytic theoretical perspectives, she continues her research by pursuing a Doctoral degree. Her current PhD thesis is entitled *Eros and Thanatos: A Psychoanalytic-Feminist Approach to Human Understanding of Fear and Premature Death in Fantasy Literature and Science Fiction.* Felicity's research interests include examining fantasy and science fiction genres concerning their reflection of culturally constructed norms (such as gender and social hierarchies), as well as Gothic and Monster literature and postmodern literary perspectives.

Alicia Fox-Lenz is an independent scholar currently pursuing a graduate degree in English Literature and Language with a dual concentration in Tolkien Studies and Germanic Philology at Signum University. She is interested in studying Tolkien through a Cultural Studies lens and expanding the mantle of mythopoeic literature to interactive narrative platforms. More specifically, her work examines the applicability of Tolkien to a modern audience through audience reception and comparisons to other pop culture media and contextualizing the *Legend of Zelda* franchise as a work of mythopoeia.

Giovanni Carmine Costabile holds an MPhil in Philosophy from the Università della Calabria in Italy. Independent scholar, freelance translator, writer, and private teacher, he has published on Tolkien, War, and Medieval Literature in several Tolkien journals and presented papers at Tolkien events in Leeds, San Marino, Oxford, Florence, and Birmingham. His first monograph, *Oltre le Mura del Mondo: Immanenza e Trascendenza nelle opere di J.R.R. Tolkien*, including a foreword by Fr. Guglielmo Spirito, an introduction by Fr. Alberto Quagliaroli, and an afterword by Oronzo Cilli, is forthcoming.

Walking Tree Publishers

Zurich and Jena

Walking Tree Publishers was founded in 1997 as a forum for publication of material related to Tolkien and Middle-earth studies.

http://www.walking-tree.org

Cormarë Series

The *Cormarë Series* collects papers and studies dedicated exclusively to the exploration of Tolkien's work. It comprises monographs, thematic collections of essays, conference volumes, and reprints of important yet no longer (easily) accessible papers by leading scholars in the field. Manuscripts and project proposals are evaluated by members of an independent board of advisors who support the series editors in their endeavour to provide the readers with qualitatively superior yet accessible studies on Tolkien and his work.

News from the Shire and Beyond. Studies on Tolkien
Peter Buchs & Thomas Honegger (eds.), Zurich and Berne 2004, Reprint, First edition 1997 (Cormarë Series 1), ISBN 978-3-9521424-5-5

Root and Branch. Approaches Towards Understanding Tolkien
Thomas Honegger (ed.), Zurich and Berne 2005, Reprint, First edition 1999 (Cormarë Series 2), ISBN 978-3-905703-01-6

Richard Sturch, *Four Christian Fantasists. A Study of the Fantastic Writings of George MacDonald, Charles Williams, C.S. Lewis and J.R.R. Tolkien*
Zurich and Berne 2007, Reprint, First edition 2001 (Cormarë Series 3), ISBN 978-3-905703-04-7

Tolkien in Translation
Thomas Honegger (ed.), Zurich and Jena 2011, Reprint, First edition 2003 (Cormarë Series 4), ISBN 978-3-905703-15-3

Mark T. Hooker, *Tolkien Through Russian Eyes*
Zurich and Berne 2003 (Cormarë Series 5), ISBN 978-3-9521424-7-9

Translating Tolkien: Text and Film
Thomas Honegger (ed.), Zurich and Jena 2011, Reprint, First edition 2004 (Cormarë Series 6), ISBN 978-3-905703-16-0

Christopher Garbowski, *Recovery and Transcendence for the Contemporary Mythmaker. The Spiritual Dimension in the Works of J.R.R. Tolkien*
Zurich and Berne 2004, Reprint, First Edition by Marie Curie Sklodowska, University Press, Lublin 2000, (Cormarë Series 7), ISBN 978-3-9521424-8-6

Reconsidering Tolkien
Thomas Honegger (ed.), Zurich and Berne 2005 (Cormarë Series 8), ISBN 978-3-905703-00-9

Tolkien and Modernity 1
Frank Weinreich & Thomas Honegger (eds.), Zurich and Berne 2006 (Cormarë Series 9), ISBN 978-3-905703-02-3

Tolkien and Modernity 2
Thomas Honegger & Frank Weinreich (eds.), Zurich and Berne 2006 (Cormarë Series 10), ISBN 978-3-905703-03-0

Tom Shippey, *Roots and Branches. Selected Papers on Tolkien by Tom Shippey*
Zurich and Berne 2007 (Cormarë Series 11), ISBN 978-3-905703-05-4

Ross Smith, *Inside Language. Linguistic and Aesthetic Theory in Tolkien*
Zurich and Jena 2011, Reprint, First edition 2007 (Cormarë Series 12), ISBN 978-3-905703-20-7

How We Became Middle-earth. A Collection of Essays on The Lord of the Rings
Adam Lam & Nataliya Oryshchuk (eds.), Zurich and Berne 2007 (Cormarë Series 13), ISBN 978-3-905703-07-8

Myth and Magic. Art According to the Inklings
Eduardo Segura & Thomas Honegger (eds.), Zurich and Berne 2007 (Cormarë Series 14), ISBN 978-3-905703-08-5

The Silmarillion – Thirty Years On
Allan Turner (ed.), Zurich and Berne 2007 (Cormarë Series 15), ISBN 978-3-905703-10-8

Martin Simonson, *The Lord of the Rings and the Western Narrative Tradition*
Zurich and Jena 2008 (Cormarë Series 16), ISBN 978-3-905703-09-2

Tolkien's Shorter Works. Proceedings of the 4th Seminar of the Deutsche Tolkien Gesellschaft & Walking Tree Publishers Decennial Conference
Margaret Hiley & Frank Weinreich (eds.), Zurich and Jena 2008 (Cormarë Series 17), ISBN 978-3-905703-11-5

Tolkien's The Lord of the Rings: Sources of Inspiration
Stratford Caldecott & Thomas Honegger (eds.), Zurich and Jena 2008 (Cormarë Series 18), ISBN 978-3-905703-12-2

J.S. Ryan, *Tolkien's View: Windows into his World*
Zurich and Jena 2009 (Cormarë Series 19), ISBN 978-3-905703-13-9

Music in Middle-earth
Heidi Steimel & Friedhelm Schneidewind (eds.), Zurich and Jena 2010 (Cormarë Series 20), ISBN 978-3-905703-14-6

Liam Campbell, *The Ecological Augury in the Works of JRR Tolkien*
Zurich and Jena 2011 (Cormarë Series 21), ISBN 978-3-905703-18-4

Margaret Hiley, *The Loss and the Silence. Aspects of Modernism in the Works of C.S. Lewis, J.R.R. Tolkien and Charles Williams*
Zurich and Jena 2011 (Cormarë Series 22), ISBN 978-3-905703-19-1

Rainer Nagel, *Hobbit Place-names. A Linguistic Excursion through the Shire*
Zurich and Jena 2012 (Cormarë Series 23), ISBN 978-3-905703-22-1

Christopher MacLachlan, *Tolkien and Wagner: The Ring and Der Ring*
Zurich and Jena 2012 (Cormarë Series 24), ISBN 978-3-905703-21-4

Renée Vink, *Wagner and Tolkien: Mythmakers*
Zurich and Jena 2012 (Cormarë Series 25), ISBN 978-3-905703-25-2

The Broken Scythe. Death and Immortality in the Works of J.R.R. Tolkien
Roberto Arduini & Claudio Antonio Testi (eds.), Zurich and Jena 2012 (Cormarë Series 26), ISBN 978-3-905703-26-9

Sub-creating Middle-earth: Constructions of Authorship and the Works of J.R.R. Tolkien
Judith Klinger (ed.), Zurich and Jena 2012 (Cormarë Series 27), ISBN 978-3-905703-27-6

Tolkien's Poetry
Julian Eilmann & Allan Turner (eds.), Zurich and Jena 2013 (Cormarë Series 28), ISBN 978-3-905703-28-3

O, What a Tangled Web. Tolkien and Medieval Literature. A View from Poland
Barbara Kowalik (ed.), Zurich and Jena 2013 (Cormarë Series 29), ISBN 978-3-905703-29-0

J.S. Ryan, *In the Nameless Wood*
Zurich and Jena 2013 (Cormarë Series 30), ISBN 978-3-905703-30-6

From Peterborough to Faëry; The Poetics and Mechanics of Secondary Worlds
Thomas Honegger & Dirk Vanderbeke (eds.), Zurich and Jena 2014 (Cormarë Series 31), ISBN 978-3-905703-31-3

Tolkien and Philosophy
Roberto Arduini & Claudio R. Testi (eds.), Zurich and Jena 2014 (Cormarë Series 32), ISBN 978-3-905703-32-0

Patrick Curry, *Deep Roots in a Time of Frost. Essays on Tolkien*
Zurich and Jena 2014 (Cormarë Series 33), ISBN 978-3-905703-33-7

Representations of Nature in Middle-earth
Martin Simonson (ed.), Zurich and Jena 2015, (Cormarë Series 34), ISBN 978-3-905703-34-4

Laughter in Middle-earth
Thomas Honegger & Maureen F. Mann (eds.), Zurich and Jena 2016 (Cormarë Series 35), ISBN 978-3-905703-35-1

Julian Eilmann, *J.R.R. Tolkien – Romanticist and Poet*
Zurich and Jena 2017 (Cormarë Series 36), ISBN 978-3-905703-36-8

Binding Them All. Interdisciplinary Perspectives on J.R.R. Tolkien and His Works
Monika Kirner-Ludwig, Stephan Köser, Sebastian Streitberger (Cormarë Series 37), ISBN 978-3-905703-37-5

Claudio Testi, *Pagan Saints in Middle-earth*
Zurich and Jena 2017 (Cormarë Series 38), ISBN 978-3-905703-38-2

Music in Tolkien's Work and Beyond
Julian Eilmann & Friedhelm Schneidewind (eds.), Zurich and Jena 2019 (Cormarë Series 39), ISBN 978-3-905703-39-9

Sub-creating Arda: World-building in J.R.R. Tolkien's Works, its Precursors, and Legacies
Dimitra Fimi & Thomas Honegger (eds.), Zurich and Jena 2019 (Cormarë Series 40), ISBN 978-3-905703-40-5

"Something Has Gone Crack": New Perspectives on J.R.R. Tolkien and the Great War
Janet Brennan Croft and Annika Röttinger (eds.), Zurich and Jena 2019 (Cormarë Series 41), ISBN 978-3-905703-41-2

Tolkien and the Classics
Roberto Arduini, Giampaolo Canzonieri & Claudio A. Testi (eds.), Zurich and Jena 2019 (Cormarë Series 42), ISBN 978-3-905703-42-9

Deborah A. Higgens, *Anglo-Saxon Community in J.R.R. Tolkien's The Lord of the Rings*
Zurich and Jena 2020 (Cormarë Series 43), forthcoming

Beowulf and the Dragon

The original Old English text of the 'Dragon Episode' of Beowulf is set in an authentic font and bound in hardback as a high quality art book. Illustrated by Anke Eissmann and accompanied by John Porter's translation. Introduction by Tom Shippey. Limited first edition of 500 copies. 84 pages. Selected pages can be previewed on: http://www.walking-tree.org/beowulf

Beowulf and the Dragon
Zurich and Jena 2009 , ISBN 978-3-905703-17-7

Tales of Yore Series

The *Tales of Yore Series* provides a platform for qualitatively superior fiction that will appeal to readers familiar with Tolkien's world:

The Monster Specialist

Sir Severus le Brewse, among the least known of King Arthur's Round Table knights, is preferred by nature, disposition, and training to fight against monsters rather than other knights. After youthful adventures of errantry with dragons, trolls, vampires, and assorted beasts, Severus joins the brilliant sorceress Lilava to face the Chimaera in The Greatest Monster Battle of All Time to free her folk from an age-old curse. But their adventures don't end there; together they meet elves and magicians, friends and foes; they join in the fight to save Camelot and even walk the Grey Paths of the Dead. With a mix of Malory, a touch of Tolkien, and a hint of humor, The Monster Specialist chronicles a tale of courage, tenacity, honor, and love.

The Monster Specialist is illustrated by Anke Eissmann.

Edward S. Louis, *The Monster Specialist*
Zurich and Jena 2014 (Tales of Yore Series No. 3), ISBN 978-3-905703-23-8

Tales of Yore Series (earlier books)

Kay Woollard, *The Terror of Tatty Walk. A Frightener*
CD and Booklet, Zurich and Berne 2000, ISBN 978-3-9521424-2-4

Kay Woollard, *Wilmot's Very Strange Stone or What came of building "snobbits"*
CD and booklet, Zurich and Berne 2001, ISBN 978-3-9521424-4-8

Information for authors

Authors interested in contributing to our publications can learn more about the services we offer on the "services for authors" section of our web pages.

http://www.walking-tree.org/authors

Manuscripts and project proposals can be submitted to the board of editors (please include an SAE):

Walking Tree Publishers
CH-3052 Zollikofen
Switzerland

e-mail: info@walking-tree.org

Walking Tree Publishers, Zurich and Jena, 2019

Lightning Source UK Ltd.
Milton Keynes UK
UKHW020619260220
359363UK00004B/280

9 783905 703412